creation of new communities as the city spread into neighboring suburbs. At the same time, the Church was forced to adapt itself to the needs and demands of its various ethnic constituents, particularly the flood of Spanish-speaking newcomers in the late twentieth century. Occasionally, it had to confront the secular government when city policies conflicted with Church principles, as in the conflict over the Church's care of Sacramento's hordes of homeless and hungry people.

Steven M. Avella's close study of secular and church archives, newspapers, and other sources reveals that churches and their congregations played a significant role in determining both the physical shape of Sacramento and the tone and quality of life there. *Sacramento and the Catholic Church* is a major contribution to our understanding of the development of western cities and the role of religion and religious institutions in that development.

STEVEN M. AVELLA grew up in Sacramento. He is currently on the faculty of Marquette University, Milwaukee, where he teaches courses on religion and American life, and the American West.

JACKET ILLUSTRATIONS
Background Image: North Sacramento aerial view, 1950.
Courtesy *Sacramento Bee* Collection.
Color photograph: Sacramento: Early Spring by Steve Memering.
Digital image courtesy of Smith Gallery, Sacramento.

Sacramento and the Catholic Church   *The Urban West Series*

Sacramento *and the* Catholic Church

SHAPING A CAPITAL CITY

Steven M. Avella

UNIVERSITY OF NEVADA PRESS RENO & LAS VEGAS

The Urban West Series

Series Editors: Eugene P. Moehring and David M. Wrobel

University of Nevada Press, Reno, Nevada 89557 USA

Manufactured in the United States of America

Library of Congress Cataloging-in-Publication Data

Avella, Steven M.

Sacramento and the Catholic church : shaping a capital city /
Steven M. Avella.

p. cm. — (The urban West series)

Includes bibliographical references and index.

ISBN 978-0-87417-760-2 (alk. paper)

1. Catholic Church—California—Sacramento.

2. Sacramento (Calif.)—Church history. I. Title.

BX1418.S23A94   2008

282′.79454—dc22   2008014262

The paper used in this book is a recycled stock made from
30 percent post-consumer waste materials, certified by FSC,
and meets the requirements of American National Standard
for Information Sciences—Permanence of Paper for Printed
Library Materials, ANSI/NISO z39.48-1992 (R2002).

Binding materials were selected for strength and durability.

First Printing

17   16   15   14   13   12   11   10   09   08

5   4   3   2   1

To Francis Paul Prucha, S.J.

Friend, Mentor, Scholar, Priest

CONTENTS

ILLUSTRATIONS

ACKNOWLEDGMENTS

Rugged individualism is not the lot of the academic researcher and writer. While the toil may be lonely and even enervating at times, every author realizes the extent to which he or she is dependent on the kindness of others and their labors on his or her behalf. I sincerely and gratefully acknowledge the network of scholars, archivists, teachers, and friends who have helped me along the way in preparing *Sacramento and the Catholic Church: Shaping a Capital City*.

Marquette University has given me sabbaticals and research assistance, which allowed me to devote full-time efforts to this project. My chairs, Ralph Weber, Lance Grahn, and James Marten, were always most encouraging. The Department of History provided wonderful research assistants, including James Bohl, Edward Schmitt, Paula Dicks, John Donovan, Amanda Schmeider, Matthew Luckett, Christine Jaworski, and Stanford Lester. The superb staff of the Raynor Library and especially its Interlibrary Loan Department deserve all the praise in the world.

My ecclesiastical superiors, the archbishops of Milwaukee, the Most Reverend Rembert G. Weakland, O.S.B., and fellow historian the Most Reverend Timothy Dolan, have always been supportive and interested in my scholarly work.

I am deeply indebted to the many archivists, librarians, and administrators who have assisted me. The wonderful resources at the Sacramento Archives and Museum Collection Center (SAMCC) are first in order of importance. I have spent literally thousands of hours at SAMCC, combing through various documents housed there. Every step of the way I was helped by the wonderful staff—manager James Henley and archivists Charlene Gilbert Noyes, Patricia Johnson, Stasia Wolfe, Dylan McDonald, and Carson Hendricks. SAMCC has become a second home to me and its staff and volunteers like a family. We have all grown close over the years and been with each other in good times and in bad.

Likewise, I could never repay my debt of gratitude to the staff of the Sacramento Room of the Sacramento City Central Library. This marvelous resource room contains almost everything written about Sacramento. Its director, Clare Ellis, has also become a great friend.

I spent many hours at the California Room of the California State Library. There, too, an efficient staff coordinated by Gary Kurutz provided for my every request. Other sources were procured at the Bancroft Library of the University of California—Berkeley and at the Shields Library of the University of California—Davis. At the latter, librarian Roberto Delgadillo was of particular help.

The Diocese of Sacramento allowed me generous access not only to its "official" collections but also to a wonderful treasure trove of unprocessed materials in its storage facilities. Although the days were long and hot in the former locker room where these records are kept, my toil was rewarded time and again by the discovery of many important documents that helped with critical parts of this work. For this access I would like to thank the Most Reverend William K. Weigand, bishop of Sacramento; Vicar General Monsignor Robert Walton; former chancellor the Reverend Blaise Berg; and the ever gracious chancery staff. Retired bishop of the diocese the Most Reverend Francis Quinn helped correct some of the errors in earlier drafts of this work. Other kind Sacramento priests provided access to various sacramental records or shared their recollections of events described in this book. Some of them have now crossed over to the other side.

Other ecclesiastical archives supplied various pieces of the larger story. The Secret Archives of the Vatican contain marvelous collections of records on the Diocese of Sacramento. The Archives of the Archdiocese of Los Angeles, managed by Monsignor Francis Weber—a name synonymous with the history of California Catholicism—has an abundance of information relating to Sacramento. The Archives of the Archdiocese of San Francisco, administered by my old graduate school classmate and another scholar of California Catholic life Dr. Jeffrey Burns, was a rich source for research. I also wish to thank Gary Topping of the Archives of the Diocese of Salt Lake City, Brother Matthew Cunningham of the Archives of the Diocese of Reno, Sara Nau of the Archives of the Archdiocese of Seattle and her predecessor Chancellor Christine Taylor, as well as the Reverend Jan Joseph Santich of the Diocese of Cheyenne for their help and the materials they provided.

Religious communities of men and women have wonderful archival stockpiles, which I was able to consult. The Franciscan Sisters of Penance and Charity, both of Stella Niagara, New York, and Redwood City, California, supplied many important documents for the history of their sisters in Sacramento. The Sisters of Mercy in Burlingame and Auburn opened their doors to my requests and allowed me to copy materials that helped me to better understand their role in city building. Brother Wenceslaus Farlow, O.F.M., of the Santa Barbara Province of the Franciscan Friars shared with me the wonderful files about the origins of St. Francis Parish. The Dominican Friars of St. Albert Priory in Oakland were most gracious in meeting my research requests.

Other archival collections consulted include those at the University of Notre Dame, the Archdiocese of Baltimore (the Reverend Paul Thomas), All Hallows Seminary in Dublin (Greg Harkin), and the joint Archives of the Congregationalists, Methodists, and Baptists at the Graduate Theological Union in Berkeley (Stephen Yale).

I was blessed to have a number of outside readers—long-suffering souls—who read all or parts of the manuscript. They include Jeffrey Burns, Joseph M. White, William Mahan, Gregg Campbell, LeRoy Chatfield, Sister Katherine Doyle, and Lorena Marquez. The excellent editorial eye of Marlene Smith-Baranzini went over this draft in its various incarnations.

Technical assistance and the creation of various charts and maps came with the help of Ramona Farrell, Vernon H. Petrich, and the Reverend Gregory M. Spitz. Jean Iacino lent me her computer and work space to assemble these data. A dear saint, Susan Silva—patient and competent— edited my various drafts, helped as a research assistant, and boosted my flagging spirits when this project hit occasional dead ends or frustrations.

Even historians need friends and occasionally a good meal and a bed. I gratefully acknowledge the wonderful hospitality of the Reverends Gerald Ryle, Vincent Brady, Michael McKeon, and Michael Engh, S.J., and Monsignors Francis Weber, James Kidder, James Murphy, and James Gaffey. The Generalate of the Salvatorian Fathers and Brothers in Rome provided lodging during my work at the Vatican Archives. My classmate the Very Reverend Dennis Thiessen, S.D.S., was my host.

Working with the University of Nevada Press has been a delight from the moment we first made contact. From the initial proposal through the final production of this book, I have received nothing but support and affirmation from these very fine people who honor me by publishing this work. I met David Wrobel at annual meetings of the Western History Association and always found him sincerely interested in what I was doing. Gene Moehring, whose work on Las Vegas was an inspiration to me, has always been front and center in helping make this a better book. Acquisitions editor Charlotte Dihoff has shepherded this text through its various permutations from proposal to final draft. The two "anonymous" readers who agreed to let their names be used, Ferenc Szasz and Mark Wild, provided a solid and helpful critique that I attempted to integrate into the final draft. Managing editor Sara Vélez Mallea helped to bring this project to conclusion. Copy editor Annette Wenda did a magnificent job in shaping this text into a better book.

But in saying thanks, I return to the network of scholars and fellow travelers interested in Sacramento, religion, urban life, or any combination thereof who have been at my elbow every step of the way. They include wonderful colleagues such as Tom Jablonsky, Marquette's urban historian who has helped me clarify my ideas about cities. Likewise, my graduate students in a seminar on religion and urban life provided many insights and challenges that helped flesh out the complexities of church-city relations. Also in this communion of saints are two men whom I have long admired, Ferenc Szasz, one of the leading historians of religion and the American West, and Sacramento scholar Joseph Pitti of California State University–Sacramento. I have been privileged to know both over the years and have benefited from their scholarship and knowledge in so many ways. Professor Kathleen Conzen I know only through her wonderful scholarship. More than anyone else, her work opened new vistas for me concerning the interplay of religion and urban life. Younger scholars whose papers I listened to at Western History Association conferences or whose careers I've been able to watch from afar—women such as Gina Marie Pitti and Lorena Marquez—have taught me much. I only wish I had been as smart and capable as they are when I was their age.

Although I live in the Midwest, I am a Californian and I will always consider the West my home. It was a class on westward expansion taken during the 1980s with the legendary Francis Paul Prucha, S.J., at Marquette University that resurrected an interest in my home region. His wry humor, his unflinching demand for thoroughness, his sometimes painful honesty about my writing, coupled with his personal concern for my career and well-being, have meant a great deal to me over the years. One is never afraid of Paul Prucha—but like any good and exacting scholar he creates a standard of excellence that those who respect and love him wish to meet. If I lived a thousand years I would never meet those standards as he has lived and embodied them, but that I am willing to try is my tribute to a man whom I consider one of the greatest historians of the American West. To Paul, I respectfully dedicate this book.

Sacramento and the Catholic Church

Introduction

At the corner of Eleventh and K Streets in Sacramento, California, stands the stately Cathedral of the Blessed Sacrament. Renovated and retrofitted in 2005, the cathedral buzzes with life every noon as a spectrum of worshipers—from street people to state officials—"catch mass" or confess their sins in the oak confessionals at the rear of the church. On Saturdays, wedding couples are often photographed before the terra-cotta-faced presbytery. The sunny plaza in front of the cathedral fills with hundreds of Latino/a Sacramentans who arrive at *ora mexicana* for the 1:00 PM Sunday Spanish mass.

As one strolls south on Eleventh Street from the cathedral, the church's sphere of influence remains strong as one passes the bronze statue of Roman Catholic auxiliary bishop Alphonse Gallegos. It was erected by the community to honor the late prelate, tragically killed on a dark California highway in 1991. After passing the Gallegos memorial, one leaves the penumbra of the cathedral and enters the outer ring of the state capitol. Here, smartly attired legislators, lobbyists, and state workers sporting their picture IDs head through manicured Capitol Park into the state-house to transact the business of the largest state in the American Union and the fifth-largest economy in the world.

Caught up in the "chaos of intentions" that is the American city, few probably take time to see the influence of religion on Sacramento's physical and human landscape.[1] It might never occur to those who regularly worship at the cathedral or do business at the capitol (often one and the same person) that the cathedral, once the largest west of the Rocky Mountains, was deliberately placed one block north of the capitol by a Catholic bishop anxious to help Sacramento realize its dreams of urban glory. Nor would they know that a bishop in the twentieth century contemplated selling the great cathedral to urban developers. Attorneys, bail bondsmen, and others involved in the justice system may never wonder why a parking lot near their offices on Eighth and G streets is named for St. Joseph. Only a few aging Sacramentans remember that a large convent, academy, and grade school once stood on this block and trained a number of Sacramento's early schoolteachers. Sacramento children who attend Father Keith B. Kenny Elementary School on Martin Luther King Boulevard may not know that the school is named for a Catholic priest who was a respected leader in the Latino/a community until his death in 1983.

Religion is not totally invisible in the California capital, but its presence is for many like the proverbial tip of the iceberg. Beneath the surface of Sacramento—and other cities of the American West—there is more going on than meets the eye. In fact, I argue that the Catholic Church has had an important influence on Sacramento's life and development. Conversely, Sacramento's distinct social, cultural, and economic conditions have affected the character of Catholic life in the city. This book examines the interplay between the city of Sacramento, California, and the Catholic Church from the city's beginnings to the twenty-first century, to illustrate the sometimes hidden ways religious communities help form and sustain urban communities.

The Sacramento metropolitan area, according to adjusted 2003 U.S. Census figures, has nearly two million people and is today the twenty-sixth-largest population center in the United States. The city itself is the thirty-seventh largest in the United States and the seventh largest in California. It is also one of the most culturally diverse communities in America.[2] In its origins and development, the city is a microcosm of urban development in California and in the American West. Sacramento's past is ripe for serious treatment by historians.[3]

Sacramento was an "instant city" created by one of the mining rushes that gave birth to cities all over the American West.[4] Many of these boom-towns faded into oblivion or became quaint tourist attractions once their precious metals or minerals were played out. Others, like Sacramento, found ways to reinvent themselves and became important urban centers. Sacramento's survival was the result of purposeful planning and just plain good luck. Its founding generation decided that the hastily planted Gold Rush city would remain on its environmentally precarious site even after the gold mining boom ended. Determined city leaders overcame the ravaging fires and dreaded diseases that overwhelmed the city in its early years. Even today the city continues to fight off flooding. Sacramento stands at the confluence of two rivers, the American and Sacramento, and is located at the lower end of one of the nation's most volatile drainage basins. Indomitable citizens built and rebuilt levees and raised city streets to keep the city dry—and never gave up, as new efforts were required to keep the waters at bay. Today, the city exists inside a complex high-tech infrastructure of dams, weirs, levees, and electronic monitors.

Good fortune smiled on Sacramento when it became California's capital in 1854. It also became the permanent home of the state fair in 1861, and the terminus of the Central Pacific Railroad in 1863. In turn, both the city of Sacramento and Sacramento County became an industrial site, an agricultural processing center, a government town, a host to major military and aerospace installations, and a high-tech capital.

Thanks in part to its small size and its compact city grid, Sacramento retained a small-town atmosphere for a long time.[5] Sacramento citizens met and mingled in a variety of regularly frequented city institutions. Until 1937, Sacramento had only one public high school. For many years it had only two major employers: railroads and canneries. Although it had two active newspapers until the 1990s, the voice of the *Sacramento Bee* was the major news outlet and town crier. From the middle of the nineteenth century on, McClatchy family shaped the news and the image of Sacramento. The McClatchy brothers, Charles and Valentine, both reflected and shaped the city consensus. "Old sweet Sacramento," as longtime residents nostalgically referred to the pre–World War II city, eventually gave way to the spatial diffusion of suburbanization created by the jobs at military installations and defense plants.

Demographic changes pushed the city north, east, and south over the course of its slow but steady expansion. The largest demographic shift of recent times began when a 1986 flood led to a redrawing of the maps of the Sacramento floodplain by the Federal Emergency Management Agency in 1989 (FEMA officials warned Sacramentans that they would enjoy fewer than one hundred years of protection). Then the disasters caused in the Bay Area by the 1989 Loma Prieta and 1994 Northridge earthquakes caused companies, especially high-tech firms, to look favorably on Sacramento as a place to escape seismic fault lines. These firms chose the high ground to the east of the city—particularly the cities of Folsom and Roseville—for their new plants and facilities. In the 1980s and 1990s, the rapid growth of these cities and southern Placer and El Dorado counties provided a major boost to Sacramento's sprawling metropolis, linked together by freeways and public transit.

Throughout Sacramento's history, the driving force behind much of the city's development has come from a cadre of commercial and professional elites who appeared at every critical juncture to refocus the energies of the community, to meet new challenges, to move Sacramento forward, and to build on the energy and enthusiasm of a previous generation. These "civic middlemen," first identified by historian Mark Eifler in *Gold Rush Capitalists: Greed and Growth in Sacramento,* consisted of an informal group of merchants, professionals, and others who helped the city survive at its present location during its early years.

Jesse W. Wilson exemplified this class of citizen. Wilson came to Sacramento in 1861 after trying his hand at mining and as a teamster in Marysville. He became a successful liveryman and served as sheriff and county supervisor. In 1863, he headed the committee that presided over the ceremonial groundbreaking for the Central Pacific Railroad. When he died in 1916 at the age of eighty-two, the newspaper noted, "With his death passed one of the typical Sacramentans of other days—one of the builders of community; one of the men who always was loyal to Sacramento and who loved her so much that when his finances grew from the very moderate to a well-lined purse, he followed not the example of other

Sacramentans who departed for larger cities, but remained firm and steadfast by his old home."[6]

Successors to the founding generation drew on the inspiration of their predecessors to create new programs of urban rejuvenation needed after periods of economic slowdown or perceived urban lethargy. Their goals, distilled here, I call the "urban agenda" or the "urban consensus," persist to the present time:

- *Economic growth:* the leading and most easily accepted priority. Sacramento's urban leaders wanted a city that prospered, and they continually sought to improve the physical and social climate of the state capital for business growth and investments in land.
- *City modernization:* the shorthand phrase for a cluster of initiatives that included urban beautification, infrastructure improvement (water, sewer, roads, waste), the construction of an appealing city image (boosterism), and insistence on greater efficiency in local government.
- *Social stability:* This meant creating a safe environment for work and commercial activity. On the surface it included steady upgrades in the quality of law enforcement, fire protection, and general public safety. For many years it also meant an emphasis on social homogeneity through a common adherence to Euro-American ideas and values. Sacramento's collective values were safely "middle class." Lacking the extremes of wealth or poverty, the city valued orderly public life. Its small size and common institutions maintained a level of personal familiarity and contact that reinforced its desire for social peace and harmony.

These goals could be the credo for any developing American city. Their uniqueness, however, is not at issue. These priorities, transmuted throughout the city's history, have remained dominant and are the crucible for church-city interaction. This study underscores the role of religious believers who actively and deliberately identified themselves with the priorities of the "urban agenda" or the "urban consensus."

How did religion affect Sacramento's growth and development? The answer is complex. Sacramento was not a "religious" community like Salt

Lake City, and on the face of it religion and religious faith would seem to have had little to do with either the founding or the sustaining of Sacramento over the years.[7] Sacramento churches occupied urban space and added to the array of cultural amenities of the growing city, but their active participation in the key priorities of city life and development is not easy to discern. However, a closer examination of "secular" archival and newspaper evidence and also a search in previously untapped church archives suggests a significant measure of religious agency in Sacramento's history that might not have occurred to the relative few who have studied and written about California's capital.

Even religious people might be surprised at their role in creating an urban community. Since religious faith is highly personal and private and church affiliation generally a separate sphere of people's lives apart from their "secular" daily concerns, religious people and institutions might not recognize themselves as "urban agents." To suggest that religious activities also produced "secular" social benefits to the city is in no way to deny the meaning of these activities to individual believers or to denominations.[8] Faith-motivated actions on the part of individuals and the collective endeavors of churches and congregations have had some very public manifestations. Churches joined in the larger consensus that insisted Sacramento bloom where it had been so serendipitously planted by Gold Rush entrepreneurs in 1848, rebuilding their worship sites and continuing their schools and other forms of social provision once floodwaters receded or fires burned out. Throughout Sacramento's history religious believers fed the poor, housed the homeless, and cared for the sick. Religious feasts spilled out into city streets and other public places, and even civic functions acknowledged religious sentiments. Religious leaders conferred blessings or heaped sanctions on certain civic actions. Blessings and dedications of churches were often civic events with the governor, legislators, and the mayor in attendance.

Religious congregations were sometimes microcosms of city ethnic and class realities. They also threw a spotlight on the gendered realities of life in heavily male Sacramento. Women played important roles in church life—sometimes in ways that defied the norms of male-female relations in the nineteenth and twentieth centuries. For example, religious sisters in Sacramento were among the first to claim "female space" in the heavily male city and to operate major businesses—a school, convent, and hospital—without direct male oversight. Suburbanites acquired land and through volunteer activities built parishes, schools, and halls, providing a nexus for communal action in the social and spatial diffusion of Sacramento's suburbia.

Some of this is understandable when placed within the larger context of religion in the American West. As many have long acknowledged, region has had an impact on the character of religious life in the United States. Sacramento's particular location in the West provides some insight into its religious identity.[9] Scholars of religion and the American West, such as Ferenc Szasz, have argued that the West consisted of an array of "ecological subregions" that "provided a home for differing faith systems."[10] Each of the various "Wests"—from the Great Basin to the deserts of the Southwest, the Pacific Northwest, and the broad valleys of California and its western coastal cities—had a religious character specifically calibrated to its particular locale. Sacramento and cities that shared its basic religious characteristics were no exception.[11] Sacramento's identity as a California city adds further context to its distinctive religious patterns.[12]

Contrast with other regions of the country may be helpful here. Sacramento was not like eastern cities such as Boston and New York (where Protestant-Catholic tensions occasionally erupted into violence) or midwestern cities like St. Louis, Chicago, and Milwaukee (where Catholics built parallel institutions to "ward off" the faithful from mainstream urban life). Sacramento Catholics for the most part pursued an active pattern of accommodation between the Catholic-Protestant and Catholic-urban forces. This was perhaps most evident in the behavior of clergy leaders who did not enjoy the status and resources of their counterparts in other cities of the United States who could approach civic leaders as coequals. Instead, they had to assume a more conciliatory stance toward the dominant commercial and urban political leaders. Sacramento's Catholic Church proved much more "inclusive" and less contentious than its counterparts on the East Coast or in the Midwest. Accounting for local variations, Sacramento's experience was to some degree replicated in Seattle, Portland, Cheyenne, and Phoenix.

Although indigenous faiths flourished, Sacramento and the entire Central Valley of California never had a "prehistory" of any one European religion. It grew up relatively tolerant and open to the religious systems of Native Americans, Protestant evangelicals, Catholics, Orthodox, Chinese and Japanese Buddhists, Jews, and nonbelievers. Early religious communities first formed in the hurly-burly of the Gold Rush. Each group was welcomed to write their story on the tabula rasa of the Central Valley. However, it was not until the city developed a stable government, social amenities, and a firm economic life that religious denominations built permanent churches and hired residential ministers. Churches helped western mining frontier cities like Sacramento dispel notions of backwardness and lack of civility and replicated cultural environments similar to those of eastern cities. Libraries, schools, theaters, lyceums, department stores, and churches were part of these formal and informal efforts to create and sustain viable urban communities.

Of the role of religion in "civilizing" the western city, there can be no doubt. One early San Francisco developer summed it up in the 1850s when he welcomed a minister to the rapidly growing community: "Property is worth more under the gospel, life is safer, community is happier—we can't do without it."[13] But Sacramento, like many other western cities, had low church membership and attendance rates and somewhat erratic patterns of voluntary giving. When it became clear that Sacramento's priorities were commercial, not religious, successful churches shaped themselves to these realities—even as they tried to be faithful to their core values and practices.

This book hopes to make some contribution to urban history as it examines the interplay between religion and urban life. The direct inspiration for this book comes from a brief essay by urban historian Kathleen Neils Conzen, who argues strongly for a reexamination of the agency of religious bodies in urban history. Religious institutions, she argues, were "particular agent[s]" who sought "to influence the urban order directly through its investments, services, political power, and control of space."[14] Conzen's essay emphasizes the civic impact of religious institutions and deals less with the aspects of unique religious behavior (that is, prayer, ritual, devotion). This book does the same while also acknowledging that the religious experience of Sacramentans is worth further study. Even if one is not a believer in any faith tradition or maintains strict walls of separation between "secular" and "sacred," I hope one can appreciate the energies and impact of religious individuals and groups on the "secular" urban project.

Finally, an explanation of why this study uses the Catholic Church as its primary vehicle for exploring the role of religion in urban Sacramento is in order. Many faith traditions have a long and significant record of activity in Sacramento and have affected the course of city life in significant and substantial ways. Nothing said in this book is intended to negate or underplay their influence. The reasons for selecting the Catholic Church as the case study of this book are both personal and professional. I am a lifelong Roman Catholic and a priest who spent my childhood years in Sacramento. It is the religious tradition I know best, and the religious community with whose primary source materials, religious nomenclature, and organizational development I am most familiar.

The Catholic Church is also numerically large. Rudimentary statistics suggest that its founding generation was the single largest denomination in Sacramento, and it has had the highest levels of regular church attendance. Catholics also have an institutional breadth that other denominations do not match. Catholics operated schools for all age groups and sponsored one of the city's major hospitals, an orphanage, a settlement house, and a day-care center. The number of full-time religious workers (priests, sisters, religious brothers) exceeded any other denomination. Since 1886, Sacramento has been the administrative headquarters of the Roman Catholic Diocese of Sacramento and has had among its prominent citizens residential bishops who have been important urban actors. These institutions and offices permitted Catholics to engage Sacramento's evolving community on a number of fronts and as active agents in Sacramento's development. To this day the Catholic Church occupies significant urban space and provides an array of services (such as schools, health care, and charities) that are integral to the city's effective functioning.

There are a number of ways in which the Catholic Church has supported the urban consensus. The location of the Cathedral of the Blessed Sacrament in 1889 by Bishop Patrick Manogue, situated one block from the state capitol building, was chosen to give visible expression to Catholic desires to be an important part of the city's life and culture, and to invest in its future. City leaders recognized the gesture, and often referred to the edifice as the "Sacramento cathedral" or just "the cathedral"—an acknowledgment of the prominence of the building and its acceptance as part and parcel of city life.

Educational, social welfare, and health-care facilities and programs sponsored by the church constituted the city's single largest alternative to public institutions, and accentuated their nonsectarian identity by welcoming people from all walks of life. Catholic schools operated by the Sisters of Mercy and the Franciscan Sisters of Penance and Charity, as well as the Christian Brothers, appealed to a diverse array of Sacramentans, not only contributing to the general literacy of the community but also producing influential members of its professional classes. The Catholic hospital provided the first major expansion of Sacramento's evolving health-care-delivery systems. Catholics helped ensure urban peace during periods of significant demographic change. No other church held together such a spectrum of the city's diverse ethnic populations. Irish and German communicants initially predominated, but later under the Catholic "big tent" came Portuguese, Mexicans, Italians, Croatians (also called Slavonians), French, and Japanese worshipers. Public anxieties over assimilation inspired the largely Irish church leadership to help ethnic residents negotiate their role in the city through a program of Americanization. Church officials assured city leaders that these newcomers would learn to take their place in the urban setting. When Americanization efforts met resistance, church leaders shifted gears and provided a "middle way" between old ethnic ties and a new American identity through the popular Catholic ethnic church. However, from the very beginning it was clear that these small ethnic churches were not intended to be permanent institutions but rather way stations to Americanization.

Intermarriage reinforced the relative religious tolerance (or indifference) in Sacramento. Unlike their counterparts in cities in the Midwest and East, many Catholic Sacramentans intermarried with non-Catholics. Catholic politicians were regularly elected to public office. Catholics sat on the bench, were respected members of the legal profession, and owned important businesses and industries. Most important, they were part of the close-knit cadre of commercial and professional elites who governed the city's destiny. When local fears of "Catholic power" erupted periodically during the course of Sacramento's history, the salve of a balanced Catholic reaction reassured city leaders that the church was a good urban partner and a force for civic advance and not, as bigots suggested, a threat to democratic institutions and the American way of life. In a backhanded way (although those subject to the insults would not have agreed), the sporadic bouts of anti-Catholic feeling that gripped Sacramento were something of a compliment to a religious community whose visibility and investment in the city were openly envied by other denominations.

After World War II suburban expansion shattered the spatial closeness that had once defined the city's culture. The onset of military and industrial growth began tentatively after World War I but became more permanently entrenched in the period leading up to World War II and during the Cold War. This dramatically changed the California capital and produced a new ethos for Sacramento life. "Old sweet Sacramento" gave way to a decentralized congeries of suburbs. Catholic institutions followed their communicants into suburban areas and provided a matrix for communal energies in the building of new parishes and schools. Functional postwar school and church facilities took their places with the shopping centers and gas stations along busy commercial corridors. Some were nestled in the curvilinear settings of suburban neighborhoods, sitting in the middle of huge parking lots. Suburban parishes depended in large measure on a spirit of volunteerism that in some places literally raised the walls and roofs on new centers of worship, education, and social life. Later, the memories of these early days in temporary quarters and makeshift arrangements provided an important communal memory for the "founders" of these parishes.

Back in the city, church leaders struggled with the reality of urban decline, symbolized by the fading of the grand Cathedral of the Blessed Sacrament. By the late 1950s, this once visible symbol of church-city cooperation found itself cash-strapped and unable to raise money for even the most basic maintenance. However, church-city relations were stirred to life as the church became one of the primary institutions that accommodated the increasing flood of Spanish-speaking newcomers who demanded living space and cultural recognition. Sacramento's Catholic Church played a critical role in supporting the Latino/a identity by establishing a permanent church for them—thus providing a cohesive and visible sign of their importance within the larger community. A huge mosaic of Our Lady of Guadalupe, the chief spiritual and cultural icon of the mostly Mexican migrants to the state capital, adorned the outer wall of the Latino/a church—a clear sign that Latinos/as had "arrived" and found their "place" in Sacramento.

Although this study emphasizes church-city consensus, no honest evaluation of the evidence can conclude that harmony was always the order of the day. In fact, the normally placid relations of church and city were from time to time challenged by other voices that did not readily accede to the demand for uniformity or conformity with the urban agenda. City ethnic groups, most notably Italians and Portuguese, insisted on and grudgingly received from church authorities the right to have their own ethnic parishes. Both communities persisted in maintaining their traditional patterns of language, prayer, and communal celebration down to the present day, holding on firmly until the city consensus vis-à-vis Americanization shifted in their favor by the middle and latter twentieth century. Latino/a Catholics were somewhat better positioned chronologically to develop their own religious space, and Our Lady of Guadalupe Church became a center of education and activism on behalf of Latino/a causes, and the terminal point of the famous 1966 March from Delano by the United Farm Workers under César Chávez.

The most explosive disruption of city-church relations occurred in the mid-1990s over the care of Sacramento's hordes of homeless and hungry. Here, when pressed by local government and developers to either curtail their humanitarian efforts or end them altogether, Catholic activists drew a line in the sand and refused to compromise. A major court battle ensued in 1997, which dealt the city a significant public relations defeat. These "contrary" voices perforce temper the nature of my emphasis on consensus. Church and city were not always peaceful and cooperative in Sacramento.

This history illuminates a dimension of city building not always readily apparent to urban historians and others who study the city. It speaks in particular of those in the American West who created urban culture out of distinct regional realities. It hopes Sacramentans themselves understand the role of religion in the world their forebears created and they sustain. If, as John F. Kennedy once said, "God's work on earth must truly be our own," perhaps this study, like the God of the Book of Genesis, can draw order out of the chaos.

CHAPTER 1

A Cooperative Community, 1850–1886

"To build up Sacramento and promote its prosperity"

The primacy accorded commerce and civic advancement in Sacramento provided the social and cultural framework for the city's religious communities and institutions. This was underscored in the recollection of a September 1849 Sabbath day in Sacramento by argonaut Peter Decker: "Went to church, no not church but to meeting, for it was not at the call of the church . . . bell. Neither could I see heavenward pointing spire through the trees, but found commerce had preceded the gospel when I looked at the masts of the ships crowding the Sacramento [River]."[1] Commerce had indeed preceded the gospel. In fact, commerce *was* the gospel in Sacramento.

RELIGION IN SACRAMENTO: A STRUGGLE TO FIND A PLACE

Religious communities did not have an easy time in Sacramento. Located in California's Central Valley, between two great rivers—the Sacramento and the American—Sacramento was for a time a freewheeling, transitory community with little time for religion. In the pell-mell rush for instant wealth that transformed northern California in 1848–1849, hordes of gold seekers from across the country and around the world crowded into Sacramento, coming and going to the Sierra foothills. As was common in most "instant cities" and mining camps of this era, there was a noticeable loosening of moral and social restraints. Merchant Mark Hopkins of Sacramento put a positive spin on the social climate when he wrote to his brother in 1850, "There is a freedom of thought & action that seems to characterize the people of this country." Others may have compared Sacramento to Sodom and Gomorrah. Religious faith and institutions, usually the products of more settled social conditions, struggled for a foothold in early Sacramento. As one former believer confided to Congregationalist minister William F. Taylor, many Gold Rush–era Californians "hung up their religion with their cloak" when they traveled West.[2]

Sacramento provides a good case study of the development of religion on mining frontiers of the American West.[3] Despite the lack of stable populations and apathy, ministers and preachers tried to preach the gospel in Sacramento. Early church gatherings took place along the riverfront, under stands of oaks, huddled around wagons, or perched atop quickly built levees. Later, church meetings were quartered in stables, shops, and warehouses. No early preacher could count on a regular congregation. Sacramento Congregationalist minister Joseph Augustine Benton wrote in 1849, "The citizens with a few exceptions are here without their families and not expecting to remain long."[4] The temporary locations and their transient congregations were also buffeted by the elements. The heavy rainfall of the winter of 1849–1850 brought floods, delaying the building of one church and sweeping a small Methodist chapel off its moorings. Fires raged that wiped out wide swaths of the city, including a few fledgling churches.

The Reverend Benton also noted other recurring features of Sacramento religious life: skepticism and indifference. "There were some in town then . . . who might have done much, who, it was thought would do much, and who, nevertheless, did not do much, if anything, toward establishing a church and maintaining a minister. Whether they thought the proposed preacher a very indifferent sort of a man, or suspected him of a desire to make money out of them, by going into a sort of pious speculation, or whether they were pretty indifferent characters themselves, it is

Grand Hotel ("A view from a German newspaper"), ca. 1870. Courtesy of Sacramento Archives and Museum Collection Center, Eleanor McClatchy Collection.

not necessary now to inquire." Methodist pastor Isaac Owen, writing in March 1850, could not escape the hard reality of the place: "With shame and confusion we are constrained to say that many that left their friends and homes acceptable members of the church and doubtless made fair promises to maintain their Christian character have not only failed to report themselves here as members of the church, but have fallen into the common vices of the country."[5] Even those who came with deep religious beliefs sometimes modified or abandoned them under the new circumstances in Sacramento.[6] Church founder and local Catholic physician Gregory J. Phelan observed sadly, "Many Catholics who have come to California have become very careless and indifferent." Even ministers of the gospel succumbed. Isaac Owen noted that even those "solemnly ordained and set apart to the work of ministry" had turned to waiting on tables and selling liquor.[7]

Eventually, churches were able to move from their primitive riverfront locations, and the first generation of church construction took place between I and L streets and between Fifth and Eighth. Some smaller congregations would dip south to N and east of Tenth, but the churches of the first phase of Sacramento's growth were in close proximity to one another.

An 1858 article in the *Sacramento Daily Union* indicated that the number and size of church buildings exceeded the number of people who attended them. "Much of [the number of churches] is due to our oft-boasted Californian liberality. Men who are never seen inside our churches do not hesitate to contribute handsomely to their support. . . . Were it not for this liberality, we should have much fewer churches."[8] Sacramentans may have built churches, but they did not frequent them.

Examples of religious apathy or a selective approach to religious affiliation persisted even beyond the Gold Rush era. In 1859, the *Daily Union* counted just 655 active Protestant church members in a community of 15,000. This, the writer commented, is "little leaven for so large a measure of meal," and further noted that most new members came from other cities, bearing letters of membership from their denominations elsewhere. In an 1861 sermon, the Reverend J. D. Blain bewailed the listless state of church affairs among the Methodists: "The saddest, most humiliating fact that stands out in the past has been the general lack of revivals." Even the Sunday School Union formed in September 1850 by Congregationalists, Methodists, Presbyterians, and Baptists did not bring about a quickening of Sacramento faith. Begun with some enthusiasm and an average attendance of 150 children, the school met once a month and then scaled back to meeting quarterly. When the Baptists decided to withdraw, the group went steadily downhill. By 1860, although 900 were enrolled in the program, only 475 were the offspring of active church members, meaning that children were being sent for Christian instruction without the example of parents who were regular churchgoers. When the number enrolled was contrasted with the 2,500 eligible citywide to participate, it became clear that the majority of youth did not care to participate in Sacramento's largest religious instruction program. By 1861 there were just 255 enrolled, with an average attendance of 150.[9]

The Young Men's Christian Association (YMCA), a great success in the industrial cities of the East and Midwest, had a difficult time getting off the ground in Sacramento. Begun at a prayer meeting of young men at the Baptist church in September 1866, the organization floundered, in spite of the fact that its founding president, Nehemiah Denton, worked closely with the city's Protestant clergy to broaden its appeal to the city's young men. Even taking into account the transiency of Sacramento's early population and a lack of steady leadership, the YMCA faltered because Sacramentans had other priorities. "Building their businesses, their neighborhoods, their community and their city literally from scratch . . . Sacramento just didn't have much in the middle and upper levels of society" to support the organization, notes historian Timothy Comstock. Perhaps most important, "Sacramento was not a hotbed of evangelical movement." Comstock observes, "The city had plenty of Protestant churches, with reasonably large and active congregations. However . . . those churches did not dominate the life and development of this city. . . . Sacramento developed in a state of peaceful co-existence with the churches, and not as directed by them."[10]

Organized religion also had little success as a form of social control in Sacramento.[11] Gambling, prostitution, drinking, and other social pathologies consistently resisted religious and civic efforts at cleanup during the latter half of the nineteenth and the early twentieth centuries. Religion was highly privatized in Sacramento, as it was elsewhere in the West. Sometimes people "outgrew" the religious commitments of their youth and dropped out of church altogether—never to return. Such was the case of Judge Peter Shields (1862–1962), a long-serving jurist in Sacramento County. Born a Catholic in Sacramento County, he had attended St. John the Baptist Church in Folsom and was schooled at the Christian Brothers "College." Although the brothers may have claimed him as one of their most prominent alumni (and sought his endorsement for various fundraising projects), Shields himself rejected the title "brothers' boy." By the end of his life, he described his Catholic education in remarkably nonsectarian terms. Speaking of one of the brothers who had taught him Christian doctrine, he claimed he had "little recollection" of the subject matter, "but I am sure [the brother's] faith was broad and intelligent. . . . He never attempted religious indoctrination and I left the School with a mind free to search for its own truths and to follow them when found." Shields rejected in particular Catholic teachings about a cruel and punishing God, which had scared him at a parish mission he attended as a youth. Toward the end of Shields's life, Bishop Joseph McGucken attempted to entice him back to the religion of his youth, but he gently turned the prelate away: "My dear Bishop, I have lived in this way for many years that have taken me into old age. . . . [If] I went back to the ways of sixty-five years ago I could not live differently or better than I am doing here and now."[12] Shields, like many others in the American West, did not need religion to live a life of decency and virtue. No one seemed to care whether he attended church, and he suffered no punishment at the polls from his lack of formal religious practice. His case was not unusual among many prominent Sacramentans.

Religious indifference and low rates of church affiliation persisted throughout the nineteenth century. As late as 1901, First Baptist pastor A. P. Banks complained, "The attendance is far below that of cities of like population and wealth in this state, or, so far as I know, in any state in the Union." Certainly, he moaned, "it is not the fault of preachers, for have we not had Dwinelle, Dewey, Frost, Silcox [all ministers who formerly served in Sacramento] and a score of other distinguished men, who in other cities are preaching to crowded houses?"[13]

In 1910, Presbyterian pastor J. T. Wills echoed Banks's lament, noting that even in urban booster publications, Protestant churches were given short shrift. "Are there any churches in Sacramento city and county?" Wills wondered in a newspaper editorial. He acknowledged it was "a strange question to ask," but "it has been asked by people who have read the literature sent out by real estate firms and realty syndicates, and they find that while they get a great deal of information about the climate and soil, the farms and crops, the rivers and ditches and the other advantages of the great valley, as a place in which to find homes, they find no mention of any churches." He concluded sarcastically, "Some of them say they can learn that it is a good place for raising cattle and hogs, but they want to know if it is a place where they can safely raise their children." As late as 1921, when the city was considerably developed, an eastern visitor who took in the city panorama from the capitol dome, praised the beauty and verdure of the city, but noted "one peculiarity. . . . There were no very high church spires . . . such as are usually found in a city as old and rich as Sacramento." The only exception: the Catholic cathedral.[14]

The true priests of the city were its business and professional classes. Baptist minister A. P. Banks indirectly acknowledged the primacy of business and the extensive influence of businessmen over city priorities. In his lament over low church attendance, he laid the blame for the "languid religious spirit" at the door of the very people who had built Sacramento: the businessmen. "These men, whose genius flows through every other enterprise in our city, the Churches lack."[15] Sacramento believers did eventually create churches, and various denominations established a visible presence. But there was never a critical mass sufficient enough to stamp a religious character on Sacramento in the same way Mormonism had on Salt Lake or Catholicism had on Chicago or Boston. In those cities, religious institutions attained a high level of prestige and influence in urban affairs by their sheer size and resources. In Sacramento, religion was clearly secondary to other more defined urban goals, such as money-making and city survival.

How, then, did religious institutions find their footing in western cities such as Sacramento that seemed to make a virtue of religious indifference? Naturally, as they did everywhere, religious institutions adapted themselves to their milieu. Although they retained core beliefs and practices, religious communities in the West softened the edges of their sectarian boundaries and placed more emphasis on their contributions to the social and economic development of their communities. This adaptation was best modeled, perhaps unconsciously, by the most prestigious and long-serving minister in Sacramento's first generation, Congregationalist Joseph Augustine Benton (1818–1892).

NEGOTIATING THE ROLE OF RELIGION IN "SECULAR" SACRAMENTO

Even in the heat of the Gold Rush, Sacramento was not a totally secular city. There were people who believed and prayed, and Benton found them. In the same recollections that bemoaned the skepticism and penury of early Sacramentans, Benton also mentions finding "a few at that early day who took much interest in me and my work from the very first."[16] But in order to make himself relevant to the wider community, Benton soon found a way to negotiate a middle ground between it and the unique teachings and subculture of his church. Benton's ministry provided a prototype for religious agency in the city.

Benton was one of early Sacramento's longest-serving ministers, coming to the city in 1849 and leaving in 1863. He noted in 1854, "Of the clergymen belonging to this city, there is now no one who has lived here two full years but the speaker."[17] Benton stayed long enough to understand the forces that shaped Sacramento and understood what it took to adapt his message and pastoral practices to the specific needs and ethos of the community. For example, as a gesture to his denominationally skittish Sacramento flock, he dropped the word *Congregational* from the title of First Church so as to make it more generally appealing. Likewise, he put his 350-seat church at the service of the larger community. Located at Sixth and I streets, it hosted concerts, traveling speakers (including one of the first appeals for Irish independence), and scientific demonstrations. The Sacramento Republican Party held its first convention there. Benton himself, one of the best orators in the city, occasionally lectured on secular topics. Even though the need for the church space diminished as other public halls were constructed, Benton's adept use of the church as an urban middle ground (no doubt adapted from the New England meetinghouse tradition) inserted his congregation into the mainstream of urban life.

Benton's broad-minded ministerial techniques and his far-ranging civic interests made him a sort of unofficial city chaplain during his nearly fourteen-year ministry. He appeared regularly at civic ceremonies, offering prayers and lending dignity to public events. In September 1850, he played a prominent role in one of the city's first civic "liturgies," a lengthy memorial procession to mourn the passing of President Zachary Taylor. It was a memorable occasion, with Masons in full regalia, an elegant hearse with plumed horses, the mayor and city council, and large numbers of Mexican War veterans.[18]

Apart from ceremonial religious duties, Benton swung his support behind key city priorities that had little to do with strictly religious purposes. Interestingly, he endorsed these secular ends for religious reasons. Benton viewed Sacramento's survival of flood and fire as a manifestation of divine purpose. Sacramento had been preserved for a reason; it had a destiny. In a sermon called "City-Building," he compared Sacramento to the other inland cities created during the Gold Rush, "about one-fourth of which now survive as landings or towns of some importance while most of them have left no permanent memorial and have been forgotten." Sacramento, by contrast, was "successful beyond all parallel, masterful in the struggle with fates," because it had in it "the characteristic of foresight, plan, outlook . . . enterprise."[19] Benton, in effect, baptized the survivalist consensus of the city founders.

Benton demonstrated over and over his support for Sacramento's advance.[20] He was most forceful and eloquent when he directed believers to support city development and even offered his own program of urban improvement in various sermons.[21] His orations were full of traditional moral exhortations, but also specific items that his well-heeled and socially prestigious congregation would heed. In April 1852, for example, he urged his congregants to support a new sewer system, street grading, and a new waterworks. In July 1852 he grounded his concern for Sacramento in scriptural themes lifted from chapter 29 of the book of Jeremiah: "Build ye houses and dwell in them and plant gardens and eat the fruit of them. And seek the peace of the city whither I have caused you to be carried away captives, and pray unto the Lord for it for in the peace thereof shall ye have peace."[22]

Benton's program for the "welfare of the city" meant a system of free public schools. He insisted that the "demand is urgent, it can not be done too soon. It should have been done long ago." He also pleaded for improvements in the city cemetery, where a new fence was needed to improve the "shocking barbarity and bare desolation of the place," and "the planting of the city full of young cottonwood trees—sixteen to every block, through all the streets." This, he believed, would enhance Sacramento's rude image. "Our city is perfectly level. It has not picturesque beauty of landscape—no agreeable varieties. Its only possible beauties are those of cleanliness, verdure and architecture." If trees were planted, he prophesied, "in five years we should have the most beautiful city in the state—cool, leafy, and shady. They would protect us from the sun, keep us from the dust, preserve us from the spread of fires, and hang their leaves and flutter a common joy in the face of every traveler."[23]

In 1853, after the city had again suffered flood and then fire, Benton called for a new agenda. "The conflagration changed all plans, unsettled everything. The floods and storms deranged all that was left of order and plan, almost of hope and confidence," he declared in a sermon. Plans for a city hall and a prison and his hopes for a common school system had to be placed on the back burner. He enjoined his listeners to personal austerities to pay for the needed improvements in Sacramento. "We must give over many costly and extravagant gayeties and splendors of a more private nature and not allow ourselves such latitude of personal expenditure as we sometimes do." He encouraged new priorities that would make the city safer from flood and fire: the raising of the levees, the elevation of the city grade, the creation of an efficient fire department, and the erection of brick structures. He was even willing to draft the city's well-established vice industries to serve the common good. He urged that "drinking houses, gaming saloons, and brothels—if they must be tolerated—should be taxed to the very verge of intolerableness, though they can afford to pay, strange as it may seem and lamentable to almost any extent." He noted that there were 154 taverns, restaurants, and grogeries in Sacramento and 16 saloons of some sort "where men are invited to drink something stronger than coffee." By his own computation, this came to 4 per block in the 42 developed blocks of Sacramento. He suggested a tax on these places that "would yield from 8,000 to 16,000 dollars" through a day of abstinence.[24]

Benton eventually grew weary of Sacramento, and in the late 1850s, after a tour of the Holy Land, he and his new wife (Benton had been single during his Sacramento pastorate) moved to Berkeley to help start a new college, the precursor to the University of California. Before he departed in early 1863, his last official act was to offer a prayer as the first shovels of dirt were turned for the Central Pacific Railroad.

Sacramentans remembered Benton fondly and mourned his death when he passed away in the Bay Area in 1892. When the city built a new railroad depot in 1926 and adorned one of its walls with a mural of the 1863 groundbreaking ceremony for the Central Pacific, all the "Big Four" (Stanford, Crocker, Hopkins, and Huntington) were there—but in the center was Benton, Bible in hand, standing among Sacramento's prominent leaders and presiding over the event that ensured the city's future as the most important in the Central Valley.

Perhaps other ministers endorsed similar wide-ranging and highly specific civic agendas, but in Sacramento's formative years few had the prestige, the eloquence, and the credibility of Joseph Augustine Benton. His ability to bring the resources of his office and religious authority into the service of wider civic goals laid down an important benchmark for future religious figures. Successful religious leaders who followed learned as he did to negotiate and adapt to the realities and priorities of Sacramento life. Catholics would also pick up on these lessons and work for the good of the city in ways Benton (who shared some of the traditional prejudices of his coreligionists about "Romanists") may never have imagined.

CATHOLICISM IN SACRAMENTO

Catholicism was not the religion of most Sacramentans, but it was the city's largest denomination and represented the faith of a substantial portion of its citizens. From the outset, Sacramento Catholics did not wall themselves off from their fellow citizens or seek to maintain a distinct religio-ethnic enclave. They attended public schools and welcomed non-Catholics to their own schools. With the exception of the Masons, they rubbed shoulders with people of all backgrounds in Sacramento's rich network of fraternal and social organizations.[25] They were active and visible at the highest levels of political, commercial, and professional life. Significantly, since this was officially discouraged by the church, Catholics married non-Catholics at very high rates. Above all, Catholics were actively cooperative with larger city goals. They embraced, often with enthusiasm, the goal of making Sacramento a great and respectable city. The bulwarks of their denominational identity—churches, schools, and social welfare agencies—continually emphasized their social utility to all Sacramentans regardless of creed. Individual Catholic citizens—lay, clergy, and religious—often embodied this cooperative ethos and stressed the interdependence of church and society.

Though a minority, Sacramento Catholics were numerically strong, constituting at various times a quarter to a third of the city's population. Likewise, if early fragmentary data can be believed, as well as the more substantive religious numeration compiled by the U.S. Census Bureau, Catholics were among the most faithful church members. Virtually every ethnic group in the city was represented in the Catholic Church, although the community's leadership was dominated by the Irish.

Accurate historical numbers for the earliest years of Sacramento Catholicism are difficult to find prior to 1922 (when each parish began making an annual report). Consequently, to attain a rough estimate of the number of Catholics in the city, this study uses a formula devised by Sister Marie Vandenbergh, who extrapolated approximate numbers by relating the number of annual Catholic baptisms to the number of live births in the city and county. Percentages were then determined by setting that number (admittedly rough) against the total city and county populations.

St. Rose Church, northeast corner of Seventh and к streets, ca. 1880. Courtesy of Sacramento Archives and Museum Collection Center, Eugene Hepting Collection.

Until 1894, Sacramento had only two Catholic churches, St. Rose of Lima (1850–1889) and the Cathedral of the Blessed Sacrament (1889). Most practicing Catholics in the city would have had their own names entered into the register of baptisms or marriages. With this information, it is possible to derive some basic, if imperfect, understanding of the size and nature of the Catholic community in the city and county of Sacramento.

Ascertaining the actual number of Sacramento Catholics who regularly attended church is as difficult, but the little data that exist suggest that they were quite faithful. One clue comes from the annual compendium of city statistics, which appeared each New Year's Day in the *Daily Union*. For unknown reasons, Catholics do not turn up in these numbers until 1862, when the paper reported an average attendance each Sunday for St. Rose's at 600 to 800 (the latter no doubt being the holidays of Christmas and Easter). For 1863, the average attendance grew from 800 to 1,000. In 1866, the numbers again rose from 1,200 to 1,600, but the next year declined to 1,500. Between 1870 and 1871, the number reported weekly at St. Rose's was from 3,000 to 3,500. By 1874, the number had gone down to about 1,750.[26] The religious censuses conducted by the U.S. Census Bureau reveal that 6,800 Sacramentans claimed Catholic affiliation in 1906, 7,700 in 1916, 17,253 in 1926, and 25,845 in 1936.[27]

TABLE 1.1 | CATHOLIC POPULATION OF SACRAMENTO COUNTY, 1850–1990

YEAR	ESTIMATED NUMBER OF CATHOLICS IN SACRAMENTO COUNTY	PERCENTAGE OF CATHOLICS IN SACRAMENTO COUNTY
1850	400	4
1860	5,429	23
1870	4,771	18
1880	5,171	15
1890	5,571	15
1900	8,050	18
1910	11,000	16
1920	18,844	21
1930	16,083	11
1940	33,434	20
1950	49,750	18
1960	106,394	21
1970	81,490	13
1980	110,152	14
1990	114,985	11

SOURCE: Estimates are derived from mathematical extrapolations of baptismal records (pre-1930) and parish reports (1930–1990). Sometimes parish reports are missing for certain years, and an approximation is made based on projected growth during the decade.

More indicative of Catholic growth was institutional expansion. Catholic churches, schools, hospitals, and social services grew in response to Catholic numbers. Catholic life "officially" began in Sacramento in 1850 with the establishment of St. Rose of Lima Church on Seventh and κ streets. After several false starts, church founders erected a permanent structure there in 1855, which served as the city's only parish for many years. In 1886, Sacramento became the headquarters of a new diocese, or regional ecclesiastical jurisdiction, for northern California and, until 1931, eastern Nevada. The presence of a residential bishop enhanced the prestige of Catholics in the state capital. Various bishops played active roles as urban agents throughout Sacramento's history. Catholic institutional life grew steadily, and sometimes spectacularly, during the next 150 years. The institutional growth of Catholic churches in the time frame of this study suggests that it kept pace with the spatial and demographic transitions of the area.

Institutional expansion gave the church an important foothold in city life. These buildings occupied important urban space. Each of them represented investments of financial and human resources in the community. Catholics had every reason to embrace the urban consensus and be among the most cooperative of citizens. The welfare of the city was inextricably linked to their own collective well-being. This was often modeled by local Catholics who were also civic leaders.

CIVIC-MINDED GREGORY PHELAN: CHURCH FOUNDER

Gregory Phelan (1822–1902) was one of the first Catholic Sacramentans who blended faith and civic responsibility in his career. Active in Sacramento almost from the beginnings of the city, he was an important figure in both city and church affairs until he left the city in 1870.

After attending medical schools in Massachusetts and New York, Phelan, a native of New York City, answered a call for physicians to come West.[28] Sailing around the Horn, he arrived in San Francisco in July 1849, and soon decamped for Sacramento, where he quickly became a respected physician and civic leader. In 1855 he married Cecilia Blanchet, the sister of two Catholic bishops serving in the Northwest.

Phelan joined the informal coalition of "civic middlemen," or cadre of professionals, merchants, and land speculators who shaped Sacramento's destiny in the critical 1850s.[29] He believed that Sacramento had a real future:

TABLE 1.2 | CATHOLIC CHURCHES IN SACRAMENTO COUNTY, 1850–2005

PARISH NAME	LOCATION	YEAR FOUNDED	ASSORTED DATA
St. Rose of Lima	Seventh and K	1850	Closed in 1887, and then the congregation rented temporary quarters until the cathedral was completed in 1889
St. John the Baptist	City of Folsom	1857	
St. Christopher	Galt	1888	
Cathedral of the Blessed Sacrament	Eleventh and K	1889	
St. Francis of Assisi	Twenty-sixth and K	1894	
St. Stephen	Third and O	1900	Mission of cathedral except from 1924 to 1944 when it was under the ownership of Japanese theater owners
St. Mary, Italian	Eighth and N	1906	Moved to Seventh and T in 1914; relocated to Fifty-eighth and M in 1948
Immaculate Conception	Oak Park	1909	
St. Elizabeth, Portuguese	Twelfth and S	1909	
St. Mel	Fair Oaks	1921	Mission of Folsom until 1947
St. Joseph	North Sacramento	1924	
Sacred Heart	East Sacramento	1926	Originally named St. Stephen
Holy Spirit	Land Park	1940	
All Hallows	Tahoe Park	1942	
St. Rose	Franklin Blvd.	1942	Orphanage chapel raised to parochial status
St. Philomene	Arden Arcade	1948	
Holy Family	Citrus Heights	1949	
Our Lady of the Assumption	Carmichael	1952	
St. Therese	Isleton	1953	
St. Ignatius of Loyola	Arden	1954	
St. Lawrence the Martyr	North Highlands	1955	
St. Peter	South Sacramento	1955	
St. Robert	South Sacramento	1955	
Our Lady of Lourdes	Del Paso Heights	1957	
Our Lady of Guadalupe, Latino/a	Seventh and T	1958	Began as chapel in 1944 at St. Stephen site (Third and O)
St. John Vianney	Rancho Cordova	1958	
St. Paul	Florin	1958	Originally mission of All Hallows
St. Charles Borromeo	Parkway Estates	1960	
St. John the Evangelist	Carmichael	1960	
St. Anne	Meadowview	1961	
Presentation	Arden	1961	
St. Joseph	Elk Grove	1962	Originally mission of St. Christopher in Galt
St. Anthony	Pocket area	1974	
Vietnamese Catholic Martyrs	Southern suburbs	1986	Vietnamese national parish
Divine Savior	Orangevale	1987	
St. Jeong-Hae Elizabeth	Southern suburbs	1993	Korean national parish
St. Stephen	Fruitridge	2002	To provide Latin mass
Divine Mercy	Natomas	2005	

SOURCE: Official Catholic Directory, 1850–2006, Diocese of Sacramento, California.

This is destined to be a great agricultural as well as mining country, and in a few years, no doubt, will be thickly settled. The climate is good, the soil fertile and the mines rich. A good wagon road will soon be made across the plains to Missouri, then the telegraphy wires will be laid, and before many years elapse the great Atlantic and Pacific Railroad must be constructed. Immigration will rapidly increase, lands will increase in value, and the immense resources of the State will be more and more developed.[30]

Phelan served on the city's first school board and helped to found its first medical association. In the 1860s he functioned as city and county physician as well as the superintendent of the Sacramento County Hospital. He also invested heavily in the city's future development, purchasing large swaths of land on the city's eastern extremities.[31]

Phelan was also the prime mover behind the organization of Catholic life in the city. Beginning in 1850 and using the nom de plume "Philos," he wrote regularly for the New York–based nationally circulated Catholic newspaper the *Freeman's Journal.* Phelan routinely boosted the city's image in eastern Catholic newspapers and did what he could to create a visible Catholic presence in Sacramento. He wrote in 1850, "There is much to be accomplished: churches to be built, congregations organised, religious institutions established, in fact hardly a beginning has been made in the northern part of California; everything remains to be done; there are children without schools, orphans without asylums, sick and needy but no Sisters of Charity or Mercy to assist and console them."[32] Phelan continued his occasional articles until 1858, when the "Irish and Catholic" *San Francisco Monitor* provided more than enough news about Sacramento for eastern sources.

CATHOLIC ORIGINS SUGGEST COOPERATION

The traditional story of Catholic beginnings in Sacramento is a mixture of heroic legend and hard fact. Clerical historians generally ascribe the church's foundation to the first Sunday mass celebrated by Dominican Peter Augustine Anderson in August 1850.[33] Phelan's account of the service gives us another case study of the general patterns of Sacramento's religious life: It was heavily male. Of the seventy to eighty persons gathered for the mass, only "about a dozen were ladies." Many of those who came had not been to church in a long time, and it was evident "they probably had almost forgotten many things." Anderson "reminded the hearers of the awful solemnity of the Mass and of the necessity of attentive and respectful deportment during its celebration." Finally, the first mass held the promise of the future, as three children were baptized on that afternoon. In one of those unique moments when Catholicism blended so seamlessly with the dynamics of the Gold Rush, it was noted that one of the infants who had been "born at the foot of the great Sierra Nevada mountains" was "named after our Illustrious Pontiff." The child's name was Pius Sierra Nevada O'Brien. "For this one," Phelan proudly noted, "I was asked to assume the responsible office of 'Compadre.'"[34]

However, the first mass also had non-Catholics in attendance. Phelan noted that Anderson welcomed "those who differed in religion," assuring them "that there was nothing of the mummery or show in the forms and ceremonies and dress but on the contrary, that they all tend to attract the mind and keep it fixed on the great sacrifice of Mount Calvary." The first mass also formally launched the organizational efforts to create a permanent church. Phelan reported that a committee was formed to determine a permanent location for the Sacramento flock; the committee would report to the pastor, who held veto power.[35] At this point, other laymen came forward to assist, including Peter Burnett, a Catholic convert and the first governor of California, who donated land at Tenth and I streets for a church. When this plot became tied up in squatter litigation, Burnett donated another plot, this one on Seventh and K streets, where the church was finally planted. To be sure, Burnett, an important land speculator in Sacramento and a major player in Sacramento's subsequent development, gave this land out of devotion, but he also knew that a church would add to the value and attractiveness of city property. Church and city worked to each other's mutual benefit.

The first mass suggested bonds of cooperation between civic and religious leaders that would be replicated throughout Sacramento history. Clerical historians rarely refer to the role of Phelan and Burnett, preferring to accord the honor to Anderson, who died of cholera in Sacramento four months after celebrating the first mass. However heroic Anderson's deeds, the Catholic presence in Sacramento owed more to Phelan. He represented a "type" of civic-minded Catholic leader who would appear and reappear in Sacramento life. There were other factors as well that contributed to steady Catholic support for the urban consensus.

INTEGRATING CATHOLICS INTO THE URBAN FABRIC

Phelan worried that the lack of priests and churches might dissolve ties of allegiance to the church. "Mixed marriages become frequent," he lamented. "Indifference follows and hundreds of children grow up without religious instruction."[36] Although he had married into a strong Catholic family, many of his coreligionists in Sacramento had not. In fact, intermarriage became a common occurrence during Sacramento's first generation. In 1856 the number of mixed marriages held at just 4 percent of Catholics; by 1862 that figure had risen to 44 percent. The rate then declined significantly to 28 percent and from then on averaged 22 percent until the end of the 1880s.[37]

Matrimonia mixta was a general "problem" for the church in the United States—although it diminished in some parts of the country as the Catholic population surged. In the American West, however, intermarriage was a fact of life, given the uneven ratios of men to women and the lack of clergy, religious education, and social pressures to "marry your own." Catholic clerics in western missionary areas frequently presided at the marriages of Catholics and non-Catholics even though American bishops issued a steady stream of admonitions against the practice at provincial, or plenary, councils throughout the nineteenth century.[38]

The intermarriage of Catholics and non-Catholics or nonbelievers may indeed have weakened religious identity as Catholic bishops feared, but it no doubt contributed to the general climate of religious toleration that characterized Sacramento. The chances were very good that the typical Sacramento Catholic was related to or even married to a non-Catholic. If blood or marital relationships were not enough to promote toleration, the relatively small confines (spatial and otherwise) of Sacramento society meant that Catholics and non-Catholics regularly encountered each other and worked cooperatively with one another.

Another critical factor in the character of early Sacramento Catholic life was that the church was dominated by men and women who spoke English. More specifically, a large number of its members and virtually all of its leaders were either Irish-born or of Irish descent. In particular, the advance of an Irish American identity played a significant role in making Sacramento Catholics enthusiastic urban boosters.

In 1850 there were about 250 foreign-born Irish in Sacramento County. Two years later there were 545, making them the second-largest European group after the Germans. By 1860 they reached their peak within the city, numbering 2,500.[39] Patrick Joseph Blessing's study of the Irish in Sacramento and Los Angeles between 1850 and 1880 suggests that they were a close-knit group who looked out for one another.[40] Continued immigration, especially after the Civil War, as well as healthy second- and third-generation loyalties (many of them perpetuated by Irish Catholic associationalism and Irish authority within the local Catholic church) made Irish identity a fact of life in Sacramento for many years. An examination of the baptismal statistics of the only parish in the city reveals that from 1855 through 1885, the Irish constituted anywhere from 33 to 53 percent of Catholics. In addition, 7 to 25 percent of those baptized during that same period had at least one parent of Irish extraction.[41]

Many of the Irish listed in the St. Rose baptismal register were working-class denizens, several of them simply having the title "laborer" affixed to their names in city directories. They provided manpower for the construction trades—laying gas lines, assisting in the raising of the city grade, and so on. Historians Dian Self and Elaine Connolly suggest that Irish women were also to be found in the ranks of city housekeepers, schoolteachers, and even prostitutes. Blessing's samples include a respectable number of upper (or "better") classes among the Sacramento Irish, specifically citing prominent figures such as church founder Gregory Phelan—although he was Irish American.[42] Foreign-born Irish included Antrim-born James McClatchy, who served a term as sheriff of Sacramento County in 1864 and directed the *Daily Bee,* one of the city's most popular newspapers; grocer Christopher Green, who was elected first trustee and mayor of the city in 1873; and Wexford-born Thomas Dwyer, whose fortune in the river trade and brick making made him one of Sacramento's most prominent citizens.

Irish ethnic loyalties were on display in nineteenth-century Sacramento. Beginning in 1857, local Irish citizens organized celebrations of St. Patrick, Ireland's patron saint. Veneration of the saint vied with public support for Ireland's long quest for independence on these occasions.[43] In 1854, the famous Irish nationalist Waterford-born Thomas Francis Meagher (later governor of Montana) visited the city and inspired the formation of several nationalist organizations.[44] By the 1860s, Sacramento had two branches of the popular Irish militia companies, the Emmet Guard and the Sarsfield Grenadier Guards, and a smaller Fenian Circle.[45] On St. Patrick's Day 1865, 350 people marched in support of the city's growing Fenian organization. Despite opposition to the movement from the Catholic archbishop of San Francisco (who had ecclesiastical jurisdiction over Sacramento and also opposed such revels during the penitential season of Lent), hundreds of Sacramento Irish turned out to cheer on the cause of the Irish nationalists. Irish nationalist causes dominated even after the Fenian movement declined, and interest in Irish affairs continued to energize Sacramentans well into the twentieth century. The legion of Irish nationalist speakers included Eamon de Valera, the first president of the Irish Republic, who traversed the United States in the late nineteenth and early twentieth centuries.

The celebration of Irish culture found a place in Sacramento's communal life. The city's Robert Emmett Club endorsed Irish independence at various events. A Sacramento branch of the Land League, an organization dedicated to land reform in Ireland, and the Sacramento Irish Sufferers Relief Committee both raised funds to tend to dire conditions in the homeland. In 1870, the Irish founded a branch of the popular Ancient Order of Hibernians (AOH). Begun in Ireland in the sixteenth century, the order came to America in 1836 and supported Irish Catholics experiencing persecution in Erin. The order also provided benefits for its members in the event of sickness or death.[46] All of these groups held monthly meetings, hosted social activities whose proceeds sometimes went to the church, and maintained the loyalties of the Sacramento Irish to the church.

Irish priests, brothers, and nuns exercised considerable influence over the city's religious culture.[47] For many years, even after Irish immigration slowed to a trickle and Hibernian Sacramentans were more Irish American than full Irish, the clergy and religious women were regularly replenished with first-generation residents. Indeed, Sacramento had a steady flood of Irish priests and nuns who arrived in successive waves that persisted as late as after World War II.

The Sisters of Mercy, who came to Sacramento in 1857, were an Irish foundation of a convent in Kinsale. Through the voices of these sisters, many Catholic schoolchildren, Irish or not, heard of the beauty and struggles of the Emerald Isle and were introduced to its history, its geography, and especially its Catholic culture. At the closing exercises for St. Joseph School in July 1870, the Sisters of Mercy choreographed 300 girls who marched into the convent assembly hall singing "The Wearing of the Green."[48] Likewise, the Christian Brothers, who opened a boys' school in 1876, were heavily Irish. Like the pupils at St. Joseph School, the young men at the Christian Brothers School also received a full dose of Irish nationalism and history. One of the most vocal proponents of Irish nationalism in Sacramento was Christian Brother Justin McMahon, a fiery orator who regularly denounced the British and headed up relief collections for the victims of English tyranny.[49] Even well into the twentieth century the Irish dominance of the sisters and priests left their imprint on young Richard Rodriguez, who recalled the Irish-born nuns and priests at Sacramento's Sacred Heart School in the 1950s: "'Our lovely Ireland,' the nuns would always call her. . . . Ireland was where old priests returned to live with their widowed sisters and (one never said it) to die. . . . Ireland was our heart's home."[50]

In the nineteenth century, seven of the ten men who administered the affairs of St. Rose Church were of Irish birth, and all of them had been educated in the Irish seminary system. It was All Hallows, Ireland's famed missionary seminary just outside of Dublin, that provided many of Sacramento's priests in the nineteenth century (among them James Cassin, James L. Cotter, Thomas Gibney, Patrick Scanlan, and Thomas Grace). Founded in 1842, All Hallows equipped its charges spiritually and psychologically to manage the multiple tasks of church building in missionary territories.[51] Other Irish seminaries at Wexford, Carlow, Waterford, Thurles, and Maynooth also sent men to serve in the California "mission." Perhaps the largest groups of Irish clergy came after World War II, when diocesan chancellors Monsignors Thomas A. Kirby and Cornelius P. Higgins regularly visited the seminaries of the Emerald Isle to recruit eager young men to come to the United States. Likewise, in the 1950s, the Diocese of Sacramento helped the local Sisters of Mercy erect a training facility in Ardfert, County Kerry, to recruit young Irish women for service in California.

Irish clergy were most visible and vocal as proponents of Irish nationalism. Typical were the comments of St. Rose pastor Reverand Patrick Scanlan, who declared at the city's St. Patrick's Day celebrations in 1873: "England has robbed you of everything but your flag and your cross and Wendell Phillipps says that the Irishman in America with the cross in his right-hand and his flag in his left is forever a standing menace to England. I hope they will always go on hand in hand." Later, the Reverend William "Will" Ellis carried the torch of Irish nationalism in the state capital. A native of County Longford, polished and eloquent, Ellis was a scholar of Irish literature and a supporter of the late-nineteenth-century Gaelic revival. "I cannot imagine there is one in whose veins runs one drip of Celtic blood that is indifferent or forgets his motherland," he lectured the local Irish associations on one St. Patrick's Day. On another occasion from the cathedral pulpit he lamented, "We sons and daughters three thousand miles away from our motherland are too far to wipe from her furrowed cheek the tears of suffering, yet near enough to send the message that brings consolation to her heart. That message—that we live true to the faith for which our fathers battled and for which our martyrs died."[52]

The foreign-born Irish were important players in Sacramento's first generations. However, as Blessing's study of the Irish in California observes, Irish agency in Sacramento was different from other parts of the country. "The variety of Irish immigrant institutions in Sacramento . . . was never as extensive as [it was] on the east coast," and Blessing notes that the Sacramento Irish never attained the "institutional completeness" to allow them to separate themselves from others in the city.[53] It was this factor that contributed in some degree to the high level of Catholic cooperation with Sacramento's civic agenda, making the Sacramento Irish and, even more, the city's Irish Americans key agents in developing a cooperative relationship with the city.

The first Irish who came to Sacramento in the Gold Rush period were predominantly male, unmarried, transient, and literate. Unlike the Irish in other parts of the country, the Irish in the West did not come directly from the Emerald Isle (in fact, this was true of most immigrants to Sacramento) but had lived and worked in other parts of the United States before coming to California. This made the typical Irish Sacramentan not only generally more highly skilled, better educated, and financially more secure than fellow Hibernians in the eastern United States but also less insecure about American customs and culture and hence more disposed to "fit in." As Blessing and Timothy Sarbaugh suggest, Irish-born and Irish American citizens in the West may have encountered some discrimination, but overall they found it easy to establish a business and make it succeed in the social and political milieu of "instant cities."[54]

Timothy Meagher's studies on second- and even third-generation Irish identity have some applicability to Sacramento realities. Meagher observes of generational change among the Worcester, Massachusetts, Irish "the fluidity of ethnic identifications, boundaries and cultures" and "the capacity of ethnic groups to continually reinvent themselves through new definitions of identity, expansion, or contraction of group boundaries."[55] Meagher examines the sometimes conflicted identity of second-generation Irish Americans who (quoting historian William Shannon) lived with "a foot in both worlds." In the fluid social and political conditions of the West, which threw few roadblocks to Irish upward mobility in politics, the professions, or commerce, those feet may have landed more in the American world than in the Irish world. In fact, Irish assimilation in the West took place relatively painlessly and allowed the Irish to thrive in San Francisco. Sarbaugh also insists that Irish identity in San Francisco was marked by attachment to the Catholic Church and to the causes of Irish nationalism.[56] Yet significant regional differences notwithstanding, Meagher's descriptions of Irish accommodation—even in the wake of occasional outbursts of nativist anti-Catholicism—ring true of the Irish American experience in Sacramento.

Sacramento's migration from Irish to Irish American identity came even as Irish nationalism and public displays were at their peak. Generational differences were already evident in 1869 when the young women of St. Joseph School concluded their academic year by singing "The Bonnie Flag of Green." Here a reporter for the *San Francisco Monitor* made an important observation when he noted how moved he was to be carried "back in thought to the Fatherland, when I heard it sung by children *who had never been there but who seemingly inherit the love of the 'Bonnie Flag' from their parents or maybe from their good teachers.*"[57] In fact, the young women who sang the nostalgic song were like so many described by historian Kerby Miller, yearning for an Ireland long lost, or in this case never experienced. These same young women presaged the subtle transition that would replace intense Irish nationalism with a blend of nostalgia and a new civic consciousness. Eventually, as historian Elizabeth McKee maintains, the city's Irish population "developed a dual identity as American and Irish with loyalties they grew to consider synonymous."[58]

After 1875 the St. Patrick's Day parades began to lose momentum, as did the belligerent Irish nationalism they expressed. From 1877 on, the scaled-back celebrations increasingly became city celebrations, using the general theme of Irish nationalism to showcase Sacramento's bright, young Irish American talent. At the 1877 festival, Francis DeSales Ryan, then a pupil at the Christian Brothers School and destined for a brilliant if short-lived career in Sacramento politics, delivered Irish patriot Robert Emmet's speech on being convicted of high treason. However, instead of focusing on the righteousness of the Irish cause, the Catholic press honed in on the young man's skills as a speaker. "The manner in which this young gentleman acquitted himself was excellent. His voice was clear and finely modulated." John Delury notes that the last St. Patrick's Day parade (until the late 1950s, when the Shriners revived them), in 1879, "was the most civic-minded to date, the most open to the wider community." In fact, Delury observes, the term *Irish Americans* was first used by the local press in commenting on the parade and further notes that "the old inward-turning ethnic fervor was merging with a wider sense of being American."[59] The hybrid Irish Americanism (apart from that of the foreign-born clergy) that emerged in Sacramento was the best representation of local sentiment.

There were some prominent Sacramento Irish Americans who were even anxious to shed their identification with the Auld Sod and resisted the romanticism of Irish nationalism and active membership in the Catholic Church. One was James McClatchy's son Charles Kenny McClatchy, who edited the *Sacramento Bee* from 1883 to his death in 1936. McClatchy was decidedly unsentimental about Ireland and detested "hyphenated-Americanism." From time to time his opinionated columns insisted that even though he was proud of his Irish father, he was an American. It was on this and other scores that he waged a noisy public dispute with the Reverend Peter C. Yorke of San Francisco, one of California's greatest apostles of Irish identity.[60] However, most second- and even some first-generation Irish Sacramentans cherished their Irish heritage and were also, for the most part, devout Catholics. A good number of Irish Sacramentans entered public life as city councilmen, sheriffs, supervisors, city managers, and superintendents of schools.

William F. Gormley was one of many "bridge figures" who illustrate the urban commitment of Sacramento's Irish Americans.[61] Gormley was born in 1862 in Irvinestown, County Fermanagh. Gormley's father, Thomas, a millwright and pattern maker, migrated to California's El Dorado County in 1871. The Gormley family reunited in 1872, and two years later they moved to Sacramento, where Thomas found steady work with the Central Pacific Railroad. Apprenticed at age fifteen to a bookbinder, young William soon found a very substantial job as assistant foreman of the State Printing Office. When Bishop Patrick Manogue moved to Sacramento in 1886, he brought with him his young niece Minnie Fogarty, whom he had raised since she was twelve. After Patrick died in February 1895, Minnie and "Billy" Gormley were married in 1896 by the Reverend (later Bishop) Thomas Grace. In 1897, Grace convinced the young man to become a funeral director. As the sole Catholic undertaker in Sacramento for many years, Gormley made a great many friends among the clergy and the Catholic community at large.

Gormley was probably the most visible and prominent Irish Catholic layman in Sacramento from 1897 until his death in 1935. An inveterate joiner, he was a member of the San Francisco Bookbinder's Union and the Sacramento Council of Federated Trades.[62] He was a devout cathedral parishioner and a leading force in creating associations of Catholic professionals. He participated in the founding of nearly every major Catholic men's organization in the city.

Gormley was also, for a time, a popular local politician. He first entered regional politics at the urging of the County Democratic Central Committee as a candidate for county coroner in 1898. He served in this capacity and also as sheriff on two different occasions. Eventually turned out of office, he retired to the funeral home business. Since day-to-day operations were by then handled by his sons, Manogue and Thomas, he was free to pursue his civic and political interests.

Another distinguished Irish American Catholic was Robert T. Devlin, who was born in Sacramento in 1859, the son of a prosperous grocer. After graduating from Sacramento High School, he read law in the firm of longtime Sacramento attorney George Cadwallader, and in 1881 opened his own firm, Devlin and Devlin, with his brother William. Devlin cemented his social prominence by his marriage to Mary Ellen Dwyer, the daughter of transportation magnate Thomas Dwyer. A skilled attorney, he also was an active supporter of the Southern Pacific, which in turn made possible his career in local politics and land dealing. He served on the commission to revise the city charter in 1891 and invested heavily in the development of the city's Oak Park neighborhood. From 1884 to 1912 he was a member of the state board of prison directors. From 1900 to 1904 he represented Sacramento County in the state senate, retiring from the legislature to accept an appointment as U.S. attorney for the Northern District. Devlin held this position until 1912 and then returned to private practice.

Touted frequently as a candidate for higher judicial office in both the federal and the state systems, Devlin developed a national reputation as an expert on property law. His *Treaty Power Under the Constitution of the United States* (1908) became a required text in many law schools. Likewise, *The Law of Real Property and Deeds* (1911) went through several editions.

Devlin was a member of every prestigious club in the city and a prominent member of St. Francis Church. He was often called upon to express the patriotic sentiments of Catholic citizens. Together with another second-generation Irish Sacramentan, Valentine McClatchy, Devlin was a founder of the city's prestigious Sutter Club. In the smoke-filled paneled rooms of the club, Sacramento businessmen were urged to "shake off the cares of business" and seek "the opportunity of interchanging views with other business and professional men."[63]

Other Irish American Catholic politicians included William Hassett, who governed the city in the early years of the twentieth century; city trustees James Devine and E. J. Carraghar; and local political bosses Bart Cavanaugh Sr. and Thomas Fox.[64] In business, Wexford-born Thomas Dwyer held a virtual monopoly on Sacramento's river-cargo traffic. Minnie Rooney O'Neil, a graduate of a Sacramento convent school, was the county's first female superintendent of schools. Other Sacramento Catholic women were found among the ranks of schoolteachers and principals in the city school system.

Sacramento's Irish American organizations also stressed dual loyalties. The Ancient Order of Hibernians provided the main organizational umbrella for Irish cultural and social events in the capital city. Although committed to the cause of Irish freedom, their fund-raising efforts were often directed to local Catholic institutions. After the St. Patrick's Day parades fell by the wayside, the AOH organized the annual *killegh* (social gathering) at which local Irish Americans could dance until the early hours of the morning.

AOH president Terrence Mulligan reflected the direction of Irish American life in Sacramento by the 1920s. The longtime head of Sacramento's fire department, Mulligan was a native of New York and claimed to have experienced anti-Irish discrimination as a young man. Although he cherished his Irish identity, he nonetheless diversified Sacramento's firefighting force (once thought to be an Irish enclave). Mulligan was a charming and popular man, as at home in the Oak Park Irish tavern owned by the Ryles of County Kerry as he was in the Croatian-owned Rosemont Grill and the Italian-run Espanol Restaurant. He even boasted of his ability to get along with the city's Masons—a group off-limits to most Catholics.[65]

Two largely Irish American organizations, the Young Men's Institute and the Young Ladies' Institute (YMI and YLI), flourished for a time in Sacramento. Both of these groups began among Irish Catholic laity in San Francisco. The YMI was established in 1883 by James McDade, a mechanical-drawing instructor and later a public official, and James Smith, a former governor-general of the Philippines. McDade and Smith recruited a number of young Irish Catholics to the group, which the *San Francisco Monitor* characterized as "a mutual aid and beneficial organization composed of Catholic young men."[66] The group met annually in a convention called the Grand Council, which put on public demonstrations of Catholic loyalty and held masses and street parades. The Sacramento YMI raised funds for tidal-wave victims in Galveston, Texas, after a devastating storm in 1900, came to the aid of 1906 earthquake and fire victims in San Francisco, and supported other charities.[67] The group distinguished itself primarily through sponsorship of cultural and social events for improving the social and intellectual life of its members and demonstrating their patriotism. The women's branch, the Young Ladies' Institute, soon followed the YMI and began a branch in Sacramento in 1889. The women of the YLI raised funds for charities—especially orphanages—and underwrote benevolent activities in public hospitals.[68]

CATHOLIC CLERGY AS SACRAMENTO CITIZENS

Irish priests and bishops were also supportive of the city agenda—especially of social peace. Catholic clergy in Sacramento, as in other parts of the West, were noted for their toleration of non-Catholics and even of nonbelievers. Typical was the Reverend (later Bishop) Thomas Grace, who took over as pastor of St. Rose's in 1884. A native of County Wexford, he had come to the United States in 1866 after his ordination and had worked in Catholic churches all over northern California and Nevada. As bishop, Grace lived a simple and frugal life, often traveling by himself to remote areas of the Sacramento Diocese. He was a quiet but generous benefactor of the city's annual Fourth of July celebrations, and when the city celebrated its electrification in 1895, he donated the then large sum of two hundred dollars from his own purse. He also subscribed to the fund appeal to bring the Western Pacific yards to Sacramento.

Grace's irenic approach to the religious diversity of the city was on display in a very important way early in the twentieth century. During the city's 1894 Pullman strike, Grace interceded with the leadership of the Central Pacific to reinstate workers who had joined the strikers. His close association with the superintendent of the railroad yards, Episcopalian Col. John B. Wright, established a warm personal bond between the two men. When Wright died in May 1903, Grace, by this time bishop of Sacramento, publicly appeared at the side of the local Episcopal bishop in the sanctuary to offer condolences—a first in California. Several of his priests claimed to be "grieved" by this joint appearance with a Protestant, and one, the Reverend Michael Wallrath, reported him to the apostolic delegate to the United States, the pope's personal representative. When asked to give an explanation for this unseemly "religious mixing" to his superiors, Grace calmly explained that his presence was a token of gratitude and esteem for Wright, who had reinstated many workers at Grace's request after the strike.

Grace epitomized the somewhat indulgent attitude that many western clerics felt toward those who did not either affiliate or regularly attend church. "You should go to some church," the prelate counseled, "but if you don't—then live a life that will enable you to have a clear conscience and in the end that will count." Grace's tolerance was certainly picked up by members of his flock. In 1914 when Catholics formed a corporation to raise money for the construction of a new clubhouse, two Catholic women, Minnie O'Neil and Clara Diepenbrock, urged admitting Protestants to the organization. They were opposed, however, by cathedral rector Thomas Hayes.[69]

Grace was at his best when dealing with fallen-away Catholics such as newspaper editor C. K. McClatchy. Grace presided at the 1885 nuptials of McClatchy and his devoutly Catholic wife, Ella Kelly. He baptized McClatchy's three children and served as godfather to one of the McClatchy daughters, Eleanor, who took the middle name "Grace" in his honor. Editor McClatchy could sometimes be hard on the Irish, the Catholic Church, missionaries, and religion in his columns, but it never deterred Grace, who took the published outbursts in stride. When the editor decided to take an extended trip abroad, Grace wrote letters of introduction for him to the court of Pope Pius X and arranged for a personal audience with the pontiff.

CONCLUSION

Catholics have been active urban agents throughout Sacramento's history. Their efforts, as we shall see, were sometimes very public and their contributions to the city literally monumental. But more often than not, Catholic agency was low-key and hidden. From time to time, evidence of this fruitful relationship between city and church would become manifest. When in 1908 a citywide parade brought out scores of Catholic groups to march, surprising many (including Catholics themselves), a periodical of the cathedral noted, "For years the Catholics of Sacramento have been content to go their way in a quiet, unobtrusive manner, avoiding as much as possible the searchlight of popular notice. They have kept to themselves, as it were, though of course individually mingling in the commercial, social, and civic activities of the town. For this reason the outside public has not fully appreciated the numerical strength of the Catholic body, or its importance from every point of view as a factor in the spiritual and material up building of the community."[70] These broad principles of church and city cooperation worked well for the Catholic community in the California capital. They also worked for Sacramento.

CHAPTER 2

Cathedral Building As Urban Project, 1865–1889

"It is high time we had a new church"

Sacramento's Catholics built the majestic Cathedral of the Blessed Sacrament in 1889. At the time of its dedication it was the largest Roman Catholic church west of the Rocky Mountains. Although today dwarfed by large skyscrapers, for many years its stately dome and towers loomed large over the flat city. Together with the imposing state capitol, a block away, the cathedral provided Sacramento with its first real skyline. The Cathedral of the Blessed Sacrament was no ordinary building. Its placement, size, and grandiose architecture were part of a deliberate plan by the city's first bishop to put the Catholic Church "on the map," while he materially assisted Sacramento's dreams of urban glory. All this took place within the context of a number of developments that ensured the city's social and economic dominance in the Central Valley.

BUILDING A RESPECTABLE CITY

Sacramento passed through another period of environmental travail as the city flooded again in 1861–1862.[1] This time some businesses and commercial houses evacuated the city never to return. The city population leveled off, and questions again arose about the suitability of the site for the state capital. City buildings were functional and uninspiring at best. Roads were dusty in the dry months and mud-choked in the rainy season, sewers did not always work, and the levee system around the River City had proved inadequate. Sacramento was damp in the winter and beastly hot in the summer. San Francisco, the city's rival, occasionally lobbed insults at the provincial state capital, and its "cow town" image contrasted badly with San Francisco's cosmopolitan atmosphere. The egress of the fabled "Big Four"—Stanford, Huntington, Crocker, and Hopkins—all of whom had made their railroad fortune in Sacramento, set an unfortunate pattern for those who had "made it" in the state capital, leaving as soon as they could. This was a sensitive point revealed in the 1916 obituary of local entrepreneur and politician Jesse W. Wilson quoted in the Introduction. Some of the worst critics of Sacramento were state legislators who came to the capital for legislative sessions and complained bitterly about the dismal living and working conditions. Sacramento did not have good hotels, paved roads, or decent drinking and bathing water (although it did have plenty of gaming tables and whorehouses). Some state offices, such as the supreme court, were located in San Francisco and strenuously resisted periodic calls to relocate to the seat of state government.

The floods may have discouraged some, but for others the deluge unleashed the "indomitable" energies of the city founders (in fact, the motto Urbs Indomita was added to the city seal after the floods of 1861). Within a year after the floodwaters receded, the city began a multiyear process of revamping its sewer system and raising the grade of its streets. In what even today remains one of the most remarkable feats of urban survival, residents and shopkeepers living or working along the path of the street raising spent thousands to elevate their structures to the new city level.[2]

Out of the travails of the early 1860s, a stronger, more stable Sacramento emerged. By the turn of the century Sacramento was well on the way to the respectability it craved with a stable and productive local economy, a growing number of cultural amenities, and the beginnings of a building renaissance that improved the appearance of the community. The symbolic center of this urban resurrection was a permanent and beautiful state capitol building, which Sacramentans hailed as an anchor and a benchmark for future developments.

Since 1855, the state government had been meeting in the city's courthouse, but by the late 1850s demands for a larger and more permanent statehouse became more insistent.[3] The first plans called for the new capitol to be erected on the public square between I and J and Ninth and Tenth, today's César Chávez Park. Architect Reuben Clark designed an imposing Corinthian-style three-story building, capped with a huge dome. Foundation work began on this structure in late 1856, but had to be stopped when difficulties arose over the constitutionality of its funding. A new flurry of politicking ensued, culminating in the decision in late 1860 to relocate the statehouse to four large blocks stretching from L to N and Tenth to Twelfth streets. (This land was already occupied by some, including the Sisters of Mercy.) Miner F. Butler's design, a smaller replica of the U.S. Capitol, was selected and the cornerstone laid on May 15, 1861. Construction moved slowly thanks to floods, labor difficulties, changes of architects, and shortages of supplies. Nonetheless, by 1869 the capitol's soaring dome loomed over the flat city. Gaslights flickered in the new statehouse by November, and the governor, legislature, and the supreme court moved in by the end of the year, even though the building would not be totally completed until 1874.

The new capitol building worked wonders. It reoriented the unrelenting grid pattern of Sacramento by giving it a center and a qualitative aesthetic standard for the built environment. A *Bee* editorialist noted that the new statehouse was "a masterful piece of architecture" upon which no one could look without feeling its "refining impulses." He predicted that its influence on the city would appear in the architecture of public buildings and private residences, and that even businesses would soon reflect and conform to its elegance and beauty.[4]

The construction of the capitol, according to architectural historian Joseph Armstrong Baird Jr., "necessitated the modification of the town plan." To set off the structure, state and city leaders laid out "a spacious Capitol park" on the grounds surrounding it.[5] State and "community-minded" Sacramentans raised funds to enlarge the capitol grounds by six blocks (between L and N and Twelfth and Fifteenth streets) in 1872. The city's Agricultural Society planted eight hundred saplings of two hundred species.

Other additions replicated the elegance of English gardens of the nineteenth century, and it became the model for future park creation in Sacramento.

Ripple effects occurred immediately. M Street, which led up to the capitol and would one day be renamed Capitol Avenue, was soon transformed into a modest grand boulevard that transferred "the official focus of Second Empire Paris to Sacramento." Subsequent plans by Charles Mulford Robinson and Werner Hegemann sought to use the capitol as the focal point for a more aesthetically pleasing Sacramento.[6] Other planners attempted to widen streets flowing out from the capitol to provide a panoramic view of the city's heart. But not until the urban-renewal programs of the 1950s and 1960s did a grand mall open on the west side of the building, facing the city's Tower Bridge.

THE IMPACT OF THE CAPITOL BUILDINGS

The new capitol and other urban improvements made visitors take a second look. A correspondent for the *San Francisco Call* wrote after a visit to the state fair in 1866, "[Sacramento] seems neither dead nor dying, but shows a greater life than at any period since the flood of '61–'62 and appears to be quietly entering upon a new era of healthful growth." The *San Francisco Bulletin* was even more complimentary: "Her citizens have always manifested a most courageous determination which is admirable. Despite the floods and the loss of population and wholesale trade, they are building permanently on the foundation of local energy and resources."[7]

Even though economic hard times befell the city in the general depression of the 1870s, still-devoted city boosters, such as local merchants Joseph Steffens (father of muckraker Lincoln Steffens) and Albert Gallatin, pressed for further development. Under their leadership a board of trade formed in 1877, which dedicated itself to improving the city's business climate and its physical appearance.[8] Steffens, Gallatin, and others were a local manifestation of the wider phenomenon of California boosterism that took place in the late nineteenth century. Sacramento, like other California cities, promoted its natural advantages of sunshine and good health together with plentiful economic opportunities for the savvy entrepreneur.[9] The Central Pacific Railroad contributed substantially to this marketing project and as far as Sacramento was concerned was the linchpin of its economic and social stability.

The Sacramento River continued to be an economic lifeline to the city. Barges and river steamers, many owned by the California Transportation Company, hauled imports and manufactured goods to and from the port of San Francisco. Busy docks, wharves, and warehouses received and distributed these goods and returned them with an array of agricultural products and building materials. River traffic was soon inextricably linked to the railroad, whose tracks ran parallel with the waterfront.

It is impossible to understand the significance of the Central Pacific Railroad to the development of Sacramento. The Big Four who built the line were aggressive monopolists and dominated the transportation networks of the state as smaller lines that connected Sacramento with the northern and southern valleys and the Bay Area fell into their hands. In 1868, the partners gained control of the Southern Pacific Railroad, a seventy-five-mile set of tracks that ran from San Francisco south through San Jose to Gilroy.[10] Southern Pacific tracks were then laid throughout the San Joaquin Valley to Los Angeles. Subsequent expansion pushed the Southern Pacific into Arizona, Texas, and ultimately New Orleans. In 1884 its owners abandoned the Central Pacific name and incorporated the company as the Southern Pacific. It became the West's largest corporation.

Sacramento's economic life was inextricably linked to the railroad when it became a center for the construction, repair, and refurbishment of railroad engines and cars. Virtually all of the cars in the Central Pacific and Southern Pacific systems were repaired and retooled in Sacramento. Beginning in 1873 the shops also began manufacturing locomotives and elegant Pullman railcars. By the turn of the twentieth century, the Southern Pacific shops employed an estimated 2,500 to 3,000 men, accounting for 20 to 30 percent of the salaried employees in the city. Railroad craftsmen built more than 7,000 railcars and 73 locomotives, with locomotive construction continuing until 1937.[11]

The ever expanding rail lines eventually included the Western Pacific and the Santa Fe engines as well as a series of electric lines that splayed out from Sacramento to various locations in the valley and to the Bay Area. These transportation arteries also contributed to Sacramento's economic life through food processing, especially grain milling, but also fruit and vegetable canning. Even before the railroads pushed into the interior of the Sacramento Valley, wheat farming dominated the agricultural economy. Sacramento-based flour mills ground up millions of tons of wheat into fine flour. Likewise, abundant hops fields produced enough to make Sacramento a brewing center for a time. Wheat was displaced by deciduous fruits and assorted vegetable crops that grew in abundance and came to Sacramento for processing and shipment to all parts of the nation. Sacramento Valley historian Joseph McGowan notes that by 1860, the orchards were already producing more than could be consumed within California.[12] New fruit-processing and shipping technologies, especially refrigerated cars, forged close ties between the fields and the rail lines in the 1870s and 1880s. Sacramento quickly became the hub of a major food-processing and shipment industry that nearly rivaled the railroad repair work.

Many Sacramentans, especially women, made their livelihood in the city's expanding canneries. Canning had been perfected during the Civil War and was introduced into California in the 1860s. Sacramento County's canning industry began in 1864 with a small fish-packing company on the Sacramento River. Until the advent of frozen foods, the canning season employed 3,000 to 4,000 Sacramentans annually. Cans, boxes, and other shipping materials were also manufactured in or near Sacramento, creating more jobs and steady incomes. Although Sacramento felt the effects of nationwide economic cycles in the 1870s and the 1880s, state government work, the railroad, and canning industries held relatively steady despite market fluctuations.

Sacramentans understood their dependence on the railroad and did everything they could to make certain that relations between the city and the huge corporation were amicable and cooperative. In January 1872 the *Daily Bee* reported another expansion of the rail yards and observed, "The increase of its working capacity will of course require the employment of a still greater number of mechanics and laborers by the company, all of which will result in benefit to the city."[13] Employment provided by the railroad caused Sacramento's population to grow from 16,283 to 21,420 between 1870 and 1880, according to the U.S. Census. Between 1880 and

1890, the city's population grew to 26,386, and by 1900 it stood at 29,282. A solid economy was the bedrock on which other cultural amenities could be built.

IMPROVING THE QUALITY OF LIFE

City boosters were anxious to improve the physical appearance and the quality of life in the state capital in order to attract more residents and silence critical solons who came to dread the legislative sessions. The new capitol shifted the commercial and residential districts steadily eastward and away from the West End of the city, which eventually became a slum. During the 1880s, the area between Tenth and Fifteenth and K and O streets became an especially desirable residential area because of Capitol Park, and would remain so until the turn of the century.[14] Some of these homes included the first of the city's landmark Victorians whose size and design reflected the growing wealth and class consciousness of the city.[15] The emergence of the middle class was reflected not only in the rows of elegant homes going up along H Street and fronting the fine views along Capitol Park but also in accelerating efforts to create a more refined urban culture.

Boosters were also eager to promote the state fair, permanently located in the capital since 1861, as an occasion to showcase city developments and tout its advance.[16] By the 1880s, tens of thousands descended on the capital for a week each autumn to view agricultural and technological exhibits. Sacramento's ever active gambling industry gladly relieved visitors of cash through wheel-of-fortune, poolrooms, and faro games, which ran constantly at hotels and saloons in the city.[17] Horse-racing events, held on the eastern city limits (today the Boulevard Park area of midtown), drew huge crowds, despite the disapproval of agriculturalists and local moralists who fretted about the heavy betting at the racetrack. The fair was financially rewarding for Sacramento, as hotels, restaurants, saloons, and brothels did a healthy business during the fair's run. Recognizing the economic jolt the fair provided and the prestige of having all the other California counties come within the city limits, Sacramentans did whatever they could to keep the fair. With state help, Sacramento shouldered the burden for the repair and expansion of fairground buildings and racetracks. The city also tried to improve the quality of urban life in ways that would make visitors take notice, and even overruled local moralists who wanted to do away with poolrooms for fear that overly restrictive ordinances would cut into racetrack gambling revenues.

Other improvements enhanced the respectability of the state capital. One of these was the fine arts. Sacramento already had the distinction of having established the first theater in California, the Eagle, which opened its doors in October 1849. Traveling troupes of actors came regularly to the state capital and performed in the Clunie Theater, constructed in 1885. Until it closed in 1923, the Clunie hosted the best of these visiting companies, and Sacramentans sampled the full run of drama, from comedies to Shakespeare.

Boosters and local cultural leaders promoted the visual arts—painting, drawing, and sculpture. In 1884, merchant David Lubin and others founded the California Museum Association "to foster art, science, mechanics and literature." This civic-minded group brokered the transfer to the city of a private art gallery belonging to the estate of Edwin B. and Margaret Crocker, giving Sacramento the West's first public art museum.[18] In 1885, the Ladies' Museum Association sponsored an art school. The Crockers' generosity was matched by another prominent patroness of the arts, Jane Lathrop Stanford, wife of Governor Leland Stanford, who not only donated to the Catholic cathedral but also provided a magnificent stained-glass window for St. Paul Episcopal Church. Interest in art led two Sacramento women, Alice Higgins and Frederika de Laguna, to found the Kingsley Art Club, an association for the "education, edification, and fellowship among middle and upper-class women," in 1892.[19]

The architectural, economic, and cultural quickening was the backdrop for the construction of the Cathedral of the Blessed Sacrament—the largest religious edifice in the state capital to this day. It was and still is the most prominent symbol of Catholic cooperation with urban designs.

Sacramento became a diocesan center and the administrative hub of Catholic Church life in northern California in 1886. The city's first Catholic bishop, Patrick Manogue, engineered the move of the diocese to the state capital. Manogue was one of Sacramento's most ardent supporters and placed the church firmly behind the priorities of city development. In a manner reminiscent of the city-friendly Congregationalist Benton, Manogue demonstrated his belief in a greater Sacramento not by words (he was a relatively poor public speaker) but with bricks and mortar.

Architectural historian Peter Williams notes, "The way religious groups have chosen to express themselves in wood, brick, stone, or concrete tells us much" not only about "their patterns of worship, their social standing and economic resources" but also about "their interaction with one another and with the surrounding secular realm, and their participation in the cultural matrixes exemplified in architectural style and regional culture."[20] The mammoth cathedral, which rose one block north of the state capitol building, reworked Sacramento's skyline and made the local Catholic church one of the strongest private contributors to Sacramento's dreams of respectability and urban beautification.

THE CULTURAL SIGNIFICANCE OF CATHEDRAL BUILDING

Historians of American "sacred space" have grappled with the multiple layers of meaning attached to sacred buildings and sites. Two insights provide a good framework for understanding the Cathedral of the Blessed Sacrament. One noted by Louis P. Nelson accentuates the functional aspect of church buildings when he suggests that they have a "work" to perform in secular settings. Historian Jeanne Halgren Kilde observes, "Buildings and religions are products of culture. Consequently, in analyzing religious architecture, one must foreground the cultural context in which religious meaning is created, keeping attuned to social, political, and technological changes within contemporary non-religious as well as religious arenas."[21]

Cathedrals accomplish a number of "works" for Catholics. Churches of enormous size and grandeur, they dominate urban space and are often the finest expression of their collective presence in a city or region. Theologically and sociologically, they are the central church of a diocese. Within their walls take place the most important events of the life of a local church: baptisms, confirmations, ordinations, and funerals of significant figures in the church and community. Cathedrals are also repositories of sacred art, performance venues for high-quality music, and communal gathering places in times of collective sorrow or celebration. Every Catholic diocese in the United States has a cathedral church where the local bishop presides. A liturgist at St. James Cathedral in Seattle summed it up: "Cathedrals are . . . the spiritual centers of their dioceses, cathedrals also stand at the centers of commerce, industry, learning, and the arts.

And they reach beyond a local Catholic community to become a source of civic pride for an entire region."[22]

The cathedrals of the American West reflect the diverse demographic realities of their respective regions. The Cathedral of San Fernando in San Antonio harks back to the mission era. Some, like the elegant Cathedral of the Madeleine in Salt Lake City, set within the midst of largely non-Catholic populations, replicate what historian Kevin Frederic Decker calls a more triumphalist style. Decker observes, "Roman Catholics saw their cathedral churches as a means to proclaim their faith and reproach their critics" and declare a "separatist architectural establishment." Some cathedrals of the West such as St. Eugene in Santa Rosa, California, and Sts. Simon and Jude in Phoenix reflect the suburbanization of the church and are simply large parish churches that were made cathedrals when their cities became the diocesan centers. Other cathedrals reflect the changing status of the church in various cities. A number of western cathedrals are in their second or third location or building, reflecting changes in the size and demographics of Catholic life. In Los Angeles, the tiny, old St. Vibiana gave way to the majestic Our Lady of the Angels, reflecting L.A.'s prominence as the largest archdiocese in the United States. In Oakland, the destruction of the Cathedral of St. Francis de Sales by an earthquake has opened the way for the new Cathedral of Christ the Light on the shore of Lake Merritt and contributed to the rejuvenation of the downtown.[23] The "work" of Sacramento's cathedral was to make a distinctive mark on a western city and to contribute to the cultural advancement of the state capital. This was the plan of the man who built it, Bishop Patrick Manogue.

Sacramento's cathedral was a part of the city's efforts to pull itself up by its bootstraps. Catholics saw it as a fitting temple to God's glory, but Manogue and the city boosters with whom he affiliated evaluated it also from the perspective of dollars and cents. The new cathedral represented a substantial investment in urban land. The extent to which it improved and upgraded city values and contributed significantly to the level of urban amenities determined its worth.

MANOGUE, THE MAN

Manogue was born in Desart, County Kilkenny, Ireland, in 1829, the youngest of seven children.[24] In 1848 or 1849, he left Eire permanently and arrived first in Virginia, where he sought out an uncle who had once corresponded with the family. Not finding him or "seeing any encouragement in Virginia," he moved north to Hartford, Connecticut, with its burgeoning textile mills and where scores of Irish immigrants had settled in the early nineteenth century. In 1850 Manogue decamped for a Chicago seminary to pursue a call to the priesthood. These studies were interrupted in 1854 when he and his brother James pulled up stakes to accompany their sister Mary and her husband, Timothy Dooling, to the gold fields of California. Manogue then became a hard-rock miner at a stake north of Nevada City. With his earnings, he resumed his studies for the ministry at the Seminary of St. Sulpice in Paris in September 1858.

Patrick Manogue's intellectual and spiritual formation took root during the heyday of the French Second Empire (1850–1871). Napoléon III was one of the great urban planners of modern times, and literally remade Paris during Manogue's years abroad. Drawing on the genius and organizational skills of architect and planner Georges Haussmann, prefect of the Seine, Napoléon III demolished deteriorated housing and widened narrow streets, creating the broad, straight, sweeping boulevards that would become a hallmark of Paris. Napoléon III and Haussmann revamped areas around Paris's ancient churches, while church leaders eagerly constructed new facilities that complemented the city's grand plans. One such edifice was the Church of the Holy Trinity, built in the 1860s. This majestic church, with its elegant facade and dominance of city space, must have etched itself in Manogue's mind as the *beau ideal* of church design. Manogue also understood the "work" of this great new church in the life of a newly remade Paris. It added to the city's grandeur and drew the church into a relationship with the City of Lights that was equal parts secular and sacred in its origins and its future.

Returning to the United States in late May 1862, Manogue was appointed to the church of St. Mary in the Mountains in Virginia City, Nevada, a headquarters for scattered Catholic missions and stations in the center of the Comstock Lode.[25] The small mining town grew by leaps and bounds. By 1873 and 1874, with the discovery of the Big Bonanza by four Irish miners, the population soared to twenty thousand, making Virginia City, for a time, one of the largest urban centers west of the Rockies.[26]

Bishop Patrick Manogue, ca. 1890. Courtesy of Sacramento
Archives and Museum Collection Center, Eleanor McClatchy
Collection.

Virginia City's boom times brought an explosion of home building,
new gas and sewer lines, and an array of new businesses. Newspapers, a
first-class opera house, and schools enhanced city life. Rail links, which
transferred precious ore from the mines, also connected Virginia City
to even larger markets. The six-foot-six Manogue (his height was a defi-
nite asset in the rough-and-tumble of the mining community) strode the
busy city streets like a giant and worked cooperatively with the medley
of characters in public and private life whom he met in the heyday of the
mining era.[27] With the help of parishioners and the superrich, Manogue
embellished his church as much as he could, mostly to make space for the

twenty-five hundred people who attended mass weekly. He recruited the Sisters of Charity to staff a hospital, orphan asylum, and schools for girls and boys.[28] After a fire in 1875, Manogue substantially rebuilt St. Mary in the Mountains and made it the neo-Gothic gem of the American West. Summarizing his years in Virginia City, Manogue wrote to a priest in Rome: "When having charge for 20 years of Virginia City, I put up two churches at a cost of more than $160,000, a hospital at $40,000, an orphan asylum for $30,000 and schools averaging $20,000." He concluded with an understatement: "I have been now thirty years on this Pacific Coast and I may lawfully say I have not been idle."[29]

MANOGUE AS URBAN DEVELOPER

The mining frontier was an unstable place for those with grandiose dreams. Virginia City collapsed as quickly as it rose once the mines faltered. Its demise was sealed by the shifting monetary policies of the government in the nineteenth century.[30]

The fortunes of mining enterprises in California and Nevada also affected the location of the Catholic headquarters. In 1861 a temporary headquarters at Marysville, with jurisdiction for California and Nevada above the thirty-ninth parallel, was established, with Bishop Eugene O'Connell directing it.[31] In 1868 O'Connell was transferred to the new headquarters at Grass Valley, a center of hydraulic mining. Grass Valley flourished as a Catholic center for a time, accommodating a girls' academy and orphanage.[32] Yet by the 1870s Grass Valley too was in decline. In 1884 a decision by the California Supreme Court ended the environmentally controversial practice of hydraulic mining, causing a precipitous drop in the town's population. Manogue later noted that Grass Valley was reduced "to a village of a few Cornish miners and a few Jew stores." He feared the "diocese was on the verge of becoming a thing of the past."[33]

Before agreeing to be made bishop in 1881, Manogue had extracted a promise from his religious superiors to move the headquarters of the church from Grass Valley to Sacramento. At a meeting of California's bishops, Manogue insisted that they recognize "the changed circumstances of the new region. When the precious metals fail in the mines then the towns fail too and their inhabitants are forced to seek new homes. Such an outcome befell the towns of Weaverville, Forest Hill, Smartsville, Nevada

City, Austin, Gold Hill, Grass Valley, Virginia City, and Marysville; these had been the chief towns in our diocese."[34]

Manogue's choice of Sacramento was nothing less than a vote of confidence in the city's future. No one who had lived in the region as long as Manogue could fail to notice the quickening pace of the state capital, especially since the arrival of the railroad. Like so many pioneer Sacramentans, he had come west seeking gold only to discover that the real wealth was in land development and local industry. Because of the railroad, Sacramento was destined to become the major hub of a vast agricultural empire.

Even before the final transition took place in 1886 (after nearly five years of wrangling with church authorities in Rome and San Francisco), Manogue laid plans to replace Sacramento's aging St. Rose Church. Writing to Roman authorities in 1885, who had no idea of the dynamics of Sacramento's growth, Manogue emphasized the poverty of the church in relation to religious rivals: "There is but one sorrowful little Catholic Church in Sacramento while the Protestants have fifteen attractive edifices."[35] St. Rose's, he argued, was inadequate since the size of the congregation had increased significantly. Moreover, the raising of the city grade had left St. Rose Church three or four feet below street level. Manogue wanted to build a cathedral to match the beauty of the churches he had seen in Europe and also befitting the prominence of his new diocesan headquarters in the state capital of California.

The location of the cathedral was the first important decision. Manogue, faithful to the Catholic tradition, knew that cathedrals were intended to hold a place of prominence in urban centers. Historian Kevin Frederic Decker observes, "Siting these buildings was a very deliberate and conscious act, for not only were prominent and, when possible, elevated locations selected, the churches themselves were situated on the site to show them to their best advantage when viewed from the surrounding area."[36]

American bishops often chose carefully the place where their cathedrals would be built. When Bishop Edward O'Dea moved the headquarters of his diocese from Vancouver to Seattle in 1903, he immediately sought to "supply a suitable Cathedral Church." O'Dea picked a choice spot on the summit of First Hill, a well-to-do neighborhood, which commanded a panoramic view of the city.[37] St. Joseph Cathedral in Sioux Falls was also situated in a posh neighborhood (later preserved as the first historic site to be listed on the National Register of Historic Places in South Dakota) on a hill overlooking the city. Salt Lake City's Cathedral of the Madeleine was careful to avoid competition with the imposing Mormon temple and tabernacle, but it too sat high over the city.

But unlike Seattle, Sioux Falls, or Salt Lake City, Sacramento's cathedral was not intended to be removed from the main channels of urban life; rather, it would become an intimate part of it. Other bishops of capital cities in the West would do likewise. For example, Cheyenne, Wyoming, bishop James John Keane moved the site of his original cathedral to a location three blocks from the state capitol. According to one source, "Bishop Keane was aware of the potential civic significance of the building and its site."[38] As early as 1885, Manogue had chosen "a most eligible place" in the shadow of the capitol. With the help of shipping merchant Thomas Dwyer, the prelate began quietly assembling land in the block surrounded by J and K and Eleventh and Twelfth streets—exactly one block north of the state capitol building.[39] In May 1886, as soon as the transfer of the diocese from Grass Valley was formalized, excavations began for Sacramento's grandest religious building.

AN OPPORTUNITY FOR URBAN COOPERATION

The erection of Sacramento's cathedral was cheered by citizens of all faiths. Manogue confided to a Roman friend, "The people of Sacramento are delighted in fact with joy at the prospect of having a respectable church and resident bishop. . . . I might be permitted to say that our future in building up the church here is most flattering."[40] Manogue naturally welcomed the goodwill and support of city economic leaders. At one point he seized an opportunity to show his support for the city when the building of the cathedral and the construction of a new government building intersected in an important way.

On the wish list of new buildings for the city was a modern post office to handle the increasing volume of mail and mail-order merchandising done by city merchants. Joseph Steffens of the board of trade lobbied local congressman Joseph McKenna for a federal appropriation for a new federal building in early 1885. Overcoming opposition, McKenna secured a $150,000 government appropriation. Even though the U.S.

MAP 1 Catholic Churches and convent in downtown Sacramento

Senate pared the amount back to $100,000, the task of site selection began in June. To Manogue's delight, postal commissioners selected the site of the former St. Rose Church as their choice.[41] A series of complex three-way negotiations involving Manogue, officials of the federal government, and the trade board then took place related to the site of St. Rose's. Of the $100,000 Congress had appropriated (for acquisition of property and construction), the amount provided for the land purchase was only $30,000—or about $7,500 less than the appraised value of the St. Rose property. Consequently, the government cut corners and purchased only part of the property. Although less than Manogue had hoped for, he agreed to the price, retaining title to the adjoining lot.[42] By 1887, however, government planners realized the original appropriation was too small for the structure they were planning and decided they needed the additional land to complete the building. By this time, of course, the property had appreciated steadily and was continuing to go up in value as the beautiful sandstone post office and federal building was erected. Steffens and postmaster Russell D. Stephens asked Manogue to reserve the lot and to hold the price at $10,000—as it would turn out, considerably less than he might have gained had he sold it on the open market. By this time, the cathedral was well under way, and Manogue was in great need of cash. However, he agreed to hold it until Congress appropriated the needed $10,000.

Congress dragged its feet, and a bill assigning an additional $150,000 for the building languished in the Senate.[43] Summoning Steffens, S. Prentiss Smith, and Stephens to his home in May 1888, Manogue informed them that he could no longer wait. He told the men that he would give the government a week to make its decision on the stalled appropriation but then would put the property on the open market.[44] Anxious to keep the property off the market and to work with Manogue, the board of trade assembled a consortium of businessmen who guaranteed a loan to Manogue from the D. O. Mills Bank for the needed $10,120. This provided Manogue with the cash to move forward with the cathedral. If the government did not make a decision before the end of the session, Manogue was free to put the property on the open market and repay the loan. The assembled businessmen agreed to pay the interest. Eventually, the congressional logjam was broken, and the additional money was appropriated.

When the cathedral was completed, Steffens expressed the gratitude of the city for Manogue's patience with the frustrating government negotiations: "It was the long and tedious negotiation to get the general government to round out and complete the building site which was so desirable to have done." Steffens concluded, "The appreciation of value with the lapse of so much time would have canceled any bond but the word of Bishop Manogue was found to be more endurable and far more elastic than could any written bond possibly have been made."[45] Manogue had made it clear to the city's commercial and political elite, of all religious denominations, that he wanted the Catholic community to be an active force in the development of Sacramento.

The Catholic press fanned enthusiasm for Manogue's project. "The people are jubilant over the prospects of seeing a beginning to what they ardently hope in time will be a lasting temple to Almighty God and an ornament to Sacramento City." Manogue selected a building committee of ten Sacramento residents that included the Reverend Thomas Grace and other local Catholic notables, including Judge John Wesley Armstrong, cigar manufacturer Anthony Coolot, shipping magnate Thomas Dwyer, and former mayor Christopher Green.[46]

Manogue anticipated city planner Daniel Burnham's famous admonition, "Make no little plans." The cathedral church was to be the largest west of the Rocky Mountains, and its size exceeded the needs of the Catholic population of the city at the time. Building big may have reflected Manogue's own ego (and his desire to best the cathedral put up by his clerical rival, Archbishop Patrick Riordan of San Francisco).[47] But Manogue's long experience in Virginia City and his constant rebuildings of St. Mary in the Mountains primed him for the challenge of building a major cathedral. Not only did his own religious tradition provide examples of important churches, but he also had an instinctive feel for the importance of size in the American West and the role of public buildings in creating a respectable urban environment. Two important strands came together in Manogue's plans: His Catholic community needed the prestige a beautiful cathedral could offer, and developing Sacramento needed buildings of beauty and size to realize its aspirations to respectability. He chose an architect who like himself was of Irish birth, but also well skilled in the use of location and materials in the American West, Bryan James Clinch.

Clinch was born at Maryborough, County Queen's (now County Laois), Ireland, in 1842. Educated first at Belvedere College in Ireland, he graduated from the Catholic University of Dublin in 1865.[48] Clinch, who never married, had a lifelong interest in Catholic life and culture and was accomplished in a number of areas. A distinguished writer and speaker as well as an architect, he edited the pro-Irish *San Francisco Monitor* (the official newspaper of the Archdiocese of San Francisco) on two different occasions (1891–1892 and 1899–1900) and was—as must have been a prerequisite for that job—an ardent Irish nationalist.

Arriving in the United States sometime in the 1870s, Clinch fell in love with California. He absorbed as much as he could of its scenic beauty and distinctive culture to share with audiences in the East and abroad. His fascination with California's Catholic culture found expression in two volumes on the history of the missions that appeared in 1904. Clinch had worked on a number of prominent Catholic buildings in northern California and was well equipped to translate Manogue's vision.[49]

In 1886, Clinch began work on the Cathedral of the Blessed Sacrament with clear instructions as to its basic design. In 1873, Manogue had taken a health leave from his Nevada parish and traveled back to Paris to visit the now completed Church of the Holy Trinity. Memories of its beauty and preeminence were refreshed. For Manogue, its siting within the context of an improving Paris was as impressive as the building itself.

Although the Sacramento church was scaled down in size and scope from the Parisian model, their exteriors were strikingly similar. The cathedral's magnificent facade, crowned with a soaring central bell tower and two smaller flanking towers, boldly etched its presence on the low Sacramento skyline. A dome reminiscent of Brunelleschi's Renaissance masterpiece in the *duomo* of Santa Maria del Fiore in Florence would cap the large and spacious interior. Because the streets around the new cathedral had already been raised, the cathedral entrance could be scaled by a relatively low flight of granite steps. In late spring 1886, work began. By fall, with the excavations completed, workers poured the concrete foundation. The basement construction proceeded on into the fall, as workers hoped to finish it before the onset of the rainy season.

In the spring of 1887, Manogue took up permanent residence in the capital city. Daily he inspected the construction site and watched as Sacramentans gaped in awe at its gigantic proportions. Layer after layer of bricks were mortared together to form walls that rose sixteen feet above the main floor. Giant columns of Sacramento brick supported the clerestory and the roof. The cruciform image of the building became plainly clear, with the main shank of the supporting roof beam extending 204 feet from front to rear, while the crossbeam, at 116 feet, spanned both transepts. With the walls in place, work began on the outer facade, where

Cathedral of the Blessed Sacrament, 1915. Courtesy of Sacramento Archives and Museum Collection Center, Frank Christy Collection.

space was set for a huge central rose window. Smaller semicircular windows were placed over the doors. Finally, rising at the intersection of the transepts and nave was the massive dome.

The public events heralding the cathedral's building and dedication drew some of the largest public crowds in Sacramento's history. On June 12, 1887, more than eight thousand people turned out for the formal cornerstone laying. On that occasion the leather-lunged Jesuit James Chrysostom Bouchard extolled the future glory of the rising temple. The *Daily Bee* noted the civic significance of the edifice: "It may stimulate other religions to improve their property. There is nothing that so beautifies a city as handsome temples of God, and the Catholics have shown a magnificent example."[50]

For two years the building moved along, the pace of construction ebbing and flowing. By March 1888 the building was under roof, and the three towers of the outer facade stood in relief against the skyline. The two flanking towers were 14 feet square at the base and rose 120 feet in height. The center tower stood 25 feet square at the base and spiked up 216 feet. Crowned with a gilded cross, it rose to a total height of 230 feet. The cathedral dominated K Street, towering over every other structure in the city except the capitol dome. In fact, it provided a counterpoint to the nearby capitol building.

By May the belfry of the tower was ready to receive the bell that had been cast for it, and the two other towers were ready for painting. Plastering and stuccoing on the outside and inside proceeded. By the end of 1888, the full power of the building's size and magnificence was apparent for all to see. A golden cross, taller than the apex of the capitol, capped the stunning main tower. The ceiling inside was painted, the columns had been enclosed, and the walls were plastered. The sanctuary was 3 feet above the main floor of the vast church, with a set of stairs and a railing running its full length. A communion rail with wood carvings set it off. The cathedral's pulpit was perched on the right of the sanctuary, and the main altar was set near the back wall, with space behind for the celebrant to enter from a passage that led from the sacristy. Flanking the sanctuary were two alcoves that contained shrines to the Blessed Virgin and St. Joseph. In both transepts rested altars, one containing a statue of St. Patrick, the diocesan patron, and the other a statue of the Sacred Heart of Jesus. The nave itself provided seating for about seventeen hundred in pews made of pine and redwood. To the rear of the cathedral were two galleries: The upper one, containing an organ, was reserved for the choir, whereas the lower gallery was set aside for children.

At the end of June 1889 the cathedral's formal dedication turned out thousands in what was one of the most spectacular public events in the history of the city. After the rites were completed, the crowds poured into the church. "Fully four thousand people were in the church," the *Monitor* reported with some exaggeration. Bedlam erupted as they shoved each other aside for a better view. Some wiped their hands across the newly plastered walls, gaped in awe at the interior of the huge dome and the stained glass, and fanned themselves to endure the heat and the crowds. After taking in the grandeur, the reporter noted that one woman expressed the admiration of all: "Oh! Ain't it beautiful."[51] That evening, solemn vespers were chanted in the new church, and the inner and outer domes were illuminated brilliantly with twinkling electrical lights. The Reverend John Quinn preached the concluding sermon of the day.

SACRAMENTO'S ARTISTIC SHOWCASE

The architectural majesty of the cathedral added another benchmark for city builders and planners. Winfield Davis's *Illustrated History of Sacramento County*, a booster publication, extolled the structure: "For grandeur, architectural magnificence and artistic finish, it has no equal in the West, and is a noble addition to the attractions of California from a scenic standpoint." He observed that because of the cathedral, "new life has been infused into the veins of what has been heretofore the somewhat sluggish city of Sacramento." But just as important, the cathedral added to the cultural depth of the city by providing a space for civic-minded Sacramentans of all faiths to showcase the city's newfound love for art. As John Quinn later observed in his funeral eulogy of Manogue, "Note the names of the donors of these beautiful windows and these works of art on the walls about you and you will find they are the names of the loyal sons of Abraham, the Protestant, the scoffing infidel, and the honest skeptic."[52] Boosters worried less about "scoffing infidels" and "honest skeptics" but wanted to silence those who derided the state capital as a backwater. The new cathedral gave them plenty of evidence that the city had now attained a level of sophistication previously unknown.

Wealthy Catholics vied with each other to select the stained-glass windows that would adorn the apse and transepts. These lavish benefactions—with their donors' names prominently etched at the base of the windows—spoke of the affluence and influence that many Catholics had already attained. Above the high altar stood a beautiful row of elegant custom-made stained-glass windows, imported from the Tyrolean region of Austria. Rich in reds and blues designed to refract the radiance of the morning sun, they drew gasps from visitors and elicited devotion from the Catholic faithful. A mammoth three-paneled stained-glass representation titled *The Last Supper* dominated the group. The gift of Anthony Coolot, undisputedly the wealthiest Catholic citizen of Sacramento, it had cost twelve hundred dollars to manufacture, ship, and install. Flanking *The Last Supper* was Ellen Dwyer's donation of *The Nativity,* whereas Daniel McCarthy provided funds for the window titled *The Ascension.* These two windows alone cost about a thousand dollars. In the north clerestory of the sanctuary, a stained-glass grouping of the four evangelists was bestowed by Elizabeth Harley Hooker, a wealthy Sacramento widow, and James McNasser, a successful hotelier, cattle merchant, and land speculator. To the left of the sanctuary, next to the altar dedicated to the Blessed Virgin, Mrs. Michael Rigney, the wife of another associate of Dwyer, installed a window called *The Assumption of the Blessed Virgin Mary.* To the right of the altar, in the shrine to St. Joseph, Mrs. James Kaseberg, wife of a prominent Placer County rancher, donated a window titled *Flight of the Holy Family into Egypt.*[53]

In addition to individual gifts, Catholic associations contributed to the embellishment of the building. The Catholic Knights of Sacramento, a men's fraternal society, donated a stained-glass window named *Christ Delivering the Keys to St. Peter,* whereas the YMI provided the funds for the stained-glass depictions of four Latin doctors of the church in the northern clerestory of the sanctuary: Sts. Jerome, Augustine, Ambrose, and Gregory.

In the transepts were reminders of Manogue's early roots in Nevada, his friends generously donating to their former pastor's monument. Two of the transept windows were donated by the daughters of Theresa Fair, the ex-wife of Big Bonanza partner James Fair and friend and benefactor of Manogue. In the south transept stood a depiction of St. Patrick converting the Irish, a window donated by Manogue's former parish in Virginia City.

Of the twenty-five windows in the apse, side shrines, and transepts, women donated nine of them. When one includes the nave windows and other works of art, women were the primary artistic benefactors of the cathedral—as they were in the advancement of art in general in Sacramento.

Most significant were the gifts of non-Catholics whose extensive travels abroad made them aware of the role of cathedrals as repositories of great art and fitting objects for their philanthropic impulses. Margaret Crocker, the wife of Central Pacific general counsel Edwin Crocker, provided the cathedral with a series of six colored-glass insets of the stations of the cross, which she had purchased from a European church.[54] She also gave an elegant rendition of the prodigal-son story that crowned the windows of the north transept. In memory of her son Leland Jr., Jane Lathrop Stanford donated a replica of Raphael's *Sistine Madonna,* which she had found in a Dresden gallery. Decorated with an elaborate frame, the painting was one of the priceless art treasures of the church. Jewish merchant David Lubin donated a copy of Guido Reni's masterwork *St. Michael Defeating Satan,* which hung in Rome's Capuchin Church. These donations reflected not only the benefactors' generosity but also their appreciation of churches as places of cultural uplift.

On the day of the cathedral's dedication, its last outstanding debts had been paid off with the proceeds of an on-the-spot collection. Manogue had received thousands of dollars from benefactors such as mining millionaires John W. Mackay and Theresa Fair (although we do not know how much, as financial records disappeared long ago). But there was still more to do. Manogue apparently intended to replace the wooden altars and plaster statues in the church with marble ones. His plans to decorate the walls and ceilings had to proceed in piecemeal fashion. The outer niches of the cathedral facade went without statuary, and the upper parapets were not crowned with angels blowing trumpets to the four corners of the earth as planned. Until sidelined with a fatal illness in 1894–1895, Manogue continued to raise money to complete the cathedral. When he died in February 1895, the scaffolding of a local artist was in the sanctuary. External improvements went even slower. For many years, the only addition to the cathedral's exterior was a Seth Thomas clock installed in the bell tower in 1902.

Like the capitol, the cathedral made an impact on the city of Sacramento itself. The *San Francisco Monitor* noted, "The progress of the

David Lubin, ca. 1913. Courtesy of Sacramento Archives and Museum
Collection Center, Weinstock's Collection.

Church has also materially assisted in helping along both the temporal
and spiritual interests of the Catholic elements in the Capital City." Citing
the resurrection motif that was now part of the city's official narrative,
the paper declared, "Sacramento—like all other portions of the State—has
passed through many vicissitudes during its past career, but it now enjoys
a stability, a commercial prosperity and a thriving population which
augurs well for its future."[55] A bright forecast was ahead for Sacramento.

INVESTING IN "GREATNESS NOW UNKNOWN"

The cathedral was first and foremost a Catholic building. Its mammoth
size was a sign of hope that Catholic numbers would grow. Its interior aesthetic beauty was intended to encourage new levels of faith and devotion.
Its location continued the reordering of urban space begun by the construction of the Greco-Roman statehouse. There were other meanings to

the cathedral design that may have become evident to Sacramento residents and visitors. The cathedral's Italian Renaissance facade, soaring towers, and Romanesque dome clearly distinguished it from the classical lines of the nearby capitol. If Greco-Roman design memorialized classical civic virtue, the cathedral represented the traditional Catholic values of prayer, morality, and charity that complemented the life of the state. The City of Man stood one block away from the City of God. Manogue believed that cathedral and capitol served as two sides of the same coin of civic order. His eulogist recalled sitting with the prelate one evening and noted that the setting sun had briefly illuminated in the same beam the golden cross atop the central spire of the cathedral and the waving flag atop the capitol. In what no doubt was an embellished recollection, Manogue extended his arms toward the sun-wrapped cross and flag and said, "God grant that it be ever so! And when the sun sets to rise no more, may the sign of man's redemption from the slavery of sin be still bound by chains forged in heaven to that flag, the emblem of liberty to all mankind!"[56]

As has been already noted, Manogue viewed the cathedral as part of the city's developing landscape—melding its private religious character with the larger goals of Sacramento's urban advance. City leaders, many of them of no particular religious persuasion, recognized Manogue's intentions and hailed the new structure as an urban masterpiece and a major contribution to city life. Comments offered at a celebratory banquet hosted by Manogue for his friends and associates prior to the cathedral's dedication in 1889 issued in a "flow of good cheer," as Sacramento's civic elite celebrated the cathedral as an urban achievement in language usually reserved for public events and civic holidays. Col. T. W. Sheehan, a local military figure and member of the Sarsfield Grenadier Guard, acknowledged, "Sacramento is indebted to His Grace for the grand Cathedral which is to become one of the future attractions of the city." He continued, "It is high time we had a new church in keeping with the business importance and population of the city." Manogue's longtime friend Judge John Wesley Armstrong remarked that fifteen years prior, he "had talked with rich Catholics who thought of settling permanently in Sacramento, but who were deterred upon seeing the kind of church we owned. . . . Nothing could be done so effective to boom [promote] the city as the building of this grand Cathedral." Sacramento postmaster

Russell D. Stephens, who felt a special debt of gratitude to Bishop Manogue, paid special tribute to the prelate's business savvy. "The Catholic Bishops were far seeing men and never made investments in places where there was not a bright prospect. . . . Bishop Manogue would not invest so large an amount in Sacramento if he did not see in its future signs of greatness now unknown." Thomas Dwyer, who had negotiated the land deals and supplied brick for the huge cathedral, also hailed the economic and social boon the prelate brought to California's capital: "When Bishop Manogue came to Sacramento, nobody was buying lots and nobody seemed to want any. Now, however, property that was lately worth $3,000 is held at $5,000. These facts," he claimed, "indicated clearly that the Bishop had started the boom." Even the normally circumspect Reverand Thomas Grace noted the desired "ripple effect" of the church: "The quiet boom inaugurated by Bishop Manogue is more effective than all that has been done by all other citizens of Sacramento. It has started one of the largest hotel owners to enlarge his building and has induced a great mercantile house to add to the beauty of their property by building two new stories." He concluded, "It has given employment to our mechanics and laborers, increased value, and in other ways contributed to the material advancement of the city." In the midst of the bubbling cheer sat the aging Dr. Gregory Phelan, who had helped build the first St. Rose's and been instrumental in the development of Catholic life in the city. Recently returned from a lengthy period abroad, he predicted that one day people would come to Sacramento to see this cathedral just as they visited the cities of Europe to see the cathedrals of old.[57]

A second banquet, held in September 1889, underscored what had been said earlier. According to the engraved vellum invitation, Manogue was honored "in recognition of his eminent services in the erecting of the Grand Cathedral of the Most Holy Sacrament in Sacramento City." Rising to speak his praises were many of his congregation, but his admirers also included those outside his faith, among them department store mogul David Lubin, California secretary of state William C. Hendricks, and board of trade president Joseph Steffens. Steffens's toast in particular reflected a common attitude toward religion in Sacramento, even as the banquet itself acknowledged the positive role the church played in advancing the civic agenda. "Some of this same delegation which you have seen fit to call in from the 'byways and hedges' of the world, are people who do not handicap any church to much extent and yet are buying pools in all of them. They have a religion, the basis of which is the orthodoxy of everyday life."[58] Steffens's "orthodoxy of everyday life" was the kind of civic religion that Sacramentans really valued. The value of churches was measured by their ability to advance the common good and contribute to the urban agenda.

Manogue never gave up in his devotion to the city. In 1893, efforts to create a new industrial improvement association found the Catholic bishop in full assent. He added his name to the list "for the industrial onward march of our city." With a zeal comparable to any urban booster, he declared, "Let our energy practically assert itself; let the hum and bustle of activity and industry be heard in our midst and strangers will be attracted to come and remain. . . . I hope our people will take active part in this laudable work, quadruple our population, and enhance the value of their own property."[59]

Manogue's health declined shortly after the dedication of the cathedral. He traveled abroad with Thomas Grace to restore himself, but by mid-1894 he was unable to leave his rooms in the episcopal residence. Even from his sickroom, however, he continued to work on his beloved cathedral. In late 1894 he commissioned frescoers under Sacramento artist Thomas L. O'Neil to decorate the sanctuary. He also ordered a bell cast at a Cincinnati foundry to be hung in the cathedral tower. When Manogue died in 1895, at the age of sixty-four, the new bell was rung for the first time—in a funereal toll.[60]

Although he had been a resident of Sacramento for only seven years, Manogue stepped into the stream of the urban consensus. Few Catholic bishops have ever had such a sense of themselves as urban developers as did Patrick Manogue. Sacramentans acknowledged what he was trying to do and referred to the Catholic temple merely as "the cathedral"—a sobriquet of affection and an acknowledgment that the structure was an integral part of the fabric of city life.

Ordinary Sacramentans esteemed Manogue and composed a ditty that they hummed to an unknown tune upon completion of the cathedral: "Of All the Bishops that are now in vogue, the greatest of all is Bishop Manogue!"[61]

CHAPTER 3

Religious Sisters As Urban Agents, 1850–1920

"Deborahs of the new faith"

In February 1851 Gregory Phelan regaled eastern readers of the *Freeman's Journal* with details of the dedication of Sacramento's St. Rose Church. The "neat little chapel" now stood where only a few months prior "there was scarce a vestige of civilization." Another "vestige of civilization" caught the eye of the observant physician. "Among the congregation there were a greater number of ladies than we have seen together before in this city, and their rich attire as well as number was another evidence of rapid progress."[1] For Phelan and others, women were an important key to civilizing the raw and rough Gold Rush city. For many years, women were a minority in Sacramento. As historian Florence Nina McCoy points out, "Sacramento in 1852 was literally a man's world." The 1850 census recorded the presence of slightly more than 600 women compared with 8,529 men in Sacramento County. By 1860, even though the number of women had risen to nearly 7,000, the ratio of men to women was two to one. By 1880, women nearly evened out the count when the census enumerated 12,271 men to 9,149 women. In fact, although the numbers have often been close, males outnumbered females in Sacramento County up through the 1960s.[2]

A growing literature has accentuated the role of women in the shaping of the American West.[3] As with so many other topics, the "gendered" history of Sacramento demands additional study.[4] In one important pioneering account, historians Elaine Connolly and Dian Self note that Sacramento women struggled to carve their niche as active participants in the creation of urban culture. Sacramento women "forged ahead to help create a society where they could be granted their due as citizens." Churches provided one outlet for the creative energies and agency of Sacramento women.[5]

RELIGION AND WOMEN IN SACRAMENTO

Early ministers in the city noted the absence of women in their fledgling congregations. For example, shortly after building the Baltimore Chapel on Seventh and L, Methodist minister Martin Briggs preached to full congregations in 1851—but observed that there were only two women present.[6] Only a dozen women were among the seventy or eighty who gathered for the first Catholic mass in Sacramento in August 1850. However, as the number of women living in the city grew, their visibility in church congregations naturally increased. Their rising numbers contributed to stable memberships and a greater degree of financial security. In 1873, when the Sixth Street Methodist Church invited a female revivalist, Maggie van Cott, to preach, Minister David Deal reported a positive financial result, which he attributed to the "glorious revival under the labors of Sister Van Cott, to inspire the congregation."[7] Catholic laywomen contributed to the success of St. Rose's by running frequent fund-raisers to retire its heavy debt.[8]

Ministers were anxious to have women in their congregations, because their presence brought refinement and stability. Methodist pastor Isaac Owen noted the calming effect of women, even upon those men who had not professed any religious beliefs but "whose tempers and manners were sweetened by the associations of pious wives, affectionate daughters, fond mothers and devoted sisters." Owen declared that with more women in Sacramento, the "state of society here will be greatly improved as churches become more permanently established and families more numerous and business more stable [and] when churches, schools, colleges shall have taken the place of grogeries [sic], gambling houses and houses of ill fame." The rector of Grace Episcopal, the Reverend William H. Hill, exhorted the women of his flock not to dwell on the comparative lack of creature comforts in the developing city but to exercise their influence for the good of their spouses and thereby the larger community: "Knowing well the influences which women always exerts [sic], for good or ill, on the other sex—ten fold greater in California than elsewhere—I plead for my God, my church, my city, state and country—for all that is dear to us, that that influence may be thrown into the scale of right, and tell its full force in the mental, moral and spiritual elevation of our community." Urging women to reject the "peevishness" of their eastern sisters when deprived of "real or imaginary comforts or associations," he pleaded, "Be helpmeets, I pray you to those who so willingly lavish on you their gains. If adversity in pecuniary matters comes, that need not banish from the fireside the cheerful smile of welcome and sympathy that makes the distressed man forget his losses, and only remember that his richest treasures of wife and children are still left him."[9]

Religious benevolence, a favored outlet for Protestant women, was common in Sacramento. Most churches had women's groups that raised money for church debts, spearheaded religious education, sponsored mission activity, and cared for the poor. Sacramento had an array of these associations. In 1904 the newly formed Sacramento Women's Council (an outgrowth of the Tuesday Club, which had begun in 1896) included most of them: the Daughters of the King, the Ladies' Hebrew Benevolent Society, the Ladies' Auxiliary of the YMCA, the Ladies' English Lutheran Society, the Sacramento Branch of the Women's Christian Temperance Union, the Ladies' Aid Society of the Sixth Street Methodist Church, the Women's Home Missionary Society (also of Sixth Street Methodist), and the Catholic Ladies' Relief Society (CLRS).[10] Forty years earlier, the women of the Congregationalist church had established the Protestant Orphanage.

A unique group of Catholic women, religious sisters (or nuns), made a powerful impact on Sacramento. Their various services—health care, education, and child care—were critical to the civic project.[11] There is an added dimension to their work and presence in Sacramento that is worth noting. Not only did sisters provide critical social services, but they also

Mater Misericordiae Hospital, ca. 1907. Courtesy of Sacramento Archives and Museum Collection Center, Robert Tutt Collection.

represented a significant instance of female autonomy and agency that was remarkable in the nineteenth and early twentieth centuries.[12] Viewed from this perspective, their convents and various charitable and educational enterprises represented "female-centered" space—enterprises owned, operated, and totally controlled by women. Their authority over their day-to-day lives and over the scope and nature of their work exceeded that of most other women of the nineteenth and twentieth centuries. Understanding their activities contributes to a better understanding of the gendered realities of Sacramento life but also adds another layer to the story of Catholics as urban agents. C. K. McClatchy's glowing encomium to the Sisters of Mercy in 1907 could also be said of many congregations of sisters in Sacramento: "To a very large extent," McClatchy declared, "the history of charity, the history of humanity, the history of beneficence in this community is the history of the Sisters of Mercy."[13]

Religious women were welcomed because of the services and refinements they could bring to the city. Dr. Gregory Phelan continually pressed for "charitable and literary institutions" to be staffed by "pious and charitable ladies" who could instruct both Protestant and Catholic children "in virtue and kindness." Even a fallen-away Catholic, *Bee* editor C. K. McClatchy, acknowledged them as significant figures in the city's life. In his florid Victorian prose he likened them to the "Rebekahs of the olden, the golden, and yet mournful days of Sacramento's springtime."[14]

> Like unto Deborah they were warrior maidens, and like unto Deborah did they rejoice and make glad. But unlike Deborah they were warriors of peace—the black-robed Amazons of the white Christ—Amazons who fought under the banner of universal love; Deborahs of the new faith who won many a hard-fought battle against suffering and disease and sin; Deborahs whose voices rose in hymns of praise and victory—not Deborahs whose warlike souls found martial vent in a "Marseillaise" of Israel, but Deborahs from whose tender lips beneath their streaming eyes rose the touching "Ave Maria" and the majestic, "Kyrie Eleison."[15]

Although many congregations of vowed religious women would come to Sacramento and labor for church and community, two major groups, the Sisters of Mercy and the Franciscan Sisters of Penance and Charity, dominated church work for many years. The Sisters of Mercy, who arrived in 1857, were the first to root themselves in the city, making their local convent the center of an autonomous branch of the community and the hub of its other ventures. The Franciscan Sisters, who arrived in 1901, were a branch of a larger community that had its American headquarters in Stella Niagara, New York.

BRINGING SISTERS TO SACRAMENTO

Shortly after his consecration as bishop in Rome in 1850, Archbishop Joseph Sadoc Alemany visited convents in Europe, bringing back with him communities of Dominican Sisters to assist in serving the new San Francisco diocese.[16] Alemany and his clerical agents traveled abroad on several later occasions to entice more religious women to come to California to advance the mission and visibility of the Catholic Church on the Pacific Coast.

The first to arrive in Sacramento, the Sisters of Mercy, were the spiritual progeny of Catherine McAuley, a wealthy Irish heiress. She had devoted herself to educating and caring for Ireland's urban poor. As a laywoman, McAuley established a House of Mercy on Baggot Street in Dublin in 1827.[17] Although she had no intention of becoming a religious sister, in order to preserve her mission and work she made vows as a Sister of Mercy in 1831. Her original plans for a religious sisterhood called for a less conventionally structured order than defined by tradition. The nuns would live a communal life, wear simple attire, and pray together as they engaged in public acts of charity. McAuley's undertaking represented a common impulse in nineteenth-century religious communities that wished to modify the demands of traditional cloistered life in order to serve the increasing number of urban poor. In Ireland and in their missions abroad, the Sisters of Mercy assigned a high priority to working with young girls and women. This "gender-bias," as one historian calls it, defined the work of the Sisters of Mercy in San Francisco and Sacramento.[18]

Irish sisters from numerous small religious communities came to the United States in great numbers between 1812 and 1914.[19] In 1843, the first Sisters of Mercy came to serve in the Diocese of Pittsburgh. Led by Mother Mary Francis Xavier Warde, the order grew steadily and branched out to Chicago and Providence. A house in New York was founded by Mother Agnes O'Connor from the Baggot Street community. Another house was opened in Little Rock from a Mercy community in Naas, County Kildare.

Hearing of the Sisters of Mercy from the Reverend Hugh Gallagher, who had come to San Francisco from Pittsburgh, Archbishop Alemany sent the priest to Ireland to request their services in far-off California. The sisters in Dublin turned down his request, but directed him to a sister convent in Kinsale, where Gallagher received a warm reception. When he related the needs of the California mission, a number of religious, including Sister (later Mother) Mary Baptist Russell, volunteered to go.[20] Gallagher's descriptions of conditions in California included a rendition of Sacramento's spiritual and civic needs, and he managed to persuade a second Irish community, the Sisters of the Presentation, to come to the new state capital as well. All of the religious, in company with Gallagher, departed Ireland in late 1854 and made their way to San Francisco by sea, crossing from the Atlantic to the Pacific through Nicaragua, then traveling by steamer up the coast of Mexico to San Francisco.[21] Arriving on December 8, 1854, a Catholic feast day in honor of Mary, the eight Mercy

Sisters lodged temporarily with the Sisters of Charity, who had preceded them by two years. On January 2, 1855, the sisters opened their own convent on Vallejo Street near the San Francisco city hospital.

Within months of the completion of the new brick St. Rose Church in 1856, rumors surfaced in the local newspapers that nuns were coming to Sacramento.[22] In fact, however, because the city's reputation was so rough, it actually scared sisters away. The Sisters of Charity had considered Sacramento, but quickly rejected it.[23] The Presentation Sisters, whom Gallagher recruited, refused to come once they heard of the floods, fires, and social disorder in the city. They lamented Sacramento's relatively small population and noted in their community annals that the city "was then even less developed than San Francisco" and "gave little promise as a suitable location for a cloistered teaching order."[24]

Alemany then pleaded with the Sisters of Mercy to consider a Sacramento mission. On April 21, 1857, Mother Mary Baptist Russell traveled with Sister DeSales Reddan to Sacramento and inspected its possibilities. Mother Mary Baptist also tested the feasibility of opening a convent near Mount Shasta. Rugged and remote Shasta was soon ruled out, but they stayed in Sacramento until early May, "reporting favorably on the undertaking" but insisting on adequate living quarters if they were to come. A return visit by Russell and Reddan in July brought a promise from the Reverend John Quinn of St. Rose's to give up his own home to the sisters, and the deal was sealed. Sister DeSales Reddan contracted a fatal illness shuttling back and forth from San Francisco to Sacramento and died shortly after the agreement was made—a blow to the small community. Nonetheless, on August 9, 1857, five sisters were appointed to start the new Sacramento convent: Sisters Mary Gabriel Brown, Mary Paul Beechnor, Agnes Stokes, Martha McCarthy, and Madeline Murray. The details of preparation delayed their actual entrance into their new mission, but they finally arrived on October 2 under the leadership of Russell. "The arrival of six Sisters of Mercy in this city was hailed with joy," wrote an exultant Phelan. In early January, Phelan's brother-in-law, Archbishop Francis Norbert Blanchet of Oregon City, and Alemany traveled to St. Rose Church to bestow the religious habit on Nora Bouse, who took the name Mary De Sales in religious life. "This being the first public reception in Sacramento, the church was densely crowded with a very respectable and attentive audience."[25]

Forty-three years later, in 1901, the Franciscan Sisters of Penance and Charity came to Sacramento. They were founded in 1835 by Magdalen (Catherine) Damen, the daughter of a Dutch farmer who had become acquainted with Franciscanism through the Third Order group in Maaseik, Holland (now Belgium).[26] Damen affiliated with three other women Franciscan tertiaries (a group of laypeople who devote themselves to the Franciscan life), and they began living a life of evangelical simplicity while dedicating themselves to works of mercy. This group was invited by a parish priest, Peter Van der Zandt, to help in his parish in Heythusen. Damen gathered around her several women, and in May 1835 they took up residence at a dilapidated estate near Heythusen, and lived a "formal" religious life, that is, more like religious sisters, with a convent, rule, and vows. In 1874 their order was welcomed to the United States, where they worked with German-speaking Jesuits in the Diocese of Buffalo, New York. Their first establishments were schools in Buffalo and a school and orphanage in Columbus, Ohio. Before the turn of the century, these Franciscans had opened houses in Nebraska and among the Native Americans of South Dakota. Thanks to the visibility they had in their educational ministries and later hospital and child-care ministries, the community attracted new recruits in the United States, surging to nearly 175 sisters by 1900. The American sisters established a permanent central administration at Stella Niagara, New York, which in 1928 became the headquarters of an independent province, or administrative unit, of the community. In 1929 they founded a province on the West Coast, with headquarters first in Monrovia and later in Redwood City, California.

In 1895 the Reverend Augustine McClory, the Franciscan pastor of Sacramento's St. Francis Church, invited the sisters to come to Sacramento to staff his newly opened school. Community leader Mother Cecilia Steffen did not believe the time was right for such a foundation so distant from the motherhouse. McClory then recruited the Sisters of Mercy to teach at the school. But when they were withdrawn in 1901, a new St. Francis pastor, the Reverend Godfrey Hoelters, once again begged the Franciscan Sisters to come to California. This time the answer was affirmative. Mother Cecilia dispatched Mother Bertha Gores and Sisters Aloysiana Schmidt, Aquina Miller, Henrietta Lakas, Clement Finkel, and Pacifica Kirschel to the California capital. The sisters' first impressions of Sacramento bear repetition: "Sacramento is about one-fifth the size of Buffalo. It is a clean, bright city with friendly houses, each with a lawn, flower beds and palm trees, and what with the balmy air and the blue sky over head, the first impression is a most pleasing one."[27]

The sisters welcomed 95 pupils crowded into the classrooms in September. By the end of the year the student number climbed to 150, and in the summer of 1902 Hoelters added an additional four rooms to the school to accommodate the growing number of students. The number of sisters serving in the school grew steadily as well.

Both the Sisters of Mercy and the Franciscans operated grade schools, which provided secular and religious instruction for scores of Sacramento children, Catholic and non-Catholic. The Mercy Sisters also ran a successful academy for girls, where in addition to the traditional three R's curriculum they taught domestic arts (sewing and food preparation), music, art, and foreign languages. Training and education at the academy empowered Sacramento women to assume positions of leadership and influence in city life. A number of these parochial-school graduates became public schoolteachers, and one became the first female county superintendent of schools. The Mercy Sisters also upgraded and expanded the city's health-care systems by establishing a hospital, whereas the Franciscans provided needed day-care facilities for working-class women.

The Franciscans also undertook the sometimes challenging ministry of charity and religious education to the city's diverse ethnic populations on the West End of Sacramento, the significance of which will be explored in a subsequent chapter. In later years, the Franciscan Sisters at St. Francis School established a second Catholic high school for girls.

SISTERS AS AUTONOMOUS AGENTS

Religious sisters tended to their own business affairs, managed increasingly complex personnel issues and technological advancements for their health-care centers, and maintained control over their living space—all within the context of a church structure totally dominated by men.

For the Sisters of Mercy, the demands of convent life, as well as their desire to establish a degree of autonomy from the local clergy, provided the incentive to create separate living and educational facilities. This in itself was not remarkable, since all congregations of religious women did the same. However, in Sacramento as elsewhere, the decision to create a separate convent space—to literally mark out urban space that belonged exclusively to them—created one of Sacramento's first "female-centered" spaces.[28]

The Mercy Sisters began a school in the basement of their own small residence. This first school was swamped with students, but the use of the residence (a shanty, in fact) was intended to be only temporary. Their plans for a more permanent space were ambitious, so they soon launched a general fund drive and also began offering classes "for a small consideration" in the "higher branches that are not taught in the public schools, including French, music, painting, needlework, etc." With the funds gathered from the drive, the sisters purchased a half-block between L and M and Tenth and Eleventh streets for $4,850. "It is their intention," noted Phelan, "to build a Convent, House of Mercy, Asylum, School, Hospital, etc., as soon as possible."[29] This would be a virtual replica of the sisters' "female-centered space" in San Francisco.

When it came to raising the money needed to build on the land, though, things became more difficult. As other religious denominations experienced, Sacramentans could be generous the first time a new project was presented, but not so free with their money the second time around. By the end of December 1859, Mother Mary Baptist wrote to Mother Mary Francis Xavier Warde that the Sacramento efforts were stalled at a school enterprise, consisting of a day school averaging 120 students and the sisters' practice of home visits, called the "visitation." Plans for a new convent and orphanage were halted because "it is pretty hard to raise the necessary funds even in this so-called golden country." On top of it all, the summer heat and cramped quarters of their home brought on health problems. At one point the fledgling community was under the directorship of a novice after the superior became ill.[30]

The lag in fund-raising was to some degree providential, for if the sisters had built on the property they might have found their early investment swept away when the state demanded the M Street property for the erection of the state capitol. The penurious legislators paid the sisters only the $4,850 they had originally invested in the property, absent any interest.[31] The sisters then purchased a half-block consisting of four lots at Ninth and G streets, which included the residence of Col. Ferris Foreman, for $8,000. The adjoining half-block was purchased for $5,000.[32] The Foreman home became their new convent, and they quickly built a one-story building for the primary and grammar grades of their St. Joseph School. This "convent block" was dominated by the convent itself and became their general headquarters, the training center for their recruits, and a major educational site for Sacramento youth, housing a primary school and later an academy with a normal-school program.

Although Sacramento women owned property and directed businesses, there was no other place in the city where the scope of female agency was as evident as the convent. Protestant women had social clubs, dominated church organizations and benevolent societies, and were to be found in the ranks of teachers, but no other group of women in Sacramento could claim urban space and point to physical structures that they themselves had built and exclusively directed extensive social and religious activities. The convent was their "beachhead," and to it they attached ties of deep affection. The sisters demonstrated their fierce proprietary interest in their original site when they resisted the efforts of clerics to move them.

As early as 1867, Mother Mary Baptist pondered spinning off the growing Sacramento enterprise into a separate "foundation" (an autonomous convent).[33] Although this idea was turned down at the time, the sisters were anxious to expand and above all wanted a new convent and orphan asylum on their property to replace the now cramped Foreman home. A friend of the sisters, Isaac Allen, who represented a "company of gentlemen of Sacramento," began planning a fund drive centered around a "grand gift concert" with the idea of donating part of the proceeds to the sisters' orphan asylum.

This plan immediately elicited opposition from St. Rose pastor Patrick Scanlan, who worried that the sisters' fund drive might interfere with his own efforts to retire long-standing parish debts and build a school for boys. He complained to Archbishop Alemany, who sent a "card" to the local press disclaiming any sanction of Allen's concert.[34] Alemany and Scanlan further pressed for a relocation of the convent and school to another part of the city. St. Joseph's was, Alemany explained, "in a corner of the city with railways and rivers very near on the west and on the north which will prevent any extension of the City in those directions." He lamented that "the population convenient to the Sisters is almost

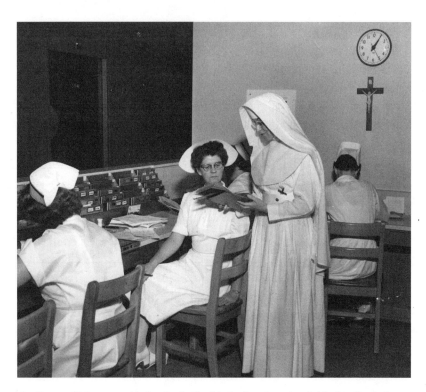

The Sisters of Mercy provided active leadership in the advancing field of medical administration. Courtesy of Sacramento Archives and Museum Collection Center, *Catholic Herald.*

exclusively Protestant and it is very difficult to get the children to go there, most of our people live South and south east." He gently urged the sisters "to sell where they are and purchase in a more convenient place even if they could not secure as much ground."[35]

Mother Mary Baptist appeared to have been sympathetic to the idea of a move, especially since the street raising "had the effect of backing the water on our end of the city," but the Sacramento sisters were vehemently against giving up their location. Although they acknowledged the need for a second school on the other side of the city, they insisted that "the chief attraction of the present place was the high state of cultivation for it truly was a lovely shady spot and no where else could a *whole* block be secured." Anxiously, the sisters placed small statues of St. Joseph on each corner of the block, "charging the Saint not to allow their grand place to be taken from them and it was not."[36] Facing this stiff resistance, Scanlan and Alemany backed down, and local businessmen (some of whom may have had daughters who attended the school) raised enough money to erect a four-story brick structure on the site. Archbishop Alemany himself came to lay the cornerstone on September 8, 1872, and on the feast of St. Joseph, March 19, 1873, the structure was complete.

This conflict with the clergy over the retention of their convent block emphasizes the desire of the sisters to maintain control over their lives and location. Even needs for expansion did not shake them. In 1887, when the Sacramento sisters became an autonomous congregation and the number of women seeking admission to the convent created demands for more space, the sisters instead added on to the buildings rather than move. Likewise, another plan to relocate the flourishing academy was doused in 1892 when additions to existing buildings were made. Bishop Manogue even paid to have the walkways around the convent paved and erected a fence around the property.[37] This remained the administrative center of the Sacramento Mercy Sisters until 1940, when its motherhouse and sister-training operations were transferred to a new site in Auburn. The block continued in operation as an educational center until changing demographics and urban renewal finally closed the academy in 1968. The convent remained open until the mid-1970s. Today, the property is a parking lot in the heart of Sacramento's legal district and is surrounded by bail bondsmen and attorneys' offices.

CREATING THEIR OWN ENTERPRISES:
THE STRUCTURES OF SELF-GOVERNANCE

Following the creation of the Diocese of Sacramento in 1886, the Sacramento sisters became an autonomous (that is, self-governing) branch of the Sisters of Mercy in 1887. At the time of the split, the sisters were given a choice: to remain permanently or for a shorter time at the new Sacramento foundation or to return to San Francisco. Sister Vincent Phelan, who had been in Sacramento for nearly her entire religious life, chose to remain (although she retained the right to go back to San Francisco). Sister Mary Liguori Madden had earlier severed ties to the San Francisco group and remained in the state capital. Sisters Aquin Martin, Cecilia

Downing, Helena O'Brien, Genevieve McCue, and Rose Smith volunteered to remain for a few years until new recruits were taken in from the area and from Ireland.[38]

The sisters were not exactly "orphaned," since they had received many years of solid tutelage in the rudiments of religious organization from San Francisco. However, the newly self-governing Sacramento community faced serious challenges. They now held the primary responsibility for staffing their institutions, raising funds, recruiting new members, and expanding or contracting their ministries to fit the needs of the Diocese of Sacramento. Two Irish-born women, Sisters Vincent Phelan and Liguori Madden, shepherded the young community through its first generation of independence, trading off terms as mother general from 1887 to 1905.

To welcome new members the Sacramento branch opened a training center, called a postulancy (a program for young women interested in entering the community), and novitiate (a year—or longer—of intense introduction to religious life culminating in the taking of temporary vows) with Sister Mary Liguori Madden as novice mistress. New recruits came from American and also from Mercy convents in Kerry and Westmeath, Ireland. The sisters also absorbed detached members of other religious communities that had faltered in California.[39] The administration of convent affairs offers another example of the kind of administrative work done by these Sacramento women.

The mistress of novices was, comparatively speaking, in the position of a midlevel manager evaluating prospective employees. She had to oversee the details of their admission (that is, documentation, testimonies of good character, and dowry) and also size up intellectual and physical attributes that would presage success or failure in convent life. She would also have to determine whether the candidate was going to be admitted to the choir sisters (a more exalted status that included academic study and teaching) or become a lay sister (one assigned domestic tasks). If the candidate was admitted to the convent, the mistress of novices was in charge of training and educating the new sister and offering advice, guidance, and negotiation through the inevitable adjustments to community life. She had a major voice in determining whether the candidate should be permitted to take vows and become a permanent member of the community. These were demanding tasks—and ones the various Sisters of Mercy exercised regularly.[40] All decisions eventually were referred to the mother superior, who functioned not only as the chief executive officer of the various enterprises owned and operated by the sisters but also like a mother who tried to monitor the sisters' lives and work, to ensure unity and harmony among them.

Until 1895, the work of the sisters primarily involved the administration of St. Joseph Convent and its schools. The mother superior ruled the community, assisted by the mistress of novices and a general council, which advised on questions of religious discipline and primarily on the admission of young women to the various stages of membership. It also helped to direct the placement of the sisters—allocating their scarce human resources in endless configurations of talents, skills, abilities, and the chemistry of community life.

First-generation leaders—Mother Liguori Madden and Mother Vincent Phelan—exercised a sphere of influence well beyond that of most Sacramento women of their times. Likewise, two American-born superiors, Mother Mary Gertrude King (1862–1944) and Mother Carmel Naughton (1885–1957), demonstrated exceptional leadership skills at various times in the community's history.

A native of New York, the future Mother Mary Gertrude was born Elizabeth King, the daughter of Mr. and Mrs. Peter King, who came to California with their eight children about 1870 and purchased a farm near Sacramento. Typhoid fever claimed the life of Mrs. King and three of the children. "Lizzie" King attended St. Joseph Convent boarding school, where she graduated in 1876 with high honors. After passing the state teacher's examination in 1880, she taught in the public schools of Sacramento County, maintaining a lifelong friendship with schoolmates Mary Rooney O'Neil and Ella Kelly McClatchy. King, like O'Neil and McClatchy, became an important figure among women who played public roles in Sacramento. In 1887, Elizabeth King was the first postulant to enter the Sacramento Sisters of Mercy novitiate and was given the name Sister Mary Gertrude. A prominent teacher at St. Joseph Academy for many years, she also served as superior at the convent for two terms in the 1900s and was director of the popular devotional societies, the Sodality and the Children of Mary.[41] In 1907, Mother Mary Gertrude King presided over the celebrations of the sisters' fiftieth jubilee in Sacramento—a significant civic event that accentuated the contributions of the Mercy Sisters to Sacramento. King steadily upgraded the quality of education at St. Joseph Academy, affiliating it with the University of California, ensuring its college-bound graduates an easy transition to the state's university system.

As the community expanded and grew during the decades of the thirties and forties, Mother Mary Carmel Naughton played an important role. Born Winifred Naughton in Eureka, California, she entered St. Joseph Convent in 1909 and made her profession of vows in 1912. Sister Mary Carmel was clearly an able administrator, serving as superintendent of the old Mater Misericordiae Hospital at Twenty-third and R streets and eventually overseeing the construction of the new Mercy Hospital at Fortieth and J.[42] She held the position of mother superior for five three-year terms between 1932 and 1956 and proved her skills as a builder and organizer. During Naughton's years in authority, the Mercy Sisters undertook major building projects at their hospital. It was Naughton who transferred the administrative and formation tasks of the community to a new motherhouse in the Auburn foothills. Naughton also faced the challenges of a steady increase in membership during a general vocational "boom" after World War II. Once again, young women from their academy and also from a prepostulancy house in Ardfert, County Kerry, brought new blood into the community. Phelan, Madden, King, and Naughton were women of substance who oversaw complex corporate activities, which in their eras were still largely the preserve of men. Their work also served the larger good of Sacramento, and this is where Catholic sisters made their largest impact on city life and development.

MERCY SISTERS AS URBAN AGENTS

Public education took off slowly in early Sacramento. Even though the California legislature passed enabling legislation in 1851, a school system was not launched in Sacramento until January 1854, when H. W. Harkness, George Wiggins, and Gregory J. Phelan were appointed school commissioners. By February a school building had opened at K and Fifth streets. The following year the city had six schools in operation, with accommodations for 414 pupils. That same year a school opened for African American children.[43] The first public high school was erected in 1876 and served Sacramento until a new structure was built in 1906–1907.

Although the city took its time establishing its public schools, private schools flourished in Sacramento. In 1850 Joseph Augustine Benton founded a school in a makeshift building. By June 1852 there were nine private schools in operation. One of the most prominent, about two blocks south of St. Rose Church, was the Sacramento Academy, under the direction of James Stratton. The Pacific Seminary opened its doors on Fourth Street between κ and l.[44] By 1864 Sacramento had thirteen private schools, serving 1,200 pupils. Phelan, who served on the school board, tagged moral education as an important civic need. "Protestants as well as Catholics desire to have a school where their children may be instructed in virtue and kindness."[45]

When the Mercy Sisters arrived, they found a somewhat poorly run Catholic school on the St. Rose grounds. Begun in 1851 as a Sunday school, St. Rose School was for boys only and experienced a perilous existence for a number of years. (It was not until the imposition of mandatory attendance laws that the school registered an enrollment of 200 boys in 1875.)[46]

In addition, as noted earlier, the sisters began a school in the basement of their home and in 1860 purchased the convent block where they built their St. Joseph School. By the beginning of the school year in 1861, the sisters had moved the girls and young women to the new site, and in 1862 welcomed 334 children to their institution. The boys were left behind in the old quarters near St. Rose's, but the difficulty of securing stable teachers for the lads led the sisters to take the younger ones at the g Street school where "some 75 or 80 boys were taught until the opening of the [Christian] Brother's College [sic] in 1875."[47]

Placed under the patronage of St. Joseph, the school became the first permanent location for Catholic education in the city. The clientele of St. Joseph's encompassed elementary-age to teenage students. The academic program consisted of "primary, grammar, high school and academic studies; and there are various departments which embrace business and commercial courses, music, painting, and embroidery."[48] Literary exercises were held annually at the end of the school year.

According to Mother Mary Baptist's wishes, the school charged no tuition, but accepted voluntary contributions from the parents of the pupils. To bolster finances, the sisters gave private lessons in music and foreign language. They formed a subscription library, which charged a small fee for taking out books. The sisters also hosted raffles, bazaars, and fairs from time to time. On occasion, the proceeds from Sacramento's popular St. Patrick's Day celebrations were turned over to the sisters. During the community's jubilee in 1907, academy alumnae spearheaded efforts to collect funds for the sisters and presented a large check to Mother Mary Gertrude King.

The "donor base" of the sisters was large, because they opened enrollment in their schools to anyone who wanted to come. St. Joseph School provided a first-class education for girls of all faiths, and a number of non-Catholic girls (mostly Protestant but some Jewish) were educated by the sisters. In Sacramento as in other parts of the United States, a convent education was the emblem of a refined upbringing, and this trumped sectarian concerns about exposure to Catholic ritual, doctrine, or practices. Non-Catholics regularly patronized the nuns' school until the 1880s when public schooling became the norm. From 1860 until 1870 non-Catholics constituted anywhere from 10 to 38 percent of the school's enrollment.

By the time the sisters celebrated their centenary in 1957, nearly 1,600 young women had passed through the school's doors. The sisters inspired an abiding loyalty among the alumnae and made friends with a wide range of Sacramentans. To their pride, some entered the religious life as Sisters of Mercy or joined other religious congregations.[49] Others remained in Sacramento, married, and reared children. Years later Mother Mary Gertrude wrote, "Many of the Alumnae preside, nobly, over truly Christian households, 'queens of the domain of home,' and their children to mold their lives by the precepts taught them in the happy 'Convent Days' by loved sisters."[50] Interestingly, the celibate nuns who lived in community actually instructed young Sacramento women in wifely duties and child rearing and proudly listed the married names of their alumnae in their yearbook.[51] St. Joseph graduates also made their presence felt in the ranks of administrators and educators and in the offices and commercial enterprises throughout the city.

The further strengthening of the public school system and the increasing demand for teachers provided the sisters with another opportunity to serve the larger community. In 1874 a new mandatory attendance law required more schools and teachers. This in turn gave birth to another bevy of private schools devoted to preparing young women as teachers for Sacramento's classrooms. These included the Sacramento Business College, Bainbridge College, Howe's High School and Normal Institute, and Monaghan's Business Institute and Normal School. In June 1875 St. Joseph Academy was incorporated by the state and empowered to confer diplomas. Among the early recipients was Ella Kelly, who later married C. K. McClatchy. St. Joseph's also began a normal-school course in 1878 that ran in tandem with its academic program and bestowed teaching licenses on its graduates. In 1880 the first three women to receive the coveted licenses were Mary Rooney, Margaret Keegan (later a Notre Dame sister), and Elizabeth King.

The academy turned out a number of graduates who spent their entire professional lives in the Sacramento city and county school systems. These included future principals Lizzie Griffen, Nettie Hopley, and Emma von Hatten. Griffen headed the Mary J. Watson School for many years, until it was torn down to make way for the Memorial Auditorium. She also doubled as the organist and chief musician for the Cathedral of the Blessed Sacrament, playing at every important function from the dedication of the church in 1889 until her death in the 1920s. Hopley was the principal of the ethnically diverse Lincoln School on Fourth Street. Ernesto Galarza memorialized Hopley in his memoir, *Barrio Boy,* as a true friend of the multiethnic students who passed through Lincoln School.[52] Von Hatten, teacher and principal at Marshall School at Twenty-seventh and G, graduated from St. Joseph Academy in 1894. She served as principal of Marshall School for thirty-two years until her retirement in 1944. Like Griffen, von Hatten kept active in church affairs, even serving as the treasurer of the National Council of Catholic Women (NCCW).[53] In terms of Sacramento history, however, the most visible graduate of the academy was the first female superintendent of schools, Mary Rooney O'Neil.

Mary Rooney was born of Irish immigrant parents John Rooney and Mary Clark in 1862.[54] Her parents were hop farmers who sent young Mary to school at St. Joseph Academy. Once she received her teaching certificate in 1880, she taught general subjects in public schools in both Perkins and Brighton (Sacramento County) until her marriage to Thomas O'Neil in 1887. O'Neil was a prominent local artist who produced original paintings on the ceilings and walls of the Cathedral of the Blessed Sacrament. He also served one term as Sacramento County sheriff and tax collector. In

1905 O'Neil suddenly dropped dead of a heart attack, leaving Mary with seven children under the age of seventeen. Pressed by the financial plight of her large family, Mary threw her hat into the ring for the elective post of county superintendent of schools. Even though she did not yet have the "right" to vote herself, she won handily, and was reelected in 1910 and served until 1914. She was then appointed assistant superintendent of city schools in 1916, a position she held until her death in 1932.

O'Neil maintained her connections with the network of friends and acquaintances she had formed from her years at St. Joseph Academy and helped broker a broader role for women in Sacramento's Catholic community. In 1920 the Diocese of Sacramento sent her to Washington, D.C., where she participated in the formation of the National Council of Catholic Women, a federation of Catholic women's organizations from around the nation. The NCCW lobbied for Catholic issues in the public sphere such as the care of "working girls" in industrial cities, religious education for public school youth, and financial support for Catholic immigrants. O'Neil organized the Diocesan Council of Catholic Women, the local affiliate of the NCCW, and remained active in its affairs until her health declined.[55]

While the academy provided a number of teachers for Sacramento's growing elementary-age population, St. Joseph's also offered course work to students entering the ranks of clerical workers in city businesses. In 1893 a commercial course was introduced, promising that "young ladies will receive a thorough business training." The commercial course taught skills such as shorthand, typing, and other subjects to prepare them for service as secretaries, switchboard operators, and office administrators. The sisters also opened a new department that taught practical dressmaking. "This class," the school announced, "is intended for young ladies, who are through with their studies or who do not wish to attend school."[56] The entry of these young women into the city's prestigious law firms and businesses reinforced the sisters' hope that the school would be helpful to civic advancement. It also endeared the sisters to members of the city's professional and merchant classes who often gave generously to the sisters' occasional fund campaigns.

The Franciscan Sisters plowed their own religious fields in Sacramento. As St. Joseph Academy grew and developed, the Sisters of Mercy were no longer able to staff St. Francis School and had to withdraw from it in January

1901.[57] The Franciscan Sisters who came in 1901 found a large, well-equipped convent and a growing school, which kept them quite busy. An unexpected departure from a school they had accepted in Colusa (where they clashed with the pastor) freed up enough of them to take over a new school in a refurbished coach house on the city's multiethnic West End. St. Stephen School on Third and o streets opened in 1906, and Mother Tarcissia Mulbay headed up the first contingent of nuns to teach at the school.

At first the Franciscan nuns lived at St. Francis's and took the streetcar to the West End school. However, the convent facilities at St. Francis Parish soon grew cramped.[58] In 1908 the sisters opened a new convent in the heart of the neighborhood around St. Stephen's. Living in closer proximity to some of Sacramento's poorest and working-class citizens created new opportunities for the Franciscan Sisters. In addition to the classroom instruction for the immigrant children, St. Stephen's became an important source of social services for the decaying and sometimes dangerous neighborhood. Sister Mary Manuela Dieringer, who arrived at St. Stephen's in 1917 to teach the combined seventh and eighth grades, recalled years later, "The area around St. Stephen's . . . was in 1917 rapidly deteriorating and the school, an old wooden structure that had once served as the Crocker stables was not too safe. . . . After school we often went to visit the sick and the poor and took baskets of food to them. People were so generous to us that we always had much to give away."[59] The sisters also helped to evangelize the fallen away—learning of them from the children. Not only by taking children off the street, the school aided in attacking the causes of juvenile delinquency. The school became an important social anchor of the West End. It provided an inexpensive form of day care for the working-class parents of the area who labored in the railroad yards or in nearby canneries. The school also prepared the youngsters for the sacramental celebrations and holy days that were part of the Catholic subculture.

In 1924 St. Stephen's closed (temporarily, as it turned out), and a new school was erected on Eighth and s called Holy Guardian Angels (Holy Angels for short). The Franciscan Sisters moved their entire school operation to the new brick structure, which provided all the amenities of a modern educational institution. Until its closure in 1973, Holy Angels provided a strong Catholic educational presence in the community.

Schools were only one way the Mercy and Franciscan sisters served Sacramento. Both congregations also engaged in acts of charity and mercy that contributed substantially to the city's growing network of social services and advanced the urban agenda. Health care and day care were also provided. In fact, the Sisters of Mercy made an enduring contribution to city life by creating a reputable community hospital. Here, too, their skills as administrators, builders, and entrepreneurs were significant in the history of women in Sacramento.

In addition to their hospital and school work, the Sisters of Mercy oversaw works of benevolence in the city. This part of their labor was directly related to the original inspiration of their founding by Mother McAuley in Ireland. Even as they were getting their first school off the ground, the sisters undertook the "visitation" practiced by their order. They literally went out two by two into the streets and homes of early Sacramento to bring supplies, spiritual guidance, and support to people who needed them. They visited public hospitals, the city and county jails, and the homes of the sick and dying. Likewise, they organized classes for children who did not attend their school, teaching not only catechism but also arithmetic, grammar, spelling, and "accounts" to Sacramento's working-class young women "whose days were spent in earning a livelihood."[60]

The Sacramento Sisters of Mercy benefited from a tradition of nursing and hospital care propagated by their order long before they arrived in California's capital.[61] They were world famous for their work in health care, having nursed the injured and dying in the Crimean War as well as in the American Civil War. Much closer to home, Mother Mary Baptist Russell, who had sent the first Mercy nuns to Sacramento in 1857, had also established St. Mary Hospital in San Francisco, considered one of the premier health-care facilities in the city. Until 1887, when the two communities split into separate jurisdictions, the Mercy Sisters who served in Sacramento often exchanged places with those at St. Mary's. The technological and administrative capabilities of the sisters in the field of nursing and health care responded to the need for an improved hospital system in the growing capital city.

Sacramento's medical establishment evolved over the course of time. From the outset the community had an array of doctors. Given the lack of professional standards at the time, the range of physicians went from those with formal training to self-proclaimed healers who tried various therapies on their ailing patients. After a few failed efforts, the Sacramento Society for Medical Improvement was founded in 1868, chaired by city doctors anxious to upgrade and standardize the quality of city health care. A board of public health was founded in the 1860s to address issues of sanitation and situations that threatened the health of the populace.

As was typical of nineteenth-century American cities, Sacramento's early hospitals were a mix of municipal and private institutions.[62] The first was an adobe hospital on the grounds of Sutter's Fort, which included various "pesthouse" facilities. A city hospital was begun in 1850. After the original structure was blown down in a windstorm, a new jointly owned city-county hospital opened at Tenth and L, which remained on the site until the mid-1860s when it was torn down for Capitol Park. In the late 1860s, sixty acres were secured on Stockton Boulevard, and in 1870 a 216-bed hospital was erected there. This Stockton Boulevard site became the permanent location for the public hospital. By 1915 there were 500 beds. Around the hospital were other county institutions that cared for the poor, the elderly, and the chronically ill. The county hospital was probably the most used health-care facility in Sacramento. Sacramento also had an array of private health-care institutions. Among them was one for which there was an obvious need—the Southern Pacific Railroad Company Hospital founded to care for those injured on the job.

Hospitals in the nineteenth century underwent a dramatic transformation. Originally refuges for the poor and the socially marginalized, they were sustained by tax collections or the generous benefactions of wealthy donors. Physicians worked for free or for a nominal fee. Nursing the sick back to health was important, but so was the moral instruction in good habits of cleanliness, abstinence of various sorts, and overall good social behavior. Middle- and upper-class people were often nursed in their own homes. However, by the late nineteenth century advances in medical knowledge revolutionized medicine and hospitals. Hospitals became for all economic classes the chief location for surgery and soon achieved a reputation as places of healing and recovery. Physicians played an important role in creating the modern hospital, with assistance from medical associations, especially the fledgling American Medical Association. They insisted on standards that differentiated scientifically trained practitioners from homeopaths, quacks, and self-proclaimed healers. Hospitals served as training facilities for new physicians and for apprentices in the medical field. They soon supplanted the medley of smaller institutions that had evolved in many cities.[63]

By the 1880s the growth of the city's population and important changes in medical knowledge and technology compelled Sacramento to upgrade its health-care systems. Civic leaders actively advertised the city's medical establishments as "modern" and "up-to-date," just as California marketed itself as a land of sunshine and health, especially to midwestern and eastern audiences. In Sacramento as well, the number of citizens who desired a private health-care alternative to the large wards of the county hospital and a facility more centrally located than Stockton Boulevard was increasing.[64]

Dr. Gustavus Lincoln Simmons, a leading Sacramento physician, sought to expand health-care options for Sacramentans when he took over the Ridge Home (on Twenty-second and R streets), which had been donated to the city by Margaret Crocker. The operation, however, soon proved to be a financial disaster for Simmons, who was forced to supplement its deficits from his own purse. His efforts to find a professional association of doctors to take over the facility failed. As a last resort he turned to the Sisters of Mercy.

When Simmons and fellow physician Dr. James Parkinson first approached the Sacramento sisters with their "bail-out" request, Mother Superior Mary Vincent Phelan turned down their proposal. Mother Mary Vincent noted that the thriving academy and the administrative tasks of forming an independent branch of the Mercy community absorbed all the energies of the small band of sisters. But in 1893 a new superior, Mother Mary Liguori Madden, reevaluated Simmons's proposal. Madden may have been swayed in favor of expanding the sisters' health-care role by the arguments of the highly respected Dr. Thomas Huntington, chief physician of the Southern Pacific Railroad Company Hospital and one of Sacramento's most respected doctors. A pioneer of modern hospital operations in Sacramento, Huntington was a Harvard-trained physician with several years of experience on the staff of Massachusetts General Hospital. Prior to coming to California he had practiced in Nevada. As the chief surgeon for the railroad in 1882, he introduced the first antiseptic operating room on the West Coast.[65] His great respect for sister-nurses as well as his pledges of support convinced Madden to undertake the Ridge Home enterprise. On June 24, 1895, Simmons conveyed the property to the Sisters of Mercy for the reduced price of twelve thousand dollars, which included the land, building, and equipment. The sisters had to borrow to cover these costs—a not inconsequential risk for a relatively small congregation (fewer than one hundred sisters). The nuns named the institution "Mater Misericordiae" (Mother of Mercy), but most Sacramentans knew it as "Sisters' Hospital."[66]

The hospital showed the sisters to be as bold in taking risks as any Sacramento entrepreneur. After borrowing the twelve thousand dollars, Madden negotiated with doctors, hired staff, and trained and assigned sisters to nursing and support positions in the facility. In 1896 she engaged an Oakland firm, Basset Brothers, to construct an entirely new building on the Twenty-third Street side of the property. "The new hospital will be four stories in height," reported the San Francisco Monitor. "The building will be illuminated throughout with gas and electric lights, and hot water heaters and electric bells." Plans included special wards for different medical disorders, an operating-room wing, and balconies and solariums to assist in the healing of the patients.[67] When it opened, the new hospital provided only thirty beds but had the facilities to perform the kind of surgery Huntington had pioneered in the West.

The new structure was a decided improvement over its predecessor, and surgery was performed sometimes ten to twelve times a day. Sacramentans with a variety of maladies—industrial accidents, typhus in the summer, and pneumonia in the winter—found relief at the new hospital.[68] It soon supplanted the private hospitals, and even the injured employees of the Southern Pacific found their way to the Sisters' Hospital. Sisters with nursing experience from St. Mary's in San Francisco took the lead in providing services, but their ranks were soon augmented by the graduates of a nurses' training school that lasted until 1950.[69] Though anxious to maintain their Catholic identity (in particular, they kept on the alert for deathbed conversions and the need for baptism of infants in danger of death), the sisters opened their hospital, as they did their academy, to all people of Sacramento, and there was no effort to actively proselytize patients. The habited sisters and the presence of religious statues, crucifixes, a chapel, and eventually a full-time priest all bespoke the values of the sisters, underscoring the reason for extending their concept of mercy beyond its original boundaries of caring only for the young women of Sacramento.

Keeping the enterprise afloat financially must have weighed heavily on the community, but generous ad hoc benefactions from the local clergy helped the project along. A substantial gift in 1900 from Bishop Thomas Grace enabled the construction of an even better operating room.[70] In 1905 a local priest, the Reverend Alexander DeCampos, donated the princely sum of ten thousand dollars for a hospital chapel.[71] Under Mother Mary Gertrude King another wing was added in 1908, providing twenty new beds, additional surgical space, and a new x-ray room. In 1914 the sisters added seventeen more beds to the north wing and in 1918 another twelve small private rooms, bringing the hospital to its peak capacity of ninety beds and twenty bassinets.[72]

By 1919, however, the old Mater Misericordiae had about run its course. The influenza epidemic of 1918 had seriously overtaxed its limited facilities, and the steady improvements in health care and medical technology required new and improved facilities, especially ones that were fireproof. The Sisters' Hospital was eventually relocated to a new site on Fortieth and J streets in the 1920s and renamed Mercy Hospital in 1934.[73] It soon became an integral part of the growing Sacramento health-care network, which included the county hospital and Sutter General Hospital.

Once committed to the hospital, the sisters provided active leadership in the advancing field of medical administration. The decision to take over the Ridge Home and transform it into a functioning city hospital must have challenged the creativity and imagination of the various mothers superior as they scrambled for funds and sisters to staff their ministries. Continual improvements in medical technology and the need for more and better trained sisters in the various departments of the hospital required constant planning, fund-raising, and negotiation with civic and medical leaders. Two members of the Mercy community, Sisters Mary Carmel Naughton and Mary Peter Carew, rose to the forefront as hospital administrators. Naughton, as noted earlier, oversaw the erection of the new Mercy Hospital in the 1920s. Carew's long career in the hospital included a major expansion of its facilities and its outreach in the 1950s and 1960s.[74]

FRANCISCAN SISTERS PROVIDE CHILD CARE

Other needs generated by Sacramento's economy were also met by religious sisters. The rise of canning and the demands of a busy cannery season created an opportunity to develop child care for the working women who staffed the busy canneries from March to November. Women who lived near the canneries on the West End were in particular need.

The opening of a day-care center for cannery workers came almost naturally to the Franciscan Sisters, who observed recurring absences in St. Stephen School during the canning season. They had even watched from their convent as older children wheeled buggies with their younger siblings onto the school grounds to watch them from windows while trying to pay attention in school. When it rained, the sisters took the children into the convent for protection. The sad case of a Portuguese girl, Leonora Santos, goaded them to action. Leonora was brought to the sisters by her parents, who ran a restaurant "in a very disreputable part of the city." The sisters agreed to watch the child, who eventually contracted diphtheria and died. The Santos case convinced some of them a facility was needed, especially on the West End, where children could be sheltered and also given basic health care. At about the same time, a Mrs. Kyle, the matron of one of the canneries, pledged financial support if the sisters undertook child-care services. At first the Franciscans contemplated renting property near St. Stephen Church, and sometime in 1917 Mother Mary Pacifica Kirschel approached Bishop Grace, who generously offered to pay the rent. Later that year Kirschel gave up on the idea of renting a building and asked Bishop Grace for permission to raise funds for a new building. Although he pledged no diocesan funds, Grace allowed the sisters to go door to door. In this manner, Kirschel and Sister Mary Tarcissia Mulbay raised nearly sixteen thousand dollars. These funds were augmented by contributions of war bonds and a large gift from Magdalen Gehring, a wealthy matron from St. Francis Parish, who gave two thousand dollars and left another seventeen hundred dollars in her will for the project.

The influenza epidemic of 1918, which hit Sacramento hard, provided the Franciscan Sisters an unexpected opportunity to hone their caretaking skills. However, when city officials beseeched the sisters to open up an emergency hospital on the West End, the sisters demurred (they did not have nursing training). Instead, the sisters offered to transform their school into a care facility for children whose parents were sick.[75] Religious rivalry came into play as the sisters learned that members of the Protestant Church Federation contemplated opening a new center in the district. To their aid came Rebecca Coolot, the primary Catholic representative to city benevolent societies, who blocked this move and cautioned the federation to "desist from any attempt to open a day home . . . for the Sisters of St. Francis are to have it."[76]

On July 22, 1919, the sisters purchased a plot of land near Southside Park from Robert Callahan and another parcel from Mrs. Katherine McCarthy for a total of seventy-five hundred dollars. The architectural firm of Barton and Dudley designed the building, and the sisters broke ground in May 1920. By mid-December Mother Mary Pacifica and Sisters Mary Helen Seibol and Mary Camillus Kruse moved in. Eight days later an ailing Bishop Grace dedicated the edifice, which would later be named Grace Day Home in his honor. The facility was a godsend for the hardworking people of the area. Every day hundreds of youngsters were dropped off at Grace Day Home. The sisters charged twenty-five cents a day or a dollar and a half a month to those who could afford it, but many could not. Many of the children had only one living parent. Most of the custodial parents were women, who would have lost their children to an orphanage had they not been able to support them by the seasonal cannery work.

At first the home pulled in anywhere from 120 to 150 children daily. It was most crowded during the packing months from late spring to early fall. However, when one of the canneries burned, the number of children needing care diminished rapidly, leaving the sisters for a time with about 60 children per day. The sisters supplemented their work by catechetical instruction at nearby St. Mary Church and in summer schools of religion for Mexican children. Financial support for the endeavor was always a challenge, but charitable contributions continued, including a five thousand–dollar bequest from the Reverend Peter Van Schie, who died in

September 1921, and seven thousand dollars from Grace when he died in December 1921. The state licensed the home in 1922. The sisters purchased another plot from Callahan for twenty-five hundred dollars (replete with an old brick building from early Sacramento) in 1923. With a grant of six thousand dollars from Bishop Patrick Keane, they erected a new wing, which included a long-desired chapel. Its long-term financial success was ultimately ensured when, in 1923, Rebecca Coolot added it to the list of institutions that received funds from the recently created Community Chest.[77] In 1924, directly behind the home, the diocese built a new Catholic school, Holy Angels, to replace the aging St. Stephen's.

CONCLUSION

Grateful Sacramentans publicly acknowledged the importance of these privately run institutions to the development of Sacramento. The fiftieth anniversary of the Mercy Sisters' arrival in Sacramento was a citywide event, spearheaded by Mayor Marshall Beard in 1907 and including among its sponsors some of the city's civic and business leaders.[78] Thousands came to pay their respects and descended on the convent yard for refreshments and a musical concert. A collection taken up by prominent citizens netted six thousand dollars, which allowed the sisters to put in a heating system at St. Joseph Academy.

These religious sisters were not the only Sacramento women who cut a major swath in city affairs, though. Other congregations of sisters and the increasingly visible presence of Catholic laywomen, many of them trained by the sisters, were active as well. However, the Sisters of Mercy and the Franciscan Sisters illustrate the ways in which Catholics contributed substantially to the welfare of the city. As the city developed they would all prove particularly effective in nurturing the various Catholic immigrant groups who sought to find their place in Sacramento's life.

CHAPTER 4

Catholics and the Ethnic Consensus, 1880–1930

"Quietly accomplishing a distinctly valuable service"

Sacramentans reveled in the results of a 2002 study by Harvard University that acclaimed the city "the most diverse" in the country.[1] *Time* reported approvingly that Sacramento had a "Crayola culture" in which you could see a "Sikh casually strolling into a Mexican restaurant for takeout" and "an Eskimo and a white punk hanging out together downtown." Mayor Heather Fargo declared, "Sacramento has been a diverse city throughout our history. From the earliest days of incorporation through today, our city is home to families from all cultures."[2] Literally speaking, the mayor was correct. Sacramento has always been home to a medley of ethnic groups. But diversity was not always celebrated.

Sacramentans of earlier generations sometimes reacted to the foreign-born with suspicion and even outright hostility. Active nativist movements flourished at different times in the city's past. These targeted not only the city's "unassimilable" Chinese and Japanese but also other foreign-born groups who were the alleged source of certain social pathologies—for example, drunkenness, prostitution, petty theft, and so on.[3] Certain ethnic groups were excluded from city housing by restrictive covenants. Eventually, the care and handling of the foreign-born became a Catholic "problem" since so many immigrants were Catholic. It was an easy step for some to equate Catholicism with social decay.

To be sure, it was hard to tar all Catholics as bad citizens. As noted earlier, intermarriage and Catholic participation in commercial, civic, and political life made blanket accusations of disloyalty anomalous. In the small spatial and social confines of Sacramento, chances were that one either lived near or was related to a Catholic and found them to be good neighbors and loyal citizens. Likewise, prominent Catholic leaders like Bishops Manogue and Grace and groups like the Sisters of Mercy and the Franciscans were beloved public figures to whom it was impossible to attribute malice and of whom one could scarcely be afraid. But the foreign-born, many of them Catholics, did pose a problem for Sacramento. They were the "other."

Sacramento was not exempt from California's history of racial exclusion. These attitudes and policies were directed mainly at people of color, especially Asians, but they also created a hostile climate toward foreign-born or other nationalities. Policy and opinion makers in the state capital at times regarded the foreign-born in their midst with suspicion and insisted on their assimilation into American culture (for instance, speaking English, practicing temperance, and dutiful hard work) as a condition for social peace. Sacramentans who came from abroad were expected to shed their "foreign" ways, learn English, and integrate themselves into the wider community. In 1920 Harry Muddox, executive secretary of the Chamber of Commerce, summed up Sacramento's expectations of its foreign-born citizens: "I am not so much concerned with the actual naturalization of the foreigner, neither am I so much interested in knowing that he can write his name legibly or say American words, but I am deeply concerned as to whether he and his wife and children learn to fit in and become really Americanized."[4]

Sacramento Catholic leaders at times embraced the racism inherent in exclusionary policies and were disposed to go along with the city consensus. However, it was not easy. Although they were sympathetic to the demand for assimilation, they had to contend with those who insisted on another course. Foreign-born Catholics of southern and eastern European backgrounds in particular and their patrons in the American hierarchy rejected an overly hasty assimilation process into American culture. They demanded distinctive national churches to preserve their Catholic faith. Caught up in the pressures within the church, Sacramento's Catholic leaders initially temporized and permitted ethnic churches, while insisting that they be way stations to Americanization. When this solution proved unsatisfactory, though, the demands of lay Catholics and their clerical supporters had to be accommodated despite the urgent requests of the local community.

THE CALIFORNIA LEGACY OF RACIAL DISCRIMINATION

A look at the larger context of intergroup relations in California provides a context for Sacramento's conditions. Among the first to feel the sting of discrimination were African Americans of the Gold Rush era who resented measures to exclude them from the state. One delegate to the 1849 constitutional convention in Monterey, former Kentuckian M. M. McCarver, had urged the body to exclude free blacks who not only would give competition to free white labor but were also "idle in their habits, difficult to be governed by laws, thriftless and uneducated." This was rejected, but antiblack feeling persisted. California's first governor, Peter Burnett (who as noted earlier donated the land for Sacramento's first Catholic church), proposed to exclude free blacks from the state. The legislature rejected this idea, but passed statutes that, historian Malcolm Edwards writes, "humiliated, restricted, and periled any blacks who chose to enter California."[5] McCarver and Burnett had come to California from Oregon, where they had advocated similar policies. Both of them made their homes in Sacramento.

Antagonism toward Asians is one of the best-known features of antiforeign sentiment in California's history.[6] Already in 1850 California was imposing a steep tax on foreign miners, enforced principally against the Chinese and Latino argonauts. Official hostility to the Chinese limited their rights, but Chinese laborers were used extensively in building the Central Pacific Railroad. Acts of violence against the Chinese escalated in the 1870s when hard economic times created bitter rivalry for jobs between Chinese and Caucasian workers.[7]

A good bit of agitation was centered on Chico, where local community leader John Bidwell employed Chinese laborers in his various businesses—paying them considerably lower wages than he paid Caucasian labor. Chinatowns in Yreka, Chico, and Weaverville were burned. In 1877 Chinese workers were driven out of Rocklin, Penryn, and Grass Valley. The rise of the Workingman's Party in 1878, led by Irish demagogue Denis Kearney, pushed hard against the Chinese and made life even more difficult for them. Although Chinese immigration had been temporarily restricted by an 1882 treaty, anti-Chinese agitation continued nonetheless in California. Historian Joseph McGowan notes that the year 1886 was the "peak of the anti-Chinese movement in the Sacramento Valley." An Anti-Chinese Convention was held in Sacramento on March 10, 1886. The Chinese were permanently barred from the United States in 1904.[8]

Anti-Japanese sentiment also churned to the surface in California politics. Difficulties in San Francisco over the segregation of Japanese children from whites led to serious tensions between the United States and Japan. In 1913 California passed the Alien Land Act, barring Japanese from owning land. This law was extended by the initiative process and by subsequent action of the California legislature.[9]

A GROWING FOREIGN-BORN PRESENCE

From the outset Sacramento mirrored the ethnic realities of northern California. In the heat of the Gold Rush, people of every language and race poured into the new city. Gregory Phelan observed of the small group that turned out for the first Catholic mass in 1850, "These few represented different portions of the globe. I noticed a pious Mexican young lady, as well as persons from Ireland and the United States."[10] Emerging Sacramento initially welcomed the Irish, the Germans, and the Chinese. Later, the so-called new immigrants from southern and eastern Europe came along—Italians, Portuguese, Slavonians (a generic name for Croatians and Serbians)—as well as Japanese and Mexicans.

Immigrants came to California and Sacramento initially for gold and later for more steady jobs. Work at the railroad yards (Sacramento's largest employer) and seasonal labor at the canneries on the West End attracted foreign laborers. These newcomers also ran hotels, bakeries, laundries, restaurants, and saloons. Sacramento built its economic life on their labor. By 1880 one of every three Sacramentans was foreign-born. Table 4.1 provides data relating to the number of foreign-born residents (excluding those of foreign parentage) in Sacramento County.

TABLE 4.1 | FOREIGN-BORN IN SACRAMENTO COUNTY, 1880–1920

YEAR	NUMBER OF FOREIGN-BORN	PERCENTAGE OF FOREIGN-BORN IN SACRAMENTO COUNTY
1880	12,494	36
1890	13,212	33
1900	12,736	28
1910	19,166	28
1920	14,998	17

SOURCE: U.S. Census Bureau, 1880–1920.

By the end of the nineteenth century Sacramento's most recently arrived ethnic groups tended to cluster in relatively small enclaves in the city's West End, near the commercial and industrial districts. The spatial closeness of the city grid—confined by its rivers—precluded the kind of ghettoization that existed in larger cities. Sacramento's various nationalities attempted as best they could to maintain some form of communal cohesiveness.[11] Immigrant groups formed fraternal and benevolent societies, held ethnic festivals, and even built clubhouses and social halls to preserve their identity. Religious institutions were integral to the life and identity of these groups. Later, the city developed inexpensive public transportation, which permitted greater movement between neighborhood and work. As upward social mobility occurred, city inhabitants moved east and south.

INSISTENCE ON AMERICANIZATION

The foreign-born were an important part of Sacramento's labor force, and their work contributed to the city's wealth. However, their increasing visibility evoked negative reactions from some quarters, especially when they were associated with public disorder. It did not help that some of the seediest taverns, gambling joints, and brothels were located in the West End, where many immigrants lived. But city newspapers reinforced a climate of suspicion, with articles highlighting the participation of the foreign-born in acts of murder, divorce, marital infidelity, larceny, arson, gambling, excessive drinking, violations of the Sunday Sabbath, and prostitution. The key to immigrant salvation was to become Americanized as rapidly as possible.

Public schools, especially Lincoln Elementary at Fourth and Q streets, in the heart of the city's most diverse district, conducted classes in English and reinforced lessons of public patriotism and American nationality expected by the city school board and city leaders. Ernesto Galarza, recently arrived from Mexico in 1913, recalled of Nettie Hopley, principal of Lincoln School (and a devout Catholic), "Miss Hopley and her teachers never let us forget why we were at Lincoln: for those who were alien, to become good Americans; for those who were so born, to accept the rest of us." Likewise, the city's only public high school taught a version of U.S. history that inculcated respect for American heroes and reverence for the founding ideals and documents of the nation.[12]

Pressures for Americanization also came from Protestant ministers, who formed the Ministerial Union in 1890 to tackle adverse local moral conditions.[13] Anxious to uplift the foreign-born whose lives they considered morally inferior to their own, they endorsed a Sunday Sabbath "blue law" in 1891, prohibiting certain forms of entertainment and work on Sundays. One of their spokesmen, Congregational minister J. B. Silcox, declared patronizingly that the "Sunday law is demanded also for the welfare of the workingman."[14] Ministerial concern for the "proper" role of women also stirred up a move to ban women and young girls from entering taverns.[15] However, a member of the organization, the Reverend R. M. Stevenson of Westminster Presbyterian, made it clear that many of Sacramento's serious social problems could be laid at the feet of the foreign-born. In a sermon on Washington's Birthday in 1891, titled "Our Country and Our Church," Stevenson stated, "Not only is the tide of immigration swelling with rapidity, but it is bringing us the most filthy and degraded and undesirable classes." He warned of the dangers of taking in "a great mass of peons whom we cannot assimilate" and singled out among its many evils the saloon. "Nothing so increased the number of criminals and the number of paupers as the saloon, and it is a great producer of lunatics and idiots."[16] The anxieties of the Ministerial Union reflected a growing discomfort among Sacramentans with the presence of the foreign-born. In the mid-1890s this led to one of the worst eruptions of anti-Catholic nativism in the city.

ANTIFOREIGN SENTIMENT

The American Protective Association (APA) was founded by Henry F. Bowers in Clinton, Iowa, in 1887 and surged in membership and popularity in various areas of the nation. This group was particularly fearful of the specter of "Catholic power" and resurrected old fears of a Catholic take-over of American political and social institutions. Once in charge, members of the APA believed, Catholics would seek to impose their doctrines and forms of authority on God-fearing Protestants, they would eliminate the use of the Bible in public places, and they would make the U.S. government subservient to Rome. The APA targeted the hordes of immigrant Catholics who were swelling the voting rolls of big cities and sometimes installing corrupt politicians (mostly Irish) in positions of authority. Members of the APA also feared Catholic dominance in the ranks of public-school teachers and in the police and fire departments—believing that such coveted jobs would gradually be handed out only to fellow Catholics.[17]

The APA came into California in early 1893 and began organizing chapters in various cities.[18] In Sacramento an ailing Bishop Manogue warned his fellow Irish citizens in northern California that the APA bore a strong resemblance to the hated "Orangemen" of the Auld Sod.[19] In March 1894 a former priest, Joseph Slattery, and his wife, Elizabeth, a former nun, both of whom had left the church, hosted a series of widely attended anti-Catholic lectures at the Pythian Hall on Ninth and I streets. The Slatterys' coarse allegations and sensationalism opened up a space for local Protestant clergy to give vent to similar concerns. APA organizers formed three chapters in Sacramento. Although many local ministers would disavow any formal affiliation with the group, a few openly joined and supported it.

APA speakers attacked Catholic doctrines, retooled Reformation-era polemics about the "machinations" of the Jesuits, and questioned Catholic loyalty to American institutions and freedoms. They persistently questioned the number of Catholics who received jobs with the police and fire departments as well as in the public schools.[20] During the election campaigns of 1894 they forged a tight link between their nativist appeals and anti-Catholicism. At an evening service in his own church First Baptist pastor the Reverend A. P. Banks warned Sacramentans about Catholic political power: "Men who have taken possession of our land are foreign and strange to our institutions." He urged his fellow citizens to "gaze upon the spectacle of he who stands behind the incense in yonder Cathedral, and you will see whose hand is upon the politics of this country." Congregationalist minister J. B. Koehne cautioned, in the midst of the 1894 campaign, "We should not shut the gates on account of birth, but against those who are under the dominion of a foreign potentate or pontiff." The city and county election results were mixed, but provided enough APA victories to give the movement some impetus. Of the nineteen candidates they endorsed (some of whom denied affiliation with the organization), six won election (one of whom denied APA membership) and one tied.[21]

Buoyed by their modest successes in the 1894 campaign, APA organizers planned the next year to take over Sacramento's newly reformed city government and exclude Catholics from city jobs by using the new appointive and executive powers of the mayor. In this campaign the anti-foreign invective was harsh—and crudely targeted the Irish. J. E. Denton of the First Christian Church unloaded on the Irish and the Catholic Church in a sermon on the Sunday evening before the November election: "Let us as Protestants stand together against every Catholic in the land. Let us be true to the APAs. The APA is against the Irish. It is time for Americans to take office and for the Irish to take to the woods. . . . Let us for once have an American government, an American state, and an American city where we can hang our banner on the outer wall, 'No Irish need apply.'" Before a crowd of five hundred Sacramentans, another APA speaker, former state deputy attorney general Oregon Sanders, mimicked the accents of ethnic Californians, sneering at "Dagoes" and deriding the Irish immigrant as having "a Gothic brow and hair on his teeth." Sanders advocated the direct election of the president, because he "was afraid a time might come when there might be a sufficient number of Catholics chosen as electors." He also warned that churches were becoming obscenely wealthy because of tax exemptions for their properties, which by his account tallied up to two million dollars. "They bury a Dago there and call it a cemetery. When in the course of time that property becomes worth millions of dollars that festive Dago experiences a premature resurrection and he is carted off to the sand dunes, while the cemetery is cut up into town lots and sold."[22]

Thanks to a split in the opposition forces, APA sympathizers managed to elect hardware merchant Cyrus Hubbard to the mayoralty. However, the Hubbard "victory" was a fluke, as the new mayor found his efforts to purge the city of Catholic influence blocked at every step by the city trustees (city council) and the continual harassment of the *Sacramento Bee*.[23]

Most Sacramentans had not embraced the bitter nativism that erupted during the campaign. However, these outbursts must have made local Catholics apprehensive.

After the APA passed from the scene, antiforeign sentiments were perpetuated by an organization of Protestants called the Church Federation. The Church Federation was a national organization devoted to the moral uplift of urban communities. Sacramento's federation had these interests as well, but thanks to the influence of its chief organizer, Charles Matthias Goethe, its agenda was also nativist and anti-Catholic. After a trip abroad during which he had seen the positive effects of unified church action, the independently wealthy Goethe organized a meeting of city ministers at the Sacramento Hotel in 1914 to do the same thing. He hoped that the federation would tackle some of Sacramento's seemingly intractable social problems: alcoholism, petty crime, and the like. Unlike federation organizers in other parts of the country, however, Goethe had well-developed ideas about the origins of social problems. Enriched by his marriage into the opulent Glide family, Goethe was a proponent of the pseudoscience of eugenics (a popular belief that certain racial groups are inherently superior or inferior to others).[24] As a result he was fairly certain that many of Sacramento's problems could be laid at the door of the "racially inferior" foreign-born. Because the Catholic Church was one of the few that opposed eugenics and any artificial "tampering" with the processes of human reproduction, Goethe considered it a menace.

The group sponsored lectures and luncheons and disseminated its points of view on the national, state, and local issues of the day. However, they also took swipes at the Catholic Church when they could. The federation sponsored a talk in 1921 by Miss Burke McCarty of Oakland, who launched a bitter verbal assault on Catholic schools. After this meeting copies of the anti-Catholic Klan publication *New Menace* were distributed throughout Sacramento's residential districts. It included a personal attack on the city assistant superintendent of schools, Mary O'Neil, who was singled out in part because of her Catholic faith.[25] As late as December 1935, Goethe pressed the federation to put a copy of an anti-Catholic tract, *Rome Stoops to Conquer,* on city library shelves to see how long it would remain.[26] The federation managed to rile C. K. McClatchy, who occasionally denounced it as an agent of intolerance (as he had the APA) and scoffed at its allegations that the *Bee* was a Jesuit organ because the editor had attended Santa Clara College.[27] Goethe might have been dismissed as a malevolent eccentric if he had not also been a major supporter of public parks and later a benefactor of Sacramento State College and University.

In the lead-up to World War I and in the wake of war-generated propaganda, suspicions of the foreign-born and demands for assimilation were even more intense in Sacramento. Sacramento had its own Council of Defense, which closely monitored "subversive" activity—especially war dissent by ethnic groups who did not support the Allied cause.[28]

Progressive Era concerns about Americanization were voiced regularly by the *Sacramento Bee*. The McClatchy brothers, in private and public, were strong proponents of Americanization, and the columns of the *Bee* often railed against "hyphenated-Americans." As World War I approached, patriotic sentiment ran high, and in an April 1916 article C. K. McClatchy derided ethnic clubs that perpetuated dual loyalties. "No man can serve two masters. And neither can any man serve two countries. A man is either an American or he is not an American. He cannot be a 'German-American' nor an 'Irish-American.' And any man who says he is either such a hyphenated contradiction is not a good American citizen." The brothers insisted, in season and out, that the foreign-born assimilate as soon as possible. "What do you think about this, Americans?" McClatchy lectured. "And when *The Bee* says Americans, it means Americans of Irish blood and English blood, and German blood, and French blood, and Russian blood, and Scandinavian blood, and Italian blood, and the blood of all the other Nations of the earth that have come into this melting pot to make up the citizenship of America."[29] If assimilation was deemed "impossible," as it was with the Japanese and other "Asiatics," they argued for their exclusion. In fact, Valentine McClatchy spearheaded efforts to exclude Japanese from the state.[30]

Other civic officials and leaders echoed the sentiments for Americanization. Superior court judge C. E. McLaughlin reminded a group of Portuguese young people from St. Elizabeth Parish that they had "the duty of becoming true Americans resting upon them." He warned those who dissented, "If there are men of foreign birth who are listless and disloyal, I call upon them to go back to the day when they stood looking from the land of their discontent to the land of their desire over which floated the American flag and ask them to remember the motives which prompted them to come hither where their higher affection is centered."[31]

The McClatchys viewed with a skewered eye religious groups that perpetuated ethnic separatism. When sympathetic clergy attended an April 1916 meeting of German Americans (before American entry into World War I) and dared to express solidarity with the Central Powers, the editor noted acerbically, "Among the speakers last night were Father Appolinaris of the Catholic Order of Franciscans; Reverend Charles F. Oehler of the German Lutheran Church; and Father Ellis of the Oak Park Catholic Church. The latter, of Irish birth, evidently brought his hatred of England over to this country."[32] Clearly, the pressure was on the church to do something to curtail these kinds of activities and to demonstrate absolute loyalty to American values.

Even if their rhetoric against the foreign-born was at times belligerent, the McClatchys were no friends of the revived Ku Klux Klan. Restored in 1915, this nativist organization dramatically appeared in Sacramento on Palm Sunday of 1922, when several hooded Klansmen strode down the aisle at an evening service at Westminster Presbyterian. Klan organizers in Sacramento generally avoided the crude nativism of the APA and portrayed themselves to God-fearing Sacramentans as guardians of public morality and especially as enforcers of Prohibition laws. They could not evade their strongly anti-Catholic feelings, though. In an interview, local Kleagle Edgar Fuller tried to portray a balanced and moderate image for the Klan. "We are not anti-Catholic, anti-Jew, or anti-Union labor, as has been charged, but are simply anti-wrong." However, he left no doubt that his tolerance was conditional. "We believe in the tenets of the Christian religion, that lets out the Jews. We believe in the separation of church and state, and that lets out the Catholics."[33]

The Klan questioned Catholic loyalty to the United States and linked the church with tolerance of Sacramento's well-known bootlegging operations. The undertow of the Klan's appeal, though, was a residual suspicion toward foreign-born Catholics. In late April 1922 Fuller held a major initiation of new Klan members at Muddox Hall in suburban Oak Park. Nearly three hundred men knelt before the fiery cross and swore allegiance to the Invisible Empire.[34] Another major Klan initiation took place on

May 5, 1922, on lower Stockton Road and drew nearly four thousand people.[35] The Klan managed to make some mischief for Catholics (for example, in demanding that Catholic properties be assessed a full share of property taxes), and the size of these rallies must have distressed Catholics.[36] Again and again they paid allegiance to the demand for social homogeneity.

CATHOLICS CONFRONT THE ISSUE

Sacramento Catholics also believed that social peace required assimilation. At times they were as overtly racist as their fellow Californians. They proved this early on by providing support to Sacramento's anti-Chinese activities.

Sacramento's Chinese community developed during the Gold Rush and expanded substantially when their labor was used on the Central Pacific Railroad. Sacramento's Chinese formed their own associations and had their own markets, restaurants, newspaper, gambling dens, theater, joss house, and houses of prostitution. Most religious groups worked with the Chinese, and Catholics initially made some effort as well. Already in 1852 Phelan reported the presence of eighteen Chinese at mass. In 1854 Father Thomas Cian, a Chinese convert, tried unsuccessfully to begin a mission to the Sacramento Chinese.[37] Chinese resistance to Catholicism may have stemmed not from any aversion to Christianity (there was a thriving Baptist mission) but from an antipathy to the Irish. Prominent Sacramento Catholics were in the forefront of movements to exclude the Chinese.

A serious depression lasting much of the 1870s created intense competition for low-wage jobs between the Chinese and Caucasians. In April 1876 Sacramento citizens gathered at Pioneer Hall to demand the abrogation of the 1868 Burlingame Treaty, which allowed a trickle of Chinese to enter the country. At the behest of Sacramento county state senator Creed Haymond, the state legislature held a series of hearings on the impact of the Chinese on California politics, morality, and social relations. The Sacramento phase of these hearings produced an array of witnesses, many of them Irish, who attested to the depravity and social degradation that the Chinese brought to the city. One longtime police officer, and a member of St. Rose Church, Charles O'Neill, drew from his experience walking the beat along the heavily Chinese I Street and declared, "As a population, the Chinese are largely criminal." He also scoffed at efforts to convert them to

Christianity.[38] O'Neill's comments were only the beginning, as an increase in anti-Chinese sentiment built in the California capital.

Northern California's leading Catholic newspaper, the *San Francisco Monitor,* expressed Catholic opposition to the Chinese. Lamenting in an 1873 editorial "the great evils sure to attend the influx of these heathens," the paper praised the formation of organized opposition to the Chinese in Sacramento in March of that year. Prominent city Catholics like Christopher Green and John Wesley Armstrong continually urged restrictions on Chinese immigration. Catholics were among the three thousand who turned out to hear a speech by the sinophobe Denis Kearney in 1879. One Catholic who played a major role in Sacramento's anti-Chinese activities was Robert T. Devlin, a successful businessman and attorney, and later state senator and U.S. attorney. Devlin was an organizer of the Citizen's Anti-Chinese Association of Sacramento and a public spokesman for the cause. Speaking at a rally at Turner Hall in December 1885, Devlin urged his listeners to refuse to rent houses and land to the Chinese and suggested a boycott of those who did. "I would never defend another Chinaman," he declared, "if the other lawyers would agree not to do so." In March 1886, when a statewide anti-Chinese convention was held in Sacramento, Devlin was one of five committee members in charge of drafting the convention's resolutions. The resolutions adopted during the convention included a boycott of all businesses that could "dispense with Chinese help" but were not doing so and a certificate that was to be "given to dealers, hotels, restaurants, etc., who neither employ Chinese, nor handle the products of their labors." The committee further drafted a "memorial to Congress," calling for "relief" from the "Chinese evil."[39]

DEFENDING THEIR LOYALTY

In 1894, during the APA campaign, Sacramento Catholics responded to attacks on their patriotism and loyalty to the Republic by reassuring community leaders that they were trustworthy citizens. During the controversies, Robert Devlin, perhaps the city's most prominent lay Catholic, stepped into the breach. At the dedication of a new flagpole in the Civic Plaza, Devlin spoke for his fellow religionists when he declared, "And what is the freedom symbolized by the Glorious Stars and Stripes?" he asked. "It is the freedom to express honest thoughts, to recognize no dominion of man over man, to enjoy our natural rights, to respect the rights of our neighbors, to make the laws by which we shall be bound, to choose as sovereign our servants in public places, to commune with our Maker as we wish, to worship God according to the dictates of our conscience or to worship not at all." Catholics were not seeking to undermine basic American institutions, Devlin insisted, but supported "free schools, free thought, free speech." He warned, "Whoever would stifle honest thought or deny his fellow-men the same freedom he claims for himself, or attempts to deprive them of enjoying the inalienable rights vouchsafed to all and preserve that for which this nation was baptized in blood is a traitor to that flag."[40]

Local Catholic youth assured the community of their loyalty. The Young Men's Institute sponsored an annual celebration on Washington's Birthday, which included well-publicized patriotic speeches and events stressing loyalty to their faith and to their nation. One other patriotic group was the popular Catholic fraternal order the Knights of Columbus, which came to Sacramento in 1905. The Knights publicly celebrated their patriotic Americanism and reminded their fellow citizens that the discoverer of America was a Catholic.[41]

JOINING THE CONSENSUS ON IMMIGRANT ASSIMILATION

Although they found it easy enough to stress their patriotic loyalties, Catholic leaders found themselves pressed on the issue of assimilation. Ironically, the Irish could distance themselves from the foreign-born with whom they may have shared the Catholic faith, but not much else. Even Irish-born citizens, such as Bishop Thomas Grace and city coroner and sheriff William F. Gormley, were not lumped into this general category. For example, the *Bee*'s obituary of Thomas Grace noted that in "the days when the APA was rampant some of its most ardent supporters were friends of Bishop Grace."[42] In fact, the Irish-born seemed to concur with the critics of their foreign-born coreligionists. Immigrants were more prone to vice and public corruption. Middle-class Catholic leaders, like their Protestant counterparts, wanted a clean city, did not approve of gambling, and hoped to see some restrictions on city vice—if not its outright abolition. Catholics actively supported efforts to clean up Sacramento and improve the city's image. As we shall see in the next chapter,

Catholics were among the most ardent city boosters and some of the best city and public works supporters. The Reverend John Quinn, rector of the Cathedral of the Blessed Sacrament from 1899 to 1906, publicly supported the Ministerial Union's campaigns to end poolrooms—a reform to some degree directed against the foreign-born.[43] Other Catholic leaders threw their support behind efforts to exclude saloons from residential districts.[44]

Irish Catholic leaders also slowed and even blocked the creation of "nationality" parishes, one of the chief requests of foreign-born Catholics. When they could no longer evade the demands of local ethnic groups or the Vatican to create ethnic churches (churches that ministered to those who did not speak English), Irish Catholic leaders did whatever they could to "dilute" them from being "pure" ethnic enclaves or kept them in an ecclesiastically subservient status (that is, missions and chapels rather than parishes). Nationality churches in Sacramento were treated like stepchildren: They received almost no financial or moral support from the diocese, and even found their fund-raising capacities were carefully circumscribed. When it did permit them, the diocese pushed these ethnic churches to become way stations to Americanization.

The first "nationality" Catholic church in the United States, Holy Trinity Church, opened for the German-speaking Catholics of Philadelphia in 1791.[45] In most cities, membership in a congregation depended on where you lived. Parish boundaries encompassed certain streets, and the church within one's particular area determined where one would go to receive the sacraments. Catholics within this territory were obliged to attend this church and support it, and from it they received spiritual ministry. National churches, on the other hand, had no fixed boundaries but welcomed any and all of a particular ethnic group who wished to go there. Ethnic (or nationality) churches were formed by foreign-speaking Catholics (for instance, Italians, Poles, and Germans) who desired their own worship space and a place for the maintenance of their own unique religious devotions and practices, and above all the perpetuation of their language for public services and confession. Church leaders permitted the existence of nationality parishes, often within the boundaries of territorial parishes, to meet the spiritual needs of the ethnic groups who formed them.[46] This was a common reality in the larger cities of the East and especially in the industrial Midwest. The nation's Irish-born or Irish American bishops, however, did not encourage them. In their view, they not only prevented Catholics from Americanizing but also spread church revenues too thin. In Sacramento, Bishop Thomas Grace worried that too many churches would overburden the slender finances of Catholic citizens.

In the West, American Catholic bishops approached ethnic parishes with caution. Historian Jeffrey Burns notes that in California, "ethnic national parishes were turned to only as a last resort, and were often regarded as temporary institutions." Throughout California, Burns observes, "reluctance to establish national parishes reflected a fear in the Catholic community of appearing too foreign to the American host society."[47] Sacramento's history of parish formation bears out the validity of Burns's observations.

DILUTING ETHNIC IDENTITY: THE CASE OF THE GERMANS

Thanks to its wealth and social prominence, Sacramento's German-speaking contingent represented a significant subculture in the city.[48] During the 1850s, as historian Carole Cosgrove Terry observes, German speakers were drawn to Sacramento by prospects of economic advance and added to the city's merchant and professional classes.[49] The 1852 census counted 730 German immigrants in Sacramento, most of whom had come to California after earlier stays in other parts of the country. This first, largely male, cohort of German-speaking Sacramentans grew steadily over the century. By 1860 the number had nearly doubled and continued to grow slowly, reaching its peak in 1890 when 2,182 Sacramentans were of German birth. Many of them became skilled laborers, barbers, butchers, shoemakers, and hoteliers.[50] Sacramento's Germans developed an active social group, replete with popular organizations such as the Turnverein (established in Sacramento in 1854), which sponsored social and cultural events to keep German identity alive.

Religion was part of the network of German culture; however, separate churches were initially difficult to sustain. The Methodists organized a church in 1856, but small membership and debts crushed it by 1866. German Lutherans, on the scene since 1850, formally organized in 1861. In 1867 they opened a church at the corner of Twelfth and K, directly across the street from the residence of the Catholic bishop. The success of the

Lutheran church inspired the city's German Catholics to seek their own church. Over the years, German-speaking Catholics had grown tired of worshiping at St. Rose Church. Antagonisms between the Irish clergy and German parishioners simmered for a long time. Church support must have been a very sensitive issue. "It's the old story," wrote German Franciscan the Reverend Godfrey Hoelters in late 1900. "The Germans and the Irish can't get on, and it's hard to get the Irish to support the church and school regularly."[51] Local German-speaking millionaire Anthony Coolot collected funds from approximately 100 people and purchased a lot on Twelfth between K and L (very near the German Lutheran church) for a German Catholic church. Soon after the public notice of the purchase, tensions between Sacramento Irish and German Catholics burst into view when the two groups differed over the outcome of the Franco-Prussian War. When the Prussian armies smashed into Paris in early 1871, more than 1,500 exulting Sacramento German citizens marched in a torchlight parade, igniting bonfires at street intersections, shooting off fireworks, and singing.[52] Other Sacramentans, some of whom were of French descent, watched glumly as their fellow citizens celebrated the Prussian triumph. The Irish, sensitive to the jackboot of foreign occupation on their native soil, quickly came to the support of the French.

On St. Patrick's Day that year, Sacramento's Irish expressed solidarity with the humiliated French by hanging the tricolor inside St. Rose Church and making the French consul general the guest of honor at the mass and subsequent banquet. German-speaking Catholics were incensed at these decorations in supposedly "neutral" St. Rose's. Shortly thereafter, famed German preacher Franz Xavier Weninger fortified their resolve to do something about the situation. The eloquent Jesuit, a nationally known apostle of German Catholics, visited Sacramento with the same message he carried everywhere: He urged German Catholics to build their own churches and schools and especially to preserve the German language, which he insisted was necessary for adherence to the Catholic faith. Sacramento's German Catholics were more than ready to respond to his exhortations.

Opposition to a new German church in Sacramento developed from the Archdiocese of San Francisco (under whose jurisdiction Sacramento was until 1886). Even though they permitted German churches in

San Francisco, officials made it clear that Sacramento could not finance another parish. In addition, a German exodus from St. Rose's at that time would have complicated the Reverend Patrick Scanlan's efforts to pay off church debts and raise money for a boys' school. At Scanlan's urging, a compromise of sorts was reached. German Catholics would abandon their plans for a new church, and the Archdiocese of San Francisco would see to it that a German-speaking priest would be stationed at St. Rose's. This worked for a time, but after the last German-speaking priest, the Reverend Leon Haupts, left Sacramento in the early 1890s, German Catholics clamored for their own church. By 1890 there were still more than 2,100 foreign-born Germans in the county, plus more in the distant farming village of Nicolaus in Sutter County.

A contingent of German Franciscans from Teutopolis, Illinois, heard of conditions in Sacramento and sent the Reverend Michael Richardt and his associate (called a "definitor" in Franciscan nomenclature) the Reverend Clementine Deymann to visit Bishop Manogue in March 1893. The Franciscans offered to establish a ministry to Sacramento's Germans. Manogue listened respectfully but discouraged the two friars, noting that local economic conditions were not robust enough to sustain a second parish. The Franciscans were further discouraged by the active opposition from the Irish clergy, especially cathedral rector Grace, who stayed Manogue's hand. Several months later Richardt once more pressed Manogue for admission to the diocese, but the prelate again turned him away, commenting that "the dullness of the place and times" precluded such a move.[53] Later in the year, however, opposition ceased when one of Manogue's closest confidants, the Reverend Matthew Coleman, the Irish-born pastor of St. Joseph's in Marysville, concluded that "something must be done for the Germans" in Sacramento.[54] Coleman had himself approved a new German church in Marysville.

In May 1894 Manogue sent word to Richardt that he "should be pleased to see him on important business on his next visit to the coast."[55] Richardt and Deymann visited the prelate in September 1894, and an obviously ill Manogue invited the Franciscans to establish a church in Sacramento. He insisted, however, that the new church be territorial rather than national. He sketched out the parish boundaries to include a relatively undeveloped area stretching from Eighteenth Street east to the city limits (then at Thirty-first Street) and then swinging northeast as far as the American River (the northern limits of the city), "four or five miles into the country and south as far as three miles from Freeport." (He preserved a three-mile limit from Freeport, because of the existence of a Portuguese church there.) Manogue noted that there were many Swiss dairymen living in the county and insisted that the friars take care of the Sacramento County institutions (the poorhouse and hospital) and, he added, "I think four or five breweries." As things were wrapping up, Deymann asked Manogue, "What about the Germans who live in the cathedral parish—will they have the privilege to come to us?" The prelate "hesitated to answer." Jumping into the silence, Deymann inquired who would hear confessions for the Germans outside the parish boundaries, to which Manogue replied, "Oh, yes, I give them all liberty about that." But once again Manogue insisted that the new parish would be English speaking and sharply restricted any potential plans to raise funds outside the specific territorial boundaries of the parish.[56]

Manogue also directed that the friars borrow the money to start their church and school so as to not overtax the financially strapped Sacramento Catholic community. The new St. Francis's was built directly across from an aging Sutter's Fort and opened in April 1895. In November of that year the school began.

St. Francis Parish operated on what would later be called a multicultural basis for many years. German Catholics heard German sermons and could confess their sins in their native tongue, and the friars perpetuated other German Catholic customs and traditions, particularly in decor and music. The Irish clergy, for their part, kept an eagle eye on the activities of the Franciscans. One Franciscan pastor, the Reverend Godfrey Hoelters, complained to his superiors, "The Rev. Ph. Brady [a member of the cathedral clergy] . . . works against us at every turn, but comes here for confession."[57] Nonetheless, Hoelters held the parish together, and large celebrations were always bilingual. From the beginning St. Francis's was a polyglot parish—even though it had a German character. St. Francis pastors learned to live with the requirements of dual-language ministry.

By the time a new church building was erected in 1910, St. Francis membership appeared comfortably balanced between English- and German-speaking communicants. Its rich inner decor was reminiscent of

German Catholic designs elsewhere in the United States, but its lavish windows were donated by parishioners with both German and Irish surnames. German-language services persisted until World War I, but, inevitably, the Franciscan friars shed their Germanic shells and became even more visibly Americanized than the Irish.

"THE ASSIMILATIVE POTENCY OF A COMMON FAITH": ST. STEPHEN'S

Keeping the Franciscan parish reliably "American," by insisting on a territorial ministry, had been accomplished with relative ease thanks to the demographics of Sacramento growth. The area simply filled up with people of mixed ethnic heritage who attended St. Francis's as their parish church. However, when the obvious need for specialized ethnic ministry surfaced in another section of the city, Catholic leaders did nothing until their hand was forced.

Sacramento's ethnic crossroads were the neighborhoods of the West End. Ernesto Galarza, who grew up in "lower Sacramento," describes the "kaleidoscope of colors and languages and customs that surprised and absorbed me at every turn." In addition to the Mexicans were Japanese whose

> women walked on the street in kimonos, wooden sandals, and white stockings, carrying neat black, bundles on their backs and wearing their hair in puffs with long ivory needles stuck through them. . . . Chinatown was on the other side of K Street toward the Southern Pacific Shops. . . . In the hotels and rooming houses scattered about the barrio were where the Filipino farm workers, river boat stewards and houseboys made their homes. . . . Hindus from the rice and fruit country north of the capital stay[ed] in the rooming houses when they were in town. . . . The Portuguese and Italian families fathered their own neighborhoods along Fourth and Fifth Streets southward toward the Y-Street Levee. The Poles, Yugo-Slavs and Koreans, too few to take over any particular part of it, were scattered throughout the barrio. Black men drifted in and out of town.[58]

Religious institutions still existed in this original part of the city, including the old Congregational church whose square towers still loomed large. Others, like the Catholic St. Rose Church, had moved away from the district. The distance between this neighborhood and the cathedral seemed far, especially in the rainy months. In spite of the arrival of more foreign-born, many of them Catholic, there did not appear any great interest in creating a mission station. Finally, a pious woman named Mary Ellen "Ella" Bowden forced church leaders to minister on the West End.

Ella Bowden was the youngest of the four children of Irish-born Richard and Margaret Bowden. The couple immigrated to California in the 1850s and settled in Sacramento. Ella went to school at St. Joseph Academy, and the family belonged to St. Rose's and the cathedral parish. Ella and her three brothers lived with their parents on the west side of the city. Tragedy befell the couple as their three sons—James, Stephen, and Richard—all died before reaching adulthood. As the sole surviving child, Ellen foreswore marriage to remain with her parents until their deaths. Her father lived until the age of eighty-four, dying in 1898; her mother followed two years later at the age of eighty-eight. Encouraged by the Reverend Philip Brady, a curate at the cathedral, young Ella turned to religious pursuits and charity to fill her days. The passing of her parents left her a sizable inheritance, which she lavishly gave to the Catholic church. Her priestly friend was one of the chief recipients of her largesse.[59]

Anxious to make provision for the scores of Catholics on the West End who found the trek into the city center to the cathedral impossible, Bowden purchased the stable house and servant quarters of the Crocker mansion, located on Third and O streets. The structure was a two-story building with two huge rooms on each level. Bowden renovated the building, transforming the lower portion into a church. In April 1900 she presented this as a "gift" to Bishop Grace, along with a five thousand–dollar endowment for the care and upkeep of the building.[60] Later she donated an additional five hundred dollars for improvements to the new church. Grace dedicated the structure on December 2, 1900, to honor the memory of Bowden's brother Stephen.[61] This stable house-turned-church would become the home base for virtually every major Catholic ethnic group in Sacramento: Italians, Portuguese, Croatians, Japanese, Mexicans, and Filipinos/as.[62] Over the years, hundreds of Catholic Sacramentans received their first formal religious instruction in the upper quarters, which had been transformed into classrooms. St. Stephen's was a microcosm of the diversity of Sacramento's West End.

Margaret Crocker by Frank Pebbles, 1877. Crocker's coach house at Third and o became a church and school (St. Stephen's). Courtesy of Sacramento Archives and Museum Collection Center, Eleanor McClatchy Collection.

As a gathering place for Catholics of many nationalities, St. Stephen's was an instant success. "Every Sunday since the dedication of the Church its capacity has been heavily taxed," wrote a correspondent for the *San Francisco Monitor.* "The congregation has proved too much for the church and a second Mass has become necessary."[63] Virtually every Catholic ethnic group attended St. Stephen services—a veritable United Nations of nationalities—listening to the mass in Latin while they strained to understand the words of the sermon delivered in the Irish brogue of the visiting priest. In addition to the liturgical celebrations held in the building, a Sunday school, located on the upper level, provided space for children of the parish to prepare for the sacraments and gain proper religious instruction from the catechism.

St. Stephen Church, ca. 1948. Courtesy of Sacramento Archives and Museum Collection Center, Frank Christy Collection.

Even though the new church was packing in communicants every Sunday, Bishop Grace tried to slow the pace of its development by insisting that it remain a mission of the cathedral. This status may not have meant much to the scores of churchgoers on the West End, but it was a practical expression of his distaste for ethnic parishes. Its missionary status meant that its finances and ministry were conducted by Irish-born clergy who would compel the immigrant parishioners to learn English and donate regularly, for although the priests said mass in Latin (which was mostly inaudible), they preached, heard confessions, and conducted devotions in English. Grace and the cathedral clergy reinforced the English-only policy by having the Paulist Fathers of San Francisco conduct annual "missions" (that is, parish revivals). That this particular community specialized in this kind of activity, with an avowed goal of Americanizing immigrant Catholics, was perhaps no coincidence. As Jeffrey Burns points out, church leaders sought to make good, practical American Catholics of immigrants. As Los Angeles archbishop John Cantwell said, "In making better Catholics of them, we shall be making better citizens of them."[64]

To assist in this process, church leaders acceded to the creation of a school that inculcated "fitting in" in the minds and hearts of young immigrant Catholics who came to study. In announcing the eventual establishment of a school, the *Evening Bee* commented approvingly that the church bell "will call not only to prayer but to moral uplifting and intellectual training."[65]

The school was part of Ella Bowden's "master plan," but it took time. Nonetheless, by 1906, after a series of fund-raisers, the empty upper portion of the old coach house had been transformed and made ready for use as a school.[66] In 1906 the Franciscan Sisters from St. Francis Parish began their work at St. Stephen's, traveling by streetcar every day from St. Francis Convent.[67] In 1908 a new convent adjacent to St. Stephen's opened.

St. Stephen enrollment leaped from a mere forty on the first day to more than two hundred by the end of the 1906 school year. The multiethnic school was a challenge. The sisters' "chronicle" (a diary of events in a local convent) reveals that ten different nationalities were represented, with the Portuguese and Italians leading the way.[68] The growth of the school required additional classroom space in 1908—built with a grant from Bishop Grace—to house the kindergarten and first grade. The growing enrollment meant an increase in the number of sisters needed to teach and put a corresponding strain on convent space at St. Francis Parish.[69] In 1912 the community erected St. Stephen Hall to serve as an overflow classroom and assembly hall. By the time the outmoded structure was abandoned in the early twenties for a brand-new facility, the school had enrolled approximately sixty-two hundred students. Bishop Patrick Keane, Grace's successor, had purchased a plot of land directly behind Grace Day Home and broke ground in August 1923 for a new parish school. Discarding the name St. Stephen's, signifying that "the purely local character of the present institution will cease," Keane renamed the new school Holy Guardian Angels and put it under the direction of the cathedral.[70] Holy Angels was an up-to-date structure with fireproof corridors and stairwells, good exposure to sunlight, and modern furnishings.[71] This school, too, continued for a time to be a major meeting ground for Catholic students of every nationality. The Franciscan Reverend Virgil Cordano, a graduate of Holy Angels, remembered, "Our school had an ethnic mix resembling our neighborhood [he lived near the Italian church at Seventh and T]. Italian,

Portuguese, Croatians, and Irish, and a few Mexican Americans made up the student body. Neither can I remember any ethnic tensions among the kids at school."[72] The elaborate preparations for a 1949 homecoming celebration reflected Cordano's recollection of multiethnic harmony. In a well-designed memorial book, the names of reunion organizers provide a perfect picture of the diversity of the school, with graduates whose surnames included Bakotich, Flores, Carvahlo, Shanahan, Barbeau, Selby, and Hauser.

A STRATEGY FOR AMERICANIZATION

The school's diverse nationalities were a challenge. "The sisters found it very hard to prepare [the pupils] for their first Holy Communion, since, most of them had no religious ideas at all, and these had to be imparted to them in a tongue which was foreign to them." However, thanks to strenuous efforts to teach English, American history, geography, and a program of patriotic observance, "the influence of the school is gradually, but surely molding the children of many diverse stocks into a homogeneous whole of bright young Americans."[73] The integrative function of the rapidly growing school was highlighted in the cathedral bulletin: "The school is quietly accomplishing a distinctly valuable service to the community apart from the purely intellectual and moral training of hundreds of little citizens. The constituency of St. Stephen's affords an interesting and instructive study of the assimilative potency of a common faith and juvenile association in the parochial school classroom."[74]

The Franciscan Sisters also worked with diverse cultures in other venues besides their two schools. They provided catechetical instruction to adults and conducted summer schools of religion for children of the Italian parish as well as for youngsters of diverse national backgrounds at Grace Day Home and also across the river in Broderick. "The Sisters must adapt themselves to the various national peculiarities of their little charges," wrote an effusive account in the local Catholic newspaper. "For besides the many children of American parents, there are tiny Mexicans, Portuguese, Italians, Chinese, Spaniards, etc., all to be trained to know and to love our great flag."[75]

Americanization was also stressed through sports. The schools seemed especially proud of the fine athletes they produced. Sports appear to have been an important tool for bringing together the diverse youth. Father Virgil Cordano recalled, "We had teams in basketball, baseball, and soccer. Baseball was my favorite sport. . . . I think I knew more about baseball than I did about religion."[76] St. Stephen and Holy Angels alumni excelled in wrestling, football, boxing, and in particular baseball, America's most popular sport in the first half of the twentieth century. Among their proud boasts were big-league stars Alex Kampouris and Henry Steinbacher. Kampouris spent nearly ten years in the major league, playing with Cincinnati and several other major league teams. Steinbacher began his career as a shortstop for the Coast League and then graduated to the Chicago White Sox.

The schools prospered for a time, and their programs of Americanization succeeded in turning out "bright young Americans." However, the polyglot St. Stephen Church was another matter. When it came to worship and special devotions, some of Sacramento's ethnic groups yearned for their own church and complained that the Irish clergy were neglecting their special needs. Sacramento's immigrant Catholics, like their counterparts in other parts of the country, soon loudly demanded separate churches and clergy who understood their language and traditional religious culture. Bishop Grace, who was often away from the city (and delegated no authority), responded indifferently at first. He was opposed to additional churches, claiming (with some justification) that they could not sustain themselves financially. Frustrated ethnic Catholics then took their demands to Vatican officials, who sympathized with them and pressured Grace to stand down from his no-ethnic-parishes policy.

INSISTING ON AN ETHNIC CHURCH

Italians were the first to win their own worship space. Italians were attracted to Sacramento by work in the rail yards. Some ran commercial enterprises such as hotels, retail shops, and barbershops or engaged in service work. Hailing mostly from central and northern Italy, they steadily increased in number from the second half of the nineteenth and into the early twentieth centuries. In 1852, only forty-one Italians resided in Sacramento County; by 1930, three thousand Italians were enumerated. These numbers, however, did not include people who had one Italian parent or those whose parents were both Italian Americans.[77]

Italians initially clustered in the city's Alkali Flat area. By 1910 they began migrating out of these neighborhoods to the southern half of the city—especially to Oak Park. Community leaders such as Commercial Hotel owner Luigi Caffaro promoted Italian interests in the city such as a short-lived Italian school in 1908. He also lobbied the school board and the state legislature to offer Italian classes in public schools.[78] An Italian-language newspaper, *La Capitale,* was established in 1907 and served as a medium of communication throughout the Italian colony.

Sacramento's Italians grew restive in St. Stephen Church and made it clear to Bishop Grace that they wanted a national parish. Helping them overcome the prelate's reluctance was Father Michael Gualco. Gualco, a native of Capriata d'Orba, near Genoa, was ordained to the priesthood in Milan in 1864. After a stint in the East, he came to California in 1868 and held a number of posts in the Bay Area, eventually working in Placerville and Folsom, where he became the first Catholic chaplain at the state prison. After a brief time in rural Galt in southern Sacramento County, Manogue dispatched him to Chico, in 1889, to head St. John the Baptist Parish and its missions at the small agricultural communities of Gridley, Oroville, and Cherokee.[79] At that time he was the only Italian-speaking priest in the Sacramento Diocese.

The articulate Gualco became the spokesman for Italian Catholics in the Diocese of Sacramento. When Grace ignored his pleas, Gualco turned to the apostolic delegate, Archbishop Diomede Falconio, in Washington, D.C., an Italian-born U.S. citizen appointed by Pope Leo XIII. Here he found a sympathetic ear, because the pontiff had specifically charged his personal emissary in the United States to investigate claims that local bishops were ignoring the spiritual needs of Italian Catholics. Falconio paid a visit to California in 1903 and stopped in Sacramento to visit the Italian community. At a meeting with Grace, Falconio insisted that the bishop do more for his Italian flock and no doubt waved away Grace's protests that St. Stephen's was "handling" the Italians. Falconio insisted on a separate church in Sacramento and a foreign-language mission for them in Reno. Grace meekly complied. Obtaining priests came next.

In 1905 Grace and Gualco journeyed together to Rome, where Grace made a report on his diocese to Pope Pius X. En route, the duo stopped in Washington, D.C., for one more visit with the delegate. After the papal visit was over, Grace turned over the selection of the Italian priests to Gualco and departed for a vacation to Ireland. Gualco soon found two priests, Temistocle Eugenio Mela and Dominic Taverna, who agreed to come to California.[80]

Trouble started immediately for the two priests upon their arrival. Taverna, who was assigned to Reno to minister to the Italian colony there, was soon sent packing by the Reverend Thomas Tubman, the local pastor, who did not want or need another priest in Reno—especially an Italian. Taverna would then be dispatched to Sutter Creek in Amador County.[81] Mela, who was assigned to start the new Italian church in Sacramento, went first to Chico to learn English under the tutelage of Gualco. Sometime in 1906 he came down to Sacramento and organized the first members of the community and in December purchased a lot on Eighth and N streets—next door to the Stanford Lathrop home. A fund-raiser at Serra Hall, the newly purchased Catholic hall, realized a "net sum" that enabled him to build a small church structure on the property. The little church was dedicated in honor of St. Mary on June 9, 1907.[82]

Money was a problem from the outset. Bishop Grace and the clergy at the cathedral offered no financial or even moral support to the Italian cleric. Nor did they allow him to collect funds from the cathedral parishioners. On one occasion, as bill collectors descended on the hapless Mela, the anxious priest sought out the bishop for help, only to be informed that Grace had decamped for his annual vacation. Mela then turned to San Francisco archbishop Patrick Riordan, writing, "Almost every day some collector call upon me and this makes me sick. Yesterday one of them was insist that I had to promise to pay at least half of a bill of $130 before night. I do so. I was formed to make a debt of 60 dollars with one good french lady and to give away the only ten dollars I had and which was given to me the day before for ten masses." Riordan offered no support. Matters grew worse when Mela next came in for criticism from his parishioners, who discovered that the priest, with no knowledge of property laws in the United States, had titled the church property in his name and not the bishop of Sacramento. Gualco, his former patron and mentor, soon became his antagonist and offered a sympathetic ear to local dissidents and reported the matter to Falconio.[83]

In the meantime, financial problems grew worse, as prominent Italians withheld support for the church. In desperation, Mela asked Grace to mandate that the city's Portuguese- and Spanish-speaking residents become members in order to attract needed financial support. In fact, this had been Mela's hope from the outset, and early fund-raisers for the parish touted the cooperation of Italian and Portuguese women in building the church. Grace agreed and decreed that Mela be "the recognized pastor of all the Italian Catholics of Sacramento . . . [and] also of all the Portuguese and Spanish . . . [and that] all of those Catholic people will contribute liberally to help him build a church."[84] Mela scheduled a 7:00 AM mass for the Portuguese and a 9:00 AM for the Italians. No services for the Spanish-speaking were scheduled. This seemed to settle the problem for the time being, but in fact the combination of Italians and Portuguese did not produce the hoped-for harmony and financial stability. The Portuguese may have been a bit reluctant to assume a secondary role in the church and were further pressed to form their own independent church. The consensus for communal homogeneity was set aside for ethnic demands that would not go away.

THE PORTUGUESE

The Portuguese were an important part of the ethnic medley of the West End. Nearly 90 percent of all Portuguese who lived in Sacramento came from the Atlantic islands of the Azores, Madeira, and Cape Verde. The Azores alone accounted for almost 80 percent.[85] Later Portuguese immigrants came from the mainland, the island of Faial after a disastrous volcanic eruption in 1957, and Portugal's colonies in Africa and Asia. California's Portuguese immigrants were shepherds and dairymen, settling primarily in the Central Valley. Others became urban dwellers in all California cities and were especially strong in Oakland. In the 1890s large numbers of rural Portuguese moved to Sacramento, making it their second-largest population center in the state.

On both sides of the Sacramento River a vibrant Portuguese colony developed known as the "Lisbon District." Portuguese laborers also worked in the Sacramento brick-making industry. Portuguese who moved into Sacramento tended to cluster on the undeveloped areas of the city's south side, near the site of the present Southside Park. Before long a visible Portuguese colony thrived east and north. This enclave became known as "Arizona," a corruption of the term *Azores*. Social and cultural life flourished, with fraternal and mutual-aid societies, ethnic businesses, and public celebrations. In 1900 a former Catholic priest, Guilherme Silveira, produced Sacramento's first Portuguese newspaper, *A Liberdade*. Another journal, *O Imparcial*, began in 1903. Within the Portuguese community pressures soon began to build for a separate church. Already in 1893 Manogue had allowed a Portuguese church, St. Joseph's, to be built in Freeport and Clarksburg. As the number of Sacramento Portuguese grew, the demand for separate space increased.

Portuguese Catholics had been among the most fervent devotees and supporters of St. Stephen Church, and Portuguese children attended the church school. Mela made a good-faith effort to welcome the Portuguese and hired a priest to celebrate an early-morning mass and to deliver a sermon in the Portuguese language. The baptismal register at St. Mary's saw a major increase in the number of Portuguese names. However, some never joined St. Mary's and took their children to Portuguese churches in Freeport or San Jose to be baptized and attended mass at the cathedral. Portuguese businessmen like Manuel S. Williams, owner of a grocery store at Eleventh and Q, began pushing for a separate church. A further catalyst was the 1908 visit of a Portuguese bishop, Enrique DaSilva, who gave support to the separatist impulses among the Sacramento Portuguese. In 1909 DaSilva visited Sacramento again and once more touched base with the leaders of the community. By this time discontent with Mela and the arrangement at St. Mary's was churning, and DaSilva no doubt encouraged them to pursue their own parish. In league with the Portuguese priest who served at St. Mary's, Father Silveira, the Sacramento Portuguese drafted a petition to Grace, requesting a separate parish.[86]

Mela reacted badly to the news of the petition and in retaliation discharged Father Silveira when he showed up for mass one April morning in 1909. News of the dismissal galvanized the already disgruntled Portuguese, and a number of them at the mass that was to be celebrated by Silveira left, vowing never to return. Another petition to Grace, this time in even stronger terms and signed by 319 heads of households, representing 1,400 Sacramento Portuguese, demanded a new parish. They insisted on "having a Portuguese priest to preach to us in our native language." They also warned that they would "appeal to the pope and submit their cause to him" if Grace did not comply.[87]

Grace, who was away at the time of the uproar, calmed passions on his return by giving over the old St. Stephen's to the Portuguese until a solution could be obtained. The Portuguese remained there through the spring and early summer of 1909. If Grace hoped that this would slow the demand for a separate church, he was mistaken. In the late summer, he consented to the erection of a new church and appointed Terceira native the Reverend John V. Azevedo, then assisting at Sutter Creek, as the first pastor. The new church, named for St. Elizabeth, formally began on October 24, 1909. Manuel Williams donated land, and San Francisco architects Frank Shea and John Lofquist designed the church, replicating the model of a church in Angra do Heroísmo in Terceira. Grace dedicated the church in February 1913.[88]

Under Azevedo, the church maintained a steady existence and served as a focal point for Portuguese cultural life. Azevedo was a fixture in Sacramento until his death in the 1950s. The Portuguese church continues to flourish under Portuguese pastors to the present day, even though they no longer dominate the neighborhood around the church.

THE ITALIAN TRANSITION

The Italian community continued to struggle to maintain their church as a communal endeavor. After the Portuguese secession, Mela did what he could to keep his parish alive. Anxious to make a new start he eventually relocated the church on Seventh and T streets, right across from Southside Park. Unable to build a new facility, he dismantled the old St. Mary's and reassembled it on the new property. A dedicated and hardworking man, he lived humbly in the sacristy of the church until he succumbed to the flu in the epidemic of 1918.

After Mela's death, his successor, Dominic Taverna, had a hard time keeping the parish together. Already by 1910 Italians were leaving the downtown area and moving into the new suburb of Oak Park, where their names turned up in the baptismal registers. By the 1920s and '30s, Father Michael Lyons, the pastor of Sacred Heart Church in East Sacramento, had experienced a steady increase of Italian members.[89] Italian immigration waned after World War I, and changes in pastors only partially

Dedication of St. Elizabeth Catholic Church, Twelfth and s streets, 1913. Courtesy of
Sacramento Archives and Museum Collection Center, Sacramento Portuguese
Historical and Cultural Society Collection.

revived the downtown Italian church. After World War II, a new Italian
church was built in East Sacramento.

CONCLUSION

The resistance of the Italians and Portuguese may have brought about
some degree of change in the policies of the church. After the death of
Bishop Grace, new Catholic leaders proved more flexible with ethnic
Catholics. When Croatians requested their own parish, Bishop Patrick

Keane readily agreed and recruited Croatian-speaking priests to serve the Sacramento community. Croatian Sacramentans came very close to having their own church until a financial scandal erupted and tragically halted their plans on the eve of the Great Depression.[90]

Although nativist movements such as the Klan derided Catholics as a source of urban crime and Prohibition violations, not all civic energies were bent toward "taming" the foreign-born. In fact, Sacramento entered a new season of reform and beautification between 1890 and 1930. If Catholics were ambiguous about the need for assimilation, they were anxious to help the city move forward.

CHAPTER 5

Building the City Beautiful, 1890–1930

"An active and prominent part"

Nearly fifty thousand people from all over California and Nevada turned out on the night of September 9, 1895, as Sacramento celebrated the forty-fifth anniversary of California's admission to the Union. But Admission Day was only the pretext for celebrating a major milestone in the history of the state capital. Earlier, in the wee hours of July 13, a steady electrical current began coursing from a powerhouse twenty-two miles away in Folsom into a substation on Sixth and H streets. Sacramento now had a stable electrical power supply, and the prospects for its future seemed literally brighter than ever. To celebrate this benchmark of progress, city leaders illuminated buildings and the state capitol. Blazing floats processed down the main business district past throngs of residents. One of them, created by the copper and pipe shops of the Southern Pacific, had an electric pump that shot fifteen streams of water three feet into the air. The illuminated slogans on its side proclaimed, "Sacramento—City of Destiny" and "Sacramento—100,000 by 1910."[1] Sacramentans were not only proud of the twinkling lights of the 1895 electrical parade and excited by the possibilities of an illuminated downtown but just as proud that they themselves—a city of only about twenty-nine thousand—had raised the one hundred thousand dollars for the spectacle through private donations. Even Father Grace of the cathedral had given two hundred dollars—although he did not allow the facade of the cathedral to be illuminated.

The lights of this Sacramento "Great White Way" also signaled the intention to create a "city beautiful" that would enhance the city's stature and rank, especially among its rivals in California. The generosity and civic pride of Sacramento commenced another season of fast-paced development that proceeded in two phases. The first ran from 1893, the year of a new city charter, to the eve of the Great War in 1917. The second began with another reform of city government in 1921 and extended to the eve of the Great Depression. Catholics played an important part in these developments.

A QUICKENING PACE OF URBAN LIFE

The years from 1895 until 1917 witnessed a concerted effort to streamline city government and services and to remove perceived obstacles to growth. Sacramento's municipal regime underwent multiple reforms between 1891 and 1921, each change creating a more efficient and responsive city administration, which in turn facilitated progress. The city's charter of 1862 had provided for a board of trustees that oversaw various aspects of city services. As the population of the city increased, this simple administrative structure proved incapable of keeping up with the demands of urban life.[2] The weak city government could do little or nothing about Sacramento's unpaved and horse dung–filled streets that were a mire in winter and dust in the summer, its unfiltered water that was dark and unpleasant to drink, and the slow pace of urban beautification.

City government was also unable to cope with the economic slump that descended on the state capital almost as soon as the Central Pacific Railroad was completed. The panic of 1873, which began in the East, eventually made its way west, and by 1875 a general economic slowdown hit California. The sluggish economy made it difficult for Sacramento to pay off the huge bond indebtedness it had run up to build levees, improve the

Electric Parade, state capitol, 1895. Courtesy of Sacramento Archives and Museum Collection Center, State of California Library Collection.

sewer system, and raise some of its streets. The pace of civic improvement slackened, and the city seemed stagnant.

A private-sector remedy for this situation was the board of trade, formed in 1877. This organization boosted city morale and stimulated a program of civic improvement. Before it ran out of steam, the board had brought a state prison to Folsom, lobbied successfully for a new state exposition building, encouraged the holding of citrus fairs (a direct challenge to Los Angeles, which claimed to be the citrus capital of California), and helped improve the number and quality of Sacramento's rail links. The McClatchy brothers' *Daily Bee* relentlessly exhorted citizens and politicians to improve the economic and social conditions of the city.[3]

Change did come. Already in 1891, fifteen well-known businessmen drafted a new city charter that won voters' approval in May 1892, and became effective in early 1893. The new charter expanded Sacramento's city government to meet the needs of the day by creating a powerful mayor's office, an expanded city council elected by wards, and more efficient city-service operations.

City business leaders were generally behind the cause of urban improvement, but they were shocked into action when state legislators threatened to move the capital. The threat of capital removal was never truly serious, but for a time it shook the city to its roots. The crisis was precipitated in March 1893 when C. K. McClatchy ridiculed the legislature at the close of an unproductive session with a front-page article titled "Thank God" (the session was over). Stung by McClatchy's snide remarks, the legislators' simmering anger and frustration with dingy Sacramento and its poor accommodations, brackish water, and unexciting cultural life burst out. The angry solons rammed a bill through that urged the capital be moved to San Jose. Although the state supreme court rejected the legislation, it nonetheless threw a scare into city leaders. Cursing McClatchy's insouciance, an informal alliance of local leaders scrambled to make amends. In 1895 they formed a highly effective Chamber of Commerce, a successor to the by then moribund board of trade. The Chamber was the seedbed and clearinghouse for virtually every important civic initiative in Sacramento during the next seventy years. Before long, city land had been donated for capital expansion, and an array of hotels and amenities were planned to make Sacramento a better and more habitable place for all citizens. In 1908, after Sacramentans withstood another effort to move the state capital to Berkeley, famed city planner Charles Mulford Robinson exhorted Sacramentans to "make their city worthy to be the capital—so noble, so beautiful, that there will never be another thought of moving it again."[4]

PROGRESSIVE-ERA BOOSTING

Like all California communities, Sacramento produced booster propaganda generated by local trade associations such as the Chamber of Commerce.[5] The Chamber had an active committee of admen who continually "boomed" the city and made sure that it was represented at regional and national fairs, expositions, and other venues where its special wares and advantages could be on display. The McClatchys pumped out a continual flow of articles praising Sacramento and the general region as an optimal place to live and work, replete with mild climate, a long growing season, and adequate social and cultural accoutrements. In 1902 the McClatchys conferred the title "Superior California" on Sacramento and the northern valley.[6]

Links with the valley proved to be a potent advertising tool. The Sacramento Valley Development Association, founded in 1900 as a cooperative venture of six counties in the Sacramento Valley, also promoted the region's economic and social development. In 1902 the association published a booster periodical, the *Wednesday Press,* and in June 1907 W. A. Beard took over as editor and publisher. In October of that year the name of the paper changed to the more romantic *Great West.* It called for "the gridironing of the valley with railroads, transcontinental and interurban," to make Sacramento a "natural center and [the] largest beneficiary" of the ongoing development of the valley. Commenting on the changes he saw, Beard observed, "The city was looked upon as one of the most backward and unprogressive on the entire Pacific Coast." But he also noted, "This condition has entirely changed. The population of the city has increased, business has increased, property values have increased and every prominent interest in the city has been infused with new life."[7]

REMOVING THE OBSTACLES

One of the most frustrating experiences for the hustling boosters and boomers involved the naysayers and footdraggers in the city government. The city was in heavy debt, and retiring these obligations was the charge of the city's Bonded Debt Commission, which seized and sold portions of urban land for this end. When real estate sales decreased significantly in the 1870s and 1880s, the city's development slackened as well, preventing expansion and cutting off necessary tax revenue. Breaking away from the go-slow policies of the Bonded Debt Commission required maximum effort, but eventually land sales resumed as the city's population grew and the southern part of the city opened to development. Annexation also added the adjacent suburbs of Oak Park and East Sacramento to the city in 1911. These two areas not only enlarged Sacramento's territory but also increased its tax base.

In 1902 the Chamber of Commerce attempted to rouse public sentiment behind a program of urban renewal, highlighted at annual banquets held every February. At the first meeting in 1902 Chamber President Louis Breuner exhorted the four hundred banqueters to help "the municipality we live in and love to take her proper place as the commercial center of Northern California . . . the brightest and richest gem in the crown of

California's cities." At the same banquet Valentine McClatchy upbraided the city in a trenchant talk titled "What Is the Matter With Sacramento?" He lectured the banqueters on the absence of city unity and pleaded for desperately needed "good streets and roads, a proper sewerage system, clear water, handsome public buildings, an imposing hotel, and city wharf facilities." In 1903 C. K. McClatchy attacked the city's provincialism, lamenting that "she is still in many ways of the hamlet order and the village persuasion." He reminded his fellow citizens that they had the energies within to move forward. "She has gone through fire and flood. She has displayed her pluck, her energy, her perseverance, her unflagging industry and her untiring energy on many occasions. Disaster has not daunted her."[8]

The reform posture of the *Bee* and its supporters also included a good dose of nineteenth-century mugwump political reformism. Removing obstacles to the city's growth and development meant driving out corrupt and inefficient politicians and their sponsors. In the case of Sacramento, this meant taking on the most important business and chief employer of the city, the Southern Pacific Railroad. Despite the fact that the railroad had been the main source of the city's stability and the key factor in its survival, by the early twentieth century, it had become the enemy. City reformers worked hard to shake off the "oppressive yoke" of the Southern Pacific, whose monopolistic and sometimes heavy-handed control of local government and economic life was seen as a drag on Sacramento's future. Railroad dominance of California politics had been up for public discussion since the 1880s. Although scholars today debate whether the huge company was the "octopus" immortalized by Frank Norris's 1901 novel, at least in Sacramento its power over land and local politics was quite palpable.[9] As the city's major employer, the railroad openly manipulated the levers of civic power for the protection of its own interests and the extension of its holdings. If Sacramentans balked at the giant company's demands, the railroad threatened to pull its shop operations out of the city and award them to a more compliant community.

Illustrative of this attitude was the company's decision to build a new steel rolling mill at its Sacramento shops in 1875. Railroad officials insisted that Sacramento simply donate the land, pointing out that the new site meant more jobs. They also demanded a broader right-of-way, which would cement their ownership of more city land—including the city's riverfront. When the *Daily Union* flayed the company's tyrannical demands and counseled resistance to its domination (the other major paper, the *Daily Bee*, defended the corporation), the railroad made its displeasure known to city officials. Fearful of losing the rolling mill, a group of Sacramentans, led by the mayor, traveled to San Francisco to reassure railroad leaders that the city was receptive to whatever the railroad company required for its mill. When the commission returned to Sacramento, it held a mass meeting of six hundred citizens in Turner Hall and voted ten resolutions, capitulating to the demands of the railroad.[10] After accepting the obeisance of city leaders, the railroad silenced the obstreperous *Daily Union* by having its own *Daily Record* buy it. The *Sacramento Daily Record-Union* was from that point on the company's official organ in the state capital.

By the turn of the century Sacramentans were not so compliant. The railroad itself had undergone leadership changes, and it had lost a great deal of its local clout. Sacramentans defiantly voted in October 1907 to break Southern Pacific's monopoly and gave the rival Western Pacific Railroad a competitive right-of-way through the city—despite efforts by the Southern Pacific and its operatives in city government to obstruct the route. City leaders also collected money to provide a rail yard for the Western Pacific.[11]

The campaign for mayor in 1907 reflected the change in public mood then emerging. The antirailroad candidate, Republican attorney Clinton F. White, linked Sacramento's future with deliverance from the oppressive hand of Southern Pacific. In the precursor of the Progressive juggernaut that would propel Sacramentan Hiram Johnson to the governor's chair, White decried Southern Pacific as the reason for the "neglected opportunities, discouraged enterprises and dominated administrations" of the city and challenged voters to "cast out the evil political influences that have so long kept the city down."[12] In the hard-fought election, White narrowly edged out his Democratic opponent, Marshall Beard. Although Western Pacific never matched Southern Pacific in size or job creation in Sacramento, the city now had two lines, two rail stations, and two repair yards. This and other innovations in transportation gave an important psychological boost to the city, which had long been under the dominance of the huge company.

Even though population figures fell far short of the 100,000 predicted by the copper and pipe workers of Southern Pacific in 1895, Sacramento's populace had risen to 44,696 by 1910. In 1911 the annexation of lands to the south and east of the city trebled Sacramento's physical area and added to an increase in population. By 1930 Sacramento was home to 93,750.

To further purge its politics of the taint of corruption, the city imposed another government reform in 1911, creating a city commission system and a complicated format for electing city councilmen at large. This, it was hoped, would eliminate the ills of ward or special-interest politics.

Sacramentans also began to rethink the basic gridiron layout of their city. In 1907 two members of the Women's Council, Mrs. A. J. Johnston and Mrs. Robert Devlin, brought Professor Charles Zueblin of the University of Chicago to lecture in the assembly chamber of the state capitol. Zueblin, a proponent of the "City Beautiful movement," delivered five lectures that had Sacramentans buzzing about possibilities. In 1908 local businessmen arranged for famed Rochester city planner Charles Mulford Robinson to come to the city. Robinson's 1908 report called for diagonal streets, new parks, and control of the rivers and led to the purchase of the eight hundred–acre Del Paso Park.[13] This marvelous tract, dotted with weeping oaks, became the site of the city's most prestigious golf club.

In 1913 the Chamber of Commerce next invited Dr. Werner Hegemann to the capital. Hegemann, who had overseen the construction of port and railway terminals in Germany and playgrounds in Berlin, organized a public educational campaign to build support for a city plan. At the same time, Sacramento native son Governor Hiram Johnson pressured city leaders to develop a plan and formed the State Capital Planning Commission to study state needs in the capital. City leaders, unsure of the financing for civic improvements, dragged their feet until fears of a proposed factory in the "Homes" section mobilized citizens to push for some order in urban planning. In 1912 yet another civic planner, Dr. John Nolen of Massachusetts, called for expanded capital facilities and the widening of Capitol Park, thereby making the central section of the city the commercial and business hub of the downtown. Nolen also pressed for the development of the extension to the northeast of the city and to Del Paso Park, giving a boost to the growing demand for parks around the city.[14] Later, Sacramento city government formed the Department of City Planning, and in 1922 the city adopted zoning as a method of controlling and directing urban growth.

In this exciting atmosphere prominent Catholics did their part to boost the city. Everyone, church leaders argued, benefited from a city on the move. Once again, church and city agendas were so intertwined that it was difficult to determine where one began and the other left off.

CATHOLIC SUPPORT FOR URBAN DEVELOPMENT

Sacramento Catholics took pride in the belief that their own beautiful cathedral was one of the stimuli for this season of urban advance. City boosters enthusiastically pointed to the presence and activity of the church, especially when touting the state capital to outsiders. Two prominent Catholics, a priest and a layman, lent their voices and public relations skills to the cause as well.

A brief digression is necessary to fully understand the role of a Roman Catholic priest in business transactions. Christian clergy of every denomination are not only men and women of the gospel but also, in some cases, very smart businesspeople, land speculators, and even financial wizards. Many erroneously believe that all Catholic clergy take a vow of evangelical poverty. This vow is taken only by members of religious orders, such as Franciscans or Jesuits, who hold all things in common and cannot officially own anything. In fact, many clergy are rather poor because they are paid low wages or given church-supported housing and living allowances. Likewise, many of them shrewdly avoid ostentatious lifestyles, especially if they serve poor congregations. However, diocesan or secular priests do not vow poverty and can own land and build wealth just like other citizens. They also, unlike religious orders, pay taxes on their property and income. This does not mean that they are free to engage in any kind of business proposition, but they are at liberty to pursue their own financial well-being as their time, genius, and good luck permit. This will help us to better understand the activities of Sacramento's most prominent Catholic clerical entrepreneur, the Reverend John F. Quinn, cathedral pastor from 1899 to 1906.

Quinn was born in 1847 in Albany, New York. He was educated in public schools and by the Christian Brothers School in Albany. When the Civil War broke out, he signed up as a youth of fourteen in the Twenty-fifth New York Volunteers but was turned aside because of his age. Two years later he tried again to serve the Union army by enlisting in Morrison's Black Horse Cavalry—and was again discharged because of his age.[15] Subsequently, he joined the ammunition corps at Watervliet Arsenal and was in the Battle of Petersburg with Grant's armies. After the end of the war, his martial spirit undimmed, he secured a lieutenant's commission in the Fenian Army, assembled for an invasion of Canada. When this endeavor failed, he entered Niagara University in January 1867 and graduated in June 1870.

After graduation Quinn edited a journal called the *Catholic Reflector,* published in Albany. He then enrolled in Albany Law School, and upon passing the bar he formed the law firm of Quinn and Cohn. As a lawyer, his gifts with pen and word marked him for a career in local Democratic politics, and he garnered the nomination for city judge in 1875. There was talk of putting him up as a congressional candidate the following year, but Quinn abandoned law and politics to enter the seminary of Our Lady of the Angels in Niagara Falls. Bishop Stephen Ryan of Buffalo ordained Quinn to the priesthood in 1877, and Bishop James O'Connor, the Vicar Apostolic of Nebraska, "adopted" him.[16] After a brief stint as an Omaha pastor, he departed for Denver in 1881, where Bishop Joseph Machebeuf accepted him.

Quinn's parochial assignments included the rectorship of the Church of St. Mary in Denver. He began the first Catholic newspaper in Colorado, the *Colorado Catholic,* which he edited from 1884 until 1886, when he was called farther west, to Sacramento, at the request of his friend Patrick Manogue.[17] Quinn arrived in Sacramento in 1886 and was appointed to Sacred Heart Church in Red Bluff. In 1893 he was transferred to St. Joseph Parish in Yreka. A strong, vigorous man with a head crowned by a high shock of hair, Quinn was a dynamic and eloquent public speaker. His passion for certain issues was honed by years of defending people's rights—whether in the cause of the Union or Irish nationalism or as a lawyer. His considerable skills in the pulpit were noted by the *San Francisco Monitor,* which reprinted in full the text of a very florid Fourth of July oration he delivered to his congregation in Yreka.[18] His grandiloquent style made him Manogue's choice as eulogist when planning his funeral. In 1899 Grace appointed Quinn rector of the Cathedral of the Blessed Sacrament. His seven-year term was a whirlwind of activity.

Quinn came to the cathedral without fanfare in the early months of 1899 but embarked on a highly visible and sometimes controversial career as Sacramento's leading Catholic clergyman, occasionally tangling with editor C. K. McClatchy.[19] In 1902, in a bid to protect the morals of downtown clerks (mostly women), Quinn actively endorsed their unionization in order to set earlier closing hours, which was opposed by downtown merchants.

He was soon taken with the beauty and prospects of the state capital and became one of Sacramento's leading promoters, especially to other Catholics. In an article for the *San Francisco Monitor,* written immediately after the earthquake and fire of 1906, Quinn called Sacramento "an earthly Eden." Sacramentans held Quinn in such high esteem that in 1902, when he celebrated his twenty-fifth anniversary of ordination, fifteen hundred people jammed into the assembly chamber of the state capitol. They heard him praised by state and local politicians, the prelate of his own church, and several Protestant ministers. Years after he had left Sacramento, Quinn was best remembered as one who "took an active and prominent part in every public movement for the religious, social, and civic advancement of the community. He associated himself with all who sought to achieve these ends no matter under what banner they were enlisted."[20]

Quinn's boosterism was more than rhetorical. He personally invested heavily in Sacramento properties and was one of the leading figures in efforts to develop Sacramento's south side. At some point the enterprising priest associated himself with a group of speculators anxious to develop Sacramento south of R Street. This loose coalition of real estate developers, businessmen, and city politicians formed itself sometime in the late nineteenth century into the Southside Improvement Club and lobbied for municipal decisions that would aid and support development of that

part of the city. Quinn, city developer J. G. Martine (who helped to preserve Sutter's Fort), and Dr. H. S. Graven acquired nearly eleven acres in
February 1906.[21] These lands gave Quinn title to about ten acres in the
vicinity of Eleventh and W streets. Quinn, in turn, gave his associates one-
fourth interest in the land, apparently retaining half the property (valued
at about forty thousand dollars) for himself. To make sure that the parcel
increased in value, Quinn and Martine also gathered a group of inves-
tors to build a belt line of railroads around the city. When interviewed
about the railroad, he declared, "This would give speedy transportation
to those portions of the city which are not reached by the present system
and would in my opinion be very advantageous to the working man who
desires to own his own home on the outskirts of the city." The *Bee* praised
Quinn as "a shrewd man of business. . . . Zealous as he is in the service of
the Lord, his vocation has not blinded him entirely to some things which
are of this earth." How Quinn acquired the money for such a transac-
tion or under what circumstances the seller decided to part with such a
lucrative piece of city property is a mystery. However, the cleric apparently had a penchant for making friends with people in positions to help
him. In 1905, for example, he inherited title to a ninety-acre ranch near
Dunsmuir, as well as a vacation spot at Soda Springs.[22]

Not everyone, however, looked favorably on Quinn's activities. His
"unclerical" behavior (priests are forbidden by canon law to engage in
certain kinds of business) aroused the concern of the normally tolerant
Bishop Grace. Events came to a head in the late summer of 1906 when
Grace gave Quinn an ultimatum to dispose of his holdings and detach
himself from these activities. Quinn decamped from Sacramento in
early October, going to Dunsmuir for a "rest," and then left on a tour of
the Holy Land. He held the controversial Sacramento property until his
death, and when it was eventually developed into lots for homes, one
of the smaller streets—really an alley—was named Quinn Avenue in
his honor.

THOMAS AUGUSTUS CONNELLY:
CATHOLIC JOURNALIST AND BOOSTER

After Quinn, Thomas A. Connelly, the editor of Sacramento's first Catholic
weekly, the *Catholic Herald,* carried on the tradition of promoting Sacra-

mento. Born in Philadelphia in 1858, Connelly was educated in parochial schools and at the University of Notre Dame.[23] In the 1880s, in Baltimore, he took up employment at the *Catholic Mirror,* a lay-owned weekly.[24] There he met and married Mary Eucebia Fink at nuptials attended by Cardinal James Gibbons of Baltimore. A friend, author and diplomat Maurice Egan of Notre Dame, helped him secure the position of editor at Cleveland's *Catholic Universe,* the weekly of the Diocese of Cleveland.

In 1898 Archbishop Patrick Riordan of San Francisco invited Connelly to edit the *San Francisco Monitor.* With some misgivings but assured by a pledge of support from Riordan and the promise that he could hire a capable business manager, Connelly uprooted his large (he had ten children) family and moved to the Pacific Coast. Arriving in June 1899, he made changes to the image and style of the *Monitor* that broadened its appeal.[25]

Connelly took to the West like a duck to water. A fervent Irish nationalist, he moved easily among the Irish clergy, who were grateful for his reports on conditions in Ireland. Connelly was a gifted booster, adept at writing the boilerplate that promoted the glories of life in the American West, and especially in California. Like Phelan many years prior, he regarded the church as an agency of civilization and a force for social and cultural uplift.[26]

His hopes of improving the *Monitor's* finances floundered. Riordan did not provide the business manager he had promised, and the paper limped along with a weak revenue stream. Even his personal finances were in disarray. In 1901 he had borrowed one thousand dollars from the archdiocese at 4 percent interest to cover his bills.[27] In 1907, when his contract came up for renegotiation, Archbishop Riordan finally agreed to hire a separate business manager, but for reasons of personal pride Connelly then refused the support and asked for additional time to bring the *Monitor* back to fiscal health—even foreswearing his own salary.[28] Riordan would not hear of it, and so in June 1907 Connelly was replaced.

Separated from the *Monitor,* Connelly moved to Sacramento. From June 1907 through February 1908 he became an associate editor of the *Wednesday Press* (later the *Great West*), the journal of the Sacramento Valley Development Association. Here, he honed his skills as a booster, writing glowing articles that promoted regional growth and development.

Thomas Connelly family, ca. 1921. Courtesy of Sacramento Archives and Museum Collection Center, Julia Connelly Collection.

Work on the *Great West* was supplemented by a small press on J Street, which he purchased and renamed the Capital Press. He obtained a steady flow of contract printing jobs from the state and local governments. He became a member of the cathedral parish, where he was a daily communicant. Here he forged friendships with Bishop Grace and the Reverend John Ellis, the cathedral rector. Connelly also sent his children to Catholic schools and developed strong ties with the network of Catholic fraternal organizations that linked Catholic businessmen and professionals.

When the journalist approached Grace in early 1908 with plans to start the *Catholic Herald,* the bishop offered no funds but gave his blessing to the project. "With at least ten thousand Catholic people in Sacramento alone, not to speak of the countless others outside who look to the Bishop of Sacramento in all their spiritual needs, I anticipate for *The Herald* a bright and useful future." The *Herald* had Grace's blessing, but it was not the official organ of the Diocese of Sacramento. In fact, some of the clergy in the diocese did not support the paper because Connelly did virtually no reporting of events outside the Sacramento area. Nonetheless, for two decades, until Connelly's death in 1929, the *Catholic Herald* rolled off the presses in his shop.[29] The paper covered national and local church news and Irish events and gave extensive space to boosting Sacramento.

Imitating McClatchy, Connelly hectored those who lacked civic optimism and pride. In one of his first editorials, "For a Greater Sacramento," he chided "the deplorable lack of local patriotism and proper civic pride" in the community for not enthusiastically backing the new Western Pacific Railroad yards.[30] He supported public water and power utilities and the development of new streets and civic buildings. He frequently urged the Catholic community to support large development projects, such as the water-filtration plant, and to make their own contributions to the uplift and beautification of Sacramento. Connelly exulted as loudly as any member of the Chamber of Commerce when in 1913 the city passed a bond issue for urban improvements. He urged passage of additional municipal bonds for more sewers and better improvements in recently annexed Oak Park and favored a municipal ice plant and more electrical power.

Connelly joined ranks with other local promoters who were in the midst of an active campaign to combat Los Angeles's efforts to attract citizens to the southland. "For a long time the only part of California that the outside world knew much about was that portion lying south of the Tehachapi," he complained in 1913. "All the vast territory of the San Joaquin and Sacramento valleys and the coast counties from Santa Barbara to Del Norte has been a terra incognita to the average citizen in the East—and yet from our point of view this end of the State is far more desirable than the south."[31]

Changes in tax laws in 1901 pushed Catholic Sacramentans to build a new hall to accommodate its growing number of associations.[32] (Catholic associations in the city also wanted a central gathering spot separate from church structures.) During this time, Father John Quinn sought to ease the burden on the cathedral. "We shall build a hall beside the Cathedral for the purpose of holding entertainments to which we desire to charge admission."[33] The hall would eventually become one of the first major efforts of Catholics to participate in the beautification of downtown Sacramento following the building of the cathedral. In May 1903 the

Gentlemen's Sodality of the cathedral parish organized to raise funds for a meetinghouse. The Fraternal Hall Association formed and was capitalized at twenty-five thousand dollars, with stock at a par value of fifty dollars per share. To start the ball rolling, chapters of the YMI and a division of the Ancient Order of Hibernians bought one thousand dollars worth of stock. At about this time, the property of Westminster Presbyterian Church became available. Built in 1866, the structure had a seating capacity of more than six hundred. Catholic leaders decided that this was a good location, so they purchased it for sixty-five hundred dollars in July 1903. Lacking money to build an entirely new structure, the Hall Association renovated the old church. Serra Hall, as it was christened, opened for business in early 1904, with upper and lower sections containing rooms for meetings and banquets. Meanwhile, more elaborate plans for a new and architecturally elegant Catholic Hall sputtered and faded.[34]

Despite their failed efforts, the drive to build a hall highlighted Catholic efforts to enhance the beauty of Sacramento's skyline. Catholics were given a second chance with the design of St. Francis Church. Their response mirrored more powerfully than ever the close cooperation between church and city.

GIVING SACRAMENTO A MISSION CHURCH

St. Francis Parish grew rapidly and by 1899, four years after it was established, found itself cramped in its small wooden church and meeting halls. The Reverend Pius Niermann, one of the Franciscans in residence at the parish, began beating the drum for expansion and urging the construction of a new church and a parish library. As the parish was unable to build right away, Franciscan architect Adrian Wewer suggested raising the existing structure six or seven feet and creating a more capacious space under the church.[35] Then, early in 1901, a new pastor, Godfrey Hoelters, raised the church nine feet above its former foundation to allow a hall fourteen feet in height to be built under the church, with a seating capacity of five hundred and costing forty-five hundred dollars. The parish continued to flourish as the streets within its boundaries filled up with homes, many of which housed Catholics.

As the church grew, Hoelters purchased an adjoining parcel of land for future expansion.[36] Hoelters was temporarily transferred, but when he returned in 1907 he continued to raise money for the new church and school. As Hoelters and his church councilmen were pondering the size and design of the proposed church, events taking place around them, in particular the renovation of nearby Sutter's Fort, came to play an important role in the design of the new St. Francis Church.

St. Francis's not only stood in the midst of Sacramento's growing residential district but was also directly across from Sutter's Fort, viewed by many as Sacramento's Plymouth Rock. The fort had tumbled into ruins, and in 1888 Sacramento city trustees proposed running a road right through the center of the remaining building. Local Sacramento developer General J. G. Martine took steps to preserve the fort and wrote a letter to the *Record-Union* on June 4, 1888, proposing a public subscription of funds to save it for posterity. The letter was circulated statewide, and small donations came in, supplemented by hefty gifts from Charles Crocker and Leland Stanford. With twenty thousand dollars, Martine bought the two city blocks on which the fort was situated and in 1889 turned over title to the Native Sons of the Golden West. An appropriation from the state legislature helped the Native Sons to reconstruct and maintain the fort.[37] (Sutter's Fort was designated a historic state park in 1947.) The lands around the fort, once a desolate waste with bawling cows, were completely reworked. The neighborhood around the park soon became prime property, hosting the new Sutter Hospital and the relocated First Congregational Church.

Sacramento promoted the renovated Sutter's Fort in a fashion similar to other California cities that used the old mission churches or gold miner themes to market themselves to newcomers and tourists. The proximity of the fort to the Franciscan church offered a unique, if ahistorical, opportunity to construct a link with an image that had worked wonders for other parts of the Golden State. One of St. Francis Parish's councilmen, Thomas Cody, who had taken an active role in making Sutter's Fort a historical site, urged Hoelters to build the new church directly facing the restored fort, with the older church structures moved behind. Cody urged that the new church architecture be made to resemble the original California mission style, thereby visually linking the restored fort and the new "mission." Hoelters and his Franciscan superiors in St. Louis quickly endorsed these ideas, including its seventy-five thousand–dollar price tag, publicizing them in the spring of 1908. Since the church was now more elaborate than had been originally planned, the cost, initially fifty thousand dollars, had been upped by twenty-five thousand. St. Francis parishioners had already raised thirty-five thousand and brought in pledges to 80 percent of the entire amount. The cautious Hoelters, however, mandated that the first spade of earth could be turned only when the building fund contained forty thousand dollars.[38]

The Sacramento Chamber of Commerce, which had pushed the efforts of the Native Sons of the Golden West to restore the fort, joined in the plans for the new church. At a meeting in April 1908, Cody managed to convince the Chamber to endorse the fund-raising campaign. A stellar cast of public officials and prominent Catholics joined forces with Hoelters and his assistant, the Reverend Ferdinand Kenny. To his great delight, Hoelters found the Chamber of Commerce did not view the enterprise as "merely . . . a new Catholic church edifice for St. Francis Parish," but "owing to its peculiar style of architecture . . . so characteristic of the State of California since the missionary days . . . [as] an attraction for the Eastern tourists and an advertisement for the city of Sacramento." The chamber agreed to provide 20 percent of the funds needed, selecting a committee to approach other businessmen with "a manly, business-like appeal, based as much on civic pride as religious sentiment." Hoelters and Kenny agreed to accompany the group "as the men behind the gun." Because the solicitation was now civic and not a religious affair, Hoelters had to raise only an additional thirty-two thousand dollars, rather than forty thousand. When door-to-door visitations became difficult for the busy friar, a meeting with the parishioners in May 1908 solicited pledges, and pictures of the new church were heralded in the newspaper.[39]

The design of the new church was executed by Brother Adrian Wewer, the Franciscan architect who had designed the original St. Francis Church and a number of other churches and buildings of note across California and throughout the Midwest.[40] "The new St. Francis Church will be a perfect copy of the design of the early Franciscan Fathers, the historic Mission Style," wrote Thomas Connelly. "The building, most appropriately situated face to face with Sutter's Fort, will be an ornament to the city. . . . No similar structure exists in Superior California." The cornerstone was blessed by Bishop Grace in October 1908 after a procession to the site amid flowing banners held aloft by parish societies, a local band pumping out religious airs, and songs rendered by the St. Francis choir. Ecclesiastical and civic dignitaries were on hand for addresses in English and German, which emphasized the significance of the event. "It is a pledge of the future social and moral development of the city along the best and most enduring lines."[41]

Despite the glories of the cornerstone laying, fund-raising proceeded slowly. The business leaders' decision to mount a low-key campaign did not produce the substantial donations needed. Thomas Cody then wrote a circular letter to his fellow citizens in which he linked the success of the church to Sacramento's "wonderful and surprising strides toward metropolitan greatness." He argued that the new St. Francis's provided Sacramento with a chance to emulate the use of mission-era churches so successful in marketing Southern California. Such sites drew "wealthy tourists to its cities and towns." Cody appealed for an additional thirty to forty thousand dollars.[42]

Cody even suggested that Sacramento's "mission" would be superior to the originals: "The building, constructed of the best of materials and with the best of modern workmanship, will not be for a day, or generation, but will remain as a monument an attractive example of mission architecture, long after the original mission buildings now crumbling into a condition of hopeless decay shall have passed away." Other civic leaders weighed in. At a Knights of Columbus banquet in February, Mayor White waxed hyperbolic on the new church, echoing Cody's letter: "We will soon have in Sacramento a piece of architecture far superior to Santa Barbara's mission."[43]

Enough money must have trickled in to complete the church by October 1910. Its exterior symbolized "ancient" California. Some 1,125,000 bricks were used in its construction, plastered over with cement to give it an adobe appearance. Galvanized steel mission tiles crowned the building. The facade faced the developing Sutter's Fort Plaza, with some insisting it was a virtual replica of Mission Santa Barbara. In reality, the church was a more generic mission style.

The mission-style theme was carried only in the facade and nowhere else. The interior represented the German church-building traditions with which architect Wewer was most proficient. Colorful mission tile floors adorned the outside entryway, the small vestibule, the baptistery,

and the two side chapels and sanctuary. Warm walnut paneling gave soft-
ness to the interior. The polished-oak pews held nearly nine hundred
worshipers—enough to absorb the standing-room-only crowd that had
crammed into the former church. Leading up to the choir loft was an elegant mahogany staircase with black walnut inlay that had been reclaimed
during a renovation of the original state capitol and recycled into the new
church. Executed by French craftsmen, the staircase was crowned at each
landing with a carved artichoke—one of the prides of California agriculture. Portions of the same wood were used to build the organ loft and the
pulpit in the main sanctuary. Frescoes depicted various Franciscan saints.
Artisans of the Tyrolese Art Glass Studio, a major supplier of decorative
glass for American churches, created magnificent stained-glass windows.
One of the window donors was Father John Quinn, now long gone from
the capital but still vitally interested in its development.

As Cody and others had foreseen, the restored fort and the mission
church complemented each other and allowed Sacramento to share in the
élan of "Old California." The church itself was a brick-and-mortar testi-
monial to the convergence of city and ecclesiastical interests. Manogue,
who had invited the Franciscans, might have been proud of their accom-
plishment, but to be sure he would have winced at the efforts of his immediate successor, Bishop Patrick Keane, to beautify downtown.

POSTWAR URBAN BEAUTIFICATION

The First World War slowed further development. But once the guns were
silenced, Sacramento resumed its growth and expansion. In yet another
government reform aimed at greater urban efficiency, Sacramento created a city-manager form of government in 1921 with no-nonsense
Illinois-born Clyde Seavey as the first occupant of the post.[44] Inspired by
greater efficiency and catching the crest of brisk new municipal growth,
city infrastructure now received long-overdue attention. After multiple
failed efforts, Sacramentans finally built a modern water-filtration system
in 1923. In that same year, the city provided even more services in the
rapidly developing areas it had annexed in 1911, including call boxes for
police and firefighters, new water mains and sewage service, and an enormous garbage incinerator that markedly improved city sanitation. Part of
the general thrust of Sacramento's steady rise was a major reconstruction

and expansion of its downtown between 1890 and 1930. In the early years of the twentieth century, partly in order to placate state legislators, the city erected new hotels, theaters, and clubhouses.

In the rush of this new prosperity, building projects flourished as never before. In the pre- and postwar period between 1912 and 1928, nearly thirty building projects were completed. The Fruit Exchange and Pacific Mutual Life were among the first to reshape the downtown district. A number of architecturally significant landmarks went up during this period, including the Rudolph Herold–designed city hall, the Capital National Bank, and the Masonic temple. A new city library was erected in 1918. In 1920 writer William Wade singled out Sacramento's development in the leading trade journal of architects, the *Architect and the Engineer,* noting the state capital's "transformation from a mining town into an agricultural and manufacturing center," which was followed by "an awakening to the uses of beauty in commercial architecture."[45]

Postwar gems included architect Julia Morgan's Public Market, which opened in 1923. In 1924 the Senator Hotel and the California State Life building were dedicated. Also in 1924 Sacramento's venerable Weinstock, Lubin, and Company department store relocated to a new building that copied the Parisian Le Printemps emporium. A new Southern Pacific depot opened in 1926, replacing the shopworn rail station on Front and K. Also in 1926 the Elks Tower spiked taller than the nearby cathedral, and the next year Sacramento's most elegant movie palace, the Moorish Alhambra on Thirty-first Street, later renamed Alhambra Boulevard, once the city's eastern boundary, welcomed the growing number of Sacramento moviegoers just as talking pictures were making their debut. After lengthy delays the capitol-extension project, consisting of two elegant bookend buildings that faced each other off the west wing of the capitol, was completed in 1928.

The renewed campaign for architectural elegance found its apotheosis in the construction of the beautiful Memorial Auditorium, which occupied an entire block. Completed in 1927, it was designed to honor the fallen of World War I and was the crown jewel of the remarkable building program. Its location on the site of the now demolished Mary Watson School, once a revered institution in city history, reflected a willingness to reorder public space to meet new civic needs.[46]

Sacramento looked forward to its future and relished a reputation as progressive and thoroughly modern. Actively promoting the city was the rejuvenated Chamber of Commerce, which had hired a bright young man, Arthur S. Dudley, as its executive secretary in 1921. Dudley, who would be around for many years, was a major builder of modern Sacramento. In his first stint of service to the Chamber (he left Sacramento temporarily in the late 1920s), he organized the popular "Days of '49" celebration that took place in May 1922. Anxious to invigorate communal pride, Dudley and festival organizers created a series of events and entertainments based on Gold Rush themes centered near the city's rail yard. In the fall of 1923 the city hosted the annual meeting of state real estate agents, with the *Sacramento Bee* boasting, "In Sacramento the visiting real estate men will find a home city, full of progressive business establishments, the location of great industrial plants, the center of the richest potential and producing territory to be found in California."[47] As they had done in the past, Catholic leaders were eager to play a role in these developments that literally remade the city.

THE EMERGING DOWNTOWN AND CATHOLICS

The completion of the cathedral in 1889 represented the opening gun for Catholic energies to assist in the crusade to beautify downtown Sacramento. The quarter million–dollar structure stood like a solitary gleaming jewel high above the flat landscape and the wooden homes and businesses on K Street. Even Baptist minister A. P. Banks, not the warmest admirer of the Roman Catholic Church, acknowledged that Catholics had the upper hand in creating the most attractive worship site in the city. "The Cathedral is abreast of the times," he wrote, "and in beauty of architecture and proportions is worthy of being the chief church of the diocese."[48]

The Reverend John Quinn managed to raise the already strong profile of the cathedral when he cajoled Mrs. Mary Bethel, who had donated four of the five cathedral bells, to purchase a Seth Thomas clock for the cathedral's tower. The bells in the tower pealed the news of Christ's birth at the Christmas celebrations of 1902, and they also announced the electrical illumination of the sanctuary that Quinn had arranged that year.

By 1920 the very elderly Bishop Grace, now a relic of the gold mining days, was on his last legs. Even C. K. McClatchy, who revered Grace, acknowledged that the bishop was "too old to cope with considerable of modern conditions even if his temperament were not far removed from business habits and business systems." McClatchy further noted that "some man with a business head may be badly needed." A new Catholic bishop who fitted that description was soon identified and placed alongside the ailing Grace. This was Patrick Keane, who came to Sacramento in 1920 as an assistant to Grace. After Grace's death in December 1921, Keane was appointed his successor in March 1922.[49]

An efficient and "modern administrator," Bishop Keane ushered in an era of vigorous leadership for the Catholic Church in the city. Undertaking projects long delayed and denied by both Grace's conservatism and his poor health, Keane introduced modern business and professional techniques into the conduct of diocesan business. Within a year of taking over, he mandated regular reporting to diocesan headquarters on the state of sacramental and financial activity in the parishes and in the other major institutions of the diocese. These would provide not only records of income and expenses but also vital statistics of sacramental activity such as baptisms, marriages, and funerals, and thereby a demographic picture of Catholic life year by year. In 1923 Keane also affiliated the main Catholic social welfare agencies—the Grace Day Home and the Catholic Ladies' Relief Society—with the newly founded Community Chest. Catholic participation in this citywide fund-raising organization ensured a steady flow of income into these agencies and to others that would come during the 1930s. The sheer energy Keane brought to his administration corresponded with the muscular expansion of Sacramento life. Chamber of Commerce president Hilliard Welch captured the heart and soul of Keane's style when he observed that the prelate had "molded himself into the life of the community."[50] The "life of the community" no doubt meant a continuation of the patterns of accommodation and urban development that had been the motif of his predecessors, Manogue and Grace.

A NEW DOWNTOWN

The city's building renaissance included the remaking of the retail district. Twelfth Street, once the outer edge of the retail district, was now its center, thanks to a significant land deal on the part of the Catholic Church. As generous urban cooperators, Catholic leaders moved with

Young C. K. McClatchy, ca. 1884. Courtesy of Sacramento Archives and Museum Collection Center, Eleanor McClatchy Collection.

alacrity and even daring to accommodate the designs for the new down-town. The most obvious sites for development were the decrepit buildings of the Christian Brothers School at the corner of Twelfth and K.

The school had been a Sacramento institution since 1876. As Sacramento modernized, however, it seemed more and more a quaint relic of the distant past. Enclosed by a high wooden fence and surrounded by stately elms, the old Georgian-style building still included a small "farming" operation as late as 1918, including a chicken coop. The last addition to the school was a wing that Mrs. Mary Bethel built in 1903. After that time the structure began to deteriorate rapidly, and by 1915 the building was condemned and repairs no longer permitted. The brothers themselves were frustrated by the increasingly cramped and substandard condition of their facilities. "Material discomfort of sundry sorts . . . inconvenience, cold, want of privacy from the boys . . . [and] a plethora of elements that [make] for dissatisfaction in community," wrote Brother Z. Joseph Fenlon, provincial visitor, when he assessed the living quarters. The classroom situation was worse. Still using old pedagogical methods that kept the students of all grade levels in one room, one of the brothers, Conrad Deschler, recalled teaching the entire first and second years of high school, sixty-four students in all, in one room.[51] Furthermore, Christian Brothers School had no athletic facilities of any kind. There was no gymnasium or any playing fields for football, baseball, or basketball teams to compete with other schools. Even before World War I there were active plans to abandon the old structure and build a new one, but Bishop Grace's refusal to spend money stymied all of them. Pressure mounted nonetheless from the Christian Brothers, alumni, and students themselves, especially after the new Sacramento City High School opened in 1924. The modern high school, with its up-to-date curriculum and facilities, including playing fields for active sports teams, set the new standard for secondary education in Sacramento.

Shortly after his formal appointment as bishop, Keane put the Christian Brothers' property up for sale. To the surprise of the city, he also placed his own episcopal residence on the block. "The [land] frontage, now used by the Brothers' College, has been holding up business development along the south side of K Street," he told reporters. For Catholic education, he noted, "a new location can be secured and a new school built, where we can do better work than in the present quarters." Keane contacted the architectural firm of Dean and Dean to begin planning the new school. After several months a bid for the Twelfth and K property came from Weinstock, Lubin, and Company, which had long been considering a move from its location at Eleventh and J. Ultimately, Keane accepted an offer of $210,000 from the department store, with the proviso that the school be vacated by June so that demolition could begin.[52]

Allison Ware, the head of Chico Normal School and a longtime land speculator, purchased the episcopal mansion in 1924 and tore it down to put up a commercial outlet.[53] Meanwhile, the sale of the episcopal residence necessitated the building of a new cathedral presbytery on Eleventh and J streets. Dean and Dean built the narrow structure, which they promised would "conform architecturally" to the cathedral.

In his most dramatic gesture of urban goodwill but to the shock of many, Keane announced his willingness to sell the Cathedral of the Blessed Sacrament. "We have been approached by the people holding the option on the bishop's house property with a proposition that we allow them to select a site containing a similar amount of ground and in a location suitable to the church where a new Cathedral on the mission style and a new bishop's residence will be erected." Keane further noted, "In exchange, we are to let them have the present Cathedral and bishop's house properties with a suitable bonus to us." Here he pushed the limits of church and city cooperation too far, even drawing negative comment from outside the Catholic flock. *Catholic Herald* editor Thomas Connelly remarked that in fact the "curiosity of non-Catholic citizens seems to be keener than that of Catholics in the matter." Opposition to the plan must have been intense enough to let it sink into oblivion. But Keane's actions suggested once again that Catholic Sacramentans were anxious, indeed in some cases overeager, to cooperate with plans for urban growth.[54]

CONCLUSION

The era described in this chapter represents one of the most dynamic periods of church-city cooperation in Sacramento's history. The level of explicit interaction between church authorities and improvement-minded civic leaders exceeded even that of Manogue's days. Their not inconsiderable efforts resulted in growth and prosperity, and Sacramento eventually attained its long-awaited goal of one hundred thousand residents in the 1930s. The city's appeal, enhanced in no small measure by the kinds of urban amenities and architectural elegance planned and provided for by the Catholic community, helped put Sacramento on the map. The golden dreams of the 1920s, however, gave way to the hard economic realities of the Great Depression and World War II. Here were forces that no one could control.

CHAPTER 6

Catholic Social Provision

The Depression and World War II, 1930–1945

"The gentle sunshine of charity"

"Sacramento is starting a new decade confidently expecting the next ten years will be as prolific in accomplishments and development as the past," wrote the relentlessly upbeat Bradley Riter in the January 4, 1930, edition of the *Sacramento Bee*.[1] However, the decade of the thirties was anything but pleasant as the city and county coped with an economic cataclysm that was the equivalent of the floods, fires, and disease of the 1850s.

The Great Depression traveled relatively slowly across the United States—slithering out from the corridors of Wall Street, devastating the financial and industrial colossus of the East and Midwest, driving farmers and ranchers into poverty and off their land, and setting in motion an internal refugee crisis that eventually made its way to California. Sacramento initially absorbed the shock waves of the October 1929 crash and subsequent industrial collapse. But by late 1930 the number of unemployed rose ominously.[2] Sacramento's fragile social services fell apart under the deluge of jobless residents and also the thousands of transients who camped along riverbanks and in the vacant lots of the California state capital. The Depression finally broke down the purposeful volunteerism that had made Sacramento an "indomitable" city. Sacramentans of this era could not push back the onslaught of the Depression as they had done with the raging waters of the Sacramento and American rivers. They could not lift their city above the flood of economic despair as they had lifted their streets so long ago. The Depression completely overwhelmed private enterprises like the Catholic Church, which had traditionally aided the city by helping the indigent. Church leaders did what they could, but they simply could not come to the city's assistance as they had in the past. In order to survive, social services had to be supplemented by federal dollars—either in direct relief payments or through wages and salaries that came from the new defense bases located in Sacramento County.

SACRAMENTO AND THE DEPRESSION

Sacramento's economic decline came gradually. But almost overnight the city became painfully aware of bad times when the huge California Co-operative Producers Canning Company closed its doors in September 1930, at the height of the canning season, leaving its employees without wages. The failure of this important industry threw shock waves into the other local canneries. Taking advantage of a glutted labor market, cannery operators reduced the wages of those they did employ and favored minority workers, who were less inclined to complain about the diminished income. This jolt to an important local industry was doubled in the winter of 1932 when a killing freeze virtually destroyed the citrus and many of the vegetable crops of the valley.[3]

The ripple effect reached into the rail yards. Demand for railroad cars lagged, as did the ability to fund repair work on engines and cars. Southern Pacific found its business reduced by 22 percent during the 1930s, with a $34 million loss. More than 2,200 Southern Pacific employees were reduced to three-day weeks.[4] Layoffs and work reductions hit Western Pacific, too. Unemployment soared to 10 percent in Sacramento County in 1930. By 1932, 27,000 were without work.[5]

The national scourge of bank failure hit in January 1933 when the California National Bank and the California Trust and Savings Bank closed their doors. The California National Bank had more than 9,000 commercial accounts, including some Catholic parishes, and the Trust and

Savings some 36,000.[6] In order to prevent additional closures, airplanes and armored vehicles, carrying $13 million in cash, were quickly dispatched from San Francisco.[7]

Declining wages, layoffs, and straitened budgets created expected downturns in Sacramento consumption. Annual family income, pegged at $1,805 in 1929, fell to $1,344 by 1933. Railroad shop payrolls, one of the major employers of the city, fell from $5.4 million in 1929 to $1.7 million by 1933.[8] In 1932 only 2,579 cars were sold in Sacramento County, representing a 43 percent decline from the previous year.[9] Building permit valuations fell from $5 million in 1928 to $3.6 million in 1931.

THE HUMAN FACE OF THE DEPRESSION

Statistics tell only part of the story of Sacramento's struggle with the Depression. The specter of homelessness and hunger grew substantially in the city, causing its nineteenth-century systems of social provision to falter.

Hungry and homeless transients, who had for years alighted in Sacramento, now flooded into the state capital.[10] The scores of trains that entered and left the city daily brought men desperate to find work or who had been driven out of other communities. According to a report prepared for the State Emergency Relief Administration (SERA), Sacramento had particular appeal due to the presence of large commercial employment agencies and the needs of surrounding farms, ranches, lumber mills, and construction projects. Sacramento, the report declared, was "one of the main centers for homeless men and migratory workers in the United States."[11]

Sacramento had a love-hate relationship with this migratory workforce. On the one hand, they provided needed labor for service jobs and other tasks. On the other hand, respectable Sacramentans suspected some of them of bringing crime and vice to the city. Sacramentans remembered with disgust the industrial armies of unemployed men that periodically swarmed through the Central Valley during the late nineteenth and early twentieth centuries. Some of these transients had even been influenced by radicals of the International Workers of the World and brought strange and alien ideologies into the sacred precincts of capitalist Sacramento. These marchers had brazenly camped out in the city and virtually demanded food, shelter, and work. Sometimes they were bribed to keep moving on, but in March 1914 violence erupted between an "Unemployed Army" of 1,400 men and city police and national guardsmen.[12] C. K. McClatchy frequently denounced them as "bummers" and even in the depths of the Great Depression scorned "the pest and plague of professionally unemployed blatherskites, windbags, and 'sons of rest'—men upon whose sensitive nerves a sawbuck has the same chilling effect a snake has upon the average woman."[13] Even though a 1901 revision of the state constitution insisted on a residency requirement for county relief and imposed penalties for "dumping" indigents on other counties, still the drifters came to Sacramento—often in search of labor. Although city leaders were suspicious, transients found sympathetic private or public charities to tide them over.

The Great Depression sent thousands fleeing from other parts of the nation to California and increased the number of unemployed residents and transients in the state capital. By 1931 fruit vendors appeared on Sacramento street corners, trying to raise a few cents by selling produce. In late February more than 200 men literally fought for twenty jobs at the Sacramento docks loading riprap for transshipment to Freeport. After the melee, the *Bee* observed, "The twenty best fighters completed the work and drew their pay early in the afternoon." Even more pathetically, hordes of scavengers: Men, women, and children foraged the city dump for the remnants of groceries discarded after a 1931 fire at the Mebius-Drescher wholesale grocery store. The scorched and seared food, some of it cans of fish, fruits, and vegetables that had burst in the fire, were set upon by the hungry. "Men and women, Sacramento fathers and mothers, penniless, jobless and desperate for food for their little ones, scrabbled in the debris for salvage. Here was a woman with a bent and broken bucket . . . busily scooping handfuls of scorched and seared beans from a torn stack." A federal worker who visited all the transient camps around the city in 1935 wrote about desperate conditions in a dump off the Marysville highway, where Mexican and white families camped, waiting for the fruit-picking season to begin. Of the white families he wrote, "Their camp, tents and shacks were the dirtiest spots on the dirty camp and dump ground. Dirty, ragged children of all ages played among the dump heaps and wrecked automobile bodies. The women washed their clothes in the river water and hung them on the brush to dry, while the 'men folks' worked on their old cars or went to town."[14] These conditions only grew worse as the decade unfolded.

THE STRUCTURE OF SOCIAL PROVISION PRIOR TO
THE GREAT DEPRESSION

The onslaught of human misery totally submerged the powers of public and private agencies that had traditionally cared for Sacramento's poor. Like many western cities, Sacramento had a loosely structured system of social provision that spread out responsibility for the poor among several different agencies. The county had many responsibilities. In 1853 the county opened its first public hospital; in 1870 it built a larger county hospital and poor home and sponsored a farm whose produce fed the inmates. The county also sustained a residence for "old folks" and an institution for the mentally ill.[15] What "outdoor" relief existed went only to bona fide county residents and was dispensed by a local official who offered meager cash vouchers for groceries and some rent.

Sacramento County's charitable officer from 1911 until the end of the 1930s was Mary Judge, a Sacramento institution in her own right. Educated in public schools, Judge was also a devout Catholic, having received some of her training at a convent. Before she had taken on the charities job, she had been a laundress and was not all that far removed from the poor people she encountered daily. Her hard work and austere life (she never married) made her less than sympathetic to perceived indolence of any kind. Wrote one admirer, "She had no use for moochers and soon got rid of them."[16] Her toughness with the "unworthy poor" won her plaudits from C. K. McClatchy and others, yet her hardness was allegedly tempered by acts of personal charity and kindness.[17] Until the Great Depression, Judge handled all county charity cases entirely on her own. Sacramento was small enough that she knew most of the area's indigents and easily applied the residency rule on the spot. In 1922 a county charter revision created the Board of Public Welfare, headed by Judge, that enjoyed "a controlling voice in all matters relating to the management and control of the Sacramento Hospital, detention home and other charitable work." Judge was ruggedly honest, and it also helped that she kept overhead and expenditures low. In 1926, for example, eight hundred families sought assistance, and Judge reported that her payouts per month ranged from twelve to fifteen hundred dollars—mostly for groceries and other needed supplies. Judge also handled a state and county program that provided a small stipend per month for each child of indigent widowed mothers.[18]

The city also took a role in relief for the poor. Like the county, it contracted out some indigent and child-care services to private agencies and administered large charitable bequests given by philanthropic Sacramentans for the care of the poor. The most important was a two hundred thousand–dollar fund left by hotelier and former mayor William Land in honor of his wife, Ann. The interest on this capital was paid out in two installments and directed to organizations that helped the needy. Local merchant Isador Cohen also left a fund to buy shoes for poor children.

Public relief agencies were heavily dependent on the network of private charities and organizations that supplemented the social welfare of Sacramento's poor. Fraternal organizations provided widows' benefits and burial policies. One of the earliest benevolent organizations was the Howard Benevolent Society, founded in 1857 to dispense charity in times of need. The Marguerite Home, founded by Margaret Crocker, cared for elderly indigent women. However, religious groups took a major lead in helping the poor. The Episcopalians sponsored the Home of the Merciful Savior for invalid children, and the Congregationalists underwrote the Protestant Orphan Asylum. The Peniel Mission was established in 1900 in the former Crocker mansion "for the benefit of homeless girls, erring ones who have but started on wayward lives." The most important organization was the Salvation Army, which came to Sacramento in May 1885. The first appearance of the uniformed evangelicals drew catcalls and missiles from Sacramento street urchins. However, the "Hallelujah" lads and lasses soon became an indispensable part of the city's network of social provision and opened their first barracks on Third Street; in 1929 they erected a building on Fifth Street. These groups fed, clothed, and sheltered countless poor and indigent in Sacramento, including those who did not qualify for county assistance (but who were referred by the softhearted Judge).[19] They generally accompanied this charity with some preaching, church services, and insistence on personal rehabilitation through conversion to religious beliefs. However, most private agencies ministered to all improvident Sacramentans regardless of creed, targeting especially families rather than single indigents.

Nine Sacramento women founded the Catholic Ladies' Relief Society on April 18, 1888. This was a branch of a larger statewide organization. The CLRS was organized "for the purposes of giving aid, assistance and care for the indigent poor within the Diocese of Sacramento and to aid in support of indigent orphan children of and in said diocese and to aid in the support of charitable institutions and to found new ones, and subordinate societies in said diocese." Branches of this society blossomed in virtually every city in the diocese under a federated organizational structure with a central leadership presided over by a "grand president." As with other sectarian charities, the group imposed no creedal requirements for assistance: "Although Catholic in name, we adopted as our principle, work of an entirely non-sectarian character, neither creed, class nor color interfering with our sympathetic interest in the applicant."[20] The common needs of Sacramento's poor brought the Catholic group into contact with the well-established Howard Benevolent Society as well as Traveler's Aid, the Salvation Army, the Tuberculosis Association, the YMCA, and the Red Cross. It also shared information and made referrals to the Ann Land Fund. In its first year, the CLRS recorded assistance to sixteen impoverished Sacramento families and care for one orphan.

As Sacramento grew, the demands on the organization became heavier. Ultimately, the CLRS engaged the services of a social service worker and a staff of officers who coordinated the dispensation of relief. A popular used-clothing drive began in 1906, netting hundreds of discarded items every year for cleaning, mending, and distribution to the poor. Early day-care services for cannery workers' children and Christmas baskets for the needy were added to the group's evolving program. Members spent hours with the inmates of the county institutions as well as the local and diocesan orphanages. They sewed and repaired clothing for children and others—providing poor Catholic children with their first-communion attire. From the time of its founding to the years of the Great Depression, the CLRS was the major dispenser of private charity for the Catholic Church in Sacramento.

The CLRS and a host of other charities and "character-building" organizations were partially funded by Sacramento's Community Chest. Established in Sacramento in 1923, the chest sponsored a highly successful annual drive that funded more than twenty private agencies. In 1924 the CLRS and the Grace Day Home began receiving regular allotments from the newly chartered Community Chest. Catholic interests were advanced and protected by Rebecca Coolot, who played a major role in establishing the chest and was later eulogized as its "godmother." Catholics supported it wholeheartedly, as Monsignor Horgan of the cathedral noted at a 1930 rally for the annual appeal. "The one thing that brings us all together, no matter how much we may differ in ancestry, attitude toward life or creed, is the Community Chest. In this cause we can all join."[21] The chest attempted to serve as a clearinghouse for eligibility and referrals for the needy.

THE OLD STRUCTURE COLLAPSES

Sacramento had enough resources to manage its own "homegrown" poor, but it was the swelling transient population that strained the network of social provision to the point of near collapse. Homeless men created at least five sprawling shanty villages, known nationwide as Hoovervilles, which could be found on the banks of the Sacramento River, in the small town of Broderick, along Jibboom Street, and eastward along Twelfth Street. These largely male communities held at least three thousand, often in tar-paper or scrap-metal shacks and always in desperately filthy conditions.[22]

The city government attempted a variety of schemes to cope with the increased demands for charity. One technique, adapted from the Hoover administration, was to boost city spirits with public-relations campaigns and the convening of study groups, which could diagnose and solve common problems. City government leaders convoked a mass meeting of industrial, social, and labor leaders in October 1930. The groups directed Mayor C. H. S. Bidwell to form a committee to study unemployment conditions and make recommendations. Committee member Carl Lamus, the president of the Chamber of Commerce, summarized the spirit of the committee: "The business depression is largely a matter of psychology and . . . if the committee could find some way to get people to start thinking in terms of prosperity again, it would have reached its objective." After

Hooverville at the edge of Gardenland, looking north from the Natomas levee (now Garden Highway), 1940. Courtesy of Sacramento Archives and Museum Collection Center, Eugene Hepting Collection.

a November 6, 1930, conference on unemployment, the committee urged citizens to provide make-work jobs for the unemployed—cleaning yards, garages, attics, and basements. Employers who retained their workforces during the Thanksgiving and Christmas holidays of 1930 had their names enrolled in a *Sacramento Bee* honor role.[23]

But unemployment grew worse. The Recreation Department of the city and the Community Chest sponsored a homeless shelter in an old waterworks on Front and 1 streets. The Community Chest served as the central intake for the city shelter and required applicants to register at the chest headquarters to secure a niche in the huge dormitory. The shelter at times crammed in more than five hundred men at night. Each resident was given a bath and had his clothing deloused with a kerosene "dry-cleaning." The YMCA, the Salvation Army, the Volunteers of America, and the Traveler's Aid ran other shelters. Some of the homeless just slept in vacant homes, sheds, and buildings. One spot check in 1934 found more than twelve hundred single men living in shelters in Sacramento.[24] The Salvation Army operated a separate feeding facility as well.

Cash shortfalls made matters worse. In early 1930 an already slow flow of city revenue had caused the city to back away from several building projects that had been on the boards for a while. Tax delinquencies, shortages in water collections, and even fines fell short of the optimistic projections of the city council and created a budget deficit of fifty thousand dollars by the end of the year.[25]

The unemployed grew more and more militant over the slow pace of relief. When the city proposed to turn over the administration of its shelter to the Salvation Army—which, as noted, doled out religious instruction along with relief—the unemployed protested and presented a set of demands to city leaders, seeking a weekly allowance, free food and clothing for their children, and the abolition of private employment agencies, which often collected fees from workers but never produced jobs. Mini-riots also broke out at the shelter when an ad hoc feeding program ran out of food before all were fed. Officials then moved all feeding off-site. Nightly, hundreds of men crowded into the old waterworks, sleeping on floors and in bathrooms just to get in out of the cold. Between December 16, 1935, and January 26, 1936, nearly seven thousand of the eleven thousand seeking shelter stayed at the city shelter.[26]

In January 1930 the Salvation Army, perhaps the private charity most skilled at relief, opened a wood yard at which unemployed men worked for an hour to qualify for relief. It ran two shelters for the homeless and found its resources stretched. It had budgeted to feed four hundred men a day, but by 1931 the number showing up hovered at nearly double that figure. By March the kitchen had run out of money, and the organization's officers turned to the city for assistance, warning of transients swarming through residential districts, defying police, demanding food of housewives, robbing pedestrians, and looting homes.

The county tried to meet the needs and even added on to the indigent home on the county grounds in 1931. However, tax delinquencies made revenues plunge even more precipitously at the same time demand for social welfare services went up. In November 1931 Mary Judge reported to members of the Ann Land Commission (on which she sat) that the county was expending relief funds at a rate of nine thousand dollars per month since the previous July, "with no prospect of this amount being diminished." Nearly thirty thousand dollars in relief alone was expended in December 1932 and January 1933. Faced with only sixty-seven hundred in the fund for indigent relief, Judge began handing out staple groceries at commissary sites opened in various parts of the county and run by her office, the Volunteers of America (a Salvation Army group), the Catholic Ladies' Relief Society, and the Ann Land Commission.[27]

The Community Chest also hit the skids. Already in 1930 the annual collection came up a whopping thirty-two thousand dollars short. The chest campaign faltered so badly that people feared it would cease to exist. A 35 percent cut in its 1933 budget required some chest-supported agencies to suspend activities. Faced with this shortage, the Ann Land Commission (which received chest funds to supplement its endowment) reduced its rent-assistance program, and the Salvation Army pulled back on its meals from two to one a day and then suspended them altogether after May 16, 1933. The Ann Land Commission could take on no new cases, and Judge stepped forward to fill the void.[28]

Unemployed workers grew even more militant and challenged county officials to provide more work or greater relief. *Sacramento Bee* reporters "infiltrated" the homeless camps and shelters and heard the mutterings of the unemployed and homeless. Frustration with Judge and the inadequacy of county relief boiled over into occasional outbursts and in petitions by the homeless or jobless to the city council, demanding jobs, free food, and shelter. Occasionally, these men and women descended on Judge's offices. At first the fearsome charity chief waved away police assistance and dispatched the workers on her own. Eventually, though, even she had to call for help. Judge dealt as best she could with the human suffering that came her way, but even as late as 1932 she seemed somewhat clueless about the nature of the Depression, telling an audience just before Christmas that the transient problem was the fault of the automobile and not deeper economic conditions. Depression-era police chief William Hallanan maintained a zero-tolerance policy for "radicals" and monitored their activities with an eagle eye. The "radical" agitation of the unemployed created the conditions for a major police crackdown on suspected Communists and labor agitators in July 1934, when a local Communist Party headquarters was raided and arrests were made.[29]

By early 1933 the county welfare fund was depleted, and the prospect of inducing merchants to accept food warrants was pondered. Finally, state and local officials made a pitch for a fifty thousand–dollar relief loan to the Reconstruction Finance Corporation to fund public works. Hopes were raised when the money was approved in late March 1933, but were quickly dashed when only twenty-three thousand dollars was sent. Still, with this fund the county hired five hundred heads of families to work on local improvement projects—paying them two dollars per day. Demands for Judge's ouster mounted as it became evident that her old-fashioned way of doing business no longer worked. With the help of loyal supervisors she resisted efforts by state and local critics to remove her. However, her office soon began to be transformed by the "modern" professional methods that she had always resisted.[30]

A slow turnaround began in 1933 when a modest increase in cannery work lifted some income levels. The railroad yards slowly brought back workers to five-day weeks. The halting recovery of the private sector was aided by Franklin Roosevelt's New Deal, which not only supplemented faltering or collapsed relief programs but also created public works programs that employed idle Sacramentans. In late 1933 county executive Charles W. Deterding Jr. applied for federal dollars for deferred building projects. The Federal Emergency Relief Act of 1933 created the State Emergency Relief Administration, which served as a conduit for federal funds. One of its branches, the Federal Transient Service, began to assist Sacramento in coping with its flow of homeless men and women. Other SERA money provided temporary jobs through the winter of 1933 and into 1934, bringing some relief to county finances. By early 1935 SERA joined with a revived Community Chest and city officials to organize a feeding program for the homeless. In November 1935 a State Emergency Relief Administration intake center opened to care for a limited number of transients and homeless. In late 1935 and early 1936 the Works Progress Administration took over some of the programs funded under SERA and poured in even more direct federal aid. Ultimately, millions of federal dollars flowed into Sacramento County in direct relief, and other federally funded projects helped create new jobs.[31]

CATHOLIC WOES

The economic collapse adversely affected all churches. Shortfalls in income impacted Catholic parishes and schools, which were totally dependent on voluntary giving. As the graph suggests, Sacramento parish income reflected the general trend of the depression, hitting a real trough in 1933 and again in 1936.

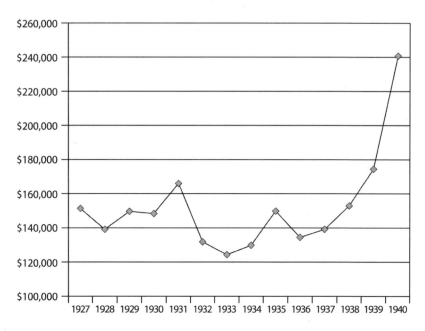

CHART 6.1 Sacramento Parish income, 1927–1940. SOURCE: Annual parish reports, ADS.

As the crisis unfolded, Catholics joined in the campaign to keep employment alive by moving forward with plans to erect a 750-seat auditorium at St. Joseph School. As the Catholic press explained, "Construction has been undertaken at this time in adherence to the appeals of the social leaders for contracting all necessary work in the current depression as an aid towards industrial rehabilitation."[32] However, building projects were nearly the undoing of some parishes, including Sacred Heart Church in East Sacramento, St. Joseph's in North Sacramento, and the new school for Immaculate Conception Parish in Oak Park. Shortfalls in revenue made it seriously difficult for these institutions to keep up with loan payments and jeopardized their future.

Mercy Hospital also carried a debt of $375,000 held by the San Francisco–based Bank of America at 6 percent interest. With the help of San Francisco archbishop John J. Mitty, the Hibernian Bank of San Francisco agreed to refinance the buildings.[33] With reduced interest and a small trickle of cash from investments made with monies from the Pious Fund (an endowment fund for the missions, provided by the government of Mexico, and paid briefly to the Catholic dioceses of California), Bishop Armstrong paid back a large portion of the money borrowed from the Bank of America for Sacred Heart and Immaculate Conception parishes.[34] Armstrong also worked to keep Christian Brothers High School from being put on the auction block and to rescue the brothers from financial ruin.[35] But the threat of foreclosure on churches was minimal.

CATHOLICS AND DIRECT RELIEF

The Catholic Ladies' Relief Society was the only Catholic charity that dealt directly with the needs of poor and unemployed Sacramentans. Struggling to keep up with the tide, the women of the society provided meals, nightly lodging, clothing, hospital and clinical care, private medical and dental care, household equipment, and rent for needy families. The CLRS minute books, despite their somewhat imprecise accounting methods, lay bare the increasing demands for relief, revealing an increase of 54 percent from 1930–1931 to 1931–1932. When the Community Chest faltered, the CLRS's efforts sputtered, but the ladies continued to collect and distribute used clothing and do what they could with the cases they received. By 1935, however, the CLRS was running short of funds and volunteers.

Other avenues of church relief fell short as well. Ad hoc efforts including meals and alms, assistance with a night's lodging, transportation, and any number of needs presented themselves daily, particularly to the priests and sisters. But here, too, the ability to keep up proved too much. For example, the Franciscans at St. Francis's began a feeding program for those who came to their door. But the numbers quickly exceeded the slim resources of the friars, and the program ended. In 1934 the Reverend Stephen Keating of the cathedral distributed four hundred baskets of food on Christmas Eve and brought gifts to twenty-five Mexicans in the county hospital. However, the efforts were quickly stretched thin there, too. A clothing drive the same year noted that "contributions . . . were not as plentiful as last year," but its proceeds were distributed "to residents of Hooverville" two days after Christmas.[36]

One organization, the House of Hospitality sponsored by the Catholic Worker movement, came in at the very end of the Depression and promised some hope, but its efforts missed the worst part of the Depression years. The Catholic Worker movement, a form of radical Catholic social activism, was begun in New York City by Dorothy Day and Peter Maurin in 1933.[37] During the Depression, Catholic Worker–sponsored Houses of Hospitality fed and sheltered the poor without question. Sacramento's House of Hospitality began its operations in January 1941 when a former Christian Brother, Arthur Ronz, with the help of thirteen Sacramento priests, obtained three houses on Second Street in the middle of Sacramento's skid row, rented out two of them, and with the proceeds opened Queen of Peace House. The priests of the diocese purchased a car for Ronz, and the Sisters of Mercy, the Legion of Mary of Sacred Heart Parish, and other Catholic groups donated food and volunteer labor. City officials sent clothes and hauled away garbage for free. With volunteer labor, the house fed nearly ten thousand people (many of them poor Mexicans, according to Ronz) between January and April 1941. The house soon became deluged with referrals from Traveler's Aid and the Salvation Army. Ronz himself struggled to keep it afloat until 1942, when he reluctantly reported for military service.[38]

GREATER RATIONALIZATION OF SOCIAL SERVICES

The sheer magnitude of the crisis made it impossible for Catholics or other social providers to really help the poor of Sacramento. However, the Depression did provide a catalyst for upgrading and professionalizing Catholic social services, particularly for dependent children. Orphan care had been a ministry of the Sisters of Mercy since they arrived in 1857. In 1861 the sisters opened an orphanage in the city, which was transferred to Grass Valley in 1879. There, two facilities, St. Patrick's and St. Vincent's, were built and staffed by another branch of the Sisters of Mercy. These orphan asylums received per capita state aid for administrative operations.

Progressive Era reforms revised child-care practices and insisted on trained staff to manage public child-welfare services. Even private agencies—especially those that received public funds—were required to be licensed and periodically inspected. Accordingly, the Diocese of Sacramento opened the Catholic Social Welfare Bureau in 1930. It not only became the clearinghouse for the five Catholic agencies participating in the Community Chest—the Grace Day Home, the Stanford Lathrop Home, the Grass Valley orphanages (which held children from Sacramento), the Catholic Ladies' Relief Society, and the welfare bureau itself—

but was also the main contact with the California Department of Social Welfare. In 1930 Bishop Robert Armstrong hired Mary Frances Grogan, a graduate of the University of Southern California's School of Social Work, to head the new bureau. A five-year veteran of the Los Angeles Catholic Welfare Bureau, Grogan had been executive secretary of its Ventura County branch for three years. In early July Grogan set up shop in a spare room at Holy Angels School.[39] Sacramento's child-care situation, long overdue for reform, took an important step forward.

Grogan visited the decrepit Catholic orphanage buildings in Grass Valley and was shocked by what she found. The nineteenth-century-era buildings hosted about 150 waifs in separate institutions for boys and girls. In the fall of 1930 state authorities had condemned the buildings. *Sacramento Bee* reporter Bradley Riter graphically described all that was wrong with St. Patrick's: jerry-rigged fire escapes, study halls converted into dormitories, and poor heating, ventilation, and plumbing. He echoed others' fears for the safety of the orphans at the dilapidated site. At Grogan's urging and really having no other choice, Armstrong made plans to build a new orphanage in Sacramento on a fifty-acre parcel along Franklin Boulevard, which had originally been a Catholic cemetery, about three-quarters of a mile outside the current city limits.[40] The diocese then moved quickly to raise the needed funds.

The citywide fund drive kicked off in February 1931, just as hard times were coming, but Sacramentans donated generously. Hilliard E. Welch, president of the Chamber of Commerce and vice president of the local branch of the Bank of America, spoke for many when he said, "It is just as much a duty of men to care for these orphaned children as it is to pay honest debts."[41] Funds flowed into the collection coffers, and in October 1931 an exultant Armstrong turned over the first shovel of dirt. In July 1932 the structure was complete, and 100 orphans, 14 sisters, and the Reverend Patrick Bennett, the priest-director, moved into the new St. Patrick Home. St. Patrick's became an important Sacramento institution, and its directors provided for the care of orphaned and troubled youth. Grogan was later replaced by Alice Coughlan, another social worker.[42] The Reverend Thomas Markham, trained at the Catholic University of America's School of Social Service, took over from Coughlan in the mid-1930s and directed the agency until the 1970s.

St. Patrick construction had ripple effects on other child-care agencies, especially the orphanage run by the Sisters of Mercy in the Stanford Lathrop Home. The Mercy Sisters had received the home as a bequest from Jane Lathrop Stanford in 1900. For years it housed 30 to 40 young girls from ages six to sixteen. State subsidies, contributions from the religious order, and funds from the Community Chest underwrote the facility. When St. Patrick Home was completed in 1932, the younger girls were transferred there, taking along their share of the state subsidy. At Markham's urging in 1936, Armstrong replaced the Sisters of Mercy with the Sisters of Social Service, a religious community that specialized in settlement-house work. Headed by Sister Lucille Klein, a contingent of 4 sisters arrived in the summer of 1936 and surveyed the area. "We were on the edge of the downtown district," recalled Sister Gerarda Fawcett, one of the "pioneer" sisters. "There were many old buildings converted into rooming houses, with dark dingy halls. There was also a recognized 'red light' district and we were advised not to go to the 1/2 numbers on a certain street. It was a multi-ethnic district with a predominance of Mexican and Italian families." The sisters transformed the residence into a care center for teenage girls and added a settlement-house program to provide social services to the denizens of the area. In the mansion's capacious quarters the sisters carved out club rooms and a small auditorium and created a library and other facilities to attract local inhabitants. In the former primary school on the ground floor, the sisters opened a community center that offered classes in art, music, cooking, homemaking, and other skills. Dramatic presentations and other theatrical events added to the home's cultural programs.[43] The orphanage, the Grace Day Home, and the settlement house all provided critical social services for the city of Sacramento. Under Markham, the new social service structure was up and functioning. The Depression itself began to loosen its grip on Sacramento's economy as federal spending via New Deal agencies and new military installations began to pump new life into the economic veins of the community.

Markham would eventually be called away to serve as a chaplain in World War II. If the Depression had transformed the social-provision services of the county, preparations for the war and the war itself changed Sacramento's economy.

Sacramento benefited from heavy expenditures for military readiness and wartime needs, becoming an important part of "Fortress California."[44] Sacramento County welcomed three new military installations that remade the economic and social life of the area by providing millions of jobs.

Sacramentans had their first taste of military investment during World War I when the War Department built Mather Field, a training school for aviators. Mather had been actively courted by local officials who all but begged the military to use the flat and sunny lands around Sacramento as a training facility. City leaders and businessmen put together a package of economic incentives (the likes of which, in the twenty-first century, would be reserved for new hotels, upscale housing, and major league teams) to lure the facility to the area. The field was an economic boon for the Sacramento area, as spending by the War Department and the aviators coursed into the local economy. However, this first Mather Field had a short life. The war ended in November 1918, and rapid demobilization meant that only a few people staffed Mather during the twenties. It temporarily burst back to life in April 1930 as a site for war games but afterward was shuttered and its first buildings razed by an economy-minded Hoover administration. The economic boon brought by the air base remained in Sacramento's collective memory.

Lobbying for a new military installation became an important priority for Chamber of Commerce factotum Arthur S. Dudley.[45] He and others beseeched sympathetic congressmen to establish supply depots in coastal states to support troops in the Atlantic and Pacific areas. In August 1935 Congress authorized two hundred million dollars for the proposed new bases, one of which was in Sacramento County. The government purchased 1,200 acres on the original Rancho Del Paso tract north of the city, which became the site of the Army Air Force Depot. On September 8, 1936, ten thousand gathered to watch Governor Frank Merriam push the dynamite plunger that began the excavation for the Sacramento Army Air Force Depot. The new facility, which opened on December 1, 1939, was named McClellan Field for Hezekiah McClellan, an army pilot who had crashed and died while testing a new plane three years earlier. As a supply and aircraft-maintenance base, McClellan became a vital link in the war effort once World War II erupted in the Pacific.[46]

Dudley also convinced War Department officials to reopen Mather Field and to transfer the tiny Rockford Aviation School and its four hundred employees from San Diego to Mather. By 1941 the base had been rebuilt, and it hummed with activity as a school for advanced pilot and basic navigation training. During the war it serviced the huge fleet of B-29s, which rained bombs on Japan. These two bases employed more than eighteen thousand workers during World War II, exceeding the combined employment of both the rail yards and the canneries. During the Cold War Mather continued to be a training facility for navigators and bombardiers. Dudley and army colonel Joseph Healy also obtained a site for the Army Signal Depot in 1942.[47] Located initially in temporary buildings, the depot relocated to a new 485-acre site at a railroad stop near Polk Station. All three Sacramento bases were retained and expanded during the Cold War era.

With Mather, McClellan, and the signal depot at the forefront of Sacramento's mobilization during the war, Sacramento's economy hummed once again. Cannery orders picked up, while railroad repair and maintenance needs brought in hundreds of new workers, many of them women, to the Sacramento Locomotive Works. Catholic churches were compelled to adapt to this dynamic. In order to accommodate the defense workers at nearby McClellan, St. Joseph Church in North Sacramento (the parish in closest proximity to the base) changed its schedule by adding a 5:30 AM mass and a mass at McClellan Field at 8:00 AM. Catholic priests were often called to help with special needs. For example, when German prisoners of war were lodged at bases near Sacramento, the diocese sent the German-speaking Reverand Raymond Renwald to minister to their needs. "Since I knew some German," he recalled in a 1981 interview, "I was called on to say Mass once or twice in a little base for prisoners right outside of Sacramento, but then they got another priest for that." At the end of the war, Renwald shuttled every Sunday to Camp Beale near Marysville to hear confessions and celebrate mass for German POWs. "I'd get quite a kick out of hearing those men sing those German songs at Mass. An all men's choir, and the Germans have a kind of penchant for singing."[48] As we shall see later, the influx of Mexican braceros, brought in as workers during the war, also required special ministry from Catholic priests, sisters, and laity.

Catholics in Sacramento—even Germans and Italians—were supportive of the war, and there was no organized Catholic opposition to it. Indeed, even before Pearl Harbor, in November 1940, forty-three hundred Catholics gathered at a faith and patriotism rally sponsored by the Holy Name Society (an association of Catholic men). During his talk, Jesuit Father Joseph Vaughn lashed out at the dictators in Europe. "We need no Hitler to turn and twist the beautiful white bars of our flag into a hideous, flamboyant and meaningless swastika." One of the few critiques of the mobilization came from the Catholic Worker House. Since Catholic Worker founder Dorothy Day was an avowed pacifist, she urged members of the movement to resist the slide to war and wrote this in the periodical *Catholic Worker*, which was distributed at all of the houses. Day's pacifism, which remained firm even after Pearl Harbor, created serious divisions within the movement—with some of the young men rejecting her advice and marching off to war, while others sought conscientious-objector status. In Sacramento, Day's views had little appeal and even rubbed some the wrong way. When Arthur Ronz was asked how many copies of the pacifistic *Catholic Worker* he wanted, he gently noted to Day, "As for the papers—if they are as strong pro-pacifist as they were in the last two issues, I'm afraid a few would be enough."[49] Ultimately, even Ronz, who agonized over it for a time, reported for induction.

Wartime mobilization brought scores of Catholic young men into the armed forces, gradually emptying clubs and organizations of their male membership. As young men reported to induction and training centers, anxious parents and sweethearts appeared in greater numbers at church services. Holy Spirit in Land Park sponsored a popular form of Catholic devotion called a novena (nine days of prayer) "to ask His blessing and protection for our country" and "for the men in the armed services . . . particularly the boys from Holy Spirit parish."[50] Other Sacramento parishes held similar services for young men sent off to war and provided the consolations of religion when a Sacramentan fell in battle.

Catholic chaplains dealt with the needs of enlisted men and service personnel who now roamed the town. Another area of concern was the well-being of young women, many of whom came to the capital city for the jobs generated by McClellan Field, which was hiring young women from all over the country to work in its warehouses and shops. Although McClellan eventually built dormitories to house and chaperone them, Catholic welfare chief Thomas Markham occasionally received letters from anxious pastors asking that their young female parishioners be given lodging with good Catholic families. Markham (soon to depart for the army himself) urged Catholic citizens to open their homes to the young workers. Perhaps experience in the confessionals and in private conferences with soldiers led him to urge that Catholic men needed housing as well. Although he noted that "the plight of the men is not so serious inasmuch as men do not need the same protection as women," he warned that "no young man can live in an unhealthy environment without becoming affected in some way. Weaker men are contaminated." Catholic priests tried to direct young service people away from the gambling joints and houses of prostitution on the West End. One successful program was launched by the Reverend Richard Dwyer.[51]

Dwyer converted the northern side of the cathedral basement into a drop-in recreation center for servicemen and -women and named it the St. Thomas Aquinas Library and Catholic Center for Military Personnel. Formally inaugurated in July 1943, the Aquinas Center offered service people religious events, communion breakfasts, roundtable and book discussions, and catechetical instruction. It also provided religious articles and counseling for scared or homesick GIs. The basement had a three thousand–volume lending library, a social center for conversation and dancing, a place to write letters, and even a dark room (the largest in the West!) for camera buffs anxious to develop their own film. By July 1944 more than thirty thousand service people had visited the cathedral basement.[52] Dwyer and fellow assistant the Reverend Vito Mistretta linked up the lonely GIs with friendly families who had them over for Sunday dinners. After the war both priests kept in touch with many of the young men who returned to Sacramento—presiding at their marriages and baptizing their offspring.

CARING FOR THE JAPANESE

The war also focused special attention on another ministry of the Catholic Church: care of the city's Japanese population. Japanese settlement in Sacramento had begun in 1884 when the Japanese government lifted emigration restrictions. Many Japanese had come to the United States to make money, and California was a desirable destination. The number of Japanese working in Central Valley agriculture and in Sacramento began to grow steadily. By 1910, 1,437 Japanese resided in Sacramento and 3,874 in the county. Whereas Sacramento had the third-largest number of Japanese citizens in the state, they were the number-one ethnic group in the city, registering 5.6 percent of the total. As with most immigrants, newly arriving Japanese settled in the older housing of the West End. Japanese children attended Lincoln School and met the kind but firm Nettie Hopley, who worked closely with them. (So grateful were the Japanese parents for Hopley's kindness that they awarded her a trip to Japan.)[53]

The strong growth of the Japanese community evoked similar reactions as had the presence of the Chinese in the nineteenth century. A period of initial acceptance was soon overtaken by concerns about labor competition from the unskilled and lower-waged Issei (the term for a first-generation Japanese) and sentiments of racism. Sacramentans were particularly hard on the Japanese, spearheading efforts to restrict the economic life of the growing community in the state, pressuring local politicians to curtail residency in various city neighborhoods, and contributing to state-wide efforts to limit Japanese landownership in California.[54] The steadily escalating antagonism against the Japanese was the context for a new goal of St. Stephen's, the Catholic church in the heart of the West End.

The increasing number of Japanese and their restriction within the parameters of "Japan-Town" compelled them to adapt their lives and resources accordingly. A thriving commercial and service sector developed within this part of town, catering to Japanese and those Caucasians who chose to frequent their businesses, which included barbershops and laundries. Religious institutions were also part of the mix. The most important religious organization was the Japanese Buddhist mission, begun in 1899 and located just a few blocks north of St. Stephen's. It later moved to Fourth and O, where a permanent temple was established in a former residence.[55] Upper- and middle-class Japanese who attended the temple stressed Buddhism's core belief in "a gospel of universal brotherhood" and sought to dispel the notion that they were "heathens." Nonetheless, Christian churches in Sacramento engaged in active proselytization of the Japanese community. The Methodists opened missions in 1893 and 1894 with Japanese pastors, the Japanese Independent Mission opened in 1900, in 1911 the Presbyterian Mission opened, and a Bible Institute began in 1920, which evolved into a Japanese Baptist church.[56] City churches also provided an array of social services, including English-language instruction, employment referrals, and general urban-adjustment assistance.

Given their history of anti-Asian sentiments, Catholics did not have much official contact with Sacramento's Japanese community. In fact, during California's general debate about the growing number and influence of the Japanese, Sacramento Catholic spokesman Thomas Connelly indicated his belief, like that of the McClatchys and others, that it was impossible to assimilate them. Connelly darkly warned of "race suicide" if "Asiatics" continued to reproduce at a faster rate than the white population. The editor even implied that "Asiatic control" of California would be a sign of divine displeasure with Caucasians, whose lower birthrates were the result of artificial birth control, "the most terrible of sins—that of murder in its worst form."

The growing number of Japanese around St. Stephen's did not go unnoticed by the sisters and priests who visited the mission. In 1914 the Reverend Albert Breton visited Sacramento in the midst of pastoral work among Japanese citizens on the West Coast.[57] Breton, a native of France, had joined the Paris-based Society for the Foreign Missions in 1901. After his ordination to the priesthood in 1905, his superiors sent him to Japan, where he remained until illness forced him to return to France. After his recuperation Breton called on Pope Pius X in Rome, who informed him of the pastoral needs of Japanese emigrants in the American West. Still unable to go back to full-time missionary work, Breton worked with Japanese Catholics in western cities for ten years until he was finally permitted to return to Japan.

Breton, who would later become a bishop in Japan, arrived on the doorstep of the Franciscan Sisters' convent in 1914 and urged Mother Pacifica Kirschel, the superior of St. Stephen's, to accept Japanese children into the school.[58] Although sympathetic, Kirschel pointed out the language barrier—already a difficulty in the school with a wide array of European languages but even more so for a non-Western language. Breton returned the next summer with two Japanese sister catechists who formed a kindergarten in St. Stephen Hall and taught religion to a bevy of four- and five-year-olds in their Japanese. They gradually introduced the children to English and made it possible for them to join in the regular school classes at St. Stephen's. By 1917 the number was up to thirty-four.

However, when the Japanese catechists left, the Franciscan Sisters were unable to continue the work, and the Japanese kindergarten closed in 1924. It was revived in the summer of 1928, when the Reverend William Stoecke, a priest of the Divine Word (a missionary order that worked in Asia), offered to send priests to Sacramento to restart the project.[59] In June 1929 the Franciscans sent Sister Roberta Clauter to begin the program afresh. A disciple of Breton, Sister Clauter had run a Japanese kindergarten in Los Angeles, where she learned enough about the Japanese culture and language to work effectively. The old St. Stephen building had been sold to Japanese theater owners, and plans were made to place the new Japanese kindergarten in the Portuguese Holy Ghost Society hall.

Sister Clauter began her Sacramento work in August 1929, hosting a tea and inviting Japanese women to come and hear of the new venture. Only eight women attended, and none of them offered to send their children to the new school. Sister Clauter then began to canvass the neighborhood around the Grace Day Home for pupils. The Japanese had little interest in a Catholic-run kindergarten so far from the heart of Japan-Town (a seven-block walk), so Clauter quickly solved the problem by obtaining a room at Holy Angels School. The Catholic press reported on the "fine work being done among the Japanese in Sacramento," referring to the "five little cherry blossoms" that formed the first class."[60]

Armstrong helped by providing a better site for the work. With a three thousand–dollar grant from the national office of the Propagation of the Faith, he erected a two-room bungalow on leased land across from the Grace Day Home. By August 1930 twenty-four Japanese children came into the school program, which offered instruction from kindergarten to third grade. Armstrong dedicated the new site and officially named it Holy Family Japanese Catholic Mission. The next year the school affiliated with the Grace Day Home and received some Community Chest funds. Clauter's pioneering work was supplemented for a time by Father Stoecke's regular visits. When Stoecke withdrew, the Reverend Thomas Kirby replaced him.

Kirby's work with the Japanese would be the entr'acte of his long stretch of administrative service to the Catholics of Sacramento.

Clauter and Kirby worked well together, as the priest managed to supplement the diocesan subsidy with donations from the Catholic Daughters of America and other benefactors. They hired a Japanese lay teacher to assist them, and the sisters were able to make a number of conversions among the Japanese, their Grace Day Home chapel being the site of baptisms, confirmations, and weddings of the Japanese converts. The mission grew steadily, if not spectacularly.[61]

In 1935 when the lease came up for renewal, the diocese purchased an adjacent lot and transferred the bungalow, fence, shrubbery, and even sidewalks to the new location. The mission offered religious instruction through regular school and Sunday school classes and also dispensed charity. In 1939 Sister Teresita Beeler replaced Sister Clauter. Beeler would be on hand to witness the end of the mission, which occurred during the internment crisis of World War II.

With the attack on Pearl Harbor, Japanese Sacramentans came under increasing suspicion of disloyalty, fanned by the reporting of the *Sacramento Bee*.[62] Anxieties about fifth-column activities led to the now infamous Executive Order 9066, signed by President Roosevelt in March 1942. This gave the U.S. military the right to designate "restricted" military areas and to evacuate all suspected people—aliens and U.S. citizens alike—from those areas. On March 3, 1942, the Western Defense Command mandated the evacuation of *all* Japanese. Sacramento's Japanese community received its official notice on May 7, 1942. Preparations for the evacuation were particularly hard on the small group of Japanese Catholics that had been slowly and steadily increasing. Ironically, the Holy Family Mission was a site for the Office of Evacuation, and on March 31, 1942, more than one thousand Japanese came to receive directions for relocation. The evacuees were directed to report to Camp Walerga, an assembly center fourteen miles northeast of Sacramento between the newly opened McClellan Field and the rural community of Antelope. Here, two hundred barracks were hastily erected in an oak grove to accommodate the group.

Kirby and the sisters helped the Catholic Japanese cope with the uprooting of their lives. Scores who lost their jobs (even those holding civil-service jobs were dismissed) appealed to the mission for food and shelter. As evacuation day approached, a number of Japanese stored some of their most valuable possessions in the mission, and Kirby personally interceded with authorities in a number of cases. On May 10 a small number of Japanese Catholics held a farewell May Crowning at the mission chapel, but already the effects of relocation were felt, as the sisters' chronicle notes: "Those from the country could not enter this zone."[63] Three days later Sacramento's Japanese reported to the Memorial Auditorium, where buses transported them to Camp Walerga. By May 16 the evacuation was complete. In early June Kirby and Beeler began a summer-school class for nearly fifty children at Camp Walerga. Meanwhile, Kirby held regular mass at the camp.

Even after many of the Japanese were transferred to a remote internment camp three hundred miles north of Sacramento at Tulelake, Kirby continued to raise funds to continue the Catholic ministry among them.[64] A grant from the American Board of Catholic Missions helped underwrite the expenses of Maryknoll priests in the camps. Kirby and the sisters made periodic visits to the camp and through letters inquired about the status of the Japanese Catholics they had worked with in Sacramento. A Maryknoll priest, the Reverend Joseph A. Hunt, carried on the religious instruction and ministry, assisted by a Mrs. Hiroshima, who taught catechism to the Japanese youngsters. "I baptized Jean and Lily Tamaki before Mass yesterday," Hunt wrote to Kirby, regarding two young girls whom he had known in Sacramento. "The mother and other members of the family were there. They say the mother shed tears of emotion and all were happy."[65] The Tulelake facility finally closed in March 1946, and Kirby and the sisters welcomed back some of their flock. The recently baptized Tamaki girls were admitted to St. Patrick School and later St. Francis High School. But others had no wish to return, and Sacramento's Holy Family Mission never reopened.

CONCLUSION

The grueling experiences of the Depression and World War II significantly transformed California's capital city. The city had known economic downturns in the past, but nothing prepared it for the magnitude of the collapse of the 1930s. Although no one knew it then, it was the beginning of the end for the railroad yards—Sacramento's economic mainstay since the mid-nineteenth century. Likewise, the canning industry began its slow, steady decline, in part because new processing techniques gradually replaced traditional canning methods. As the older patterns of Sacramento life faded, new ones appeared. The advent of the three major military installations was destined to reorient the area's economic life and create new job opportunities that drew people out of the city proper. Newcomers included not only military personnel—some of whom returned to the capital once the war was over—but also a new array of civilian workers who made the Sacramento area their permanent home. Quietly as well, Latino/a workers made their presence felt in area agricultural and industrial work, welcomed by the 1942 Bracero Program, which invited Mexicans to help alleviate U.S. labor shortages.

Catholics, as part of the private network of charity that had sustained Sacramento's social safety net, could do comparatively little to alleviate the suffering of the period. Even in the midst of economic gloom, however, traditional patterns of church-city cooperation manifested themselves. The changing demographics and economic realities in Sacramento posed a more pressing challenge, especially during the war years.

On August 14, 1945, the day President Truman announced the final victory over Japan, cathedral assistant Reverend Vito Mistretta climbed into the cathedral tower and began pealing the church's bells, which had stood silent since 1927. Below on K Street wild celebrations erupted, as Sacramento, the state, and the world prepared for a new era. The bells of August chimed out the old order and chimed in the new.

CHAPTER 7

Carving a Space and Creating Community

The Catholic Church and the North Area, 1940–1970

"The spirit engendered almost immediately"

In post–World War II Sacramento, Catholic parishes popped up like dandelions in suburban lawns. One of the first was named for the legendary St. Philomena. Its origins were typical of suburban parishes all over the country. Begun in 1947 in the Bungalow Club, a dance hall on Auburn Boulevard to the northeast of the city, it caught the crest of a wave of suburban migration. By 1953 the church presided over a highly visible six-acre tract along El Camino Avenue, one of the major commercial arteries of Sacramento's burgeoning North Area. Its school packed in nearly eight hundred pupils, and its parish plant included a hall, convent, rectory, and church—all designed in a modified Spanish-mission motif. The three bells in its campanile, erected in 1961, rang out the church times for the surrounding homes. Next door, a girls' Catholic high school, Loretto, soon welcomed uniformed young women from some of Sacramento's "best" Catholic families.

This tale of brick and mortar, replicated all over suburban Catholic America, was only the veneer of an even more important story. Local

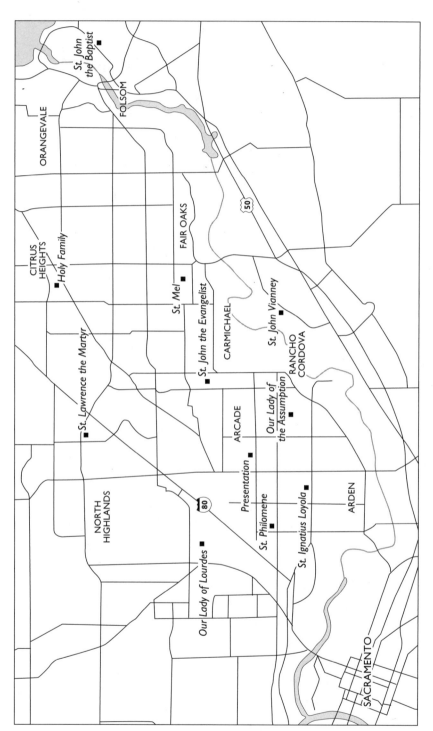

MAP 2 Catholic Churches in the northwest corridor of Sacramento County

Catholic leaders seemed to understand that something special was taking place, as the editor of the Catholic newspaper declared: "The founding of the new parish was not so astounding physically. What made the new parish unique was the spirit engendered almost immediately in the people. Content to haul chairs every Sunday and assist at a Mass in a still warm night club, the parishioners showed as much interest in the new parish as they did in their own new homes."[1] St. Philomene's and its sister parishes in the growing North Area not only were spiritual homes but also helped build a sense of community in "fractionated" areas struggling to create social networks and adjust to their new environment.

Sacramento suburbanized in virtually every direction except west, enhancing its status as a major metropolitan center. By 1963 Yolo and Placer counties would be tributary to it. Historian Thomas Norris notes simply of postwar Sacramento that "urban growth slipped the bounds of the city limits." Between 1940 and 1970 the population of the county skyrocketed from 170,333 to 634,373. Home building grew exponentially during the postwar era, as a 1957 account relates: "Homebuilding has set the pace in the construction industry since World War II. The city hit its high with 1,947 single dwelling units in 1950 and the county's record of 6,437 single units was established in 1955." The article also notes that subdivision starts, sporadic since 1850, took off at a sustained pace after the war, growing "from nine in 1945, . . . [to] 1955 with the development of 147 new subdivisions."[2] Growth had been especially fast and furious in the wider region where St. Philomene's began, called the North Area. This fan-shaped section, located across the American River northeast of Sacramento, extended east to the Sierra foothills and included the townships of Arcade, Center, Mississippi, Dry Creek, and Sylvan. Initially framed on the north and south by Auburn and Folsom roads and bounded on the west by the American River, the North Area also encompassed older communities such as Orangevale, Fair Oaks, Citrus Heights, Carmichael, and North Sacramento.

Between 1947 and 1961 the Sacramento Diocese opened nine new parishes in the North Area. In addition, one parish, St. Mel's, was raised from mission to parochial status and had to build a new church on a larger parcel of property; another parish founded in 1857, St. John's in Folsom, built an entirely new church and acquired additional property for a new school and convent.

TABLE 7.1 | PAROCHIAL DEVELOPMENT IN THE NORTH AREA, 1947–1961

YEAR FOUNDED	PARISH	ACRES PURCHASED
1947	St. Philomene, Arden Arcade	6
1949	Holy Family, Citrus Heights	3
1950	Our Lady of the Assumption, Carmichael	16
1954	St. Ignatius of Loyola, Arden Arcade	10
1955	St. Lawrence the Martyr, North Highlands	10
1956 (procured new property)	St. Mel, Fair Oaks (founded in 1921; raised from a mission to parochial status in 1947)	4
1957	Our Lady of Lourdes, Del Paso Heights	6.19
1958	St. John Vianney, Rancho Cordova	17/21
1958 (built new church); 1962 (built school, convent, and later a parish hall)	St. John the Baptist, Folsom (founded in 1857)	9.92 for the church and 20 for the school, convent, and hall
1960	St. John the Evangelist, Carmichael	10
1961	Presentation, Arden Arcade	6.75

These parishes provided spiritual homes, religious education, and social outlets for Sacramento's suburbanized Catholics. They also provided the staging ground for what historian Hal Rothman has called "communities of affinity"—the linkage with people who did not necessarily share your neighborhood or work space but who shared religious values and the common language of liturgical symbolism, the church year, and the ritualization of the passages of life. This the Catholic Church brought to an area where community life was harder to sustain because of spatial diffusion and dwellings that emphasized privacy.[3]

A NEW ECONOMIC BASE CREATES SUBURBIA

Suburbanization had actually begun in Sacramento in the late nineteenth century with the "streetcar suburb" of Oak Park. In 1911 a massive annexation included Oak Park and other areas to the south and east of the city limits. Farther east, toward the railroad hub of Folsom, the small fruit colonies of Fair Oaks and Orangevale had been on the map since the 1880s. To the north the large Del Paso Grant had been sold and broken up in 1910, creating the communities of North Sacramento, Citrus Heights, and Carmichael.[4] By the beginning of World War II the eastern part of Sacramento County had pockets of settlement between truck farms, hops fields, and orchards. It was also overlaid with school and utility districts.

The huge employment demands of the military bases in the North Area shifted population in that direction. McClellan Air Force Base employed 22,000 by 1943, each person working forty-eight hours per week, with around-the-clock operations. This labor force included large numbers of civilian women and schoolgirls. By 1953 McClellan encompassed 2,000 acres and continued to employ a large workforce—16,000 Sacramentans, more than a quarter of them women, with an annual payroll of $75 million. McClellan also pumped in $14 million in purchases from local businesses. In 1955 another $20 million expansion of the already enormous air base allowed it to stock more supplies than the nation's two largest mail-order houses combined. McClellan was by then the county's single biggest industry.[5]

Steadily, Mather also expanded its holdings of Sacramento property, building longer and longer runways for the huge military planes that landed regularly. However, Mather's workforce, military and civilian, was never quite as large as the giant McClellan. The Signal Depot reached its high point of 1,649 employees in 1945. By 1950 these bases employed about 11 percent of the county's total population. Until the base closures of the 1990s, these installations were the economic mainstay of Sacramento County. In fact, government at every level (federal, state, and local) provided most of the jobs Sacramentans had, displacing railroad and cannery work, which had been Sacramento's lifeblood.

The aerospace industry came to Sacramento as well, bringing more jobs and wealth to the county—especially the North Area. Thanks to the active lobbying of Sacramento mayor Bert Geisreiter and the Chamber of Commerce, the Pasadena-based Aerojet General Corporation announced its decision to build a testing facility on 7,200 acres formerly owned by the Natomas Company along Coloma Trail, sixteen miles east of the city. The $6.6 million Nimbus plant employed scores of local construction and building firms. Aerojet flourished after the war, receiving massive doses of federal money for contract work and security around its property. By 1957 these monies translated into a payroll of $36 million. For a time, Aerojet was one of the largest private-sector employers in Sacramento County. Rumbling sounds of Polaris, Titan, and Apollo test engines jarred the windows of the new suburban homes that went up in nearby Orangevale and its locale. Aerojet was later joined by McDonnell Douglas, which also benefited from government aerospace contracts.[6] Other industrial firms came to Sacramento after the war, providing good jobs and demands for new housing.[7] The result of the good wages and benefits that government and private-industry work provided is evident in the sharp spike in consumption in Sacramento County. From 1950 to 1960 retail sales jumped 46 percent. And from 1950 to 1962 the number of telephones in the county rose 33 percent. The local economy was clearly growing.

NEW INFRASTRUCTURE

These developments were preceded and accompanied by a significant reworking of the infrastructure of the region. Water projects, especially the famed Central Valley Project, controlled and redistributed the raging waters of the Sacramento River and its tributaries. The Central Valley Project created a more predictable water flow and likewise the generation of hydroelectric current that fed the increasing demands of growing Sacramento and its environs. In 1955 a huge appropriation poured $58,280,000 into the construction of the new Folsom Dam on the American River. Likewise, an additional afterbay dam, called Nimbus Dam, was created downriver, and its powerhouse generated even more electricity. The city of Folsom's economy, formerly dependent on the state prison and railroad work, now quickened as construction workers and aerospace employees moved into its vicinity. The recreational and developmental possibilities opened up by the dam poured millions of dollars into the once sleepy Gold Rush city.[8]

The Depression-era Works Progress Administration built schools, laid water mains, improved public recreational areas, and assisted in the development of air transportation to Sacramento. It also helped to create the North Area through a steadily improving road system. Freeway construction favored northeastern routes to accommodate the growing workforce around McClellan, Mather, and Aerojet. In 1955 the Elvas Freeway opened, spanning the American River and connecting with U.S. Route 40, thus tying downtown Sacramento more closely with the growing suburb of North Sacramento. It also linked up with the wide lanes of Auburn Boulevard, an arterial road that moved diagonally out of the city to nearby Placer County and the railroad city of Roseville. The 1956 Federal Interstate Highway Act pushed through Interstate 80, which stretched from San Francisco through Sacramento to Reno in time for the Winter Olympics at Squaw

Valley in 1960. Highway 50, the old Coloma Trail, jutted eastward toward the foothills and opened a corridor to Lake Tahoe by 1960. These two freeways, especially the heavily traveled Interstate 80, substantially contributed to the strong development of the northeast suburban corridor. Later, Interstate 5, which snaked up the center of the state, joined the spaghetti bowl of freeways and highways that met in the downtown.

The North Area overspread rapidly with new homes, roads, businesses, schools, emporia, and other vestiges of suburban civilization. Sacramento had its own "crabgrass frontier."[9]

THE DEVELOPING HOME MARKET IN THE NORTH AREA

As soon as World War II's guns were silent, the North Area burst into life, connecting the pockets of settlement that had been in place before the war. Developers Wright and Kimbrough established the Arden Park tract, a substantially middle-class housing development bounded by Arden Way, Watt Avenue, Eastern Avenue, and Fair Oaks Boulevard. West of Watt Avenue they began a new lower-priced development. Wright and Kimbrough marketing in the Arden-Arcade area helped kick off the rush to Sacramento's northeastern hinterlands.

Shopping centers also stimulated suburban growth. The Town and County Village was a ten-acre site on Fulton and Marconi, created by developer Jere Strizek. The center was an instant success, with individual shops playing off a rustic western motif (surplus railroad ties and wagon wheels). Country Club Centre, a $4 million project on Watt and El Camino, began building in 1951. Smaller retail centers and supermarkets soon dotted the area as well. The commercial centers provided shopping facilities for many of the rapidly growing residential tracts in the area. Strizek followed his Town and Country Village with a succession of profitable housing developments. In all, Strizek may have constructed a thousand homes in the immediate area of his highly successful shopping mall.

Strizek also built extensively in the rapidly growing area around McClellan Air Force Base, newly reenergized by the onset of the Korean War. In August 1950 he purchased a two thousand–acre tract near the base and with the encouragement of authorities at the field launched a series of projects even larger in scale than his previous ones. Some of the acreage he resold to realty firms that constructed homes, apartments, and

North Sacramento aerial view, looking northeast, Del Paso Boulevard in center, 1950. Courtesy of Sacramento Archives and Museum Collection Center, *Sacramento Bee* Collection.

four-family housing units. So intensive was the development that at one point a new home was completed every twelve hours. From an uninhabited tract on the map in 1950, the population in 1953 was an estimated seventy-five thousand. Strizek even took a hand in securing a federal post office in 1951, conferring the name "North Highlands" on the new suburban enclave—a blending of the two names of his subdivisions North Haven and the Highlands.[10]

Neat rows of tract homes arranged on the curvilinear streets of North Area communities such as Citrus Heights, Del Paso Heights, Northgate, and North Highlands welcomed people from all parts of the country. Many were veterans who had passed through the sunny climes of the state capital during World War II. Some were active-duty military assigned to one of the area's three bases. Still others were engineers and technicians needed for aerospace work. Many rejoiced to be away from the high-density urban centers of the East and Midwest. Sacramentans eagerly purchased the homes put up by builders such as Jere Strizek, Manuel Jacinto, and Milton Brock—the kings of the home-building boom of the postwar era. Sacramento's generally pleasant climate was a welcome respite from the cold and snow of the areas generically referred to as "back east."

But these homes were also self-enclosed enclaves, ensuring by their design the security and privacy that so many suburbanites desired. Sample blueprints that appeared weekly in the *Sacramento Bee* highlighted the emphasis on privacy in suburban living. One article commented, "One of the newest features used in this plan is the placing of the living room entirely at the rear. This is desirable because it means privacy from the street side." It concluded, "The old front porch is gradually giving way to this plan. After all, automobiles and very little foot traffic no longer make sitting on the porch particularly attractive."[11] Further, air-conditioning allowed residents to hide out in their homes, offices, or stores from late April until the early fall to escape the sweltering Sacramento Valley heat.

THE CRISIS OF COMMUNITY

The rapid growth also brought with it the predictable problems of civic management. Increased population, with its concomitant demands for services, called for a major reorganization of the somewhat sleepy county government. Sacramento County government had originally been set up to deal with rural realities. The first effort to cope with the growth was annexation. In 1946 the city resumed a steady program of annexation begun in 1911, raising the total number of square miles under its jurisdiction from 13.9 to slightly more than 23 by 1957. Suburbanites themselves began to put the brakes on annexation, and it slowed considerably. Sacramento acquired its last major addition in 1964, when it added the former suburb of North Sacramento. Growth issues continued to be on the front burner for county officials. Reporter and later state official Hale Champion commented on the inability of the schools in the North Area to keep up with the tremendous growth. In September and October 1955 the *Sacramento Bee* ran a series of nineteen front-page articles by associate editor Ralph Bladgen, noting the incapacity of localities to deal with the "human avalanche" that came to the North Area. Bladgen observed the rapid growth of the "urban or fringe areas beyond the 1950 census definitions," stretching eastward from North Highlands to Orangevale. "They constitute a lush jungle of subdivisions, shopping centers, commercial strips, septic tanks, sewer lines, labyrinthine tax codes and accumulating irritations, costs, and inadequate services which pester the inhabitants."[12]

The *Sacramento Bee* articles encouraged efforts to deal with the rapid growth. Elements of the North Area Chamber of Commerce, the Sacramento Area Planning Association, and the Sacramento County Grand Jury all pointed to the inadequacy of services and governance. City, county, and private leaders formed the Sacramento Metropolitan Area Advisory Committee in 1956, chaired by San Juan school superintendent James R. Cowan. The group engaged Chicago's Public Administration Service (PAS) to evaluate Sacramento's needs. The PAS report issued in the spring of 1957 cited the "lack of cohesion in the Sacramento metropolitan area," pointing to the existence of "fractionated governments." There were 208 units of local government in the county: the county, 5 municipalities, 45 school districts, and 157 special districts. The primary recommendation of the report was a dramatic merger between city and county, designed to accentuate the economic interdependence of the region and eliminate wasteful duplication of services. This plan and other similar efforts to consolidate the suburban areas were never implemented.[13]

The study and public debate over the future of the metropolitan region—especially the fast-growing North Area—generally focused on government and public policy issues. But it was also "humanized" to some degree by journalists such as John Cook, who put his finger on the quality of interactions in suburbia. Using North Highlands as a case study, he observed that the tracts were "seemingly endless and a little monotonous. From the air it looks as though an imaginative child had been playing with blocks. . . . [There] are Ways, Drives, Boulevards apparently on the theory that such names have more appeal." But, he observed, "there seems to be little time to stop and consider the larger aspects of community living. There is PTA, of course, and Little League and a club or two maybe. There is making a living and having time left over to shop and mow the lawn and wash the car and relax a little."[14]

In fact, initially, many Sacramentans did not find suburbia an easy fit. Many soon discovered that Sacramento's postwar suburbs were also revolving doors. With distressing regularity, military families moved in and out of the government-subsidized homes near the air bases. The government-sponsored work that sustained civilian employee wages was often subject to the changing moods of Congress or the state legislature. Sacramento's metropolitan residents (especially those who worked for private firms like Aerojet) came and went with a great deal of regularity as well. In Rancho Cordova—a suburb created by the proximity of Mather Field and Aerojet—it was discovered that on any given day of the 1958–1959 school year, eighteen students either arrived or departed.[15] Some transplants from other parts of the country found they simply did not like the heat, the long travel times to schools and stores, or being away from their extended families—moving back at the first opportunity.

Even matter-of-fact analysts such as Christian Larsen, the head of the Department of Government and Police Science at Sacramento State College, pondered the absence of meaningful human interaction in Sacramento's suburbs. "The bond that brings a group of people into community is a set of commonly held beliefs regarding activities that presumably contribute to the general welfare of all. These beliefs may be political, social, cultural, religious, or economic, but they must be held widely enough to create a feeling of group identity, purpose and destiny—a sense of community."[16] The suburbs needed a soul.

Some did attempt to create common bonds in the area. Carmichael, for example, marketed a romantic western motif for its commercial district and also created a huge public park in the "center" of its amorphous community. Older communities such as Orangevale, Fair Oaks, and Citrus Heights played up their fruit-colony origins. All of them had local festivals, parades, and civic celebrations to try to create a sense of civic awareness. Employers also tried to build support systems for their transplanted workforces. Procter and Gamble, the Ohio-based soap giant, which opened a factory in Sacramento in the 1950s, organized regular gatherings for picnics, sporting events, and holiday get-togethers for its midwestern transfers.[17] Aerojet built an employee recreational center with a huge swimming pool and organized family events. Likewise, McClellan Field had choruses, bowling leagues, and various clubs to help its workforce adjust to the new environment. Schools, parks, and shopping centers provided crossroads for suburban life. Little League, PTA groups, service clubs, and other voluntary organizations also brought people together. So did suburban churches.

Churches, because they often had a unique claim on people's loyalties and sense of obligation, created community based on commonly held beliefs and practices. Sacramento's suburbs sprouted churches as rapidly as they developed schools and shopping centers.[18] Mainline Protestant groups viewed suburban growth as a special challenge and set up a version of the church comity urged by the Federal Council of Churches. Church comity sought to avoid duplication of services and overbuilding and urged like-minded churches to come together under one roof for worship and Christian education. The Sierra-Arden Congregational Community Church, founded in 1946, welcomed Methodists, Episcopalians, Baptists, Presbyterians, Evangelical Reformed, and Evangelical United Brethren.[19]

Catholics in Sacramento replicated the traditionally high rates of church attendance common in other parts of the country. The average Catholic's sense of obligation to attend mass (it was considered a "mortal" sin to deliberately skip Sunday worship) quickly led them to find a spiritual home. After home, school, and shopping center, newcomers often looked for a nearby church and often a parochial school for their children. The rapidly increasing Catholic population created permanent parishes, schools, and even transparochial institutions in the North Area. They bought property, built on it, and kept the doors open despite the impermanence of parishioners.

Investment in property was soon followed by an invitation for individual Catholics to invest "sweat equity" in the land and to make it their own in a particular way—to create even before the "postmodern" suburbs the communities of affinity described by Hal Rothman.[20] In Sacramento, as in Rothman's Las Vegas, communities of affinity were created not by people who lived in proximity to each other but by those who created the "feeling of group identity, purpose, and destiny." Rothman did not see this kind of community in the immediate postwar suburbs, and Larsen suggested it was lacking in the Greater Sacramento of the 1940s and 1950s. In fact, however, another look suggests that churches brought people into contact with their neighbors in ways that shopping malls or even seasonal groups like Little League or other local volunteer efforts rarely did.

CREATING CATHOLIC SPACE

Catholics invested in large parcels of suburban land and developed them extensively. The centralized leadership of the diocese directed and monitored every step through a carefully conceived "master plan." Each suburban parish acquired a substantial tract of property and built according to this plan, which provided for not only worship space and a meeting hall but a whole host of buildings for the full complement of parish life: a church, a school, a rectory, a convent, and a social hall. The creation of these institutions gave North Area suburbanites a communitarian outlet for expression of their faith, and also a place to invest in the education of their children. Even parishioners who may not have been particularly "religious" could become quite active in endeavors to build and improve school facilities, contributing through a variety of fund-raisers to the mission of the school. In fact, the master plan was key to assembling, forming, and motivating a volunteer community in the Sacramento suburbs.

The master plan was a manifestation of a deeply held religious faith and a traditional Catholic way of claiming space. However, seen as a dimension of the functional role religious traditions have played in the creation of urban life, the master plan was shorthand for the various kinds of growth—number of parishioners, organizational, planning and fund-raising, building—that took place in the suburbs. Viewed only in dollars and cents, the investments it represented were considerable. The eleven parish master plans implemented between 1947 and 1961 in the North

Area (see table 7.1) constituted a major contribution to the development of the area and the creation of suburban community.

Few institutions, even other religious denominations, could match this aspect of Catholic communal activity in the years after the war. It is hard to determine who "invented" the master-plan concept or when it became a common feature of diocesan development. It may have spontaneously generated in a variety of locales as soon as church building took place in areas with less density than urban centers. As opposed to urban models where the parish "complex" was tightly contained on a single urban block, the suburban parish "plant" had access to space to create distance between church, school, hall, rectory, and convent. The added area was also a necessity for automobile parking, a sine qua non of suburban life. In Phoenix, for example, Monsignor Robert J. Donohoe was sent to establish St. Agnes Parish on the outskirts of the city on only two and a half acres. His bishop, Philadelphian Daniel Gercke, had explained that two and a half acres "is enough in Philadelphia and it's enough in Phoenix." But Donohoe convinced the eastern-born bishop that the tiny acreage would leave no space for playgrounds and a parking lot. Gercke then allowed him to purchase additional property. Afterward, diocesan purchasing agents in the Tucson and Phoenix diocese made ten-acre plots de rigueur for future parish development. In Seattle, which had a community similar to Sacramento in terms of the size of its Catholic populace and its dependence on defense spending, new Catholic parishes took place on expanded acreage. St. Paul Parish for the Catholics of the Rainier Beach district was built on fifteen acres of "one of the most coveted sites in Seattle," with a commanding view of the mountains and the city. The proposed master plan for St. Bernadette Parish in suburban Seattle was worked out on a six-acre tract and included a temporary church, a ten-classroom school, and a parish hall.[21] The purchase of six acres for Sacramento's St. Philomene's was the beginning of this trend in Sacramento. Even that acreage—mammoth by city standards—would require augmentation as the parish grew.

In western dioceses confronted by the same dynamic growth as Sacramento, Catholic land management was largely directed by officials in the central or chancery offices. In some instances, it was the bishop himself. In Sacramento, Bishop Robert Armstrong moved quickly to keep up with population growth through the foundation of a succession of suburban parishes. He personally negotiated with the Jesuits to staff a new parish in the heart of the growth area and provided them with land for a new church and school. Bishop Joseph McGucken, his successor (and a former Los Angeles auxiliary bishop), came particularly well trained in real estate matters. McGucken may have been the first to compare notes with planning officials, as a 1962 letter to the Sacramento County Planning Commission indicates: "We do make an effort to acquire parcels of land from 8 to 10 acres for future parish sites." Writing to the Jesuit provincial about the plans of the Sacramento Jesuits to seek another spot for an anticipated high school, McGucken urged the Jesuits to build the school near their thriving parish and with easy access to suburban parents. "In my own judgement, I think the site which you now have has the advantage of being in the *center,* rather than off at the edge of a large population."[22] Armstrong's and McGucken's interests were well served by the chancellors of the diocese, Monsignor Thomas A. Kirby and his successor, Monsignor Cornelius P. Higgins. Basically self-taught land speculators, these two men pored over utility maps, consulted with friendly real estate agents and developers, and regularly hobnobbed with local politicians in order to project the growth of the diocese.

Kirby purchased a great deal of land throughout the Greater Sacramento area for parish plants and other institutions of Catholic life. For example, three years before the parish of St. John Vianney's formed, he had already picked out the seventeen-acre Rancho Cordova site on which it currently sits.[23] Thanks to his contacts with developers like Jere Strizek, Kirby was able to buy land before it was subdivided, thereby avoiding the inflated prices that came with impending development. When the Reverend Daniel Twomey was transferred from rural Lincoln to found St. Philomene's, Kirby urged him to touch base with the developer whose Town and Country Village was responsible for the growth in the area covered by the new parish. Twomey complied. "I have been trying to meet Streazick [*sic*] before I make any arrangements and plans for room and board and some place for Sunday Mass. I would like to meet him independently of you people and pitch my own line of woo." Kirby wanted a good relationship with developers and hoped that they would recognize the enhancement to property values and the stability Catholic parishes would bring. He also wanted and expected to receive advance notice of impending development. When this did not happen, he openly criticized developers, accusing them of being heedless of the real needs of many of their Catholic purchasers.[24]

IMPLEMENTING THE MASTER PLAN

The implementation of the master plan varied with each parish. Some of the variation had to do with the skills and persuasiveness of the founding pastor. In other instances, the plan was either expedited or slowed by shifting demographic and economic realities.

For example, Twomey's master plan for St. Philomene's included an elementary school, rectory, convent, church (in a modified mission style), and a Catholic high school. Twomey wasted no time. By September 1948 he had the congregation under roof in a temporary hall built on the site. He announced building plans for the first of a series of school buildings on the property in late 1948, and in February 1949 obtained the services of the sisters of the Institute of the Blessed Virgin Mary of Loretto to teach in the school. That August the Loretto Sisters arrived and began phasing in the new elementary school, culminating in the addition of an eighth grade in 1951. In 1952, 530 pupils enrolled, and the design for the church was put out for bids and construction began. By May 1953 the church was ready for dedication.[25] St. Philomene Parish boundaries encompassed such a large territory that soon additional ecclesiastical subdivisions (new parishes) appeared.

To relieve the demand that the population boom imposed on St. Philomene's, the diocese and the California Province of the Society of Jesus (Jesuits) approved plans for a parish, named in honor of St. Ignatius of Loyola. On a ten-acre parcel that had been earlier selected for a new hospital, the Reverends Frederick Cosgrove, S.J., and Joseph T. Keane, S.J., a former chaplain in the United States Navy, laid out a master plan that included a church, grammar school, convent, and four-year high school for boys. By October 1954 two wings of the school had been built, one containing five classrooms, the other to be used as a temporary church. The Sisters of the Holy Name, from Oakland, consented to staff the new school, which soon blossomed to sixteen rooms. In 1956 Cosgrove launched a fund drive for a convent, rectory, and auditorium for the fast-growing school. More than $277,000 in cash and pledges was collected. With the completion of the auditorium, the church moved into the new structure, freeing the school wing for more classrooms. By the next year the parish was large enough to afford its own church. The design called for a twenty thousand–square-foot structure and was one of the largest churches in Sacramento, apart from the cathedral. It was designed to hold more than a thousand communicants. The building reflected the multiple needs of the burgeoning suburban congregation by providing a bride's room and a "crying" room (an area where families with restless children could participate in the mass separated from other parishioners). By the late summer of 1959, barely five years after the parish had been formed, St. Ignatius parishioners were worshiping in their own $400,000 church, surrounded by buildings bustling with schoolchildren.[26]

St. Philomene and St. Ignatius parishes were able to move forward, developing their entire complexes in rapid time. Others parishes' master plans were moved up by the demand for schools. Such was the case with Presentation and St. Mel's.

As with St. Ignatius Parish, Presentation lopped off some of St. Philomene Parish's territory (much to its pastor's displeasure). Formed in 1961, the new complex was planned on 6.75 acres purchased at the corner of Norris and Robertson avenues by Kirby in 1949.[27] The catalyst for the development of this parish was the promise of the Ireland-based Sisters of the Presentation to staff a school if it was built within a year of their offer. Diocesan chancellor and pastor Monsignor Cornelius P. Higgins cleared the hilly acreage and redirected a drainage ditch off the property. Work began quickly on a functional school complex, parish hall (where masses would be celebrated), convent, and rectory. In September 1961 the school opened its doors. The popularity of the school led quickly to another round of building, and four additional classrooms were ready by 1962. By the time he departed Presentation in 1968, Higgins had retired the debt on the buildings and left $35,000 for his successor as a nest egg for a new church, built in the 1970s.

A Catholic church in Fair Oaks had begun in 1921 as a mission to the Folsom parish, St. John the Baptist's. Catholics obtained a charming 1.4-acre parcel in downtown Fair Oaks at the corner of Bridge Street and Grand Avenue, near a bridge spanning the American River. The new mission, named for the traveling Irish missionary St. Mel, held only two hundred people but managed to attract employees of Mather Field and

the state prison.[28] Mass was celebrated twice a month, and catechetical lessons and special sacramental celebrations kept the small Catholic
community intact. Little St. Mel's was a perfect picture of simple, "down-
home" Catholic life in rural Sacramento County before the Depression
and World War II.

But the expansion of Mather Field and later Aerojet required that the
little church become more than a mission. In 1947 Bishop Armstrong
raised St. Mel's to the status of a parish and appointed the Reverend Patrick Cronin as its first full-time pastor. By 1954 the population of Fair
Oaks had grown to five thousand, and by 1959 there were fifteen thousand
people within its post office boundaries. In 1949 the assessed valuation in
the Fair Oaks Fire District, roughly equivalent to the post office zone, was
$1,626,000. By 1959 that figure stood at $8.5 million. Even land considered
worthless for grazing was fetching prices of nearly $3,500 per acre.[29]

The Reverend William Horgan succeeded Cronin in April 1956, just as
Aerojet and the military installations were beginning to break employment records. With no place to expand the church, much less accommodate the needs of children for a school or catechetical instruction, Horgan
purchased a hilly four-acre tract on the corner of Sunset and Pennsylvania avenues in Fair Oaks. Architect Devine drew plans for two units
that would stake a Catholic claim on the hilly property. One structure
was a three-room center for religious-instruction classes, while the other
served as a temporary church, slated for transformation into five classrooms.[30] The functional brick buildings were soon crowded with new
parishioners.

The pace of the master plan was accelerated, however, when Horgan
received a promise of teaching sisters from Doon, Ireland, in the fall of
1959. He moved rapidly to enlarge the school and build a convent. When
the sisters arrived in the late summer of 1959, they found new quarters
and school buildings in readiness.[31] In 1961 the parish built a multipurpose
room on the southern portion of the property that served as the church
until 1974, when the final stage of the parish master plan was completed.

On occasion, the decision to form a parish came somewhat after the
first rush of settlement. North Highlands was an example of this. In
1955 Kirby selected a longtime "missionary" pastor, the Reverend Virgil
Gabrielli, to create a new parish in the shadow of McClellan Air Force

Base. Land acquisition became a problem, as the most desirable acres had already been snapped up or were simply unavailable.[32] Gabrielli initially secured five acres along the main commercial corridor of North Highlands but soon discovered that the acreage was zoned for industrial use. Moreover, local officials refused to allow a school to be built so near an airfield landing zone. Gabrielli continued to work from temporary quarters. Scouring the area, he finally found a ten-acre site on the north edge of the Larchmont Homes subdivision. The land was mostly flat, but it sloped to a high point on which a church could one day be constructed. Gabrielli purchased the property for $21,000, and in February 1956 Bishop Joseph McGucken presided at a groundbreaking. Gabrielli completed a two-building complex, and by the end of September 1956 the St. Lawrence parishioners were under their new roof. The congregation worshiped in these temporary structures until October 1960, when Gabrielli scraped together the funds for a five hundred–seat multipurpose auditorium. Later a convent was added.[33] The church was built in 1987.

The case of the Folsom parish offered another twist on master planning. St. John the Baptist Parish had been in existence since 1857. Eventually, the old wood-frame church was handling more traffic than its weak wood floors could handle. The parish also needed a better meeting hall and a parish school and convent. Its method of proceeding was distinct. In 1958 it built a new church across the street from the old structure. Then in 1960 twenty acres were obtained at Foothill Oaks near Folsom Dam, directly in the path of residential growth and a new development in El Dorado Hills.[34] A new school and convent were built there in 1962 and later a parish hall. However, a third and permanent church did not complete the plan until 1986.

THE BINDING POWER OF COMMON ORIGINS

Just as significant as the development of a master plan and actual building of permanent structures was the sweat equity that went into these properties. Pastors began the process of church building by gathering a community of people living near a new parish site into some sort of temporary structure. The desire for mass in the vicinity of their homes mobilized local Catholics to plan and volunteer for a myriad of social events and fund-raisers. This process, repeated over and over again in the rapidly developing North Area, constituted an important channel for the creation of community in the new neighborhoods.

Of necessity, new parish communities began in temporary locations. This is true of most religious denominations, but it is especially significant for Catholics, since their notions of church membership—their parish loyalty—involve association with an actual church building. Because Catholicism is organized territorially, by parish (or nationality), and not congregationally, the migration from these first temporary structures to the first permanent church structures carries a great deal of emotional and social significance. The St. Philomene congregation first began in a nightclub. The Jesuits began saying mass in an old warehouse. Presentation held masses in a bowling alley and then a funeral home. Our Lady of the Assumption in Carmichael began with masses held in a theater. In fact, the recollections of their "pioneer" days created the first collective memories for parishes that had been nothing but empty tracts of land only a short time before. Stories of "beginnings" are told and retold in parish histories and parish oral traditions.

These histories are each unique, yet they share the common experience of humble origins. Founding conditions created an interesting variant of pioneer myths. As noted, St. Philomene's began in rented quarters in a band hall on Auburn Boulevard called the Bungalow Club. Founding pastor Twomey initially offered mass twice each Sunday morning, and his efforts drew an instant response. Describing the first Easter of the parish, freelance journalist Reba O'Neil wrote evocatively of how the growing Catholic community manufactured its community in borrowed space. "An altar on a bandstand, left-over decorations limp against the walls, logs burning in a fire-place—and a priest somehow putting holiness into it." O'Neil acknowledged, "It is not easy to go to Mass at St. Philomene's," but "there is something about this new St. Philomene's created last November."[35]

Bridging the gap between the temporary structure and the first permanent parish building (sometimes a school hall) required prodigious organizational skills and a constant round of fund-raising—as well as risky borrowing from local banks. The fund-raising and organizing meant the mobilization of large numbers of unpaid volunteers who went door to door to recruit new members for the church. Twomey held endless fund-raisers to erect his first buildings. At St. Philomene's, parishioners also dutifully took a census of the wide area encompassed by their first parish boundaries, knocking on doors and inquiring about the religious status of people whose homes were within those boundaries. Reba O'Neil described "weary census takers" who canvassed widespread areas north of the American River.[36] St. Ignatius parishioners also fanned out into their nearby neighborhoods, calling on parishioners.

New Catholics were also invited into each other's homes to get to know one another. "To get everyone together after a work week was over," noted the parish history, "some meetings took the form of cocktail parties on Sunday afternoon." Gabrielli sent members of the Holy Name Society to knock on the doors of the growing number of houses in his area and inform them that a new Catholic church was being established. When the Reverend James Healy wanted to build a new church in Folsom to accommodate its growing Catholic population, he recruited local postmaster Thomas Moore, who knew virtually everyone in town, as the general chairman of the fund campaign. However, Moore became ill, so parishioner Martin Jennings took over the task of fund-raising and coordinating the captains who made phone calls and conducted home visits, raising most of the $87,923 that the new St. John the Baptist Church cost.[37]

Historians point to voluntary cooperation in various parts of the West—such as barn raisings and harvests—that brought scattered people together for mutual assistance, sometimes demanding physical labor. A latter-day replica of this communal spirit literally created the emerging parishes of the Sacramento suburbs, as men and women devoted Saturdays and vacations to construct and embellish church facilities. In 1958 Gabrielli, with help from the men of St. Lawrence Parish, built a grotto shrine in honor of Our Lady of Lourdes to mark the centenary of the famed apparitions at Masabiele in France. Parishioners hauled rocks from the banks of the nearby American River to erect the structure. Dedicated in the spring of 1958, the grotto carried in its upper niche a magnificent statue of Mary, imported from Gabrielli's native Italy.[38]

Founding pastor William Horgan of Fair Oaks was perhaps the most demanding taskmaster in shaping his hilly St. Mel property for development. To save money for the construction of new buildings, he negotiated a reduction of prices with the general contractor "to reflect any work that could be done by volunteers." As St. Mel Parish's history notes, "Any parent of a school-age child to toddler was included in the labor force." When Horgan accelerated his school building plans at St. Mel's, he pushed his volunteers even harder, while at the same time scrimping on funds. After the land was graded, he recruited parishioners to repair damaged drainpipes and to create drainage ditches around the property. Working long hours in the winter of 1958 and into the spring and summer of 1959, Horgan's volunteers built a convent and a school, both ready for opening that fall. The parish history concluded (probably with some degree of nostalgia), "None of the stories told about those times dwell on hardship or inconvenience. Conversely, the people most involved recall the human involvement and lifelong friendships that were formed."[39]

One of the best chronicles of local Catholics literally "raising the roof" took place at St. John Vianney Church in Rancho Cordova. Aided by a professional carpenter, parishioners created the temporary church structure out of two barrack-style "day rooms," which had been purchased from nearby Mather Field and set on concrete foundations. "Every Saturday . . . was like a family picnic. Early in the morning the men came, armed with crow-bars, hammers and saws and started to work. Along about noon, the ladies arrived, many with their small children, bringing electric cookers filled with food and steaming coffee." Later, when "the harder 'man-jobs' were completed . . . the tile floor was laid by men, women and children."[40]

Parishioners with an aesthetic flair beautified the temporary structures. Our Lady of the Assumption Parish, for example, used the skills of Otto Schell, a master carver who crafted the corpus of a ten-foot cross in Assumption's first temporary church.[41]

The slow development of the county's North Area, still a mixture of farm, residential, and commercial properties, provided the necessary space for additional community-building activities. The Loyola Guild, of St. Ignatius Parish, raised funds for a new Catholic high school through a barn dance. Our Lady of the Assumption welcomed seven thousand visitors to a Carmichael Country Fair, raising a good portion of the money to purchase their parish property. Christmas tree sales, St. Patrick's Day parties, teas, and garden and fashion shows all helped underwrite the costs of building parish complexes and brought people out of their suburban homes and backyards for moments of interaction. Sometimes, deliberate efforts would be made to "mix" the crowd. One St. Ignatius parishioner began meetings with "ice-breakers" that required the fulfillment of "odd requests . . . find a bald man or a left-handed person, or someone with an 8 1/2 shoe. The search through the crowd usually resulted in parishioners becoming acquainted with new faces."[42]

Catholics also made efforts to blend with the wider suburban culture. One newspaper account relates how Rancho Cordova pastor Richard C. Dwyer met Folsom Unified School District's superintendent, Edwin C. Mitchell, while transacting some business at the Natomas Water Company. Dwyer and the superintendent were commiserating about their school woes. Dwyer lamented that he had classrooms but no teachers, and Mitchell had teachers but too few classrooms, as his nearby Cordova Lane School "was bursting at the seams" while the White Rock School was under construction. A deal was struck between the two men whereby from September 1960 through May 1961, the public school used the facilities at St. John Vianney School. "It was a very practical, reciprocal trade arrangement," said Dwyer. Said superintendent Mitchell, "Most of the families in this vicinity have a cosmopolitan outlook. They are primarily military personnel and Aerojet employees who have moved around quite a bit and are singularly free of built-in prejudices. It just never occurred to them to take exception to the fact, no matter what their religious convictions, that their children are being taught in classrooms connected to a Church school."[43] Similarly, St. Lawrence's Gabrielli also turned one of his empty school wings over to nearby Don Julio Junior High to help with its overflow and by doing so also collected rent to help retire the parish debts.

CROSSING PAROCHIAL LINES

It is easy enough to see how the collective energies required by new parish formation drew people together. But the Catholic Church provided more than parishes for its suburban constituents. The construction of community also took place across parish boundaries on a transparochial level through other voluntary institutions that brought diverse groups together for spiritual and social purposes. Catholic high schools and retreat houses for men and women served this function.

Catholic high schools helped shape the new Catholic presence in the northern suburbs. Existing Catholic high schools included St. Joseph

Academy and St. Francis High School for girls, while Christian Brothers still took in boys from sixth grade up. In 1956 the diocese erected a new high school near Oak Park, named for Bishop Armstrong; the school was unpopular from the minute the diocese announced it. Most parents, especially in the northern suburbs, protested that the new school was too far away. The existing Catholic high schools resented the fact that diocesan authorities intended to take away their upper grades to form the new Bishop Armstrong High School student body. For Christian Brothers and St. Joseph Academy this was a blow that threatened their very existence. Fund-raising lagged, and even Armstrong was publicly skeptical about the prospects for its success. Thanks to Herculean efforts by the superintendent of schools and the new bishop, Joseph McGucken, the school was finished and opened as a coinstitution (boys and girls together but in separate classes) in 1956.[44] But its attendance disappointed diocesan officials. Northern suburban parents had by then found alternatives.

For young women seeking a Catholic high school education, the Loretto Sisters opened Loretto High School in the fall of 1955. Located next to St. Philomene's, the school included a nine-classroom unit to accommodate the first two years of high school. Fully funded by the religious sisters of the Ladies of Loretto, no general drive was made on the already overtaxed Sacramento Catholic populace. Classes began in the modest buildings along El Camino Avenue, and in March of the next year McGucken led the rites of dedication. Five years later Nicholas Tomich designed two new wings, which added three classrooms, a locker room, a library, biology and chemistry labs, and an assembly hall.[45]

The Jesuits had always planned a high school for boys on their property. While Frederick Cosgrove, S.J., tended to the nuts and bolts of administering his parish, his assistant, Joseph T. Keane, S.J., began to lay the groundwork for the creation of a boys' high school with a fund-raising arm called the Loyola Guild. With the help of parishioner Elwood Maleville, Keane began a new campaign in 1962 that raised nearly $850,000 in cash and pledges, in part from appeals to the North Area parishes. Diocesan officials were well aware of the high school deficit in the North Area. In 1962 an editorial in the *Catholic Herald* noted that only 10 percent of Catholic students in the eleven-parish North Area attended Catholic high schools. Strongly endorsing the Jesuit fund drive, the paper hoped the drive's "success will go a long way toward eliminating the no-man's land in which Catholic boys of the area have found themselves after leaving parochial school."[46] By the time the project was ready to roll, however, the original property on the parish grounds was deemed too small for the proposed school. Keane procured a twenty-acre site, once a hops farm, off Fair Oaks Boulevard between Gordon Lane and Jacob Way. The first unit of the school opened in September 1963. Its finances were initially rocky, and it nearly closed, but soon its financial footing stabilized, and it became one of Sacramento's most prestigious private schools.

Two important retreat houses—quiet enclaves set aside for prayer and spiritual reflection—also brought together diverse groups of Catholics in the North Area. The sometimes fast-paced lifestyle in postwar Sacramento gave birth to the need for personal space and refuge from the demands of work and child-rearing. Most suburban families took vacations to nearby spots—the mountains, the seashore, or even to the newly opened Disneyland in Anaheim (an eight-hour drive). The Catholic rush to the suburbs also seemed to dovetail with a growing desire for a refuge of quiet and reflection—apart from the demands of modern suburban life. Suburban Catholics, wedded to their automobiles, devotees of shopping malls, and caught up in the whirl of career and family, needed an occasional break. Such pressures found an important outlet in the "retreat movement." The retreat movement had its origins in the Catholic Action movements of the 1920s and 1930s and by religious orders, who often found their houses inundated with visitors wishing to experience the quiet and savor the somewhat "exotic" liturgical solemnity of their chapels.[47] Such groups became involved in building retreat houses and delivering lectures and sermons in a structured context to provide earnest seekers tools for spiritual balance and reflection.[48] Retreats also brought people from diverse areas of the diocese together for a common enterprise. Weekend retreats, calculated for free time or coordinated with the availability of child care, were extremely popular in Sacramento. Smaller "days of recollection," too, drew groups, mostly women, for a day of prayer, instruction, and reflection. These gathering places mixed people from different parts of the diocese—rural and urban. They were also used by parish groups to draw men and women who might not have had a chance to meet in the ordinary context of parish life. The retreat movement encouraged friendships and fellowship, an intensification of Catholic life, and often an attachment to a locale of peace set amid the traffic and hubbub of suburban life.

The retreat movement began slowly in Sacramento. The first efforts were launched by the Franciscan friars in a small retreat center for men located outside the city. Interest in a permanent area retreat house for Catholic men next came from a prosperous paint dealer and his wife, Mr. and Mrs. Ray Wilkins. Wilkins knew the Passionist fathers at Sierra Madre, near Pasadena, and had begun making retreats at their newly opened retreat center in 1935. Although war intervened, in 1945 Wilkins shared with diocesan officials his dreams of creating a retreat center for men in Sacramento. He actively pursued this idea with the head of the Congregation of the Passion (the Passionists), a Chicago-based religious order dedicated to hosting retreats and offering spiritual direction. His timing was perfect. The Passionists, on the verge of a major expansion program, were looking for places to develop. Passionist Father Angelo Hamilton came to Sacramento and found a plot of forty-one and a half acres about thirteen miles north of downtown, right in the heart of the growing suburb of Citrus Heights. The owners, who did not want to see it subdivided into housing lots or the destruction of its handsome scrub oaks, gladly sold the property to the Passionists in early 1948. The first Passionist community arrived in the summer of 1948 and later moved into a small caretaker's cottage on the property in October. The Catholic newspaper included an imposing sketch of the proposed retreat house and monastery. However, like the Franciscans earlier in the century, the Passionists had their own in-house architect, Notre Dame–trained Father Neil Parsons, C.P., of Chicago.[49] On Palm Sunday, April 10, 1949, ground was broken for Christ the King Retreat House and monastery. The $350,000 modified Spanish-style structure was completed in late April 1950.

On May 26 the first scheduled weekend retreat for men was held. Scores of retreatants—middle-class government workers, local retailers, and others—descended on the facility, crowding its quarters every weekend. Parish priests exhorted their parishioners to take a "quiet weekend with the Lord." By 1951, 848 men had attended thirty-eight retreats in the new facility. The pace of retreat work picked up so rapidly that in 1955 an additional forty-room wing was added to the facility. In 1957 additional structures were transported onto the property to create even more rooms.[50] To further delineate the "zone of peace" in the midst of a burgeoning Citrus Heights, huge granite pillars, four in all, which had been procured from the entryways to the state capitol, stood like sentries at the entrance to the property.

The Passionists were only one of several religious communities of men and women who came to Sacramento after the war, largely at Thomas Kirby's urging, expanding activities long centered around the Franciscan men and women and the Sisters of Mercy. Each of these religious communities developed small bands of admirers who assisted them in the practicalities of getting settled in Sacramento and sought out the religious for counseling or attended their liturgical services. One of the first contemplative women's groups to come to Sacramento was a group of Carmelite nuns from Alhambra, California, who arrived in 1935 and established a small convent on Stockton Boulevard. Increased interest in visits to the Carmelite convent for periods of quiet reflection by both men and women led to an association of laity who attached themselves to the convent, sharing in prayers, days of recollection, and spiritual instruction. The needs of the swelling lay constituency led to an expansion of their buildings that included a public chapel, designed to seat 250 visitors, while the sisters remained behind a cloistered grille.[51] The popularity of the Carmelites and the interest of women for their own space for prayer and reflection led to the formation of a women's retreat house in Fair Oaks, called the Cenacle.

The remote origins of the Cenacle began in the fall of 1947 after a Sacramento Catholic club woman, Marie Dachauer, made a retreat on Long Island, New York, at the American motherhouse of the religious of Our Lady of the Retreat in the Cenacle, a religious community dedicated to retreats and spiritual direction for women. Their distinctive religious attire included a pie-plate-shaped coif that framed the face. Dachauer was so impressed by her experience that she contacted the newly appointed leader of the sisters, Mother Ida L. Barlow, and inquired whether the community would be interested in beginning a retreat house for women in Sacramento. Probably because of limited personnel, Barlow was unable to commit, but Dachauer worked on her own during the next few years to sponsor retreats for Catholic women. In early 1952 Dachauer again contacted Mother Barlow and her chief counselor, Mother Murphy, urging them to come to Sacramento that August.[52]

In 1953 the sisters were ready to consider a Sacramento foundation, and Barlow and her treasurer, Mother Roduit, arrived in Sacramento. They soon discovered an eight-acre property on Fair Oaks Boulevard, owned by Mrs. D. V. Saeltzer Jr., the widow of a wealthy Sacramento physician. The sisters loved the two-story home and the quiet acreage, but the initial asking price was in excess of what they could afford. After some negotiating (and a novena of prayers to St. Anthony of Padua), they purchased the Saeltzer property and began a $350,000 remodeling and expansion program. Eleven more rooms were added, and the facility could easily welcome 46 retreatants and a residence for the sisters. By late February 1954 the sisters began running days and evenings of recollection. More than 650 women attended the initial programs, and public interest in the retreat house built steadily. After its July 31 dedication, the first weekend retreat at the new facility was held in mid-August 1954 and was conducted by Father Richard Dwyer. A year later nearly 1,500 women had walked through the doors of the Cenacle Retreat House. But the rural idyll of Cenacle was not to last for long. The former mansion stood astride the development of Fair Oaks Boulevard. The sisters themselves wrote of the "whittling away of their acres."[53] Eventually, encroaching suburban development hemmed in the retreat house, and the whizzing of cars along Fair Oaks Boulevard shattered the peace of the Cenacle. The center closed in the 1980s. By that time it was no longer out in the country.

CONCLUSION

Catholic efforts played not only spiritual but also economic and social roles in developing Sacramento's most important suburbs during the postwar era. Meanwhile, the city underwent another period of physical and demographic transformation. Urban renewal policies, freeway construction, and the rapid rise of the Latino/a population placed a different set of demands before the community. Here, too, the Catholic Church participated in an important, if not decisive, way in shaping the city's social and political landscape.

CHAPTER 8

Building a Visible Latino Presence in the City, 1930–1970

"Coopere por mi templo"

On a rainy April day in 1945 hundreds of Mexicans filled the Cathedral of the Blessed Sacrament for a festive mass celebrated by Bishop Robert Armstrong. Afterward, the church emptied out on to Eleventh Street and assembled for a procession. Here was a virtual microcosm of Sacramento's growing Latino/a community. "At the head of the procession," noted the Catholic newspaper, "was borne a large picture of the Virgin of Guadalupe surrounded by flowers carried by four girls dressed as angels, and surrounded in turn by a group of boys and girls dressed as Indians." It also included nearly three hundred workers of the Southern Pacific Railroad who carried a streamer with huge lettering: "Trabajadores Catholicos Mexicanos." Mexican cultural and social organizations also fell in behind the sacred icon of Mary. No doubt as well in the march were migrant workers—braceros—who had been brought to the United States from Mexico as contract laborers to alleviate serious labor shortages in the fields and factories of the West. Among the marchers was Zacharias Esparza, who, "though 75 years of age and suffering from a broken leg," insisted on walking with his crutches from his home nearly a mile from the cathedral and then another mile to the procession's terminal point, a "new" Mexican chapel, which was housed in the former St. Stephen Church buildings at Third and o streets. The fervency and joy of Sacramento's Mexican community knew no bounds in finally having a spiritual home in the city. After the ceremonies of blessing and the enthronement of the painting, people visited the new church all day. In the evening three hundred devout Mexican Catholics returned to Our Lady of Guadalupe chapel to recite the rosary.[1]

The American West has been powerfully affected by the presence and culture of Latinos/as.[2] The mixture of religion and daily life brought from Mexico and other Latin American countries is also a part of Sacramento's history. The opening of the little chapel of Our Lady of Guadalupe was an important milestone for Sacramento Latino/a Catholics. Guadalupe chapel became a spiritual home to Spanish-speaking residents of Sacramento and also the many migrant workers who made Sacramento home between planting and harvesting seasons. It was also an important middle ground between religion and urban life. The church dispensed food and clothing to the poor, helped people find housing, and assisted often-disoriented Spanish speakers navigate Sacramento's sometimes confusing public life. It also served as a center for political activism and leadership training. In 1958 this chapel gave way to an even more imposing structure located on Seventh and t streets, directly across from one of Sacramento's most scenic parks. The large Mexican church with its impressive exterior mosaic of Our Lady of Guadalupe was a bastion of cultural pride.

LATINOS/AS AND SACRAMENTO: THE BACKGROUND

Tracking the number of Mexicans in the city of Sacramento before the mid-twentieth century is difficult. Spanish-speaking citizens resided in Sacramento from its earliest days, many as miners from the Mexican state of Sonora who settled in the city after working in the mines of the southern Sierra. Others predated the Gold Rush and ranched or farmed in outlying areas of the Sacramento Valley. Spanish-origin names appear with some regularity throughout the baptismal registers of St. Rose Church and the cathedral.

Their presence in the city has shifted over the course of the city's existence. One of the earliest and largest concentrations was on the West End (also known as the Lower Side Barrio). Here they lived side by side with the medley of other ethnic groups who came to Sacramento. Ernesto Galarza, who grew up there, wrote of this "colony of refugees" that mixed together "families from Chihuahua, Sonora, Jalisco, and Durango." Blending together were families who had arrived before the Mexican Revolution and many who had lived in Texas before migrating to California. "In the years before our arrival and the First World War," wrote Galarza, "the *colonia* grew and spilled out from the lower part of town. Some of the families moved into the alley shacks east of the Southern Pacific tracks, close to the canneries and warehouses and across the river from the orchards and rice mills."[3]

Another barrio developed in Alkali Flats, an area directly north of the downtown. This became a center for Latino/a settlement during the 1940s. Businesses, restaurants, and residences were located there, and its Latino/a inhabitants became laborers in the food-packing and railroad industries. Another settlement was in the vicinity of Southside Park, an area south of the capitol that had been developed by real-estate speculators. Connected with the Lower Side Barrio, it welcomed more and more Latino/a residents as time went on. Other pockets of Latino/a settlement were to be found on the far south side of Sacramento. Its Latino/a community was augmented by the presence of migrant workers who labored in the fields during the planting and harvest months but returned to the city between crops.

Another contingent consisting primarily of farmworkers, many of them American-born Latinos/as, lived across the river in Bryte and Broderick (today West Sacramento). Other Spanish speakers gravitated toward Sacramento, including those in outlying agricultural communities in Yolo County, including Woodland and Yolo, as well as in the farthest southern reaches of Sacramento County, near Isleton and Clarksburg on the Sacramento Delta.[4]

Historian Manuel G. Gonzales suggests that a steady migration into California had already begun in the late nineteenth century, as Mexicans moved first to Texas and Arizona. Revolutionary upheavals begun in 1910 accelerated the flow of immigrants, and in the 1920s Catholics fleeing religious persecution increased the tide. By the 1920s California surged forward as a prime destination.[5] Steadily, the California counties south of the Tehachapi Mountains witnessed dramatic increases in their Mexican populations, Los Angeles County experiencing the most significant growth. But other Mexican migrants moved steadily north, especially into the San Joaquin Valley, where cotton farming and other agricultural enterprises required a large labor pool.

Attempts to count the actual number of Latinos/as in California have always been fraught with difficulties and inaccuracies. In 1929 Governor Clement C. Young appointed a Mexican Fact-Finding Committee to assess the scope and condition of Latino/a growth in California. Consisting of the directors of the Departments of Industrial Relations, Social Welfare, and Agriculture, its 1930 report estimated that nearly 250,000 Mexicans lived in California. Sacramento County had only 1 percent of the state's Latino population, recording 215 in 1910 and 850 in 1920. To be sure, the number was not accurate, and the real number was no doubt higher. However, the percentage of increase was phenomenal. Between 1910 and 1920 Sacramento recorded the fourth-fastest rate of growth in the state, gaining 635 new Mexican residents, or an increase of 295.3 percent—exceeded only by a 339 percent gain in Imperial County, 414.1 percent in Fresno County, and 470.5 percent in Santa Barbara County. In the city itself, the number of Mexicans rose from 103 to 483 between 1910 and 1920, an increase of 383 percent, far surpassing the statewide rate of 159 percent. In Sacramento Mexican men labored for Southern Pacific Railroad and as construction workers, while Mexican women toiled in the city canneries and in other service jobs (in all, constituting 10.2 percent of the workforce, according to the Young report).[6]

Although the Young report undercounted Latinos/as in California, it was one of the first official acknowledgments of a demographic shift that would eventually change the face of California. The significance for Sacramento was its recording of the rapidly increasing growth. The state capital was on the way to becoming an important center for Latino/a growth. Latinos/as initially came to Sacramento attracted by jobs that were often available to all immigrants in the West End labor market. Latino/a workers were recruited for nearby truck gardens, hops and rice fields, and orchards in Sacramento, Yolo, Solano, Sutter, Yuba, and Placer counties.

Determining the actual number of Latinos/as in Sacramento County prior to 1990 is somewhat speculative. However, trends noted by the Young commission hold. There had been a surge in Latino/a migration during the 1920s due to labor needs in the railroad and construction industries. The Depression took its toll on the Latino/a workforce, which decreased significantly until the initiation of the Bracero Program in the early 1940s. Numbers increased significantly during the 1940s and 1950s, but the fear of deportation and the transiency of many Latinos/as have often made enumeration difficult.[7] Data reveal that in 1960 the number of foreign-born from Mexico living in Sacramento County amounted to just under 12,000, or about 2.4 percent of the county's population. The 1970 and 1980 census figures included those with Spanish surnames so are a bit misleading. By 1990 census figures were showing 121,544 Latinos/as in the county, or almost 12 percent. By 2000 the U.S. Census Bureau revealed that the Latino/a population had risen to 195,890, or 16 percent of the county's population.[8]

LATINO/A CULTURE IN SACRAMENTO

Steadily increasing numbers provided a critical mass for the formation of a large ethnic community and an active local culture. Organizations provide one window into their community formation. Latino/a citizens formed *mutualistas* (mutual-aid societies), such as the Alianza Hispano-Americana, a fraternal insurance society that had two chapters in Sacramento.[9] Social and cultural organizations provided entertainment and fellowship and kept alive memories of the home country. One organization, La Junta Patriotica Mexicana, a federation of various patriotic organizations, sponsored a Mexican Independence Day celebration each September. These two-day events included a street parade, a picnic with speech making, and traditional dancing in Southside Park and were capped by balls at the Native Sons Hall. Young women from the lodges of the Alianza Hispano-Americana reigned as queens of court for the celebrations. Attendees came from the city and the outlying regions, and at times the celebrations grew raucous.[10]

Latino/a agency in creating local culture was typified by Enriqueta Andazola, referred to in her eulogy as "la pionera de nuestra colonia mexicana." She was a native of Pinos Altos, Chihuahua, Mexico, who came to Sacramento in 1917 after her marriage at age eighteen. Enriqueta found employment with the Sacramento Wool Company and spent many years in the Del Monte Cannery, while her husband, Ignacio Ramirez, worked for Southern Pacific. Youthful and energetic, she organized social clubs for women that sponsored dances and other social events. She played a role in organizing a branch of the Alianza Hispano-Americana in 1936 and took particular pride in sponsoring patriotic and cultural programs for the Sacramento community.[11]

In 1942 the government of Mexico opened a consulate in Sacramento. One consul, Adolfo Dominguez, played an important role in helping Mexican Sacramentans bond by helping them claim urban space for their cultural activities. Community celebrations were held in rented facilities such as the Native Sons Hall, the Hotel Español, or the auditorium of Lincoln School. In 1938 city Latinos/as formed the Centro Mexicano to collect donations for a new hall. Early plans for the proposed center included a bilingual school, library, social club, and cultural center. A round of dances, fiestas, bazaars, and other fund-raising schemes raised about four thousand dollars by 1941. Lots were purchased in the Southside Park area at Sixth and w, but wartime building restrictions halted construction temporarily. When Mexican consul Adolfo G. Dominguez arrived in 1948, he revived the cultural center project. The emissary urged local leaders to abandon traditional fund-raisers and freewill offerings, urging them instead to underwrite the project through the sale of stock in a private corporation, "El Centro Mexicano de Sacramento." The board, headed by Southern Pacific worker Manuel Rey, was composed entirely of working people. Shares were sold far and wide, including a number to braceros. Architect Leonard Stark designed an eighty-by-forty-foot structure, decorated with murals painted by local artist Dolores O'Neill, highlighting the mythical Aztec past of the Mexican people. Ground was broken for the new center during the Cinco de Mayo celebrations of 1948 at a ceremony presided over by Dominguez and Sacramento mayor Belle Cooledge. Construction was completed by August. An elaborate dedication ceremony welcomed a representative of Mexican president Miguel Aleman on August 14, 1948. Speakers lauded the building as the "only one of its kind in the country." The center, it was hoped, would be the "focal point of the cultural and social life of the community."[12]

Enriqueta Andazola, active in the organization, worked hard to make the new center a place of cultural pride for the city's Latinos/as. Because her sons served in the military during World War II, she and her close friend Antima Perez formed a group called the Mexican War Mothers who boosted the morale of Latino soldiers in the area. Andazola and her colleagues hosted dances, made meals, sent cards, and visited sick soldiers at the Weimar Sanitarium near Colfax. To honor the memory and service of Mexican veterans, the war mothers raised money for a Mexican-American War Memorial, with a statue of a Mexican soldier imported from Milan, Italy. The monument was placed in front of the new center in 1951 and remained there until the center closed. In 1975 it was transferred to a spot on Tenth Street, directly across from the state capitol.[13]

The new center provided a much needed gathering spot for social occasions. But hopes that it would become a cultural anchor for the growing community never materialized, and it was abandoned in 1975. Although it is difficult to obtain an accurate picture of the hall's function and meaning to the growing Mexican community, one account of its demise suggests that the decision to create a corporation and sell stock undermined its success. The use of stock, Nemesio Tony Ortiz argues, undercut the communitarian nature of the Mexican *colonia*. It made "the Centro . . . the property of shareholders—a strange word to the Mexican community, and a word that would eventually haunt it. The community would witness the loss of its dream because it never understood corporation law and the significance of shares." Ortiz also tags the failure of the board of directors to take care of building maintenance, as well as the indifference of Mexican American youth who did not appreciate the significance of the building or the sacrifices its construction had entailed. Guadalupe Aguilar, an active community member, recalled in a 1984 interview that the center had begun to decline after the departure of Dominguez in the 1950s. Although efforts were made to revive it, she lamented that the building was vandalized and left to ruin.[14] But the hall and center also had rivals for the affections and loyalties of the Latino/a community. Even before the center was built, the Catholic Church had been tending to the spiritual and social needs of the growing *colonia*.

Latino/a Catholicism in northern California developed in tandem with the growth of the region.[15] The earliest evidence of a specialized ministry to Spanish-speaking Catholics in Sacramento was made in the 1879 will of a generous Catholic, M. O. V. Ayres, who left the Archdiocese of San Francisco a bequest for "the support of a Spanish priest, who shall administer to the religious wants of the Spanish membership of St. Rose Church at Sacramento City–California and who shall visit and instruct said people there at least twice a year."[16] It is unknown whether Ayres's wishes were carried out, but the Latino/a presence in Sacramento grew, and many worshiped at the cathedral or at St. Stephen's. When St. Mary's was established in 1906, it was designated as the church for the Spanish-speaking, and baptismal records attest that between four and seven baptisms for children with Spanish surnames took place each year between 1907 and 1917. From 1920 on, the number of Spanish-surnamed children baptized surged dramatically, with twenty-eight children receiving the sacrament in 1922.[17]

One hundred Spanish-speaking women of St. Mary Church formed one of the first Catholic Latina organizations, the Madres Cristianas. This group eventually moved to the cathedral and was renamed La Sociedad de Nuestra Señora de Dolores. Later they changed their name again, to the Guadalupanas. Many Mexican Catholics also attended the Cathedral of the Blessed Sacrament, where a 1927 parish census revealed approximately twenty-three hundred Mexicans.[18] This made them at least as numerous as the Italians and far larger than the city's Portuguese or Croatian communities. Spanish-speaking parents availed themselves of the day-care services offered by the Franciscans at the Grace Day Home, and their children attended Holy Angels School. Latino/a children also attended St. Joseph grade school and academy. Mercy Sister Patrick Kelligan, a teacher at the school, made them her special concern through the 1920s and 1930s.

The response to the spiritual needs of Latino/a Catholics came just as the Diocese of Sacramento was backing away from its earlier resistance to ethnic churches. Writing to the rector of All Hallows Seminary in Ireland, Bishop Patrick Keane made sure that potential recruits knew about actual demographic conditions in northern California. "In recent years however, there is a steady growth of population in all the counties within the radius of eighty miles of Sacramento, and this city itself numbers 70,000 souls—about 20,000 Catholics embracing all nationalities—Irish, English, Germans, Italians, Portuguese predominating—a goodly number of

Dalmatian Serbs—now designated Jugo-Slavs, Mexicans, etc." In contrast to his predecessor, Keane unambiguously endorsed separate ethnic parishes and made it clear that the Italian and Portuguese churches would be around for a long time to come. He went to great lengths to secure priests to serve the city's Slavonian (Croatian) Catholics and even approved a new downtown parish for them before his death.[19] Thanks to Keane's sensitivity to ethnic concerns, Catholic efforts among the Spanish-speaking in Sacramento paid particular attention to their native religious culture.

The spiritual history of Latino/a communities in the West, dominated as it was by Mexican immigrants, is often associated with the beginnings of public prayers to Our Lady of Guadalupe. This devotion is rooted in sixteenth-century apparitions of the Virgin Mary to a humble Indian, Juan Diego. The image of Mary impressed on the *tilma* (cloak) of Juan Diego became an object of veneration to the people of Mexico and subsequently an important icon of Mexican nationalism. As Timothy Matovina has observed, the Guadalupe devotion had a powerful and formative influence on Mexican Catholics far from home. The image, with its appeal as both a spiritual and a national icon, united Mexican immigrants regardless of their place of origin in Mexico. Sacramento's first public celebrations of Our Lady of Guadalupe took place at St. Mary Church in 1910 and were held annually.[20] Beginning on December 14, 1919, Our Lady of the Blessed Sacrament Church, located across the Sacramento River in Broderick, hosted the festivities. The Broderick celebrations were sponsored by the Francisco Ortiz family and merited the rather rare Solemn High Mass. The following year Bishop Thomas Grace celebrated a mass in honor of Our Lady of Guadalupe at the same church, and the next year Bishop Keane did the same.[21] As he had done for the Slavonians, Bishop Keane found a priest, the Reverend Stephen Keating, to minister to the Latinos/as of Sacramento.

PHASE ONE: VISIBILITY

The Reverend Keating's role in organizing the Latino/a community of Sacramento is not better known because he left the priesthood and married in 1935, long before the major exodus of priests in the sixties and seventies. Since this was considered a social and spiritual disgrace, Keating's name was rarely mentioned by church officials, and his efforts in the 1920s and

1930s were barely acknowledged. However, before his departure, Keating's multiple talents as organizer, pastor, teacher, intellectual, and priest were deployed effectively on behalf of the Spanish-speaking of Sacramento.[22]

Born in New York in 1898, Keating entered the Salesians of Don Bosco, an international Catholic religious community dedicated to working with urban youth. Keating began his Salesian life at Hawthorne, New York. He studied at the community's headquarters in Turin, Italy, and completed his theological studies at the community's Don Bosco Institute in Ramsey, New York. Ordained in 1921, he took some courses at Fordham University and then taught at the community's Salesian Institute in New Rochelle. In 1925 he was transferred to a boys' school in Watsonville, California. By early 1926 Keating's Salesian vocation was in crisis. When his father died, Keating's siblings, two sisters (one of whom was a Sister of Charity) and a younger brother, were unable to support their aged mother, and the priest became her sole support. Since his vow of religious poverty did not permit him to have an individual income, he left the Salesians (but not the priesthood) and became a diocesan priest so he could keep and share his salary with his struggling family. In early 1926 Bishop Keane of Sacramento agreed to "adopt" him, and appointed him to the cathedral. Keating wrote to a Salesian friend, "From present indications I will be stationed here at least until the Fall and perhaps longer. There is plenty to do and the pastor and the other two assistants are very kind so that I am well satisfied with the appointment."[23]

The next eight years were a whirlwind of activity. Before he departed from the priesthood, Keating created the diocesan Department of Education, tried to form a Catholic Youth Organization (CYO), lectured regularly on medical and moral ethics for the city's Catholic nurses, and assisted in the formation of the Catholic Welfare Bureau. Most important, the soon Spanish-conversant priest spearheaded Sacramento's first organized ministry to Mexican Catholics.

Keating devoted himself to the pastoral care of Mexicans who worshiped at the cathedral and taught himself enough Spanish to communicate with these heretofore neglected parishioners. He put out the word not only that Mexican Catholics were welcome at the cathedral but that there would actually be Spanish-language programs for their special catechetical and sacramental needs. Keating recruited two Spanish-speaking laypeople (both natives of Fresnillo, Zacatecas), Federico Falcon and Magdalena Martinez. Falcon worked at Southern Pacific but had been a musician and schoolteacher before moving north. Martinez was a former nun who had come to Sacramento with a nephew from Los Angeles. Although in poor health, she was a competent catechist. Falcon eventually quit his job at Southern Pacific in 1929 to work full-time with Keating and later for the Catholic Welfare Bureau. The trio fanned out into the neighborhoods surrounding the cathedral and visited every family they could find, surveying their spiritual and material needs. Thanks to their efforts, the parish reports of 1927 acknowledged for the first time the presence of 2,300 Mexican parishioners.[24]

In his first summer Keating enlisted the Sisters of Mercy from St. Joseph's and the Catholic Ladies' Relief Society to staff a six-week summer vacation school for Spanish-speaking children at St. Joseph Academy. The CLRS members also offered instruction in domestic and practical skills. As relief worker Evelyn Restano noted, "Our cooperation consisted in helping maintain the interest of the other girls by teaching them to sew and providing material for this work." Each summer anywhere from 400 to 600 young children signed up for the vacation school, and every annual report of the group dutifully recorded the numbers of dresses made, napkins and handkerchiefs embroidered, and clothing repaired. In 1932 the recording secretary wrote, "The ladies also remodeled about two dozen dresses and slips for the children who made their First Communion and Confirmation, who could not afford to pay for them."[25]

The census work and the summer school were the first steps in organizing the Catholic outreach to Sacramento's Mexicans. In 1928, at a community meeting, Keating formed religious organizations for the Spanish-speaking at the cathedral. The Holy Name Society enrolled 95 members, and the Christian Mothers (Guadalupanas)—transferred from St. Mary's—112; a Santa Inez group for young girls had 135 members, and the Junior Holy Name for young men had 81. Meanwhile, thanks to Martinez, scores of children were prepared for their first communion and confirmation. Both were celebrated in large public ceremonies in the cathedral after the close of summer school. Martinez and Falcon personally served as *padrina* and *padrino* (godmother and godfather) to scores of Sacramento's Mexican youth. In addition, couples married outside the church or merely cohabiting were given the opportunity for Catholic marriage. In December 1929 and 1930 the Mexican community celebrated the Feast of Our Lady of Guadalupe in the Cathedral of the Blessed Sacrament. The daylong events were marked by special preaching, religious devotions, and celebrations in the cathedral basement meeting halls.[26]

The quickened pace of these ministries was reflected in a report issued by the Cathedral of the Blessed Sacrament at the end of 1930. In the cathedral, there were 300 Mexican families registered but more than that came to mass. In the year between November 1, 1929, and November 1, 1930, cathedral clergy made 1,230 home visits and performed 172 baptisms, 32 confirmations, and 69 first communions for Spanish-speaking children. Likewise, 325 children attended religious instruction in summer school. At a time when the U.S. Census Bureau was reporting only 115 and the Young commission about 1,000, church workers reported there were about 5,000 Mexicans in Sacramento County, 3,000 of whom were permanent residents.[27] The remainder were agricultural workers who stayed in the city six months or less.

Religious instruction was complemented by social work, filling a void in city services. Helping city and county personnel who did not know Spanish, Keating provided language translation and helped in the placement of children in orphanages and adults in mental hospitals. He arranged free burials for paupers, made regular jail visitations, and saw to it that clothing and food cases were referred to the appropriate city, county, or private agency. He also reached out to the transient migrant workers who sometimes needed financial or medical assistance and occasional help negotiating the legal system. In October 1928 he spoke to the Grand Council of the Catholic Ladies' Relief Society and drew attention to the plight of the "Mexican peon," attracted to agricultural and industrial labor in California and willing to work for a paltry thirty-five cents per hour. Such poor wages, he argued, enforced idleness and illness and required additional assistance. The women responded generously with pledges of cash and service. The work of Keating, Falcon, and Martinez won acclaim with city and county social welfare officials, and the trio became a clearinghouse for cases that required public assistance.[28]

The Depression-triggered decline of California agriculture in the 1930s brought about changes in Sacramento's Mexican population. Many laborers who had worked in the fields and canneries were now jobless. Bitter competition for scarce jobs led to concerted efforts by the U.S. government in 1931 to repatriate Mexicans living in the United States.[29] These efforts began in early 1931 in Southern California, and by year's end Los Angeles had lost nearly one-third of its Mexican population.[30] Similar activities may have taken place in Sacramento, or many people may have returned on their own. As the Mexican community dwindled, Keating was assigned other tasks. He became superintendent of Catholic schools and a lecturer to the students at the Mercy School of Nursing. He was also asked to form a Catholic Youth Organization.[31] At about this same time, the hardworking priest began to experience personal problems that would eventually drive him from the priesthood.

In 1935 Keating married one of the secretaries who worked at the cathedral and moved to Los Angeles, where his long years of working with social service agencies secured him a job with the Los Angeles County Probation Department. There he became a resident specialist in juvenile delinquency among Mexican American youth. In the wake of the so-called Zoot Suit Riots of 1943, Keating's expertise was tapped by city officials probing the reasons for the disturbances and the deeper causes of social unrest.[32] He was one of the first to develop a popular toy-loan project, which collected and repaired old toys and gave them to needy children. Keating died at his desk in 1950 at the age of fifty-two, leaving behind a wife and five children—one of whom was one of the "problem" Latino youth he had discovered in his work for the Probation Department and adopted.[33] The memory of the beloved "El Padre Esteban" lived on among Sacramento's Mexican community. When Keating died, the Reverend Anthony Maio, then administrator of Our Lady of Guadalupe Mission, received stipends and votive offerings to celebrate masses for the repose of his soul. Only in 1986 were his accomplishments as an organizer, coordinator, and social leader recognized, when the Diocese of Sacramento celebrated its centenary in a series of articles published in the diocesan newspaper.[34]

Keating and his associates made a good beginning in providing for the diverse needs of the increasing number of Latinos/as in the state capital. Perhaps his greatest achievement was creating a middle ground for Sacramento's Mexican community by integrating customs from the old country into church practices long dominated by Irish Catholic practices. One memoir recalled, "Just like it is a custom in Mexico, we had offerings of flowers for Our Blessed Mother during the month of May. . . . In June small boys dressed in white shirts and white pants with a red sash would offer flowers for the Sacred Heart of Jesus."[35]

Falcon and Keating also instilled a sense of community pride among the city's Latino youth through the popular Santo Nombre band, a troupe of uniformed Mexican musicians who marched in public parades and provided entertainment at gatherings. The band drew attention to the presence of the Catholic Latino/a community in the city whenever they appeared. In 1935, for example, the band marched in the annual Holy Name Parade, a citywide Catholic event held every January. Their float depicted the apparition at Guadalupe.[36] These activities were part of the many steps that bonded Mexicans and Mexican Americans to the larger Sacramento community.

By their sponsorship of clubs, organizations, dramatics, and celebrations, Keating, Falcon, and Martinez did everything they could to make the cathedral welcoming. However, just as civic groups had grown weary of renting halls and gathering in borrowed spaces, cathedral Latinos/as also began to chafe at the diffusion of their meeting places. Organizations met in the cathedral's basement rooms, whereas religious instruction took place at St. Joseph Academy and the Santo Nombre band practiced in the school's boiler room. Moreover, the cathedral still had a very large English-speaking congregation, which related little or not at all to the growing numbers of Mexicans in their midst. There was not even an image with votive lights to Our Lady of Guadalupe in the vast church. The cathedral was also geographically distant from the growing concentrations of Spanish speakers who lived in inexpensive housing in the West End and near Southside Park. Even though St. Joseph's and other Catholic institutions, such as the Grace Day Home and Holy Angels School, welcomed Latino/a children, those institutions were not the kind of exclusive cultural space that the community needed. Keating dreamed of a separate place for Spanish speakers where they could enjoy cultural autonomy, one that would also provide a gathering point for the diverse spiritual and social needs of the community. He had even begun fund-raising plans for a new Mexican church in 1930.[37] However, his hopes were dashed by the

Depression and the decline in the number of Mexicans living in Sacramento. Nonetheless, Keating's dream would eventually become a reality.

PHASE TWO: A TEMPORARY CHAPEL

Keating's departure brought about a decline in the church programs he had started at the cathedral. In 1940 Catholic Welfare Bureau director the Reverend Thomas Markham noted of the parish groups that "the organizations are not in a healthy condition at the present time."[38]

However, the social and cultural needs of Mexicans only grew during and after World War II. The Bracero Program, a guest-worker policy begun in 1942, brought contract laborers into the United States from Mexico to supply needed labor in agricultural and other local industries. Legislation in 1950 formalized the program, which lasted until 1964 and welcomed hundreds of Mexican men. City dwellers were housed in the Depression-era homeless shelter on Front and I streets. When Falcon and others brought the spiritual needs of the workers to the attention of the cathedral priests, the Reverend (later Monsignor) Raymond Renwald, a curate (and later pastor) of the cathedral, taught himself enough Spanish to preach a simple sermon at a mass for the workers. "I would go down on Sunday mornings, and Saturday afternoons," he later recalled. "I did that for about a year then when the end of the war came and they were moved out then they asked for a church of their own."[39]

Renwald took charge of the small but growing chapel fund that had been started years before and kept his eyes open for a good space to begin the project. Ironically, the moment of opportunity came when the Mexican community became an indirect beneficiary of the relocation of the city's Japanese in 1942. Sometime in late 1943 or 1944, the former St. Stephen property at Third and O, which had been a Japanese theater, came on the market. When city officials offered the building back to the diocese, Renwald jumped at the offer. A committee of Mexicans reconstructed and refurbished the edifice.

The creation of this chapel of Our Lady of Guadalupe in the old St. Stephen Church represented an important symbolic "arrival" of Latinos/as in Sacramento. Although they already had an active associational life, now they had a church where community identity, symbolized by devotion to Our Lady of Guadalupe, could be celebrated. Here, too, the important passages of life and special celebrations of the liturgical year could be celebrated according to local custom.

Bishop Armstrong assigned newly ordained Carl Willman to the "new" Guadalupe. A native of Williamsport, Pennsylvania, the twenty-seven-year-old priest lived temporarily at the Cathedral of the Blessed Sacrament and struggled to learn Spanish. He even tried briefly to author a column in the *Superior California Register*.[40] In 1948 he temporarily changed places with a priest in Guadalajara to improve his command of the language. When ground was broken for El Centro (the Mexican Center) in 1948, Sacramento's mayor was flanked by the Mexican consul and Willman.[41] The priest's presence at the groundbreaking (prominently featured in the Sacramento papers) symbolized the close bonds between the Catholic Church and the growing Mexican colony.

Willman presided over a busy enterprise. The paper noted, "There are four hundred and sixty Mexican families in the Cathedral parish alone." Signaling the end of the older strategy of Americanizing immigrants, the paper urged that although the Latino/a immigrants "must be blended into our way of living," they must also "preserve the depth and beauty of the faith they have brought with them."[42] The paper concluded, "To develop these good points and to make their gifts available to our community is the work of the Mexican parish. How much more effectively it can be done through the training of our priests for this apostolate." Willman, however, proved unable to do the job. Even after five years of study and practice, he was unable to master the Spanish language sufficiently for the needs of the people. The mission floundered as attendance plummeted, and in 1949 he gave up and accepted reassignment to a pastorate in the far-off northern lumber town of McCloud. Willman's failure to bond with the community, however, was not the only challenge confronting the church and its growing Latino population. Redevelopment also played a part in subsequent events.

REDEVELOPMENT IN THE WEST END

In the postwar era the growth of the city of Sacramento slowed considerably. Suburbanizaton, described earlier, transferred part of the city's population and its businesses into the newly developing area northeast of the city. Shopping downtown became less and less enticing as suburban shopping malls offered convenient, popular retail outlets. Moviegoing, dining, and dancing, once staples of Sacramento's downtown cultural life, dwindled. Even though city officials attempted to adapt the inner city to heavier automobile usage (with one-way streets and parking garages), navigating and parking in the heart of downtown remained a challenge. Sacramento's West End, composed of the blocks from I Street to N and from Front Street to Eighth, became one of the worst slums in the West.

By the end of World War II, Sacramento's West End, long a source of civic anxiety, was to some an eyesore: a congeries of small eateries, bars, and rattrap hotels. In all, the property value of the West End declined 39 percent from 1937 to 1949. Virtually 75 percent of its structures had been erected before 1919. Mostly built of wood, many of the buildings lacked proper sanitation, and even running water, and were crowded and susceptible to the spread of disease and fire. The population of the area was mixed. Some, mostly the poor and the elderly, were permanent residents. There was also a good number of agricultural transients who resided there when their labor was not needed.[43]

State and federal urban-renewal programs began shortly after World War II. After a complex process involving both public and private initiatives, the Sacramento Redevelopment Agency was created in 1950, and the city began systematically clearing away the decrepit buildings on the West End. These plans often intersected with the politics of freeway location. Typical of these battles was the 1960s struggle over the location of Interstate 5, the main north-south freeway in California. Sacramento residents, loath to allow the new freeway to cut the city in half, wanted it to be located across the Sacramento River in Yolo County. Business interests, such as retailer Macy's, wooed by the Sacramento Redevelopment Agency, insisted on a more direct route into the downtown as the price of locating additional stores in the redeveloped area. After much wrangling a compromise was worked out, allowing the new freeway to hug the Sacramento River while providing a complex interchange near the new shopping area. Other freeways wiped out neighborhoods along the city's south side. Major expansions of Interstate 80 heading east toward the Sierra Nevada and Highways 50 and 99 going east and south also carved up older urban neighborhoods.

In December 1957 Governor Goodwin Knight officiated at the first demolition for the redevelopment plan—a two-story rooming house at Sixth Street and Capitol Avenue. With that, a decade of nonstop demolition ensued, reducing to rubble most of the buildings of the West End. In 1960 another downtown study by the city council solidified a plan, calling for a pedestrian mall approaching the capitol along K Street, a new convention center near the old Memorial Auditorium, and a Gold Rush–days theme village to be called Old Sacramento a few blocks west of the capitol, where a few early commercial buildings still stood along the original embarcadero.[44]

Urban redevelopment lurched forward and then stalled through the sixties. But the cumulative process—demolition, rebuilding, freeways, new shopping emporiums—proved to be a mixed blessing. It did bring new prospects for builders and developers, provided more efficient transportation around a city that recorded one of the fastest growth rates of automobile ownership in California, and removed blighted and dangerous buildings that were no longer fit for human habitation. However, it also displaced residents of existing neighborhoods, taking away cheap housing for many of the working-class men and women who toiled in neighboring fields and in low-paying service jobs. Many of the relocated were poor, and the area's median income level and the quantity of its rental-housing stock fell precipitously.[45]

Redevelopment schemes affected not only the urban space but also its social institutions. In the central business district, it left behind the urban poor, who now crowded into the deteriorating housing that had not yet fallen to the wrecker's ball. It also impacted downtown churches, especially the cathedral. As Monsignor Raymond Renwald, rector of the cathedral, observed in 1963, "Sacramento's redevelopment program has made inroads on the parish population of the Cathedral. With much of the parish encompassing areas typified by low income families—even before redevelopment—monetary contributions often fail to keep abreast of parish needs."[46]

IMPACT ON LATINO/A SACRAMENTANS

Redevelopment also redrew the demographic realities of the downtown and its adjacent urban areas. Many of the uprooted were Latino/a men, women, and children. Between 1950 and 1970 a large percentage of the city's Latino population moved from the West End into the central business district and Washington and Alkali Flats area just north and northeast of the downtown, where an abundance of affordable rental housing made this settlement possible. The Southside Park area, which had been · a Latino/a "beachhead" since the 1940s, also took in people as West End housing was demolished.[47]

As the 1960s unfolded, the relocation of Latino/a communities increased their presence in the Catholic institutions in the central city. The student body of St. Joseph grade school and academy in the Alkali Flats area became increasingly Latino/a. Holy Angels School near the West End also reported a steady increase in Mexican students—including many who could not speak a word of English.[48] Renwald laconically acknowledged the demographic shift, noting of Alkali Flats in 1965, "Many Mexico-born families are moving in with large families." The Reverend Sidney Peter Hall daily transported area children to St. Joseph School in an old school bus through Alkali Flats, the adjoining Washington District, near the Dos Rios housing project, and along Bannon Street—all slum areas fringing the north side of the city. Hall recalled visiting many of the homes along the route, noting that eleven of the twelve families he contacted on one block were Mexican.[49]

Just as plans for urban renewal were being hatched, the demands of the Latino/a community for more space and a more beautiful setting for their private and public celebrations—baptisms, first communions, confirmations, weddings, and *quinceñeras* (a "coming-out" party for a young Mexican woman)—pressed hard. Sympathetic figures in the church recognized the need and understood the significance of a larger and more aesthetically pleasing spiritual home. Unspoken, but implicitly understood, a new church could also be an anchor in the sometimes unsettling world of redeveloping Sacramento.

The Reverend Anthony Maio succeeded Willman as pastor of the Guadalupe community in 1949. Maio was born in Benevento, Italy, in 1921 and raised in Philadelphia.[50] After grade school he pondered whether he ought to become a teaching priest and spent a year in a seminary of the Oblates of St. Francis de Sales, but decided to do parish work instead. He entered the Catholic University of America in 1941 with the intention of studying Italian, but found he had an affinity for Spanish language and culture. After graduation in 1944, he taught Spanish for a year and then took a trip to California in 1945 to observe Spanish-speaking culture and life in the West. Interested since his youth in the priesthood, he paid a visit to Sacramento's Bishop Robert Armstrong, offering his services to minister to the Spanish-speaking. Armstrong agreed to "adopt" Maio as a seminarian, and the young man finished his studies at St. Mary Seminary in Baltimore. He was ordained in May 1949.

In June 1949 Maio reported for duty in Sacramento. After a few weeks he was assigned to Our Lady of Guadalupe chapel. Working with the congregational remnant left behind by Willman, Maio celebrated two masses every Sunday. Soon word spread about his fluency, and the numbers increased. Maio added additional masses to the schedule (and cajoled fellow cathedral priests to help with them). He lived in the cathedral rectory at first but later transferred his residence to the upper floor of the mission, which he later recalled was a firetrap. He was joined in 1955 by the Reverend Keith B. Kenny, who had just served his first year of priesthood in Colusa, north of Sacramento.

Kenny was born in Omaha, Nebraska, in 1925. Young Keith attended Catholic schools in Omaha, San Antonio, and Pittsburgh until the family settled in Sacramento in 1935. He attended St. Francis grammar school and Christian Brothers High School, from which he graduated in 1942. He then enrolled in the California Maritime Academy and served as a desk officer in the U.S. Merchant Marine during World War II. After the war he attended Sacramento Junior College, Santa Clara University, and the University of California. In September 1948 he began studies for the priesthood at St. Patrick Seminary in Menlo Park. Ordained in 1954, Kenny served a year in Colusa, where he worked with Mexican migrants. To everyone's surprise, he taught himself enough Spanish to preach sermons and offer instruction in the confessional. He improved his linguistic skills when he was transferred to Guadalupe chapel.[51] Until his untimely death of a heart attack after Christmas 1983, Kenny was a major force in Latino affairs in Sacramento and one of the city's leading social activists. He earned his spurs in the rapidly changing neighborhoods around Guadalupe. Maio's and Kenny's gifts complemented each other well as the men helped the city adjust to urban renewal and responded to the needs of its Latino/a population.

Bishop Armstrong's declining health necessitated a coadjutor (helper) bishop for Sacramento in 1955. Auxiliary Joseph T. McGucken of Los Angeles came to the state capital to aid and eventually replace Armstrong, who died in 1957. McGucken brought many needed skills to the post, but above all a deep commitment to the Spanish-speaking. He had learned Spanish as a seminarian and steadily improved his fluency over the years. While pastor of St. Andrew Parish in Pasadena, he had reached out to Latinos/as with bilingual sermons and pastoral sensitivity to their culture and needs. McGucken also chaired a state commission to investigate the Los Angeles Zoot Suit Riots. During McGucken's nearly seven-year tenure, Maio and Kenny enjoyed a measure of support that benefited Latino/a aspirations.

Kenny picked up the social service outreach begun earlier by Keating and Falcon. By 1956 the Latino/a community had grown to twenty-five thousand and was visible enough to attract Industrial Areas Foundation organizer Fred W. Ross. The latter, who was by this time the mentor of farmworker-activist César Chávez, arrived in Sacramento to develop a community service organization among the Spanish-speaking. Maio, Kenny, the Reverend Roy Peters, and a Social Service Sister of the Stanford Settlement met with organizers who held meetings at nearby Lincoln School and began registering Latino/a citizens to vote. In 1958 Ross and Chávez set up a six-week-long problem-solving clinic for Spanish-speaking residents of the city at the Mexican Center on Sixth Street. Bilingual counselors offered tips on services available to city residents. Chávez and Ross pledged to train workers to take over the clinic's operations after their departure.[52]

A pressing pastoral need was the plight of braceros and other migrants laboring on local farms as well as the numerous undocumented migrants who poured into California to work in the nearby farms and orchards of valley growers. Conditions in the agricultural camps were often abysmal, and regular visits found more and more women and children in need of spiritual and social services. In the summer and fall of 1956, McGucken, who also visited the camps, offered mass, heard confessions, and urged the workers not to lose their faith.[53] During the winter months, many of these workers came to Sacramento in need of charity, housing, and clothing. Along with other priests working with migrant laborers, Kenny was appalled by the poor working conditions and inhumane treatment given these workers.

At Kenny's urging, McGucken boosted outreach to Latinos/as in parishes close to the fields, such as Holy Rosary in Woodland and St. Isidore's in Yuba City. He also hosted a meeting of the so-called bracero priests from the Dioceses of San Diego and Monterey-Fresno and the Archdioceses of San Francisco and Los Angeles in early February 1957. The gathering included Mexican priests from the Diocese of San Luis Potosi in central Mexico. The clerics urged bishops to continue an ongoing consultation with bracero priests. They insisted on strict enforcement of federal housing standards for braceros and urged the recruitment of additional lay catechists and priests to bring the sacraments to the camps. To preserve the moral life of these men, cut off from their families, they recommended social centers be organized for the workers.[54]

PHASE THREE: BUILDING A NEW AND RESPLENDENT *TEMPLO*

Maio set to work to build a new church for the growing community, whose numbers were already taxing the well-worn Guadalupe chapel. The priest faced a number of obstacles, not the least of which was raising funds from the lower-income Mexicans. However, he also met opposition from cathedral rector Renwald, who still claimed the Mexican chapel as part of the outreach of the cathedral parish.[55] Renwald worried that fund-raising for a new church would further stress the already precarious finances of the Cathedral of the Blessed Sacrament. (He was glad, in fact, when the Italian church finally moved east in 1948, leaving only the Portuguese St. Elizabeth Church and Guadalupe under his authority.)[56]

Renwald's fears notwithstanding, Maio launched a series of fund-raisers that not only brought the community together but also created a nest egg for future development. In 1951 he began a popular *kermes* (festival) in the middle of summer on the grounds of St. Joseph Academy, which later took place at the Mexican Center at Sixth and w. This popular festival consisted of two full days of celebration and included games, raffles, dancing, and food. The net proceeds were often sizable. Maio also expanded the annual Guadalupe celebration, adding an extravagant parade that marched various groups in the Latino/a colony down κ Street to the cathedral. Elaborate floats and marching bands made the day a festive one.[57]

Even more creatively, at the suggestion of restaurant owner Angelita Ponce, Maio installed alms boxes in the Mexican cantinas on the West

End. Over each box he placed a picture of the *morenita,* the Lady of Gua-dalupe, with the words "Coopere por mi templo" (Give for my church). The results were fantastic. Every month he collected $300 to $400, usually in half-dollars. Maio eventually built up a comfortable $35,000 savings balance for future development.[58]

Maio's efforts regularly encountered opposition from Renwald, but also some skepticism from the diocesan Board of Consultors who shared Renwald's concerns about the financial impact of a new church in the downtown—especially as the cathedral's finances were faltering. McGucken may have listened to his senior clergy but shared Maio's views about the situation. The Latino/a community was growing, and the old St. Stephen buildings were no longer adequate. Likewise, urban renewal plans were demolishing housing and cheap residences, reconfiguring the urban landscape. The loss of housing near Third Street meant that the chapel would soon be off the beaten path for the *colonia.* Alkali Flats, north of the cathedral, would have been the best place to locate the new Mexican church. Latino/a families continued to crowd into single-family dwellings there, which absentee landlords carved up into apartments. But the proximity to the cathedral and the difficulty of assembling and pur-chasing properties made building in that area impossible. Maio proposed relocating the Mexican church to the site of the former Italian St. Mary's at Seventh and T. The diocese still owned much of the T Street property, and the area contained enough of the Latino/a community to make it via-ble. Maio envisioned all the components of a successful parish—church, rectory, school, hall, and even a convent. Virtually right behind it stood Holy Angels School. To the west of the property, new St. Stephen Hall had been built in 1950. The location had the added benefit of being right across from the beautiful Southside Park, one of the loveliest green spots in the city. The park offered a perfect gathering place for outdoor events and the increasingly popular *kermes.* Starting with the rectory, Maio assembled enough contiguous portions of land to create a parcel that ran along T Street from Seventh to nearly Eighth. McGucken gave the go-ahead, and Maio picked up the pace of fund-raising.

On February 16, 1958, nearly four thousand people watched as McGucken turned over the ceremonial first spade of earth at the Seventh and T site.[59] Architect Harry Devine drew the plans for a mission-style

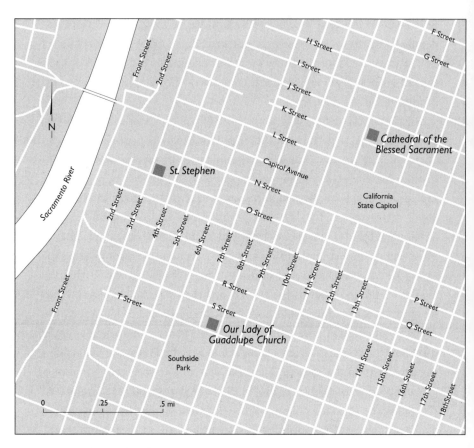

MAP 3 Catholic Churches in the Latino neighborhoods of Sacramento

concrete structure that would loom over Southside Park. The lowest bid was for around $170,000. Devine's drawings included four altars, with seating for seven hundred. However, by the time the land purchases and interior decor were completed, the church came in at nearly a quarter of a million dollars. Once he began, however, there was no turning back, and Maio borrowed money to complete the project.

From the start Maio envisioned the church as a major center of Catholic Latino/a life in the city. After his years of listening and observing, as well as occasional trips to Mexico, Maio carefully thought through virtually every detail of the new church. During his vacations in Mexico he searched for reliable craftsmen to execute his architectural and decorative wishes. Guadalupe Church would incorporate the spirituality, devotionalism, and ambience of Mexican Catholicism while at the same time providing a place that Sacramento Latinos/as could look to with cultural pride.

For the altars, Maio spared no expense. For $10,000 he commissioned artist Amado Magana to carve a handsome cedar main altar with *reredos*, embellished in gold leaf and with recessed niches for saints, reminiscent of the blend of Spanish and native Mexican culture. Above the altar were a carved crucifix and a picture of the Virgin of Guadalupe. Similar side altars were constructed as well, including one site where the bodies of the deceased could be laid out rather than in a funeral home.[60] Within the sanctuary Maio hung rich gold lighting fixtures with globes of Venetian glass in colors of blue, orchid, and yellow. In the soft pink interior, these decorations, especially the heavy dark wood of the altars, stood out for all to see. Cut-glass blocks formed the stained-glass windows, which depicted the miracle of the apparition of Our Lady of Guadalupe at Tepeyac in 1531.

Perhaps Maio's most spectacular move was to make the outside of the church itself a shrine and a reminder to passers-by of the presence of Our Lady of Guadalupe in their daily lives. On the southern outer wall, directly facing the park, he commissioned Mexican artist Victor F. Marco of Mexico City to create a ten-by-twenty-foot mosaic of the apparition of the Blessed Virgin to Juan Diego. The thousands of glass tiles, produced in Marco's Mexico City glass shop, were transported to Sacramento in 150 sections and put together by one of his skilled workers, assisted by a local parishioner.[61] The image presided over the T Street location and provided a point of devotion for those who passed by the church each day.

In December 1958 two thousand people jammed the church and crowded the street to witness its dedication. Mexico City archbishop Dario Cardinal Miranda traveled north for the ceremony. In his sermon McGucken linked the Sacramento church to the beloved shrine on the hill of Tepeyac in Mexico City, recalling Mary's insistence that a church be built on the spot of her apparition. "But the big hearted Mexicans have built not one but hundreds of churches dedicated to her. Wherever Catholics are they build churches. But, wherever Mexicans are they will build Guadalupan Churches."[62]

That the church functioned as a meeting ground of faith and culture providing for Sacramento's Latino/a community was best expressed by

Our Lady of Guadalupe Church, 1959. Courtesy of Sacramento Archives and Museum Collection Center, Frank Christy Collection.

Richard Rodriguez, who recalled being seated near the altar with two or three hundred children, "many of them dressed like Mexican cowboys and cowgirls," when his family attended the thronged predawn high mass, *las mañanitas,* on December 12 (the Feast of Our Lady of Guadalupe). He recalled scanning the congregation. "Invariably, my attention settled on old women—mysterious supplicants in black—bent deep, their hands clasped tight to hold steady the attention of the Mexican Virgin, who was pictured high over the altar, astride a black moon."[63]

Once the church was finished Maio moved to complete the rest of his "master plan" by requesting of a new bishop, Alden J. Bell, that the nearby Holy Angels School and its auditorium be transferred from the cathedral to Our Lady of Guadalupe. He noted that by 1962, of the 215 families at Holy Angels, representing 372 children, 90 families were Mexican, with 165 children among them. Likewise, the other cathedral-administered school, St. Joseph's, had become increasingly Mexican, with 99 out of 160 families of Mexican ethnicity. His proposal to take over Holy Angels, he believed, would be a relief to the cash-strapped cathedral since both schools (St. Joseph's and Holy Angels) were creating a deficit.[64]

Maio had earlier petitioned McGucken to elevate Guadalupe, still technically a mission of the cathedral, to parochial status. McGucken had in fact intended to do so, but his transfer to San Francisco in 1962 and the appointment of Bishop Alden J. Bell left the matter in limbo. The appeal for parochial status was important to Maio and his fellow clerics, for it meant that the new church was an independent entity and not merely a dependency of the cathedral parish. But strong resistance again came from Renwald, who argued that the financial strain the school caused the cathedral could be solved if Maio would pay for the Mexican children. Renwald at one point simply denied the demographic realities of the area. "I feel that the Cathedral is not ready to alienate Holy Angels. The membership of ninety families out of two hundred and fifteen still shows that the majority is not Mexican. Therefore," he concluded, "I think that Holy Angels should still stay under the direction of the Cathedral."[65] Although somewhat unschooled in these issues, Bell, with the advice of his consultors, accepted Renwald's arguments. Maio, angered by the decision, abruptly sought a transfer to a pastorate in far-off Tahoe City.

Five years later Renwald probably regretted passing up the offer to relieve himself of the administrative and financial burden of Holy Angels School. In a January 1967 report to Bell, he admitted an eleven thousand–dollar deficit for the cathedral. "The whole cause of the deficit are the schools [Holy Angels and St. Joseph's under the cathedral's sponsorship]," he admitted, "and the school situation is such that there should be one school and not two schools. I cannot think of a public school system that would tolerate, without consolidations, what has been going on in the Cathedral parish."[66] In 1973 Holy Angels closed.

Even with the setback of Maio's grand plans, the new church proved to be what he and Kenny hoped it would be: a rallying point, a *centro* for the city's Latino/a population. Each year the church drew more and more people to events as it became the spiritual hub of the Latino/a presence in the city.

GUADALUPE AS URBAN PRESENCE AND UNIFYING, SPIRITUAL FORCE

As the size and demands of the Latino/a community grew, Guadalupe Church became not only an urban center but also a regional center for

Latino Catholic life. The Reverend Keith B. Kenny, who spent some years as the head of the Catholic Youth Organization, came back to head the parish in 1962. By this time he had become very involved with local efforts to send Sacramento priests to work in Mexico and Latin America and had himself become even more immersed in Latino culture and religion. Kenny was a man of passionate beliefs. At a Marian celebration before hundreds of youth at Sacramento's Edmond's Field in May 1959, Kenny warned, "Unless we banish sin—public and notorious sin for which we are becoming a scandal to the world—our divorce rate, our birth rate, our filth production and consumption rate—our selfishness and greediness—our self-complacency in the face of the needs of others . . . then we must banish Mary Immaculate. . . . With Mary we are strong. Without her, America is doomed!"[67]

Kenny brought the same passion—absent the undercurrent of his nationalistic Cold War Marian devotion—to his pastorate at Guadalupe. He and his associates transformed it into a center for Chicano pride and activism as well as a sanctuary for prayer and religious observance. He traveled to Mexico many times in support of the Papal Volunteers for Latin America. On one trip Kenny spent three weeks in Mexico, conferring with Catholic leaders and attending Guadalupe celebrations. He returned to Sacramento convinced that the key to Latino/a mobilization was an engaged laity. He pointed out how active Catholic groups had successfully challenged communist takeovers at the University of Puebla and communist influence in business and industry.[68]

Another like-minded cleric was Eugene Lucas, who became active in Spanish-speaking ministry after his 1957 ordination. Lucas appeared at Guadalupe after Kenny's transfer to the CYO in 1958. Although maintaining a lower profile than Kenny, Lucas was no less intense. In 1962 he launched the popular Cursillo Movement in the diocese by hosting these profound courses in basic Christianity in the aging St. Stephen facility. The appeal of these retreats was overwhelming. From February 1962 to March 1963 eleven *cursillos* were held, six in Spanish and four in English for men, and one in Spanish for women. More than four hundred attended, more than half of them Spanish speakers. They also included nineteen priests.[69] Out of the ranks of the *cursillistas* came a host of committed Chicano/a leaders who worked alongside Kenny and Lucas in creating a more vocal and rights-conscious Latino/a community. Many of them pressed local church authorities hard on issues of social justice related to Chicano/a issues.

When Bishop Bell challenged Lucas's efforts on behalf of the United Farm Workers Organization, former *cursillistas* came to his defense. The Committee of Social Justice, formed from their ranks at Our Lady of Guadalupe Church, requested that Bell allow Lucas's participation "in the cause of the civil rights of workers of the field and other workers." The *cursillistas* informed Bell, "The activities of Father Lucas reflect the sentiments and aspirations of a great number of the members of the diocese where already the Mexican represents nearly 50 percent of the members of the diocese of Sacramento."[70]

Under Kenny and Lucas, Our Lady of Guadalupe Church solidified its status as a cultural and religious center for Sacramento's Latino/a community. Although other Sacramento-area churches tended to the spiritual needs of Spanish speakers, few had such a powerful public impact or sense of identity as Guadalupe, whose programs reached out to Spanish speakers throughout the region.

Continuing work begun in the 1950s, Kenny and Lucas expanded efforts to minister to the migrant camps in neighboring counties.[71] They formed the Rural Education and Advancement Program (REAP), a body of lay, religious, and seminarian volunteers who provided catechetical instruction, health care, and a "presence" to the workers' children who lacked contact with outsiders. REAP volunteers fanned out to six areas with high concentrations of migrant worker camps to provide catechetical instruction and to distribute religious articles while at the same time conducting English classes, providing health checkups and dental work, and handing out clothing.[72] Volunteers lived for three months at a time in the small delta community of Hood, located between Isleton and Walnut Grove, providing religious and charitable services. Kenny also coordinated the ministry of priests from Mexico and other Spanish-speaking countries who came to the Guadalupe Church to help with the increasing sacramental load (by then involving more than four hundred baptisms and confirmations a year). Ministry to the men and women working in the fields was also a priority.

Efforts to unionize farmworkers, the signature social justice issue of

California life and politics in the 1960s and 1970, found a sympathetic reception at Our Lady of Guadalupe. Viewing the often squalid living conditions and poor work environments of the farmworkers made Kenny a bitter critic of the government's Bracero Program. When the program finally ended in 1964, Kenny became an early supporter of César Chávez's efforts to organize a California farmworkers' union. As early as 1958 the devout young organizer had appeared in Sacramento and had gone to mass at Guadalupe. Kenny and Chávez became close friends. At one point Kenny invited Chávez to preach a homily at mass. Kenny, a private pilot, also began flying the leader to various locations in his light aircraft. In 1965 he began working with strikers in the Delano grape-picker strike (the boycott lasted until 1970). Kenny and Lucas walked picket lines and encouraged workers to leave the fields and join the ranks of the picketers.[73]

In 1966 Kenny and Lucas played an important role in publicizing Chávez's dramatic three hundred–mile march north from Delano, in Kern County, to Sacramento. Along the way both Kenny and Chávez helped add to the sense of religious pilgrimage of the march, which was led by a cross and an image of Our Lady of Guadalupe. As the protesters neared Sacramento, local seminarians went to an encampment near Clarksburg and performed segments of a popular Passion play. The climax of this profound and politically significant event took place at Guadalupe Church. On the Easter vigil, Salvatorian Father Robert Casper (a weekend assistant of Kenny) ignited and blessed the Easter fire, which was placed not only on the large Paschal candle but also on a torch and conveyed like the Olympic flame across the Sacramento River to the marchers. The next day, Easter Sunday, the marchers strode triumphantly into the city, staged a tumultuous demonstration at the state capitol, and then, in front of the church's huge mosaic of Our Lady of Guadalupe, held a benediction service with Bishop Alden J. Bell presiding.[74] The church provided a perfect backdrop to the union of religious faith, Chicano/a pride, and the demand for justice for farmworkers.

The high public visibility of Kenny and Lucas on behalf of Latino/a rights and economic justice led both of them to embrace the rising tide of sociopolitical consciousness developing, especially among young Latinos/as in Sacramento—many of them former *cursillistas*. A commitment to justice for the Latino/a members of the church led other priests who worked with Latinos/as, including the Reverend Arnold Meagher, to immerse themselves in Latin American history and culture (Meagher would even study it at the University of California–Davis). Aware of their "gringo" status, however, none of the men pushed themselves as leaders but rather worked to develop indigenous leadership. Part of this program was to press church officials to take note of Latino/a needs and to symbolically recognize the position and importance of Guadalupe as a regional center for Latino/a identity and issues. Taking up Maio's failed efforts for parochial status, Kenny, Lucas, and the energized Guadalupe laity (many of them *cursillistas*) took up Maio's earlier efforts and petitioned the diocese repeatedly to end their designation as a "mission" of the cathedral, which was now an uncomfortable reminder of their lower status. One parish group insisted that a freestanding national parish whose boundaries would then include all of Sacramento and eastern Yolo counties would be a "unifying, spiritual force among Mexicans of the area." The petition noted bitterly, "The lack of 'status' of any kind is not resented by the people. It is accepted like so many other things in their lives, without being understood, yet as somehow marking them off as 'unacceptable' by their neighbors and even by the church." They protested that the lack of a parish "is a continuing insult to the Mexican people. The Italians have a parish. The Portuguese have a parish. But the Mexicans, by far the largest and most needy minority group, have none." They adamantly opposed a counterproposal by diocesan authorities to turn Guadalupe into a territorial parish for that part of Sacramento. A new parish would have to affirm the reality of the Mexican space carved out and built by Maio. But the momentum could no longer be stopped. "The Church was built and is being paid for (albeit slowly) by the Mexicans. It is culturally Mexican. It would be unfair to turn it over to the 'gringos.'" In October 1969 the church finally achieved the status of a national parish. Kenny served as administrator until the appointment of a Mexican national, Father Jorge Moreno, as pastor in the early 1970s. In 1978 Guadalupe was designated a national sanctuary.[75]

In the aftermath of Vatican II (1962–1965) and in the midst of the social changes of the late 1960s, Kenny, Lucas, and the Guadalupe community became the focal point of Chicano militancy and the "brown power" ethnic-identity movements of the period.[76] Working with Great Society antipoverty programs, Guadalupe and *cursillo*-trained activists propelled Latino/a issues to the forefront of Sacramento life. A symbolic moment of "arrival" came in 1969 when a former *cursillista,* Manuel Ferrales, became the first Latino to win a seat on the Sacramento City Council.

CONCLUSION

From determined opposition to ethnic parishes and nationality churches, Catholic leaders of Sacramento eventually endorsed just such a facility for Latino/a Catholics. The progress was slow, in part because the Latino/a community was both poor and transient. However, the rising tide of Latino/a spirit found an important expression in the creation of the new church.

The church's engagement in Latino/a issues was inevitable, given the predominately Catholic faith of many who left Mexico for El Norte. Yet as Sacramento entered the sixties, few could have predicted the paramount role the Catholic Church would play in framing labor issues for decades to come. The social needs of Spanish-speaking Catholics had become a vital component of the work of the church in the state capital. The needs of hungry, ill-clad, and homeless Sacramentans, however, reached beyond any particular ethnic or religious group. Confronting the challenge of homelessness would provide another chapter in church-city relations.

CHAPTER 9

Homelessness and Fighting the City Consensus, 1970–2000

"Nobody wants them"

There was yet one last use for the old St. Stephen Church at Third and o streets. Urban renewal had already begun to knock down the West End flophouses and cheap hotels. One of those left homeless by the demolition of the cheap housing was Abel Chacon, a migrant worker who followed the crops in the northern valley. In 1966 Chacon approached Father Keith Kenny, administrator of Our Lady of Guadalupe Church, with the suggestion that the now vacant St. Stephen's be turned into a hostel for the temporarily unemployed. Kenny readily agreed and helped Chacon set up more than 100 cots in the decrepit structure and install rudimentary cooking facilities. The demand for the makeshift shelter was greater than Chacon or Kenny had imagined, as more than 140 persons were crammed "temporarily" into both floors of the building. Only one toilet served the sanitary needs of all.[1] This was more than the building could safely hold. Anxious to remove the building for redevelopment, the city shut it down in 1967 for multiple code and safety violations. No one knows where the homeless went. The aggressive city action to close the makeshift shelter met no resistance from the diocese, which was anxious to get rid of the aging building. In hindsight this small episode was a sign of things to come. In later years, care of the homeless and the demands of urban redevelopment would clash bitterly in Sacramento. The church and the community that had, for the most part, enjoyed an amicable relationship, eventually found themselves at loggerheads.

As we have seen, Sacramento, like many communities, relied on a combination of public and private agencies to aid the "homegrown" poor. However, when the Great Depression pushed the network of private providers to their limits, social welfare fell largely to the local, state, and federal governments and became a major part of their annual expenditures. Sacramento had long made distinctions between the "worthy" and "unworthy" poor. These too were initially swept away in the suffering of the Great Depression. Sacramentans of all faiths continued to give to the poor. Catholics in particular kept up their charity through the Catholic Ladies' Relief Society as well as branches of the popular St. Vincent de Paul Society, which were organized in various parishes. After the church reforms of Vatican II, many parishes formed social justice committees that raised money or undertook projects for the poor.

But the visible poverty of the Depression did not return in the postwar era. A healthy economy created thousands of jobs, and the Sacramento metropolitan area experienced a burst of prosperity. Suburban flight left the poor in the city, many on the now decrepit West End of Sacramento and in pockets of poverty near the downtown. However, even these "safe" quarters were falling to the plans of urban developers who were anxious to eliminate blight and make urban areas more attractive. Although redevelopment proceeded in fits and starts, its advocates in the 1980s and 1990s believed that Sacramento could now become a "major league city." In addition to a new push for urban beautification, the nation and the community experienced a backlash against the "overly generous" welfare policies of the 1950s and 1960s. This was spearheaded to some degree by a revival of conservative politics in the sixties, seventies, and eighties. Keying into middle-class resentment at paying taxes to support the "shiftless," conservative ideologues revived and rehabilitated the nineteenth-century distinction between the "deserving" and "undeserving" poor.

These dynamics created a complex and combustible political and social climate in Sacramento when a tidal wave of hunger and homelessness washed over the state capital in the late twentieth century. Some Catholics found themselves caught between their traditional impulse to support city development and the need to help the poor. When a Catholic Worker–inspired food program that laid down no means test for the distribution of food and clothing refused to move or alter its services in an area coveted by city developers and politicians, a season of controversy erupted. The old church-city consensus fell apart, and an unusual antagonism reigned where there had once been peace and cooperation.

The spectacle of people sleeping on streets or urinating in alleys, foraging Dumpsters and trash receptacles for food, or panhandling in downtown shopping or business districts became a frequent site in many western cities, especially during the 1980s.[2] Martha R. Burt notes that in 1981, Seattle, Eugene (Oregon), and Salt Lake City all had rates of homelessness exceeding 20 per 10,000 of population. In 1983 Reno joined the list. By the end of the decade, the benchmark of 20 homeless per 10,000 in population had been reached in 147 of the largest cities in the country, including Sacramento. In all of these cities, church organizations—and even coalitions of religious denominations—supplemented public agencies through soup kitchens, shelters, food lockers, clothing distribution centers, health-care facilities, and advocacy programs for the homeless.[3]

Private organizations, like churches, cared for groups of people who would otherwise rely solely on public support. They also helped "control" the homeless, by providing them sustenance and getting them off the streets for a time. But they also encountered criticism from law enforcement, who objected to the drunkenness, drug use, fighting, panhandling near local businesses, and trespassing on private property in the vicinity of caregiving sites. Urban developers of the 1980s and 1990s, anxious to revitalize downtown areas, could not avoid the phenomenon of homelessness. "Livability is incompatible with widespread poverty," argued Daniel Kemmis, an urbanist from Denver—a city with a large homeless population.[4] Yet what to "do" with the legion of homeless in cities could not be easily resolved. Wherever homelessness grew, there were unending public debates over its causes and cures. Sacramento developers wanted them out of areas they hoped to improve. Other parts of the city or its metropolitan area were unwilling to receive them or operate programs to feed or shelter them. "Not in my back yard" (NIMBY) was and is a reality of urban, suburban, and even rural life. Churches and charities could not easily turn their backs on the poor or just send them away.

POSTWAR SACRAMENTO:
PLANS FOR THE FUTURE AND REDEVELOPMENT

The onset of World War II did much to improve the local economy, as full employment once again blessed the city and county of Sacramento. But even as the war was being fought on far-off shores, Sacramento business and civic leaders were laying plans for another wave of urban development and growth.

The advent of the military installations, the availability of land and electrical power, the benign climate, and the development of air-conditioning provided the raw material for a new era of boosterism. Already in 1942 a committee of the Chamber of Commerce, led by auto dealer Claude Coffing and executive secretary Arthur S. Dudley, began strategizing on how to capitalize on the mighty flow of federal dollars being pumped into the state capital by the military and defense industries. A 1946 report, *Forecasting a City's Future,* urged an expansion of government jobs to take the place of seasonal work in the canneries and on the nearby farms. "A city which has a great many government employees, insurance men, real estate brokers, railroad workers, tradesmen and professionals, knows that some income will be coming in, rain or shine, in season and out, and that business in general will be good. In hard times, service jobs don't drop off as fast as factory or farm jobs."[5] Coffing and Dudley optimistically projected that Sacramento would grow to a city of 250,000 to 300,000 by 1960. (City population reached only 191,667 in 1960.)

Hoping that disposable income brought by new government jobs would encourage Sacramentans to "splurge a little," the report projected needs for new schools, hospitals, stores, theaters, and especially homes. Encouraging Sacramentans to "provide such a simple thing as more roofs," the report praised "urban redevelopment—the tearing down of blighted areas by government initiative, and the rebuilding of those areas with modern homes and business buildings by private initiative," calling it "a must for the slum-ridden sections of Sacramento."[6]

The relocation of the poverty stricken was an important subtext of these ambitious plans. The city had done fairly well over the years in pre-venting homeless people from loitering in public areas either by shooing them away or by shunting them to the cheap flophouses and hotels in the West End. However, the plight of the urban poor soon ran up against the demands of developers for city space and the removal of all kinds of blight—including human "blight."

By the mid-twentieth century, redevelopment and freeways were creat-ing a new demographic map for the city. They also contributed to a hous-ing shortage by knocking down old buildings—inexpensive residences for Sacramento's poor, mentally ill, and elderly. Relocation efforts were part of the urban-renewal agenda. For example, in the project that cre-ated Capitol Mall, 716 households (with varying numbers of people con-stituting a "household") were demolished and 440 of them relocated to nearby neighborhoods. At least 90 percent of those relocated, according to the plan, were supposed to receive better accommodations than what they had left.[7]

However, not everyone was able to find—or afford—other housing. Some of the city poor crowded into the nearby Alkali Flats neighborhood, where they lived in old residences designed for single-family use.[8] Large numbers of the city's African American community relocated to Oak Park or farther south to the Meadowview neighborhood. Others departed the city altogether—some were rumored to have received one-way bus tick-ets to Stockton. Thus, pockets of poverty were simply relocated to other neighborhoods or cities.

Relocation difficulties were compounded by alterations in federal and state social safety-net programs. Support for social welfare programs softened, as they required more and more of the revenue from city and county tax levies. Statewide backing also weakened during the admin-istration of Governor Ronald Reagan (1966–1974) who began to "cut, squeeze, and trim" burgeoning welfare costs, especially programs for the care of the mentally ill. Later, when he became president, Reagan slashed federal housing subsidies by nearly 80 percent. Restraints on the growth of property taxes in California were locked in place when voters approved Proposition 13 in June 1978, drastically reducing the revenue flowing into county government. Proposition 13 may have helped many home owners avoid escalating property taxes and thereby keep their homes, but it also meant less money for the urban services and for the poor. This was the context for a major collision between city needs, as defined by the traditional power elites, and how the Catholic Church applied its religious mission to social problems and public service.

A NEW DEVELOPMENT ERA

Sacramento emerged from the economically lethargic 1970s primed for a new burst of development. Once again, an important revision of city government preceded a period of growth. In 1970 a revision of the city charter retained Sacramento's city-manager system, but it also breathed new life into the mayoralty and city council. The new charter created a system whereby council members were elected by geographic districts instead of "at-large" and a mayor elected citywide (the previous charter provided that the council member who won the largest number of votes would serve as mayor). The new city council was elected in 1971 with a dynamic new slate of politicians. Voters elected Richard Marriott (a former employee of the *Catholic Herald*) as mayor. The council aggressively tackled a number of issues related to Sacramento's growth.

The office of mayor exercised only one of nine votes on the council, but the office was now popularly elected, investing it with new prestige and higher visibility. After Marriott resigned in 1975, three very strong figures held the office: Philip Isenberg, Anne Rudin, and Joseph Serna. All three were hardworking, public minded, and committed to upgrading and improving Sacramento's planning, infrastructure, transportation systems, and cultural image.

New building and renovations helped to remake the state capital. In 1976 a new community center on J Street opened its doors. Another pedestrian mall was tried on K Street that fed into a historic district of renovated and reconstituted buildings called Old Sacramento. A major railroad museum was planted in the heart of this new historic district, and in the 1990s a new urban mall opened to gateway the span between the end of K Street and "Old Sac." New restaurants, entertainment venues, and opportunities for nightlife blossomed during the 1980s. Housing in downtown neighborhoods became desirable again and was remodeled or renovated, as state workers and other professionals quit the difficult commute from the suburbs.

In 1987 the city completed the first lines of a highly popular light rail system that tooled through the downtown. By 1998 the system extended as far east as the former Mather Field–Mills Station area. In 2005 it began scooping up passengers in Folsom. Visitors coming to Sacramento in the 1990s beheld a city that now had a visible skyline of a half-dozen sky-scrapers. Sacramento received a coveted National Basketball Association franchise when the Kansas City Kings relocated to the state capital in 1985. After some tussle, team owners built a huge new arena for the team out in the Natomas area north of the city. Even the city's old Memorial Auditorium was handsomely refurbished.[9]

The cultural ferment of the 1960s and 1970s also changed the social climate of the state capital. Gender, sexuality, war and peace, and eth-nic diversity issues bubbled to the surface, especially during the term of Mayor Anne Rudin (1983–1992). As Rudin and her successor, Joseph Serna (1992–1999), worked hard to make Sacramento a more diverse and welcoming environment for all, they also contended with the economic and human fallout resulting from the closure of the county's three major military installations. In Plaza Park, right across from city hall, both of them saw the increasing reality of homelessness and visible urban pov-erty. Tending to their needs had to be balanced with the plans of city developers, anxious to make Sacramento a "major league city."

Already in the 1970s a congressional study tagged Sacramento as the sixth most needy city in the country, with 10.5 percent of its families liv-ing below the poverty line. The numbers of unemployed and poor grew in the 1980s, although the spread of urban poverty across the nation, ironi-cally, pushed Sacramento out of the "coveted" sixth place. Homelessness rose steeply in the 1980s, and the reasons for it provoked debate around the community, from dining room tables to city council chambers. LeRoy Chatfield, the executive director of Loaves and Fishes, a Catholic Worker facility for the indigent, insisted that homelessness existed in Sacramento because of "the lack of truly affordable housing (which was calculated at $200 a month for rent) and the artificially low minimum wage." Chatfield observed that other etiologies (for instance, alcoholism, drug addiction, mental illness, begging) were only "overt symptoms of homelessness."[10]

Activist Tim Brown, who succeeded Chatfield as the head of Loaves and Fishes, recalled moving to Sacramento to attend graduate school in

1982 and meeting the founders of Loaves and Fishes. He remembered that in 1983, when homelessness was still climbing, "there were very few shelter beds back in those days. And it's when homelessness was really growing. . . . [I]t grew rapidly from about '82 to '88 or so. And it coincided with the Reagan administration cutting the federal housing budget by 80 percent, cutting about 300,000 people off disability. Many of those people ended up homeless with mental health issues."[11]

City and county officials struggled to keep up with the tide of homeless, some of whom, as stated, were mentally ill. To address these needs, in part, the city opened a shelter on Bannon Street, and some of the indigent, including those released from the Sacramento Mental Health Center, were dispatched there. However, homeless advocates challenged various administrative policies, and the state supreme court forbade the use of the Bannon Street facility as a poorhouse.[12] Finding a place to assist the poor that complied with the law became a challenge. The Bannon Street facility was adapted as a homeless shelter, and in 1985 the city also contracted with the Salvation Army to care for the homeless. Homelessness had by then become a city and county problem that was absorbing more and more of the time and energy of public officials, as well as resources from private charities.

CATHOLIC RESPONSES TO THE HOMELESS

Religious institutions helped to fill gaps left by federal, state, and local welfare agencies. The Salvation Army—committed to a rehabilitative approach to urban poverty—fed, sheltered, and assisted Sacramento's urban poor. Their shelter and facilities were regularly flooded with increasing numbers of men, women, and children seeking assistance. Similarly, the Union Mission on Bannon Street provided food and gospel exhortations to those who came to them.

Catholics also jumped into the void to help the obviously needy who were at their doors. Monthly feeding programs had already begun at St. Joseph Church and Immaculate Conception in the 1980s. Weekly meals were offered at the Stanford Settlement, run by the Sisters of Social Service, and a "bounty" meal organized by Catholic lawyer and future judge James Mize at St. Philomene Parish began in 1982.[13]

One of Sacramento's most concentrated areas of poverty was the old suburb of Oak Park. Once a fashionable district with middle-class homes and palm tree–lined streets, its cohesion had been destroyed by freeway expansion. Of these developments Immaculate Conception pastor the Reverend Daniel Madigan caustically observed, "In the 1960s Oak Park was mutilated by the invasion of two intercepting freeways. Blocks of gracious living flanked by streets of established enterprises were eliminated. The freeways themselves, and their huge cloverleaf over Broadway, took out hundreds of homes. Many people were dislocated. Many more just moved away. Oak Park gradually slid into the inner-city, multi-racial neighborhood that I found when I moved there in 1976. It is truly a 'Cinderella' in reverse. Riches to rags."[14] The relocated urban poor, many of them African American, also made their way to this part of the city.

Immaculate Conception Church, which was once a relatively affluent and thriving parish community, soon emptied out, as it found itself in the center of a growing enclave of poverty and crime. In 1973 remaining parishioners created an emergency food-locker program similar to the one run by Protestant churches in South Sacramento. The first program was initially open twenty-five hours a week, five days a week. In 1976 energetic Father Madigan was assigned to the parish. Madigan brought considerable experience working with both lower-income people in Del Paso Heights and affluent Catholics at Sacramento's Sacred Heart Parish in the city's elite "Fabulous Forties" area. Madigan recollected, "Within a couple of years we were bursting at the seams." Faced with more and more mouths to feed and bodies to clothe, Madigan thought big. Under his guidance, the simple food distribution service and the food locker evolved into a major social service empire. In 1987 a local commercial real estate broker, Charles "Chuck" Sylva, helped Madigan obtained a $400,000 loan from the Diocese of Sacramento and another $350,000 from the bank and bought an old grocery store building near the parish. He quickly set to work refurbishing the building and paying back the steep loans he had taken. In early November 1987 Bishop Francis A. Quinn dedicated the new facility. When Madigan first arrived in 1976, his program was serving 789 people annually. By June 1983, 5,693 people had come for help.[15]

Madigan expanded the services, which he renamed Sacramento Food Bank Services. In addition to the food distribution program, Madigan added a clothing outlet, children's services, a learning center, a computer center, and other programs staffed by hundreds of volunteers. A bad experience with government funding led him to swear off any kind of government support forever. Instead, with the help of publicists, photographers, and his own winning personality, he solicited and received millions in private donations.[16]

Sacramentans from all walks of life (including Mayor Joe Serna, who contributed when he could) revered the hardworking Irish priest who did so much good. But Madigan's enterprise with its focus on the working poor did not reach a number of Sacramento's homeless. As Madigan himself explained, "We did not see many of the push-cart [grocery-cart] people. . . . Our folks mostly had roofs over their heads, and we provided them with enough to eat and get by until they got back on their feet." As local attorney Tina Thomas, who gave pro bono legal advice to Madigan's operation, noted, the priest's efforts seemed to be working because city leaders and others felt the working poor were more "worthy" of a helping hand than were the street people.[17]

Meanwhile, the homeless appeared in even greater numbers on the riverbanks, in abandoned buildings, and on the streets. Who would care for the increasing number of "grocery-cart people" whom some considered the "undeserving poor"?

LOAVES AND FISHES: COOPERATION AND CONFLICT

Loaves and Fishes began in 1983 through the efforts of two Sacramento activists, Dan and Chris Delany. Its first facility was a defunct beer hall, on North Twelfth Street on the north end of the city, near Alkali Flats. It was to serve as a drop-in center for the local homeless and alcoholics.[18] Its founders had no idea how big it would grow.

Dan Delany had been a priest of the Archdiocese of Los Angeles. He married Marie "Chris" Pacino, a former Sister of the Immaculate Heart, in 1968.[19] Both were inspired by the nonviolent-change philosophy of Dorothy Day and the Catholic Worker movement.[20] Day's philosophy of personalism and her nonjudgmental attitude toward the poor set her apart from other "charitable" types in the Catholic Church. She was an unflinching critic of capitalism, which she disdained for its toleration of poverty, hunger, and homelessness in the midst of great wealth. Followers of Day embraced the poor as icons of Christ who was himself a poor man and attempted to treat them with the dignity and respect they did not receive in society.

In 1976 the Delanys moved to Sacramento and began their service to the poor with a program to house and transport families of inmates at nearby Folsom Prison. They purchased and renovated an old Victorian house on Twelfth Street in 1978 and lodged families in part of it. With donations from friends and supporters, they were able to make a go of the project—even during times when Dan was jailed for various acts of civil disobedience.[21]

The start-up money for Loaves and Fishes had come from a $30,000 loan from the St. Vincent de Paul Society of the Sacramento Diocese, thereby linking the charity to the official work of the church. It enjoyed favorable support from Bishop Francis Quinn and his successor, Bishop William Weigand. Even though it eventually became an independent non-profit corporation and emphasized the ecumenical nature of its work, it retained its Catholic identity through its Catholic Worker roots and its ties to local clergy, nuns, and volunteers from Catholic parishes. In fact, Catholic congregations regularly took up collections to help Loaves and Fishes stay afloat. In its early years, mailing lists from Catholic charities of the Sacramento Diocese were used to help raise funds. Joseph Laharty, director of Catholic Charities, played an important role in the center's origins.

In early September 1983 Bishop Quinn blessed and dedicated the Loaves and Fishes Dining Room, which began serving a free hot meal every weekday at noon to needy people in Sacramento. It was easily accessible to the city's poor, who marched to the site in increasing numbers for food and some respite from the perils of the streets. Chris Delany recalled that the facility was intended at first for local indigents and street alcoholics. However, the recession of the 1980s and the policies of the Reagan administration sharply increased the number of homeless and placed increased demands on the feeding program. By Thanksgiving the 75-seat facility was attracting up to 375 diners per day. "Down the line we are going to need a permanent facility," Dan Delany commented to the Catholic press in 1983.[22] From these humble beginnings, Loaves and Fishes became one of the major private purveyors of care for Sacramento's poor and homeless. In 1987 LeRoy Chatfield was hired as its executive director and played a significant role in the charity's subsequent expansion and its dealings with the city. His intense religious zeal under-girded his work at every step.

Chatfield was born in the northern valley town of Arbuckle. In 1948 he came to Sacramento as a boarding student at the Christian Brothers School on Twenty-first and Broadway. As a young teenager he was attracted to the discipline and academic rigor of the brothers, whom he later recalled had to administer "tough love" to some of their boarding students. Chatfield joined the order after his first year of high school and completed his early formation and education by 1957. As a Christian Brother, he was known as Brother Gilbert. Chatfield taught at Catholic high schools in Bakersfield and San Francisco.

Chatfield had first heard of Dorothy Day and the Catholic Worker movement as a first-year high school student and had become involved in Catholic Action "cell" work. The simple methodology of this rather intense form of Catholic activism encouraged participants to "observe, judge, and act." Chatfield recalled how these ideas remained with him. His first direct contact with the Catholic Workers came in 1960 when he visited the St. Elijah House of Hospitality in Oakland. In 1963 he became close friends with Ammon Hennacy, a major figure in the movement who espoused anarchism and ran the Joe Hill House of Hospitality in Salt Lake City. Chatfield invited Hennacy to speak to his high school students in Bakersfield and also to local Catholic activists.[23] In 1965 Chatfield left the religious life, and the following year married Bonnie Burns.

At a National Catholic Social Action conference in Boston, Chatfield heard antiwar activist the Reverend Philip Berrigan make reference to César Chávez and his efforts to organize farmworkers in Delano. Chatfield was surprised to hear about Chávez and the efforts, since he lived only thirty miles from Delano. Later, after much searching, he finally met Chávez in a converted church building in the southwest corner of Delano. Chávez explained his plans to organize the farmworkers, one of the classes of workers not under the coverage of the National Labor Relations Act, and Chatfield signed on to work with him, becoming one of the organizer's key aides. He remained with Chávez until 1973. Work with the movement no doubt honed Chatfield's political skills and his sense of mission on behalf of the poor.[24]

Chatfield next moved to Sacramento and became involved with politics, managing the campaign of Congressman Esteban Torres of Los Angeles. In 1974 he ran the successful northern California campaign for Governor Jerry Brown. He served Brown for five years and on four separate occasions was confirmed by the California Senate for various posts. From 1980 to 1985 he worked as a real estate developer in Sacramento and also earned a master's degree in political science at the University of California–Davis.[25]

Chatfield's spiritual world meshed with his passionate devotion to the cause of the poor. Long after he left the cloister of the Christian Brothers, Chatfield wrote admiringly about the discipline of "leaving the world" that all candidates for religious life were required to undergo. It meant freely renouncing all—family, friends, possessions, even former identity—to prepare for a life of service. Though no religious fanatic, it is clear that he highly internalized the single-mindedness of the Catholic vowed religious life and developed a deep-seated concern for the poor.[26] What others, including Sacramento mayor Joe Serna, perceived in his personality as "stiff-necked" or resistant, Chatfield believed was principled and faithful to the gospel. Few Sacramento religious figures of any denomination who have had any dealings with public life have held such an uncompromising worldview.

Chatfield's wife, Bonnie, had been involved with Loaves and Fishes from the outset and recruited the critical volunteer labor that the center needed for its increasing operations. As organizational needs mounted, Joseph Laharty suggested to the Delanys that they hire a full-time organizer to help coordinate the growing demands of Loaves and Fishes. Chatfield began in February 1987 as the first full-time person to work for Loaves and Fishes. What started as a three-year contract extended thirteen years, until his retirement in 2000. A working board of directors helped to keep Loaves and Fishes on track with the basic tenets of the Catholic Worker philosophy.

Chatfield oversaw a substantial expansion of Loaves and Fishes as the charity worked to meet the cascading needs of Sacramento's homeless. His years of service with Chávez and his own passionate concern for the poor gave him a clear moral vision about what needed to be done—and also an unflinching realism about what it took to do it. In his own words he refused "to water down [the charity's] non-judgmental philosophy about homeless people or to tone down its advocacy for very low cost housing and emergency services."[27] The old pattern of accommodation to the sociopolitical status quo would no longer be operative.

EXPANSION AND CONFLICT

The challenge of meeting the multiple needs of Sacramento's homeless ultimately clashed with city development plans, and church and city would square off for major combat over an issue about which both felt moral authority. Many Catholics, who had long supported the city consensus and worked to create social peace, now found themselves in contention with neighborhoods, business leaders, and even certain city officials.

City leaders, including the mayor, members of the city council, and the police department, became anxious at the growing numbers appearing daily for the Loaves and Fishes free lunch. They also heard a steady stream of complaints from residents in the area that the homeless were sleeping, loitering, defecating, and urinating on their properties.[28] Local businesses complained that homeless and needy people frightened away customers.

From its fairly humble beginnings in 1983, Loaves and Fishes had grown rapidly. By early 1986 the Delanys had forged a network of seventeen volunteer groups to staff the meal program. New programs followed, as the needs of the poor presented themselves. A daytime women's shelter called Maryhouse opened under the direction of Mercy Sister Laura Ann Walton. The Mercy Sisters also donated substantial sums to the charity and helped set up a clinic with a nurse practitioner. With proceeds from a fund drive and a contribution of fifty thousand dollars from the Sacramento Diocese, Loaves and Fishes purchased the original property as well as twenty cottages behind the site. These would be adapted for low-cost housing. Subsequent property acquisitions took place in 1991, 1996, and 2002. Although originally attached to the diocese, in 1987 Loaves and Fishes incorporated as a separate charitable agency, but "it intentionally kept the Catholic Worker mission of ministering to the poor and homeless through the Christian works of Mercy."[29]

The larger numbers of needy coming to the site inevitably raised concerns about its impact on the surrounding neighborhood. Dan Delany remarked to the Catholic press, "We have had no complaints from neighboring businesses because we always monitor the people who wait in line for their hot meal each noon. We hope with more area and longer hours, we can alleviate lines altogether." However, some neighbors were unhappy with the homeless "invasion" and accused Loaves and Fishes of being a magnet for the poor in the region. Tensions erupted when eighty business owners, landowners, and home owners, concerned about "the transients, the filth and the crowding," examined city records and discovered that Loaves was operating without a city permit. Dan Delany expressed a willingness to comply with city regulations but noted, "Frankly, I think what's happening is that Sacramento was a sleepy town for a long time. Now the big buildings are being built and suddenly we have a problem with the homeless—nobody wants them."[30]

Delany had a point. A building boom in downtown Sacramento was renovating the area around the capitol, with new upscale hotels and restaurants, and the need for a "clear" space for legislators, staffers, and visitors to stroll without homeless panhandling was becoming more urgent. Loaves and Fishes applied for the needed permits for Maryhouse; its Mercy Medical Clinic; Mustard Seed School for Homeless Children; Guest Health Outreach, a health education and medical screening facility; and eventually Brother Martin Courtyard, a supervised waiting area for dining room guests. A women's shelter at St. John Lutheran Church was also transferred to the site. To add space for the now flourishing meal program, the St. Vincent de Paul Society helped the charity purchase an adjacent perfume factory and an unfinished concrete-block building. A new kitchen, dining room, and offices replaced the overcrowded original dining room. This was completed in 1990 as funds became available.[31] The daytime Maryhouse women's program was transferred to the perfume factory, which also served as an emergency overnight shelter for women and children—an overflow from a program sponsored by St. John Lutheran Church.

The decision to expand and upgrade the facilities won the support of the city planning office staff. But opposition came from Sacramento police chief John P. Kearns, who complained that homeless people blocked the nearby Regional Transit (light rail) tracks, panhandled, and drank in public. "While we recognize the needs of the hungry and the homeless," Kearns wrote to the city planning commission, "this department feels that this particular location is inappropriate and that the mix of proposed uses is potentially dangerous to those who would use the facilities." However, Loaves and Fishes Board spokesmen argued that most of the poor were Sacramentans and that the problem would not go away if the mission was forced to close. "We do not draw poor people from some mysterious region. That is a fantasy on the part of those who would like to wave a magic wand and have the poor go back to wherever they came from." Subsequently, Loaves and Fishes added a green space called Brother Martin Courtyard to provide a place for the homeless to "hang out" for companionship rather than loiter in public areas.[32]

The growing village of charity along North Twelfth Street was complemented by its leaders pressing the city to do more to house the homeless. Annually, the Delanys had called on the city to increase the amount of housing for the poor. Loaves and Fishes leaders floated a plan to build a thousand cottages for the homeless to occupy. Forming a separate corporation, Sacramento Cottage Housing, Inc., the organization proposed a village of one-bedroom, 310-square-foot cottages to be located on a 2.75-acre site at the Sacramento Social Services Complex north of the Southern Pacific Railroad tracks between Twelfth and Sixteenth streets. The Sacramento Housing and Redevelopment Agency promised to put up $1.4 million of the $3.2 million needed for the project, with the rest coming from the sale of state and federal tax credits.[33]

Introduced at a city council meeting on July 19, 1994, the cottage proposal sparked an intense lobbying campaign by supporters of Loaves and Fishes. This episode brought out the first stirring of the battle to come. Mayor Joe Serna, who was a backer of the project, was at the same time at the forefront of efforts to attract new investment and development to downtown Sacramento. Of course, the placement of housing for the poor did not work well with the schemes of those who wanted more upscale housing or an office and entertainment center. When Loaves and Fishes supporters bombarded him with phone calls, letters, and faxes, the conflicted mayor publicly asked the Loaves and Fishes partisans to back off. "Stop the letter-writing campaign right now; give me a little space." On March 1, 1995, the housing program was approved by the city council, but with the warning that the project would expand only if Sacramento County and the surrounding communities did more

Mayor Joseph Serna, ca. 1992. Courtesy of
Sacramento Archives and Museum Collection
Center, *Suttertown News* Collection.

to support it. Serna's chief of staff attempted to transfer some of the
political heat surrounding housing for the poor to the county government, suggesting after the vote that it "would be productive for housing advocates to begin a dialogue with the county and some of the surrounding communities." He further stated that the city "has done its
fair share and more." Groundbreaking for the first sixty cottages, named
after Roman Catholic bishop Francis A. Quinn, took place in late
November 1995.[34]

Nevertheless, homelessness continued to grow in the Sacramento area,
and the demand for homeless services swelled. Another program was
added in 1994—this one for runaways and street teenagers—when the
Sisters of Social Service won a $36,000 United Way grant to refurbish a
warehouse on the Loaves and Fishes compound.[35]

Serna's dilemma in the Quinn housing episode sent a signal that the increasing number of guests at Loaves and Fishes was going to clash with development politics. In fact, the seeds for conflict had already been sown in 1990, when the Sacramento Housing and Redevelopment Agency petitioned the city council to create a redevelopment zone in the Richards Boulevard area, close to Loaves and Fishes. This zone included the former Southern Pacific yards area that had been given up by its owner, the Union Pacific Railroad. Richards Boulevard had for many years been a corridor of warehouses, canneries, and industrial plants but now seemed ripe for the expanding office and residential needs of a growing downtown region. The promise of tax-increment funds and partial city support for office buildings, residences, and other facilities along the city's fringe pressed lawmakers to make the necessary compromises—especially with nearby North Sacramento, which also wanted these funds—and approve the area.[36] Plans to create "a huge, dazzling business and shopping district" using public and private funds soon ran aground over arguments regarding the amount of low-income housing required for any redevelopment project. Elaborate plans by the ROMA Design Group of San Francisco called for 6,932 new housing units in the redevelopment area, but only 1,040 for families with annual incomes under twenty thousand dollars.

Chatfield protested the limited number of low-income units and, as a member of the neighborhood council, cast the sole vote against the redevelopment scheme. After multiple setbacks, revisions, and changes, the city finally approved a 1,365-acre Richards Boulevard master plan in 1992. Intended to "double the size of the downtown district with a $1 billion array of parks, high-rise office buildings and housing," the plan won acclaim from many quarters. The main pillar of the plan was the redevelopment of 36 acres of the old railroad yards, now owned by the Union Pacific. But as the city became embroiled in disputes with the railroad company over the disposition of the property, developers began to grow impatient.[37]

Faced with this setback, in 1995 developers turned their attention to the riverfront portion of the redevelopment area—an area that touched on the Loaves and Fishes complex. Chatfield and others observed that the level of city antagonism toward Loaves and Fishes escalated from this point on. In the ensuing fight, however, city developers rarely criticized the charity in public, instead allowing neighborhood groups and other vocal citizens to push back against Loaves and Fishes. The charity's directors and legal team were certain that there was a link between the new development plans and the ramped-up campaign against feeding the homeless.[38]

Loaves and Fishes took two blows in mid-1995. In May the county announced cuts in general-assistance benefits, reducing the average income of some of the poorest by sixty-five dollars per month. Also, city officials insisted that a savings-and-trust office as well as the center for homeless teenagers on the property required special operating permits. Chatfield quickly dismissed this as harassment from the city manager's office and noted that the "issue with the savings and trust payee program was that the state banking department objected to the use of the terms Savings and Trust." It was not a special-use-permit issue. In early July trouble erupted over efforts to expand Friendship Park and offices of the organization when residents of the nearby Mansion Flats discovered that Loaves and Fishes had not acquired a building and special-use permit. Officials ordered the agency to also obtain these permits. As the level of tension rose, Chatfield dug in his heels and prepared for battle. He urged his project's supporters and volunteers to call and write city manager Bill Edgar in support of the planned expansion of the park.[39]

Opponents of the charity began to speak out. "We are opposed to any expansion of Loaves and Fishes," Walter F. Mueller, a local conservative gadfly declared to the press. "They will just attract more homeless people. This area is already saturated with too many homeless service providers." Others pointed to the damage done, ostensibly by homeless people, to the old Globe Mills on Twelfth and C streets, a structure that had been ravaged by fire in 1995 and stood as a wrecked hulk in the neighborhood. One aggrieved property owner in the vicinity, Johan Otto, complained that Loaves and Fishes had been "an octopus out there, just growing and growing, with no regard for how it hurts businesses and properties in the area. We won't accept another expansion. This is going to be a real show-down. This is a fight to the end."[40]

Support for the organization now wavered, even from the formerly sympathetic *Sacramento Bee*. In a scolding editorial, the paper noted, "Loaves and Fishes does important and necessary work. Without it Sacramento would have more beggars on the streets, more crime and more homelessness." But it took the agency to task for its heedlessness of the cries of its neighbors, and in a snide attack on the volunteers who wrote letters in defense of the organization, the suburban-living editors wrote, "When Loaves and Fishes closes at 3:30 P.M. and its volunteers go home to their middle class neighborhoods, the needy pour out on to the streets and riverbanks, overwhelming the patience of downtown residents." The *Bee* urged the charity to dialogue with its neighbors and appealed to it to "decentralize its operation so that no one area is so disproportionately and unfairly impacted."[41] Clearly, city officials felt they were being made to bear the brunt of caring for the poor of the entire region, expending millions of dollars in fire, police, and other city services because of the concentration along the Richards Boulevard development area. Chatfield later dismissed the insistence on "decentralization" as "a public relations ploy," noting that because "the city council had legislated such prohibitive special use permit ordinances about the siting of social services, it would have been impossible to relocate anywhere else."[42] Further, Loaves and Fishes was close geographically to the people it sought to serve.

Loaves and Fishes generated some unfavorable publicity when *Newsweek, Time, U.S. News and World Report*, and even *Sports Illustrated* ran a fund appeal, claiming that Sacramento had twenty-seven thousand homeless children.[43] Mayor Joe Serna and other city council members reacted angrily and countered that the city had "only" five hundred homeless children "on any given night." Loaves and Fishes officials themselves seemed a bit flummoxed by the figure and discovered that it had appeared three years earlier in a local publication and had drawn no attention. It had been put in the popular newsmagazines by a San Francisco ad agency that ran free public service ads and had fished the article from its files and run it without checking the facts. Loaves and Fishes officials tried lamely to defend the number, but the appearance of the advertisement in the middle of the whole permit imbroglio did not help. More scolding editorials from the *Bee* followed, and a complaint to the consumer and environmental protection division of the Sacramento County district attorney's office brought Loaves and Fishes a legal "slap on the wrist" and a suspended five hundred–dollar fine.[44]

The mayoral primaries of March 1996 made Loaves and Fishes a campaign issue—the first time a Catholic institution had been the subject of electoral concern since the contested 1895 election dominated by the anti-Catholic American Protective Association. Candidate James Hastings stood in front of the burned-out Globe Mills on c Street and "declared war on Loaves and Fishes." Only two reporters attended Hastings's event, but other candidates, though unwilling to call for the closure of the charitable site, suggested that its growth be limited or it be relocated. One perennial political candidate, bail bondsman and bounty hunter Leonard Padilla, suggested moving the facility to the old Mather Field—but offered no suggestion of how the poor would get there.[45]

Even as the mayoral race was debating the Loaves and Fishes issue, efforts were under way to negotiate a solution to the impasse between the city and the organization. LeRoy Chatfield had made what he later described as a "cold call" to attorney Tina Thomas shortly after the New Year in 1996 to ask her to represent Loaves and Fishes. Thomas had just returned from a trip to Indonesia and Australia with her daughters. In Australia she had met a dance troupe of aboriginal women who had recently been on a tour of New York. The women told Thomas that they were horrified to see people eating out of garbage cans. The remark shook her, and it was still on her mind when Chatfield's call came. She agreed to take the case. Chatfield did not know Thomas personally before he contacted her, but had closely followed her career in the newspapers. He knew her connections with developers and her familiarity with the laws of property usage. She was a respected member of the local bar, and she had also worked on Mayor Serna's campaigns. Thomas proved to be a formidable advocate for Loaves and Fishes. In addition to her ties with Serna, she also worked well with then city councilman Darrell Steinberg, who played an important role in advocating for Loaves and Fishes throughout the process.[46]

In lengthy negotiations that went from early 1996 until 1997, Thomas began with concessions on the permit issue and code violations, and offered to drop the request for park expansion. Thomas also expedited the applications for building permits and needed repairs and modifications for the facility. The teen center was to be located elsewhere. However, Loaves and Fishes refused to turn its back on the poor or downsize or decentralize its operation. In late August 1996 the stalled negotiations became even more intense when Loaves and Fishes abruptly withdrew its application for permit changes after attorney Thomas charged that city planners had attached all kinds of restrictive conditions. For example, they demanded that Loaves and Fishes serve no more than five hundred meals a day—at the time they were serving nine hundred—and mandated that its Friendship Park remain open an additional three hours so homeless people would not wander the neighborhoods waiting for the city shelters to open at night. The Loaves and Fishes request to "officially" serve sack lunches on Sunday (they had been doing it without permission) was also turned down. City officials demanded compliance.[47]

Recently appointed bishop William Weigand summoned both sides to his office to broker a deal, but compromise seemed impossible. Mediation efforts promoted by various other outsiders went on behind the scenes in October, but the issue of "illicit" Sunday feeding hardened battle lines. Denied the right to hand out bag lunches to the poor, Chatfield enlisted the help of Francis House, another agency for the urban poor supported by a consortium of downtown churches, to take the lunches and hand them out on Sundays at its Seventeenth Street location. However, the influx of people and litter brought howls of outrage from merchants and residents in the neighborhoods around Francis House, creating even more furor. When this occurred, the feeding was transferred to the Catholic Worker House at Twelfth and G.[48]

In December angry downtown business owners and residents retained attorney William Coyne to prepare a suit against Loaves and Fishes and continued pressuring city officials to crack down on the "satellite feedings." Chatfield refused to budge. He would not cut the number of meals to five hundred, he would not stop the Sunday feeding, and he would not close a counseling center for homeless teens. In a December 31 editorial the *Bee* insisted that Chatfield had to give in and suggested that the food given out by Loaves and Fishes allowed the indigent to use "spare money" to buy liquor. The editorial laid the blame at Chatfield's door.[49]

As matters grew worse, Chatfield and the board of Loaves and Fishes were advised by its attorneys, William Kennedy and Gary Smith of

Northern California Legal Services, to hit back at the city by filing a federal suit charging that the city's code demands were interfering with their First Amendment rights to conduct a religious ministry. But Chatfield and the board, Kennedy recalled, refused "to strike the first blow." The city council then threw the fat into the fire. At a closed session, the city council decided to sue Loaves and Fishes for "long standing code violations including serving food to the poor on Sundays without permits." The motion to sue was made by councilman Steve Cohn and supported by Robbie Waters, Rob Kerth, Jimmie Yee, Sam Pannell, and future mayor Heather Fargo. It was opposed by Mayor Serna and councilman Darrell Steinberg. On hearing of the vote, Loaves critic Walter Mueller declared, "It's about time. When they put Sunday feedings back in violation of permits, that was like a slap in the face. This will put them in their place and show them the city is not playing around." Chatfield replied with indignation, "This [must] be a first in the nation where a city council sues a charity for feeding hungry people on the Christian day of Sunday."[50]

In the days before the city lawsuit was actually filed, Serna tried to reach out to Chatfield. But by this point everyone was frozen into their position. Chatfield and Loaves and Fishes would not bend either on the size or on the extent of services offered—especially the feeding. Those who feared the mentally ill or alcoholic homeless in their neighborhoods would not budge, nor would others who believed that the meal program was a magnet for the poor in the region. On January 17, 1997, the city filed a thirteen-page complaint against Loaves and Fishes that sought a temporary and permanent injunction against the charity for violating its special-use permit. It insisted that the operation of its facilities constituted "a public nuisance."[51]

The subsequent fallout was a public relations fiasco for the City of Sacramento as the story hit the pages of the *New York Times, Los Angeles Times, People* magazine, and the nationally circulating weekly *National Catholic Reporter.* Bishop Weigand echoed the anger of Loaves and Fishes supporters and publicly chastised city officials: "I am embarrassed by the city action last Friday. . . . I would urge city officials to drop that approach and to provide positive leadership toward a realistic solution. . . . Trying to prevent feeding the hungry on Sundays and limiting the number on weekdays is not the answer. Harassing charities over mostly trivial regulations is not the answer."[52]

Weigand's call for calm and rational discussion was lost in the ensuing uproar. Mayor Serna, who had opposed the lawsuit, called it a "national embarrassment" for the city. He directed his most caustic comments at his rival, councilman Steve Cohn, an apologist for the lawsuit who was gearing up to challenge Serna in the 2000 mayoral race. Serna also publicly warned the council that the charity "would bring in some of the best constitutional lawyers in the country 'pro bono' to defend them" and that the charity's friends were skilled activists and organizers.[53]

In fact, attorneys for the charity seized the moral high ground and expressed incredulity that a city would sue a religious charity. As Serna had predicted, Loaves and Fishes assembled a "dream team" of attorneys led by Tina Thomas, all of whom agreed to handle the case pro bono. Joining Thomas and William Kennedy, director of Northern California Legal Services, was Jerome Cohen, a Carmel-area attorney and former general counsel for the United Farm Workers Union between 1967 and 1981.

When Serna political consultant Richie Ross heard that the defense included Cohen, he allegedly told the mayor, "I don't know anything about the city's lawsuit with Loaves and Fishes but if Jerry Cohen represents Loaves and Fishes, the city of Sacramento loses."[54] In a move that put the city on the defensive, the attorneys for Loaves and Fishes decided to file a countersuit—a first in Sacramento, where no church-run organization had ever fought back against the city in this fashion.

Cohen framed the public relations and political dynamics of the issue as a contest between good and evil. He urged (over the misgivings of some of his fellow attorneys) the insertion of a powerful introductory piece into the seventy-five-page countercomplaint. The text of this remarkable document was composed by Gary Smith of the legal team, a Yale Divinity School graduate. Reading almost like a medieval bull of excommunication, it invoked the Hebrew prophets Ezekiel and Jeremiah as well as fiery verses from the Epistle of St. James to condemn the city's action. At its core the countercomplaint repeated the religious imperative of the Catholic Workers and others devoted to the poor drawn from the twenty-fifth chapter of St. Matthew: "As you did it for one of the least of these my brethren, you did it to me" (25:40).[55] Both Kennedy and Smith agreed that the addition of the controversial preface was a risky decision. Its text read more like a church sermon or a press release and could have been subject to a legal motion to strike. Other volunteer lawyers were not comfortable with it, and even though Tina Thomas went along, it was not without a moment of hesitation. Kennedy, Smith, and Cohen insisted that the preface was essential, not only to the legal brief but also to win the critical public relations battle surrounding the controversy. Chatfield strongly endorsed its inclusion.[56]

The document dismissed the city's complaints of code violations as so much harassment and bureaucratic runaround and insisted on the larger issue at stake, freedom of religion. "This case is about the City's attempt to restrain Loaves and Fishes . . . and others from engaging in religiously mandated service to the City's homeless and poor, all under the guise of a zoning ordinance action." Reciting the multiple causes of friction between the charity and the city, the brief insisted, "The City has . . . violated Cross-complainants' rights to the free exercise of religion, to equal protection of the law, and rights against discrimination afforded by the United States and California Constitutions and federal and state law."[57]

Cohen had earlier emphasized the constitutional issues in play with the city's suit. "This is a protected activity. These guys are engaging in conduct pursuant to their religious beliefs. They have First Amendment rights to what they are doing and the City Council is going to have to face that fact." The countersuit expressed a willingness to "depose everyone from low-ranking city employees to Mayor Joe Serna, Jr., and [a willingness] . . . to take the case as far as the U.S. Supreme Court." Summing up his efforts to push back hard against the city, Cohen later recalled that the city council had given him a pretty good opening to fight back.[58]

In the midst of it all Serna expressed frustration with the unbending Chatfield. Although sympathetic to the poor and a Catholic, Serna desperately wanted compromise.[59] By contrast, Chatfield, deeply driven by his religious beliefs, was not interested in compromise where basic principles were at stake. "I was hungry and you fed me" was not a pious aphorism to be recited perfunctorily before some civic event; it was a way of life. Bucking the historical pattern of accommodation that had marked city-church relations, Chatfield refused to go along. He may have been the first Catholic church figure to ever tell the city no.

As the lawsuits played out in public, efforts to reach a negotiated settlement were under way, with councilman Darrell Steinberg taking the lead in finding a way out of the impasse. Serna himself, an old friend of Thomas's, also made it clear that he wanted to work out an acceptable deal. Overcoming his antipathy to Chatfield, he agreed to open back channels to Cohen, using aide Mark Grossman as his emissary. Cohen made clear that Chatfield would not bend on the feeding issue—and that he and his supporters were willing to engage in civil disobedience if necessary. By the end of March city leaders backed down and urged Loaves and Fishes to reapply for the Sunday feeding permission.[60] Insisting that they had never been against allowing Sunday feedings, four city council members suggested that they would change their votes. Together with Serna and Steinberg and newly elected Lauren Hammond, a majority now existed to grant the controversial permission. The only opposing voice was the outspoken Walter Mueller (not a council member), who angrily denounced the council members who had changed their minds about the feeding. However, councilman Jimmie Yee reflected the pressure put on the council: "We are getting tired of getting hammered as if we are the bad guy. We've been trying to resolve this all along through mediation, but the public hasn't been aware of that." Steve Cohn and Heather Fargo dropped broad hints that the lawsuit might be withdrawn.[61]

Rhetoric cooled as well, and Serna tried to make peace. "My job as mayor is to help the council get through this. . . . All of us, including me, need to put our passions aside. We will figure this out. There are no bad people here." Even "fight to the finish" Johan Otto sang a different tune. "We've never asked them to be shut down. All we've asked is to keep the area cleaned up." Cohn also backed away from his demand of limiting the number of meals, but hoped that the charity would help keep the neighborhood clean.[62] The most vexatious order—limiting the number of people who could come to the site—was not even mentioned. Perhaps everyone knew that there was no other place the poor could go. Even though accusations of NIMBYism were decried as unfair, it was evident, even from the satellite feeding at Francis House, that no other part of the city would take the homeless.

Anxious to extricate themselves from the public relations fiasco, the city proposed mediation by Kathleen Kelly, dean of the McGeorge

School of Law, in Sacramento, and Richard Gilbert, a retired superior court judge. The complainants and attorneys for both sides began in June 1997 to hammer out an agreement based on a draft prepared by attorney Tina Thomas. Just before the Fourth of July holiday, a settlement was announced.[63] Loaves and Fishes was permitted to apply for the necessary permits—including the one for Sunday feeding. The center for homeless youth was permitted to remain temporarily on the site but had to "diligently" pursue another location. (The search for a new location took until February 2006.)[64] As Chatfield later recalled, the search took that long because "every time the teen center proposed a suitable location, the council member of that district stepped in to prevent a permit from being issued." A desultory press conference, where all parties expressed satisfaction, was held. Chatfield called it "a fair settlement" but was not happy with the self-congratulations of city council members who had precipitated the crisis at the behest of the development cadre. "As odd as it may sound, this was the most difficult request I had to fulfill during the entire legal confrontation with the city of Sacramento," he declared. He noted that subsequent requests by Loaves and Fishes directed to the city received prompt attention "without the benefit of a contrived and antagonistic public hearing. . . . [N]eighborhood activists dropped out of sight and the redevelopment area developers were silenced."[65]

Loaves and Fishes did not come out unscathed. It experienced a drop in donations just as it was compelled to absorb nearly two hundred thousand dollars in permit fees and bills for repair work to correct its zoning and building-code violations. This forced a cutback in services in August 1997.[66] Observers like Chatfield, who had an innate sense of the underlying dynamics of city planning and politics, noted that future development efforts would have to include some provision for the homeless. The role of the church in development has been traditionally cooperative. How that relationship evolves, as the development priorities rub against the needs of the poor and homeless and the demands for affordable health care and housing, remains to be seen.

CONCLUSION

The noisy dispute over Loaves and Fishes was truly a watershed for the Catholic Church in Sacramento. Unwilling to accept the city consensus on urban development and the increasingly hostile attitudes toward the poor and homeless, Chatfield and his coworkers simply refused to budge and virtually dared the city to challenge them. Forged in the power of nonviolent resistance and skilled in the adept use of public relations, they effectively challenged the city's efforts to shut them down and move them out. Unlike Sacramento's Catholics of the 1920s, there was no intention of giving up urban space to new developments. The care of the hungry and the homeless would take place even if it meant rejecting the insistence on taking care of only the "worthy poor" demanded in a politically conservative era.

Few probably realized the historical significance of the Loaves and Fishes stand and the dramatic reversal it represented. In part this was probably because the people making the decisions were not the high-profile religious figures who had previously dominated the church's decision making. The local bishop, after some efforts to bring the two sides together, did comparatively little to bring about a settlement. There were few clerical collars to be seen in most stages of the incident. The most visible official presence was the participation of the Sisters of Mercy, who organized and ran some of the programs at Loaves and Fishes. In fact, the Catholic leaders of the dispute were laypersons and their legal allies. The confrontation left many shaken, and the Sacramentans who offered an opinion on the matter felt uncomfortable with Chatfield's combative attitude; some suggested that he seemed to be "spoiling for a fight." Perhaps some of the befuddlement or frustration with Chatfield's methods bore witness to just how entrenched the attitude of city-church cooperation had become in the city's culture. Catholics and city hall traditionally had an amiable relationship and helped each other out. Here, however, they had drawn battle lines and sued each other, and one side capitulated to the other. Even today, sharp disagreements over the care of the homeless lurk just beneath the surface of church-city relations, and some worry that it is just a matter of time before the issue explodes again.

Conclusion

The year 2005 was a major milestone in the history of Sacramento's built environment. In May a new city complex quietly opened up behind the 1910 beaux arts–style city hall on Ninth and I streets. The five-story two hundred thousand–square-foot structure overcame a number of obstacles to its completion—including the discovery of a Miwok village on the construction site. The $87.5 million project provided additional room for city offices, an expanded city council chamber, and a tasteful renovation of the old city hall itself. Linked by a sunny plaza, the two buildings symbolized the continuity of Sacramento city life from one era to the next.[1]

Two blocks east and two blocks south from the new city complex, a newly renovated Cathedral of the Blessed Sacrament opened its doors in November. Closed temporarily in 2003, the old structure had undergone a $35 million restoration—the most thorough remodeling since its erection in 1889. When the scaffolding was taken away from its exterior, the old church never looked better. The repainting of its outer walls and the regilding of its steeple crosses made it stand out even more magnificently as the architectural gem of Sacramento's downtown. The interior of the church, once dowdy and unappealing, is now a "must-see" for the city's tour guides. The cathedral's faded artworks have been refurbished, its statuary repainted, and the sun pours luminously through releaded and cleaned stained-glass windows. The magnificent dome, which had been closed off with a false ceiling in 1932, was once again reopened and painted, giving the interior of the church a centering point. Hidden from the eye were miles of new wiring, 320 tons of steel, and unknown amounts of epoxy that literally glued the major beams to the church structure.[2] Like the thousands who were awestruck on the day of its dedication in 1889, visitors to Sacramento's 2006 jazz festival during the Memorial Day weekend gaped as they toured the cathedral. Both the renovated city hall and the restored cathedral exude the new confidence of California's rapidly changing capital.

Both buildings have been catalysts for another wave of urban beautification in the downtown. On J Street, one block south of the city hall, a long-neglected stretch of this busy downtown corridor, between Eighth and Twelfth, is steadily improving, with condominiums and the renovation of old structures such as the majestic Elks Tower just a block north of the cathedral.[3] At the Elks a new dining outlet will join an array of first-class restaurants that cater to the legislators, staff, lobbyists, and even the governor himself who make the capital their home for at least a part of the year. Along K Street, new buildings are now projected westward from the cathedral at Eleventh to Seventh streets and then into a major downtown mall.[4] When completed, this stretch of Sacramento's downtown will once again be a living, dining, and recreational area. The cathedral may again have resident parishioners. Directly behind the church, on the spot where the first Catholic bishops of the city lived, a set of upscale condominiums called "Cathedral Place" is being built. Diagonally across the alley north of the cathedral, a thirty-story condominium and retail structure is proposed.

Both the city hall and the cathedral help Sacramento celebrate the diversity acknowledged by the 2002 Harvard study and *Time* magazine. The plaza linking the old city hall and the new city complex acknowledges the Miwok origins of the area and is named Sa'Cumn'e, or Big House. Miwok artifacts are displayed on the inside, and artwork depicts the racial and cultural diversity of the city. In the cathedral, Filipinos/as, Africans,

Mexicans, and Vietnamese Catholics will find their beloved icons on the walls together with the traditional images of St. Patrick, St. Anthony, and St. Therese of Lisieux. Working in city government are African Americans, Latinos/as, Chinese, and Japanese Americans. The city has already had three women mayors. The cathedral is served today by staff members named Murphy (Ireland), Ho (Singapore), and Figueroa (Mexico). In these and many other ways, both the city hall and the cathedral reflect the realities of contemporary Sacramento and exercise their own unique influence over their portion of the urban turf.

These architectural and iconic signs are only symbolic of deeper patterns of interaction between church and city. As this text has attempted to demonstrate, the Catholic Church has played an important role in Sacramento's evolution. The Cathedral of the Blessed Sacrament is the prime symbol of Catholic investment in the city, but the city's other churches, schools, playgrounds, health-care facilities, feeding programs, and various forms of social provision contribute as well. Catholics have quietly but powerfully written themselves into the fabric of the city, demonstrating their agency often in the subtle ways that religious bodies must adopt to be successful in western communities. Those who have directed the city's affairs, often men and women of no particular religious belief, accepted and welcomed them.

As in other cities of the West, Catholics in Sacramento did not set the priorities or define the city's character. This was the work of political and commercial leaders who worked hard to ensure Sacramento thrived, even after other "instant cities" had faded away. Again and again, through its leadership, the city overcame the liabilities of its location, like its torrid summer weather and inevitable flooding. It shook off the sneers of those who compared it unfavorably to San Francisco or Los Angeles and stirred the community out of periods of urban lassitude. It retained its position as the state capital despite occasional efforts to move it elsewhere and never gave up trying to end the "scatteration" of state government offices to other parts of the state. The railroad made it a major transportation hub and an industrial center. It lobbied vigorously to become a part of the military-industrial complex, and federal dollars helped to underwrite a period of explosive growth and the emergence of its suburbs. It grew to meet the needs of an expanding state government. Catholic leaders, lay and clerical, quietly and often without fanfare, generally embraced whatever it took to advance city goals. Catholicism was no bar to upward social and professional mobility, and many of the city's movers and shakers were devout Catholics. Anxious to get along with their neighbors, they stressed the social utility of their church buildings and their schools. Benevolence and organized charity on the part of Catholic women helped care for society's unfortunates. Religious sisters pioneered a practical example of female autonomy through their stewardship of schools, child-care facilities, and health care. However, the Catholic penchant for consensus was sorely tested when foreign members of their flock resisted total integration into the mainstream of city life. Catholics publicly clashed with city leaders in the 1990s, when feeding the poor and homeless became a contest over the use of city space.

Most important, although perhaps lost in this version of events, city priorities did not interfere with the worship, prayer, and heartfelt devotion of Sacramento Catholics. Nor did it take away their need for the consoling rituals of the church at important moments in life.

Sacramento tolerantly and even gratefully accepted the presence of the church and understood its importance in maintaining social cohesion and order. Even though occasional outbursts of anti-Catholic (mostly nativist) sentiment erupted from time to time, Sacramentans were not religious bigots. They showed it not only by their affection for the city's first two bishops, Manogue and Grace, and the Sisters of Mercy but also by the compliment all small communities pay to accepted and beloved institutions: a generic identity that referred to the Catholic cathedral simply as "the cathedral" (to the everlasting annoyance of the city's Episcopalians) and to the Sisters of Mercy health-care facility as the "Sisters' Hospital." Graduates of St. Joseph Academy worked in the public schools faithfully for many years. The Jesuits and Christian Brothers trained lawyers, clerks, judges, and accountants. Priests had public schools named for them. Bishop Francis Quinn, who at times slept outdoors with the city's poor, had his name affixed to low-income cottages.

Both Sacramento and the Catholic Church have changed significantly since 1850, but for many of those years, the church has been a minority religion in the California capital. As the twenty-first century opens, demographic shifts have increased the number of Catholics in the city of

Sacramento—evidenced by the founding of new parishes for Koreans and Vietnamese and the increasing number of Filipino/a Catholics who are present in most city parishes. Latino/a Catholics have become a dominant force in Sacramento, as churches all around the city celebrate masses in Spanish every weekend.

As the two rivers, the Sacramento and the American, flow together, so religious faith and city life continue to come together in Sacramento's urban life. Perhaps one sign of the future of this engagement can be found in two iconic figures of great significance to area Latino/a Catholics, both of whom are memorialized in downtown Sacramento. Lisa Reinertston's statue of César Chávez and John Houser's sculpture of Bishop Alphonse Gallegos, the city's first Latino auxiliary bishop, sit in prime urban space.[5] Both men used the language and the vision of the Catholic faith of their Latino culture and communicated it to the poor in the fields or to gang members on city streets. Both statues—one in the shadow of city hall, the other in the penumbra of the cathedral—symbolize the ongoing engagement of religion and public life in Sacramento's history.

NOTES

INTRODUCTION

1. The term *chaos of intentions* comes from Verlyn Klinkenbourg, "Without Walls," *New York Times Magazine,* May 16, 2004, 15.

2. See Ron Stodghill and Amanda Bower, "Welcome to America's Most Diverse City," or the print edition, "Where Everyone's a Minority: Welcome to Sacramento, America's Most Integrated City."

3. A number of works about Sacramento have been published over the years. The most recent overview is my own, *Sacramento: Indomitable City.* Other popular accounts include Dorothy Kupcha Leland, *A Short History of Sacramento;* and William M. Holden, *Sacramento: Excursions Into Its History and Natural World.* Dr. John F. Morse's early city history is included in a reprint of Samuel Colville's *Sacramento Directory for the Year 1853–1854.* Other works are Joseph A. McGowan's *History of the Sacramento Valley;* Thor Severson, *Sacramento: An Illustrated History, 1839 to 1874;* Joseph A. McGowan and Terry R. Willis, *Sacramento: Heart of the Golden State;* and John F. Burns, ed., *Sacramento: Gold Rush Legacy, Metropolitan Destiny.* There are also a number of county histories. Three of the most important are Thomas H. Thompson and Albert Augustus West, *History of Sacramento County With Illustrations;* Winfield J. Davis, *An Illustrated History of Sacramento County, California;* and William L. Willis, *History of Sacramento County With Biographical Sketches.*

4. A sample of the scholarship on western cities includes Gunther Barth, *Instant Cities: Urbanization and the Rise of San Francisco and Denver;* Eugene P. Moehring, *Urbanism and Empire in the Far West, 1840–1890;* and John W. Reps, *Cities of the American West: A History of Frontier Urban Planning.* Western cities since 1940 are covered in Carl Abbott, *The Metropolitan Frontier;* Gerald D. Nash, *The American West Transformed;* and Carol O'Connor, "A Region of Cities." An older but interesting article on the varieties of western cities and the creation of urban civilization is Lawrence H. Larsen and Robert L. Branyan, "The Development of an Urban Civilization on the Frontier of the American West."

5. Dennis Dingemans and Robin Datel have done important work on the implications of Sacramento's spatial realities. See "Urban Multiethnicity." The social closeness of the city is highlighted in Sacramento City College instructor Lloyd Bruno's *Old River Town: A Personal History of Sacramento.*

6. "Typical Early-Day Sacramentan Dead," *Sacramento Bee,* January 15, 1916, 2.

7. There are comparatively few studies on religion and urban life in the West. See Thomas G. Alexander and James B. Allen, *Mormons and Gentiles: A History of Salt Lake City;* and Michael Engh, S.J., who has written of the dynamics of church life in Los Angeles in *Frontier Faiths: Church, Temple, and Synagogue in Los Angeles, 1846–1888.* See also Dorothea R. Muller, "Church Building and Community Making on the Frontier, a Case Study: Josiah Strong, Home Missionary in Cheyenne, 1871–1873."

8. I fully agree with the observations of E. Brooks Holifield who insists that a proper understanding of the role of religion in public life must include an honest appreciation of the meaning of religious belief ("Forum: The Place of Religion in Urban and Community Studies"). Leslie Tentler makes a variation of the same argument when she argues for a greater integration of Catholic issues into the master narrative of U.S. history in "On the Margins: The State of American Catholic History."

9. A growing interest in the relationship of region and religion is reworking the historiographical landscape of American religious history. Geographer Wilbur Zelinsky played a major role in developing this line of inquiry in "An Approach to the Religious Geography of the United States: Patterns of Church Membership in 1952." Edwin Scott Gaustad's *Historical Atlas of Religion in America* has gone through three revisions (see Gaustad and Philip L. Barlow, *New Historical Atlas of Religion in America*). See also Jerald C. Brauer, "Regionalism and Religion in America"; and Bret E. Carroll, "Reflections on Regionalism and U.S. Religious History"; and James R. Shortridge, "A New Regionalization of American Religion." A very interesting set of volumes highlighting the region and religion theme has been produced by the Leonard E. Greenburg Center for the Study of Religion in Public Life at Trinity College, Hartford, Connecticut: Patricia

O'Connell Killen and Mark Silk, eds., *Religion and Public Life in the Pacific Northwest: The None Zone;* Wade Roof and Mark Silk, eds., *Religion and Public Life in the Pacific Region: Fluid Identities;* and Jan Shipps and Mark Silk, eds., *Religion and Public Life in the Mountain West: Sacred Landscapes in Transition.*

10. Ferenc Szasz and Margaret Connell Szasz, "Religion and Spirituality," 389. Szasz amplifies these insights in *Religion in the Modern American West.* See also Eldon G. Ernst, "American Religious History From a Pacific Coast Perspective"; Philip Goff, "Religion and the American West"; Laurie F. Maffly-Kipp, "Eastward Ho! American Religion From the Perspective of the Pacific Rim"; and Gary Topping, "Religion in the West."

11. Szasz uses the relatively neglected role of the clergy in the history of the American West to explain why religion had not been studied by earlier historians ("The Clergy and the Myth of the American West"). An emerging emphasis on social history has brought religion and religious issues back into consideration. See Patricia Nelson Limerick, "Believing in the American West"; and D. Michael Quinn, "Religion in the American West."

12. The literature on California religion is quite extensive. For a good summary of historiographical trends, see Eldon G. Ernst, "The Emergence of California in American Religious Historiography."

13. William Francis Hanchett, "Religion and the Gold Rush, 1849–1854: The Christian Churches and the California Mines," 28.

14. Kathleen Neils Conzen, "The Place of Religion in Urban and Community Studies," 111.

CHAPTER 1 : A COOPERATIVE COMMUNITY, 1850–1886

1. Helen S. Giffen, ed., *The Diaries of Peter Decker: Overland to California in 1849 and Life in the Mines, 1850–1851,* 160.

2. Mark Hopkins quoted in John E. Pomfret, "Mark Hopkins' Formative Years in California," 81. William F. Taylor quoted in Steven M. Avella, "Phelan's Cemetery: Religion in the Urbanizing West," 254.

3. See Laurie F. Maffly-Kipp, *Religion and Society in Frontier California,* 3; Szasz, *Religion in the American West;* and Killen and Silk, *Pacific Northwest.*

4. Quoted in Albion C. Sweetser, *History of the First Congregational Church in Sacramento, California,* 9.

5. "Anniversary Sermon," *Sacramento Daily Union,* July 18, 1854, 3; Isaac Owen to M. Simpson, March 26, 1850, Owen Papers.

6. Samuel Brannan himself, one of Sacramento's early developers, was a prime example of this dynamic. Mormonism had brought him to the West, and he hoped to plant the Mormon Zion on the Pacific Coast. But disagreements with Brigham Young and others caused him to abandon his denomination, and he

soon found his life dominated by commercial activity (see Louis J. Stellman, *Sam Brannan: Builder of San Francisco*).

7. "Sacramento, Cal., July 14, 1851," *Freeman's Journal*, August 30, 1851; Owen to Simpson, March 26, 1850, Owen Papers.

8. "California Protestant Churches," *Sacramento Daily Union*, August 21, 1858, 1.

9. "Sacramento Churches and Sunday Schools," ibid., January 15, 1859, 3; "History of the Methodist Church of Sacramento," ibid., January 5, 1861, 1; "Sunday School Union," ibid., January 2, 1860, 2; "The Sabbath School," ibid., January 5, 1861, 1.

10. Timothy F. Comstock, *An Honorable Heritage: 125 Years of YMCA Service in Sacramento*, 16.

11. What Patricia O'Connell Killen observed of the Pacific Northwest was also true of Sacramento: "Religion has never been a strong mechanism of social control" (Killen and Silk, *Pacific Northwest*, 11).

12. Peter Shields to Joseph T. McGucken, March 2, 1960, Shields Papers.

13. Rev. A. P. Banks, "Sacramento Needs More Modern Churches and Better Church Attendance," *Saturday Bee*, June 22, 1901, 2:10.

14. Rev. J. T. Wills, D.D., "Church Life of Sacramento," *Sacramento Union*, October 2, 1910, 16; Maude Johnston Vogtli, "Sacramento From the Capitol Dome," *Sacramento Bee*, January 23, 1921, 26.

15. Banks, "Sacramento Needs More Modern Churches."

16. "Anniversary Sermon," 3.

17. Ibid.

18. "Gen. Taylor's Obsequies," *Sacramento Daily Transcript*, September 5, 1850, 3; "Eulogy on Gen. Zachary Taylor" (delivered by Col. J. C. Zabriskie in Sacramento), ibid., September 6, 1850, 1; "The Death of President Taylor," ibid., September 5, 1850, 2.

19. Joseph Augustine Benton, "City-Building," n.d., Benton Papers.

20. In August 1850, when Sacramento was convulsed with the so-called squatter's riots, Benton publicly offered spiritual succor to the established landowners and reminded his congregants that obedience to civil authority was an ordinance of God and insisted that sedition against constituted authorities was a sin "not only against man but against God." See "An Appropriate Discourse," *Sacramento Daily Transcript*, August 19, 1850, 2.

21. Benton occasionally used the traditional New England election-day sermon—a carryover from the Congregationalist tradition of New England—to lay out his program. For general background on the election-day sermon, see Alan J. Silva, "Rituals of Empowerment: Politics and Rhetoric in the Puritan Election Sermon." See also Silva, "Increase Mather's 1693 Election Sermon: Rhetorical Innovations and the Re-imagination of Puritan Authority"; and John G. Buchanan,

"Drumfire From the Pulpit: Natural Law in the Colonial Election Sermons of Massachusetts."

22. Benton, sermon delivered April 4, 1852; sermon delivered July 25, 1852, Benton Papers.

23. Ibid., July 25, 1852.

24. Ibid., April 3, 1853.

25. Sacramento had various fraternal organizations, including the Masons, Odd Fellows, Knights of Pythias, International Order of Red Men, and Native Sons of the Golden West. See Willis, *History of Sacramento County*, 246–64.

26. These statistics are to be found in the following issues of the *Sacramento Daily Union*, all in articles titled "Churches," all dated January 1, for the following years: 1858, 4; 1859, 1; 1862, 8; 1864, 4; 1867, 3; 1868, 8; 1869, 2; 1872, 12; 1874, 5.

27. U.S. Bureau of the Census, Census of Religious Bodies, 1906, 1916, 1926, 1936.

28. John Bernard McGloin, S.J., "'Philos' (Gregory J. Phelan, M.D., 1822–1902): Commentator on Catholicism in California's Gold Rush Decade," 109–16. Phelan's influence over Sacramento Catholic life may have even extended to having one pastor, Father James Cassin, removed over the cleric's poor performance in visiting hospitalized church members. See "Removal of Father Cassin," *Sacramento Daily Union*, March 8, 1862, 3. Archbishop Joseph Alemany denied that Cassin had been transferred for that reason ("The Denial," ibid., March 11, 1862, 3). Nonetheless, Cassin was in some sort of trouble with local church authorities, which was only resolved in 1866 by a personal appeal by the priest to Rome. A newspaper report alluded to the trouble: "Father Cassin is energetic and if he thinks he has been wronged he will have his say" ("Father Cassin," *Sacramento Bee*, July 16, 1866, 2).

29. Eifler suggests that among this core group were former miners or transients who decided to settle in Sacramento. These "civic middlemen" were responsible for the bringing of order and stability to Sacramento (*Gold Rush Capitalists*, 90–94, 165–87).

30. "Correspondence, Sacramento, Cal., November 19, 1856," *Freeman's Journal*, December 20, 1856.

31. Amanda Paige Meeker, "Wright and Kimbrough Tract 24: Review of National Register Eligibility," 1:6–7.

32. "California Correspondence, December 13, 1850," *Freeman's Journal*, February 22, 1851.

33. Eleanor Doyle, "Catholic Church."

34. Philos [Dr. Gregory Phelan], "Our California Correspondence," *Freeman's Journal*, August 29, 1850.

35. Ibid.

36. "Correspondence, Sacramento, Cal., November 19, 1856," ibid., December 20, 1856.

37. Marriage Register, St. Rose of Lima Church and the Cathedral of the Blessed Sacrament, Sacramento.

38. For a sample, see the sermon Bishop M. J. O'Farrell of Trenton delivered at one of the sessions of the Third Plenary Council of Baltimore in 1884, "Christian Marriage," in Baltimore Publishing, comp., *The Memorial Volume: A History of the Third Plenary Council of Baltimore, November 9–December 7, 1884,* 120–31. See also Peter K. Guilday, *A History of the Councils of Baltimore, 1791–1884.*

39. Subsequent years record the following numbers of foreign-born Irish in Sacramento County: 1870: 2,429; 1880: 2,232; 1890: 1,979; 1900: 1,646; 1910: 1,432; 1920: 1,032. Their numbers continued to decline until the 1950s, when a burst of postwar expansion brought an increase (Elizabeth A. McKee, "The Irish in Sacramento").

40. Patrick Joseph Blessing, "West Among Strangers: Irish Migration to California, 1850–1880," 330–39.

41. Baptismal Register, 1850–1887, St. Rose of Lima Church and the Cathedral of the Blessed Sacrament, Sacramento.

42. Elaine Connolly and Dian Self, *Capital Women: An Interpretative History of Women in Sacramento, 1850–1920,* 1–20; Blessing, "West Among Strangers," 363.

43. John Francis Delury, "Irish Nationalism in Sacramento, 1850–1890," 10; Delury, "Irish Nationalism in the Sacramento Region."

44. Meagher spoke to Sacramento citizens at the Congregational church.

45. John F. Delury, "Irish Nationalism in the Sacramento Region, 1850–1890: Two Paths to Freedom—From Meagher of the Sword to T. P. O'Connor."

46. John T. Ridge, *Erin's Sons in America: The Ancient Order of Hibernians.*

47. McKee, "The Irish in Sacramento," 48–58.

48. "Convent School, Sacramento, July 19, 1870," *San Francisco Monitor,* July 23, 1870, 5.

49. Ronald E. Isetti, *Called to the Pacific: A History of the Christian Brothers of the San Francisco District, 1868–1944,* 46–48. For the Irish roots of the Christian Brothers in Sacramento, see p. 9.

50. Richard Rodriguez, *Days of Obligation: An Argument With My Mexican Father,* 206–8.

51. Kevin Condon, C.M., *The Missionary College of All Hallows, 1842–1891.* See also Rev. Thomas O'Loughlin, "The Demand and Supply of Priests to the United States From All Hallows College, Ireland, Between 1842 and 1860."

52. "Remarks of Father Scanlan," *San Francisco Monitor,* March 22, 1873, 8;

William Ellis, "Sermon Delivered at Cathedral, St. Patrick's Day," 19; Ellis, "Ireland, a Nation," n.p.

53. Blessing, "West Among Strangers," 398n93. Blessing acknowledges that "institutional completeness" was derived from Oscar Handlin's *Boston's Immigrants: A Study in Acculturation.*

54. See Timothy Sarbaugh, "Exiles of Confidence: The Irish-American Community of San Francisco, 1880–1920."

55. Timothy J. Meagher, *Inventing Irish America: Generation, Class, and Ethnic Identity in a New England City, 1880–1928,* 7–8. Meagher has a more synthetic and nuanced discussion of Irish assimilation in *The Columbia Guide to Irish American History,* 102–21.

56. Sarbaugh, "Exiles of Confidence," 161.

57. "St. Joseph's School, Sacramento," *San Francisco Monitor,* July 31, 1869 (emphasis added).

58. Kerby A. Miller, *Emigrants and Exiles: Ireland and the Irish Exodus to North America;* McKee, "The Irish in Sacramento," 86.

59. "In Sacramento," *San Francisco Monitor,* March 24, 1877, 8; Delury, "Irish Nationalism in Sacramento, 1850–1890," 25.

60. Steven M. Avella, "The Personal and Professional in the Work of C. K. McClatchy: The Clash With Peter C. Yorke."

61. McKee, "The Irish in Sacramento," 34–36.

62. William Gormley served as president of the Sacramento Council in 1893 and in 1895 was international vice president of the Bookbinder's Union.

63. "Robert T. Devlin, Leading Attorney, Dies in His Home," *Sacramento Bee,* February 24, 1938, 1. For a complete history of the Sutter Club, see Timothy F. Comstock, *The Sutter Club: One Hundred Years.*

64. "Former Mayor of Sacramento Called by Death," *Sacramento Bee,* May 7, 1919, 10; "Funeral of Ex-Mayor Wm. Hassett Is Held," ibid., May 9, 1919, 2.

65. James Mulligan, son of Terrence Mulligan, interview by author, May 1998, Sacramento. For an example of Mulligan's activities, see "Capital Irish Will Mark Milestone in Eire's March to Full Freedom on Constitution Day in Sacramento," *Superior California Register,* July 17, 1938, 5. See also McKee, "The Irish in Sacramento," 46–48.

66. Quoted in *Under the Lamp Post: History of the Young Men's Institute,* 13.

67. "A Brilliant Record," *Catholic Herald,* June 20, 1908, 5.

68. "History and Resume of Founding [of the Young Ladies' Institute]."

69. "Bishop Grace at Protestant Funeral," *Catholic Citizen,* May 30, 1903, 1; "Catholics Disagree Over $150,000 Hall," *Sacramento Bee,* March 6, 1914, 3.

70. "The Catholic Parade," 4.

CHAPTER 2 : CATHEDRAL BUILDING AS URBAN PROJECT, 1865–1889

1. Charles E. Nagl, "A Fight for Survival: Floods, Riots, and Disease in Sacramento."

2. Barbara Lagomarsino, "Early Attempts to Save the Site of Sacramento by Raising the Business District"; Marvin Brienes, "Sacramento Defies the Rivers, 1850–1878," 2–19.

3. The foregoing history of the capital is taken from June Oxford, *The Capital That Couldn't Stay Put: The Complete Book of California's Capitals*, 67–80.

4. "The State Capitol," *Daily Bee*, February 1, 1866, 2.

5. Joseph Armstrong Baird Jr., "Architectural Legacy of Sacramento: A Study of 19th Century Style."

6. Allusions to the Robinson (who visited Sacramento in 1908) and Hegemann (who was consulted in 1913) plans are found in "City Plans Drawn at Turn of the Century Still in Dream State on Postwar List," *Sacramento Union*, September 10, 1944, 13.

7. This article from the *Call* was reprinted in the *Daily Bee:* "Sacramento As Seen by Strangers," September 13, 1866, 2.

8. Davis, *Illustrated History*, 123–26.

9. Much attention to this phenomenon has been lavished on Southern California. See Glenn S. Dumke, *The Boom of the Eighties;* and Kevin Starr, *Inventing the Dream: California Through the Progressive Era.*

10. Richard J. Orsi, *Sunset Limited: The Southern Pacific Railroad and the Development of the American West, 1850–1930.*

11. D. L. Joslyn, "Sacramento General Shops: Southern Pacific Company—Pacific Lines," 17. Joslyn worked at the shops from 1902 until the 1940s. His work is distilled in a helpful article, "The Southern Pacific Shops, 1863–1950."

12. McGowan, *History of the Sacramento Valley*, 1:244–55.

13. "Improvements at the Railroad," *Daily Bee*, January 23, 1872, 3.

14. Meeker, "Wright and Kimbrough Tract 24," 1:9. The gradual shifting of the commercial district included the movement of churches as well. Three churches—the German Evangelical Lutheran (1867), Presbyterian (1868), and Baptist (1869)—opened their doors at Ninth and K, Fourteenth and O, and Thirteenth and G, respectively. Older churches would later relocate within the penumbra of the capitol grounds.

15. *Eminent Victorians*, 47.

16. Gerald Prescott, "The California State Fair in the Gilded Age."

17. Armand L'egare, *The Great Sacramento Pool Room Battle, 1896–1900.*

18. Richard V. West, "Edwin Bryant Crocker's Art Gallery in Sacramento."

19. Kay Feallock, "The Kingsley Art Club: One Hundred Years of Support for the Arts."

20. Peter W. Williams, *Houses of God: Region, Religion, and Architecture in the United States,* xiv.

21. Louis P. Nelson, ed., *American Sanctuary: Understanding Sacred Places,* 1–14; Jeanne Halgren Kilde, "Reading Megachurches: Investigating the Religious and Cultural Work of Church Architecture," 235.

22. Corinna Laughlin, "One Hundred Years Ago: The Cathedral Builders," 11. When the Episcopal Church tried to build a cathedral in Sacramento, Rev. William Moreland would write, "The cathedral is the chief or representative church of a diocese. . . . It is the seat of the bishop, the center of administration. The cathedral is the visible expression of the organic life of the whole diocese. . . . The cathedral system is the most American of spiritual institutions. Its counterpart in civil government is the State House or Capitol" ("What a Cathedral Would Mean to Sacramento," *Sacramento Bee,* April 25, 1910, 9).

23. Ellen McCracken, "'Cathedrals of the Desert' and 'Sermons in Stone': Fray Angélico Chávez's Contributions to Hispano Church Architecture in New Mexico," 75–105; Bernice Maher Mooney, *The Story of the Cathedral of the Madeleine;* Kevin Frederic Decker, "Grand and Godly Proportions: Roman Catholic Cathedral Churches of the Northeast, 1840–1900," xi–xii; Francis J. Weber, *Cathedral of Our Lady of the Angels;* http://www.christthelightcathedral.org/home.htm.

24. A copy of Manogue's baptismal certificate is in ADS. It notes that he was baptized on the day of his birth in the church of Ballycallan, County Kilkenny. This was the Diocese of Ossory. The certificate gives the year 1829 as his birth date, whereas other sources suggest 1831. Since baptism generally took place right after birth and was often recorded in sacramental books right after it happened, the 1829 date seems more plausible.

25. James S. Olson, "Pioneer Catholicism in Eastern and Southern Nevada, 1864–1931," presents a good summary of the mining booms and the pace of Catholic development in this region. See also Vincent A. Lapomarda, S.J., "Saint Mary's in the Mountains: The Cradle of Catholicism in Western Nevada."

26. The most thorough history of Virginia City is Ronald M. James, *The Roar and the Silence: A History of Virginia City and the Comstock Lode.*

27. Francis E. Weisenburger, "God and Man in a Secular City."

28. Anne M. Butler, "Mission in the Mountains: The Daughters of Charity in Virginia City."

29. Patrick Manogue to Augustine Schulte, April 30, 1885, Archives Propaganda Fidei, Rome, copy in AASF.

30. James W. Hulse, *The Silver State: Nevada's Heritage Reinterpreted*, 147–53.

31. For an excellent account of O'Connell's life and career, see John T. Dwyer, *Condemned to the Mines: The Life of Eugene O'Connell, 1815–1891*.

32. Dwyer, *The Story of Mount Saint Mary's, Founded 1866, Grass Valley, California*.

33. Manogue to James Gibbons, January 3, 1885, Manogue Papers; "Circular Letter of Right Rev. Bishop Manogue," *San Francisco Monitor*, December 15, 1886, 4.

34. Manogue to Cardinal Giovanni Simeoni, January 5, 1883, Manogue Papers.

35. Manogue to Gibbons, January 3, 1885, ibid.

36. Decker, "Grand and Godly Proportions," 59.

37. Robert Snodgrass, "History of St. James Cathedral Parish, Seattle, Washington, 1904–1929," 22–23.

38. "Cheyenne Cathedral, 1867–1974, NHRP TEXT," National Register of Historic Places Inventory Nomination Form, United States Department of Interior, date of survey 1967 (revised 1973), http://www.dioceseofcheyenne.org/history/.

39. A copy of the bill of sale signed by Thomas Dwyer and witnessed by Thomas Grace and William J. O'Brien, dated April 15, 1885, is found in the historical records of the Cathedral of the Blessed Sacrament. The exact price for the lots was $31,500. A portion of frontage on K Street was ignored in the original Dwyer purchase and had to be secured from James McCleery, a wagon maker who had a shop on K Street and owned one of the residences at the Eleventh and K site. McCleery vacated the property, although it is unknown what happened to the rest of the settlers on the cathedral site. One interesting remnant of McCleery's presence was the graceful elm trees he had planted on the property, which framed the cathedral for many years. See "Ella McCleery Left Estate of $106,113," *Sacramento Bee*, September 23, 1955, 8; and "News Jottings," *San Francisco Monitor*, April 21, 1886, 5.

40. Manogue to Schulte, April 30, 1885, copy in AASF.

41. "The Post Office Located," *Sacramento Daily Record-Union*, June 10, 1885, 3.

42. "Our Traveling Correspondent," *San Francisco Monitor*, October 28, 1885, 5.

43. Congressman McKenna apparently had to reintroduce the bill calling for the appropriation. See "Sacramento's Public Buildings," *Daily Bee*, May 24, 1888, 2.

44. "The New Post Office," *Sacramento Daily Record-Union*, May 18, 1888, 3.

45. "Honors to Bishop Manogue," *Daily Bee*, September 26, 1889, 3.

46. "Our Traveling Correspondent"; "Grass Valley Cathedral," *San Francisco Monitor*, March 3, 1886, 5.

47. Manogue's bitter dealings with Archbishop Patrick Riordan are detailed

in James P. Gaffey, *Citizen of No Mean City: Archbishop Patrick Riordan of San Francisco, 1841–1914,* 109–18.

48. "Bryan James Clinch," Biographical Information Card File, California State Library, Sacramento; Francis J. Weber, "Architect, Historian," in *Catholic California;* "Death of Bryan J. Clinch," *Catholic Citizen,* June 9, 1906.

49. A sampling of Clinch's writing can be found in the bibliography, including his two-volume *California and Its Missions.* Clinch was well known and widely respected as an architect by the time he set to work on the cathedral. Shortly after arriving in California from Ireland he entered into partnership with German architect Victor Hoffman in San Francisco. The pair commenced a successful career as church builders. In 1876 Clinch and Hoffman were commissioned to rebuild St. Joseph Church in San Jose, which had been destroyed by fire the previous year. A new church in the town of Napa was the next on Clinch's list in 1881. In 1887 the Jesuits contracted with him to build their novitiate at Los Gatos, a few miles south of San Jose. Subsequent architectural contracts allowed him to build the chapel of the Santa Rosa Ursuline Academy in 1895, St. Joseph Church in Alameda near Oakland, and Our Lady of Mount Carmel Church in Mill Valley. He was also responsible for St. Mary and St. Anthony churches in Oakland, St. Peter's in San Francisco, and perhaps thirty additional churches and other buildings throughout California.

50. "A Great Event," *Daily Bee,* June 13, 1887, 1.

51. "Dedicated! Sacramento's Grand Cathedral," *San Francisco Monitor,* July 3, 1889, 5.

52. Davis, *Illustrated History,* 252; "Sacramento Cathedral," *San Francisco Monitor,* December 5, 1888, 5; "Obsequies of Bishop Manogue," *Record-Union,* March 6, 1895, 3.

53. "Dedicated! Sacramento's Grand Cathedral"; "The Madonna: The Picture Which Now Graces the Cathedral," *Daily Bee,* April 25, 1891, 5.

54. "The New Cathedral in Sacramento," *San Francisco Monitor,* January 9, 1889, 4.

55. "The Church in Sacramento," ibid., March 30, 1887, 5.

56. "Father Quinn's Sermon," *Saturday Bee,* March 9, 1895, 1.

57. "A Lengthy Feast of Reason and a Flow of Soul," *Daily Bee,* June 13, 1887, 1.

58. "Honors to Bishop Manogue."

59. "City and Coast," *San Francisco Monitor,* April 22, 1893, 12.

60. "Death of an Eminent Prelate," *Record-Union,* February 28, 1895, 3.

61. Eleanor Doyle, "Building the Cathedral," *Catholic Herald,* September 30, 1976, 4.

1. "Catholicity in California—Dedication of a Church in Sacramento—Hospitality to Mgr. Alemany, Sacramento, February 24, 1851," *Freeman's Journal,* April 12, 1851.

2. Florence Nina McCoy, "A History of the First Five Years of the Sacramento, California, Turnverein, 1854–1859" (see also Allan R. Ottley, "Angels Without Wings: The Scarcity of Women in Pioneer Sacramento"); U.S. Census Bureau, County of Sacramento, 1850–1970.

3. A plentiful and growing canon on gender and the American West includes Susan Armitage and Elizabeth Jameson, eds., *The Women's West;* Peggy Pascoe, *Relations of Rescue: The Search for Female Moral Authority in the American West, 1874–1939;* and Glenda Riley, *Women and Nature: Saving the "Wild" West.*

4. See Maureen Flanagan, "Women in the City, Women of the City: Where Do Women Fit in Urban History?"

5. Connolly and Self, *Capital Women,* 32. See also Mary Ann Irwin, "'Going About Doing Good': The Politics of Benevolence, Welfare, and Gender in San Francisco, 1850–1880"; and Suellen Hoy, "Caring for Chicago's Women and Girls: The Sisters of the Good Shepherd, 1859–1911."

6. Edna Smith Sibole, *135th Anniversary History of the First Methodist Church.*

7. Sister van Cott's revival is noted in the "Conference Minutes" of the California Annual Conference of the Methodist Episcopal Church for the year 1874, copy in UMCA.

8. Typical of Catholic women's activities is the account of a fund-raiser in the fall of 1856 that garnered more than sixteen hundred dollars for St. Rose's. See "The Ladies' Festival," *Sacramento Daily Union,* October 18, 1856, 2.

9. Owen to Simpson, March 26, 1850, Owen Papers; "Duties of Californians: A Sermon for the New Year, Preached in Grace Church, Sacramento, January 3, 1858, by Rev. Wm. H. Hill, Rector," *Sacramento Daily Union,* January 4, 1858, 1.

10. "Minutes of the Sacramento Women's Council," February 19, 1904, microfilm, SAMCC.

11. Sisters have not been neglected in the relatively few histories of Sacramento women (Connolly and Self, *Capital Women,* 25–27).

12. Anne M. Butler, "There Are Exceptions to Every Rule: Adjusting to the Boundaries—Catholic Sisters and the American West."

13. Anne Elizabeth Hartfield, "'Sisters of Mercy, Mothers to the Afflicted': Female-Created Space in San Francisco, 1854 Through the Turn of the Century

(California)," 89; "To Honor Sisters of Mercy," *Evening Bee*, August 26, 1907, 5. Hartfield uses the work of the Sisters of Mercy in San Francisco as the case study for her examination of female agency by nuns. The growing literature on the agency of American nuns, especially in the Midwest and West, has opened a fresh chapter on the history of women in the American West. See Florence J. Deacon, "Handmaids or Autonomous Women: The Charitable Activities, Institution Building, and Communal Relationships of Catholic Sisters in Nineteenth-Century Wisconsin"; Mary Ewens, *The Role of the Nun in Nineteenth-Century America*; and Martha Smith and Carol K. Coburn, *Spirited Lives: How Nuns Shaped Catholic Culture and American Life, 1836–1920*.

14. "Sacramento, Cal., October 15, 1853," *Freeman's Journal*, November 19, 1853, 3; "To Honor Sisters of Mercy."

15. "Sacramento Sisters Honored," *San Francisco Monitor*, September 14, 1907, 1.

16. John B. McGloin, S.J., *California's First Archbishop: The Life of Joseph Sadoc Alemany, O.P., 1814–1888*, 99–100.

17. For works on McAuley and the development of the Sisters of Mercy, consult M. Joanna Regan, R.S.M., and Isabelle Keiss, R.S.M., *Tender Courage: A Reflection on the Life and Spirit of Catherine McAuley, First Sister of Mercy*; and Mary C. Sullivan, *Catherine McAuley and the Tradition of Mercy*. An introduction to the spirit of McAuley and the subsequent development of the Sisters of Mercy is given in Kathleen Healy, R.S.M., ed., *Sisters of Mercy: Spirituality in America, 1843–1900*.

18. Hasia R. Diner, *Erin's Daughters in America: Irish Immigrant Women in the Nineteenth Century*, 134.

19. Suellen Hoy provides a good overview of the emigration of Irish sisters to the United States in "The Journey Out: The Recruitment and Emigration of Irish Religious Women to the United States, 1812–1914." Hoy identifies two major waves of emigration, the first lasting from 1812 to 1881. The second wave overlapped the first during the 1870s, and continued into the twentieth century. In Sacramento the recruitment of Irish sisters continued well into the 1970s.

20. An older account of the life of Mother Baptist Russell is Mary Aurelia McArdle's *California's Pioneer Sister of Mercy: Mother Mary Baptist Russell (1829–1898)*. A more updated account is Mary Katherine Doyle's *Like a Tree by Running Water: The Story of Mary Baptist Russell, California's First Sister of Mercy*. Doyle's account includes a biographical overview of Russell's life and also an annotated selection of her letters.

21. McArdle, *Pioneer Sister of Mercy*, 26–32; M. K. Doyle, *Like a Tree*, 52–60. Both accounts retell the story of the original eight Mercy Sisters recruited for California, who missed passage aboard the ill-fated *Arctic*, which later collided with another vessel in the Atlantic fog and sank on the way to the United States.

22. One story that appeared on the pages of the *Sacramento Daily Union* related: "We are informed [that] the Sisters of Notre Dame of San Jose have purchased a lot in this city, and contemplate erecting an institution thereon, probably during the present year." However, the journal concluded, "Of the particulars of the purchase—the location of the lot, etc.—we are not advised" ("Sisters of Notre Dame," February 29, 1856, 2).

23. Citations in Archbishop Alemany's diary suggest that he had been in contact with Mother Etienne Hall, general superior of the Daughters of Charity in Emmitsburg, Maryland, for sisters to come to the Sacramento mission. However, various difficulties intervened, and at the urging of the convent chaplain, Father Burlando, the sisters withdrew their offer to come. See Alemany Diary (n.d.), AASF.

24. Citation from Presentation "Annals," reconstructed in 1907 by M. Josephine Hagarty, protégé of M. Teresa Comerford, 16–17. Provided to the author by Sister M. Catherine Curry.

25. Philos [Dr. Gregory Phelan], "Our California Correspondence, Sacramento, Cal., January 4, 1858," *Freeman's Journal,* February 6, 1858, 5.

26. Gian Ackermans, "The History of the Congregation in the Nineteenth Century," 1–13.

27. Mary Urban Archer, O.S.F., *A History of the Holy Name Province of the Sisters of Saint Francis of Penance and Christian Charity, Stella Niagara, New York,* 63, 4.

28. Hartfield, "Sisters of Mercy."

29. "Catholic Orphan Asylum," *Daily Bee,* October 9, 1857, 3; Philos, "Our California Correspondence, January 4, 1858."

30. [M. M. Clare Lunney], "Annals From St. Joseph's Convent."

31. Sister M. Evangelist Morgan, *Mercy Generation to Generation,* 91–93.

32. M. K. Doyle, *Like a Tree,* 145.

33. [Lunney], "Annals," 6.

34. Ibid., 7.

35. A copy of this letter dated April 16, 1872, is found in "Annals of This Convent of the Religious Called Sisters of Mercy of Providence, San Francisco, California."

36. Morgan, *Mercy Generation to Generation,* 121–22; "Annals of This Convent" (emphasis added).

37. Sister M. Gertrude King, "Early History of Sisters of Mercy in Sacramento, 1905–1911," n.p.

38. "Annals of This Convent."

39. Notes by Sister Mary Gabriel Spadier, "About the Early Mercy Community," 3.

40. Mary Katherine Doyle gives some idea of the challenges and problems faced by local superiors in admitting women to the congregation about whom they had misgivings. The case of a Miss Dalton of Grass Valley, a sister of the local priest, Thomas Dalton, was illustrative. See Mother Baptist Russell to Bishop Eugene O'Connell, August 15, 1864, in Doyle, *Like a Tree*, 221–24.

41. "Sister Mary Gertrude King Passes in Mercy Hospital," *Superior California Register*, November 12, 1944, 3.

42. "Mother Carmel Naughton, Mercy Sister, Dies at 72," *Superior California Catholic Herald*, December 5, 1957, 1.

43. Marilyn K. Demas, "Ungraded School No. 2 Colored: The African-American Struggle for Education in Victorian Sacramento."

44. Richard C. Rogers, *The First One Hundred Years of the Sacramento City Schools, 1854–1954*, 4.

45. Philos [Dr. Gregory Phelan], "Our California Correspondence, October 15, 1853," *Freeman's Journal*, November 19, 1853.

46. Philos [Phelan], "Our California Correspondence, July 14, 1851," ibid., August 30, 1851; "Our California Correspondence, October 31, 1851," ibid., December 6, 1851; "Our California Correspondence, November 14, 1851," ibid., December 27, 1851. The figures are cited in Sister Marie Vandenberg, "Attitudes and Events Leading Up to the Establishment of the Christian Brothers School in Sacramento, California, 1871–1876," 114.

47. Sister M. Berchmans Kennelly, "Annals," 3.

48. Willis, *History of Sacramento County*, 606.

49. A complete list of St. Joseph graduates from 1876 to 1957 can be found in Morgan, *Mercy Generation to Generation*, 261–77.

50. King, "Early History," n.p.

51. See the 1928 *Echoes From S.J.A.*, the St. Joseph Academy yearbook, which lists the married commercial alumnae, 43, ASMA.

52. Ernesto Galarza, *Barrio Boy*, 208–13. See also Wayne Maeda, *Changing Dreams and Treasured Memories: A Story of Japanese Americans in the Sacramento Region*, 163.

53. "Funeral for Emma von Hatten," *Catholic Herald*, December 5, 1963, 9. For other details of von Hatten's career, see assorted clippings in a small group of her personal papers preserved at SAMCC.

54. Much information on Mary Rooney, with the exception of her Catholic background and activity, can be found in Connolly and Self, *Capital Women*, 144–47, 173.

55. "Bishop Anxious to Make NCCW Power in Diocese of Sacramento," *Superior California Register*, April 27, 1930, 10; "First President of D.C.C.W. Dies," ibid., March 20, 1932, 10 and 3 (article begins on p. 10 and continues on p. 3).

56. "St. Joseph's Academy, Sacramento," *San Francisco Monitor,* September 2, 1893, 8.

57. Godfrey Hoelters to Father Commissarius, January 15, 1901, "St. Francis File—Sacramento," AOFM.

58. "Sacramento Catholic News," *San Francisco Monitor,* February 8, 1908, 8.

59. Sister Manuela Dieringer, O.S.F., "Recollections of Sister M. Manuela," October 1976, n.p., *Catholic Herald* Files.

60. King, "Early History," n.p.

61. Mary Patricia Tarbox, "The Origins of Nursing by the Sisters of Mercy in the United States, 1843–1910." For a helpful overview of the contributions Catholic sisters made to the development of hospital care systems, see Bernadette McCauley, *Who Shall Take Care of Our Sick? Roman Catholic Sisters and the Development of Catholic Hospitals in New York City.*

62. A helpful overview of Sacramento's hospital history is found in Eleanor Rodgerson, M.D., *Adobe, Brick, and Steel: A History of Hospitals and Shelters for the Sick in Sacramento and El Dorado Counties.*

63. Historian Barbra Mann Wall's *Unlikely Entrepreneurs: Catholic Sisters and the Hospital Marketplace, 1865–1925* accentuates the entrepreneurial role of sisters' communities that took on hospital work.

64. Many of the foregoing details are taken from J. Roy Jones, M.D., *Memories, Men, and Medicine,* 454–64.

65. Rodgerson, *Adobe, Brick, and Steel,* 35–39.

66. "History of Mercy Hospital." See also Don Cox et al., *Mercy Hospitals: The First 100 Years* (in possession of the author), which provides a concise overview of the history of the Mercy Hospital enterprise.

67. "Cornerstone Laid," *San Francisco Monitor,* December 5, 1896, 8.

68. Conditions in this early hospital were related in a 1947 interview given by Mrs. Margaret Bailey, a supervisor at the Twenty-third and R streets hospital, and Mrs. Florence Bennet, an operating room nurse. They are related in Cox et al., *Mercy Hospitals.*

69. "History of the School of Nursing, Mercy Hospital, Sacramento, California."

70. "History of Mercy Hospital," 7.

71. "Dedication of a Chapel," *Sacramento Union,* December 1, 1905, 10.

72. Jones, *Memories, Men, and Medicine,* 462–64.

73. "Name of Hospital Changed by Sisters," *Sacramento Bee,* June 16, 1934, 11.

74. Carew, a native of Tipperary, had entered the Sisters of Mercy in 1912 and provides one of the best examples of the significant responsibilities shouldered by nuns in Sacramento. From 1939 until 1968 she served as the administrator of Mercy Hospital. During her tenure she oversaw fund-raising and construction of

several major building projects, substantially expanding the size and quality of the hospital. She also enlarged the Mercy Hospital system with the construction of a major new hospital in Carmichael. See "Mercy Sisters Mourn Sister Mary Peter," *Catholic Herald*, February 3, 1986, 11.

75. "Franciscan Sisters Aiding Youngsters," *Sacramento Bee*, November 19, 1918, 15.

76. S. Liguori Mason, "History of the American Foundation, 1874–1924," 630–29.

77. "Community Chest Benefits Numbers, Says Bishop Keane," *Sacramento Bee*, February 1, 1924, 17; "Grace Day Home Pleased by Result of Chest's Work," ibid., January 5, 1924, 16; "Grace Day Home Does Efficient Charity Work," *Sacramento Union*, January 7, 1924, 3.

78. The celebration took place on October 2, 1907. See "Good Deeds of the Sisters of Mercy in Sacramento," *Saturday Bee*, September 28, 1907, 12; "Sisters Celebrate Golden Jubilee," *Evening Bee*, October 2, 1907, 14; and "Brilliant Reception in Honor of Sisters of Mercy," ibid., October 3, 1907, 3.

CHAPTER 4 : CATHOLICS AND THE ETHNIC CONSENSUS, 1880–1930

1. The report was done by the Civil Rights Project at Harvard University, which is dedicated to civil rights research and works to advance the channels through which research findings are translated and communicated.

2. Stodghill and Bower, "America's Most Diverse City"; Heather Fargo quoted in Ed Goldman, "Multicultural Sacramento," in *Sacramento: America's Most Diverse City*, by Sacramento Convention and Visitor's Bureau, n.p.

3. For discrimination against the Japanese, see Cheryl Cole, *A History of the Japanese Community in Sacramento, 1883–1972: Organization, Business, and Generational Response to Majority Domination and Stereotypes;* and Maeda, *Changing Dreams.*

4. H. S. Muddox, "Report to the Board of Directors," Minutes of the Chamber of Commerce, February 5, 1920, SAMCC, 132.

5. The information about McCarver and Burnett is taken from Malcolm Edwards, "The War of Complexional Distinctions: Blacks in Gold Rush California and British Colombia."

6. Elmer Clarence Sandmeyer, *The Anti-Chinese Movement in California.*

7. McGowan, *History of the Sacramento Valley*, 1:323–33, gives a good overview of the Chinese in the valley—including Sacramento.

8. Ibid., 327–28; "Will They Combine? Two Anti-Chinese Conventions Held in Sacramento Today," *Sacramento Bee*, March 10, 1886, 3. Efforts to restrict the number of Chinese coming into California were not completely successful.

Californians and others then moved to completely exclude the Chinese from entering the United States (Sandmeyer, *Anti-Chinese Movement,* 96–108).

9. An extensive discussion of anti-Japanese sentiment in California is to be found in Roger Daniels, *The Politics of Prejudice: The Anti-Japanese Movement in California and the Struggle for Japanese Exclusion.*

10. "Sacramento, Cal., August 29, 1850," *Freeman's Journal,* October 12, 1850.

11. See Susan Wiley Harwick, "Ethnic Residential and Commercial Patterns in Sacramento With Special Reference to the Russian-American Experience," 49–55.

12. Galarza, *Barrio Boy,* 207–14. In 1911–1912, C. K. McClatchy launched an editorial crusade against the teaching of a revisionist version of the American Revolution he called "Adrianism." Named for the superintendent of schools of Santa Barbara, Professor H. A. Adrian, this view suggested that American claims of British tyranny in the years leading up to the American Revolution may have been exaggerated. McClatchy led a heated campaign to have textbooks carrying this "errant" version of the American past banned from Sacramento schools. See "Such Disloyalty Should Not Be Permitted in Our Public Schools" (editorial), *Sacramento Bee,* December 2, 1911, 32; "Inculcation of Patriotism Is the Very First Duty of a Public-School Instructor" (editorial), ibid., December 9, 1911, 32; "Teaching Disloyalty in Sacramento Public Schools" (editorial), ibid., December 11, 1911, 4; and "Adrianism Rebuked in Legislature: Investigation Demanded Into System of History Teaching in the Schools" (editorial), ibid., December 14, 1911, 1.

13. "Pastors' Union," *Sacramento Daily Record-Union,* October 28, 1890, 3.

14. California had tried Sabbath laws in 1858, but a Jewish clothier, Morris Newman of Sacramento, challenged it. The California Supreme Court then struck it down, although the legislature later revived it, and it again passed. The law remained on the books until 1883 (Joseph B. Marks and Lisa J. Sanders, "The Blue Laws Debate: A Sacramento Shopkeeper's Story"). For Silcox's comments, see "For and Against," *Sacramento Daily Record-Union,* February 12, 1891, 3.

15. "Pastors Have a Union: They Will Strike Against Sin and Boycott the Devil," *Daily Bee,* October 28, 1890, 3; "Take Heed, Girls: Pastor's Union and the 'Ladies' Entrances," ibid., November 10, 1890, 8.

16. "'Our Country and Our Church,'" *Sacramento Daily Record-Union,* February 24, 1891, 5.

17. The most comprehensive account of the American Protective Association is Donald L. Kinzer's *An Episode in Anti-Catholicism: The American Protective Association.*

18. "The 'A.P.A.' Conspiracy," *San Francisco Monitor,* July 8, 1893, 2; "A Brave Repudiation of the APA Conspiracy," ibid., October 14, 1893, 4; "Bigotry Now and

Forty Years Ago," ibid., November 4, 1893, 4; "The Late Elections," ibid., November 18, 1893, 4; "Topics of the Times," ibid., January 27, 1894, 1.

19. "British Volunteers, Orangemen, and the APA," ibid., November 25, 1893, 4.

20. In late April 1894 one of them, the Reverend J. B. Koehne of the Congregational church, offered a series of public lectures warning Sacramentans of the perils of Catholic power. His topic titles included "The Priest and the Flag," "The Jesuits' Oath," and "Masonry and the Papacy." "The Priest and the Flag," reprinted verbatim in the *Record-Union* and summarized in the *Bee,* issued a stark warning about Catholic loyalty and questioned the compatibility of Catholic institutions with the American way of life. Catholic influence, Koehne insisted, was pervasive at every level of Sacramento life, including (and especially) McClatchy's *Bee:* "The hand of the Catholic Church was on their mouths. They would give columns to the ordination of a bishop, and a few lines to the memory or work of the most eminent Protestant divine" ("Rev. Koehne's Sermon: He Preaches the Fifth of His Series Last Night," *Sacramento Daily Record-Union,* May 14, 1894, 3).

21. "Politics in Pulpits," *Evening Bee,* November 5, 1894, 1; "Rev. Koehne's Sermon"; "A.P.A. State Ticket," ibid., November 3, 1894, 1.

22. "The Irish Must Go," ibid., November 4, 1895, 1; "Mr. Sanders' Talk," ibid., November 4, 1895, 5.

23. "Catholic Officers," ibid., November 29, 1895, 6; "No Catholics Need Apply," ibid., February 20, 1896, 5; "An Un-American Mayor," ibid., February 20, 1896, 4.

24. For additional information about Goethe and his espousal of eugenics, see Charles M. Goethe, *Seeking to Serve;* Tony Platt, "What's in a Name? Charles M. Goethe, American Eugenics, and Sacramento State University"; and Mike Spiro, "The Progressive Obscurity of Charles M. Goethe."

25. "Woman Makes Attack on Parochial Schools," undated clipping (copyright April or May 1921), Church Federation Papers. The federation also accused the McClatchy-run *Sacramento Bee* of pro-Catholic bias for opposing the federal Smith-Towner education bill in 1921, also opposed by the American Catholic hierarchy, because the two McClatchy brothers were educated by the Jesuits at Santa Clara. The *Bee* published the accusation and its reply: "Church Federation Finds Hidden Motive in Bee's Policy," April 28, 1921, 6.

26. "Minutes of Meeting," December 10, 1935, Clippings File, Church Federation Papers.

27. "Church Federation Finds Hidden Motive."

28. California's Councils of Defense are examined in Diane M. T. North, "The State and the People: California During the First World War," 197–235.

29. "Making American Citizenship Secondary to Foreign Sympathy," *Sacramento Bee,* April 7, 1916, 6. See also "Alien Millions Thriving Here and Owing

Fealty to Other Nations," ibid., August 23, 1915, 6; and "Irish-American Wind Bags Prove If St. Patrick Drove Snakes Out of Ireland He Sent Some to These Shores," ibid., May 19, 1916, 1.

30. Daniels, *Politics of Prejudice*, 91, 95–99.

31. "Neutral Citizens Disloyal to Flag," *Sacramento Bee*, June 10, 1918, 9.

32. "Making American Citizenship Secondary to Foreign Sympathy," ibid., April 7, 1916, 6.

33. "Police Question Organizer of Klan Found Here," ibid., April 11, 1922, 1.

34. "Klan Is Watched While Initiating Sacramento Men," ibid., April 26, 1922, 1.

35. Dennis M. Von Brauchitsch, "The Ku Klux Klan in California, 1921–1924," 126. For other Klan activities in California, see Christopher N. Cocoltchos, "The Invisible Empire and the Search for Orderly Community: The Ku Klux Klan in Anaheim, California."

36. "Complete Exposé of Local Klan's Workings Given by Ex-member," *Sacramento Bee*, November 2, 1922, 1, 4. In this story a Klan informant tells of the efforts of county assessor B. C. Erwin, a member of the Klan, to force Catholics to pay taxes on a heavily assessed St. Joseph Cemetery.

37. Phelan, "California Correspondence, May 31, 1852," *Freeman's Journal*, July 10, 1852; John B. McGloin, S.J., "Thomas Cian: Pioneer Chinese Priest in California"; "Religious," *Sacramento Daily Union*, July 27, 1854, 3.

38. "The Anti-Chinese Meeting," *Sacramento Daily Record-Union*, April 4, 1876, 3; *Chinese Immigration: The Social, Moral, and Political Effect of Chinese Immigration*, 117–18.

39. "The Chinese Question," *San Francisco Monitor*, May 24, 1873, 4; "Workingmen's Meeting," *Daily Bee*, July 16, 1879, 3; "Anti-Chinese Mass Meeting of Citizens at Turner Hall," *Sacramento Daily Record-Union*, December 11, 1885, 2; "Will They Combine?"; "Anti-Chinese," *Daily Record-Union*, March 12, 1886, 1, 4.

40. "An Emblem of Liberty," *Evening Bee*, November 30, 1894, 1.

41. Peter T. Conmy, *Seventy Years of Service, 1902–1972: History of the Knights of Columbus in California*, 19–20, 305.

42. "Bishop Thomas Grace Succumbs to Long Illness," *Sacramento Bee*, December 27, 1921, 1.

43. "The Clergy Will Battle Against the Vicious Poolrooms," *Evening Bee*, January 27, 1900, 8; "Father Quinn Gives His Views," ibid., January 29, 1900, 8; "Churches Resound With Denunciation of Poolrooms," ibid., January 29, 1900, 4; "Right Will Triumph: Battle Will Be Won," ibid., February 5, 1900, 2. For a good overview of the entire poolroom episode, see L'egare, *Poolroom Battle*. This work is based on L'egare, "The Great Sacramento Poolroom Battle, 1896–1900."

44. "Catholics in Fight," *San Francisco Monitor*, October 19, 1907, 1; "Catholic

California: Scatter the Saloons," ibid., February 22, 1908, 2; "Father Ellis and City Saloons," *Evening Bee*, October 30, 1907, 1.

45. Vincent John Fecher, *The Movement for German National Parishes in Philadelphia and Baltimore, 1782–1802*.

46. Jay P. Dolan, ed., *The American Catholic Experience: A History From 1850 to the Present*, 158–94.

47. Jeffrey M. Burns, "Building the Best: A History of Catholic Parish Life in the Pacific States," 49, 50.

48. For general information on Germans in California, see Erwin G. Gudde, *German Pioneers in Early California*.

49. Carole Cosgrove Terry, "Die Deutschen Enwanderer in Sacramento: German Immigrants in Sacramento, 1850–1859," 64–81.

50. See McCoy, "First Five Years." The actual figures are as follows: 1852: 730; 1860: 1,374; 1870: 1,634; 1880: 1,838; 1890: 2,182; 1900: 1,957 (Bruce Pierini, "Germans in Sacramento Area").

51. Godfrey Hoelters to Father Commissarius, November 15, 1900, "St. Francis: Sacramento File," AOFM.

52. "New Catholic Church," *Daily Bee*, March 16, 1871, 3; "The German Celebration," *Sacramento Daily Union*, February 2, 1871, 3.

53. Manogue to Michael Richardt, August 18, 1893, "St. Francis: Sacramento File," AOFM.

54. Father Leo to Father Prior, May 6, 1894, ibid. See also Carole Cosgrove Terry's "Germans in Sacramento, 1850–1859." For additional background on other German communities in northern California, see Terry's "Die Deutschen Von Marysville: The Germans in Marysville, 1850–1860."

55. Father Leo to Richardt, May 6, 1894, "St. Francis: Sacramento File," AOFM.

56. Clementine Deymann to Richardt, September 28, 1894, ibid.

57. Hoelters to Father Commissarius, March 4, 1901, ibid.

58. Galarza, *Barrio Boy*, 198–99.

59. The inheritance, thanks to good investments, was still seventy thousand dollars strong when she died in 1926. Bowden's generosity to Brady would continue throughout the priest's life. In 1907 when he was building a new Sacred Heart Church in Red Bluff, Bowden gave sixteen hundred dollars to equip the edifice with pews. She also paid for a stained-glass window of St. Patrick in honor of her parents. The next year, after the church was completed, Bowden underwrote Brady's expenses for a lengthy trip to continental Europe and a home visit to Ireland. In 1926 Brady was chosen as the founding pastor of a new parish in East Sacramento, St. Stephen's. Bowden left a considerable sum in her will for the new parish and named Brady as the executor of her estate. See "Parishioners Are Pleased," *San Francisco Monitor*, April 27, 1907, 8; "Illustrated Lecture," *San*

Francisco Leader, July 4, 1908; and Bowden's will, a copy of which is on file at SAMCC. The monies gathered for St. Stephen's, later renamed Sacred Heart, are referred to in the Catholic press. Brady seemed to be especially adept at winning large financial considerations for the cathedral. In the early twentieth century he managed to snare a huge amount of the estate of Johanna Carroll, the daughter of a prominent Sacramento business owner.

60. "City and Coast," *San Francisco Monitor,* April 28, 1900, 68.

61. "A New Church Was Opened," *Evening Bee,* December 3, 1900, 5.

62. Raymond Renwald, "St. Stephen's: Church With Eight Lives," pts. 1 and 2, *Catholic Herald,* November 4, 1976, 4; November 11, 1976, 4. The building was used variously as a church and school, day-care facility, Japanese mission, Slavonian church, Our Lady of Guadalupe Church, Filipino Center, Cursillo Center, and finally a single men's homeless shelter.

63. "City and Coast," *San Francisco Monitor,* January 15, 1901, 328.

64. "Paulists Will Hold Meetings," *Evening Bee,* December 12, 1907, 1; J. M. Burns, "Building the Best," 50.

65. "A New Church Was Opened."

66. One of the fund-raisers created a minor public uproar when McClatchy foe Father Peter Yorke spoke at one of them. See "Father Peter C. Yorke Appears As Orator—Daniel Kevane As Stage Manager," *Evening Bee,* January 29, 1902, 1; and "Working the Laborers and the Church for Henry T. Gage," ibid., January 29, 1902, 4.

67. "Sisters Open a New School," ibid., September 25, 1906, 3.

68. "Sisters Chronicle: St. Stephen's Sacramento," n.p.

69. "Free School Improvements," in "Sacramento Catholic News," *San Francisco Monitor,* February 8, 1908, 8.

70. "Cathedral," *Catholic Herald,* August 25, 1923, 8.

71. "Fine Modern Cathedral School Dedicated by Bishop Keane," ibid., January 19, 1924, 1.

72. Mario T. Garcia, *Padre: The Spiritual Journey of Father Virgil Cordano,* 11.

73. Quoted in Sister Manuela Dieringer, O.S.F., "Recollections of Sister Manuela Dieringer," p. 1 of the section "St. Stephen's School: Cathedral Parish School."

74. "St. Stephen's Free School," 8, 9.

75. "Touching Appreciation of a Splendid Institution," *Catholic Herald,* March 17, 1928, 1.

76 Garcia, *Padre,* 13.

77. Pierini, "Italian History." See also John Francis Copley, "Sacramento's Italian Immigrants in 1920," 18.

78. Susan Wiley Harwick, "Ethnic Residential and Commercial Patterns in Sacramento With Special Reference to the Russian-American Experience," 66; "Italians Want Language Taught in High School," *Sacramento Bee,* June 8, 1916, 4.

79. Gualco soon became one of the leading citizens in this agricultural community, not only by building and beautifying his church but also by working with city leaders to attract a branch of the state normal school to the community. Since the relationships between these teacher-training institutions and Catholics were frequently stormy, Gualco often attended classes and challenged professors. Moreover, he held sessions in his own parlor to explain Catholic teaching and practices (Maureen Dion, ed., *Pulpit and Pew: A Centennial History of Saint John the Baptist Catholic Parish, Chico, California, 1878–1978,* 20–29).

80. Grace to Riordan, April 17, 1905, Riordan Papers; Michael Gualco to Diomede Falconio, September 24, 1905, "Sacramento," Del. Ap. IX, Vatican Archives, Rome. Mela, who used his second name, Eugenio, was born in 1873, and became a priest of the Archdiocese of Milan in 1898 and a seminary professor at a college in Tornio, Italy. Dominic Taverna was born in Castellazzo, Italy, in 1876. He was ordained in 1900 and served in the Piedmont area of Italy until he came to California.

81. Gualco complained about Taverna's treatment in Reno and also about the ongoing neglect of the Italians in Reno and McCloud and the Germans in Woodland (Gualco to Falconio, June 7, 1910, "Sacramento," Del. Ap. IX, Vatican Archives, Rome).

82. "Church Edifice Finished," *Sacramento Union,* May 26, 1907, 7; "Dedication of New St. Mary's Church," ibid., June 8, 1907, 12.

83. Mela to Riordan, July 23, 1907, Riordan Papers (all errors in original); Gualco to Falconio, August 1, 1907, "Sacramento," Del. Ap. IX, Vatican Archives, Rome.

84. "To Raise Fund to Build New Church for Catholics," *Evening Bee,* January 7, 1907, 2; Mela to Falconio, May 6, 1909, "Sacramento," Del. Ap. IX, Vatican Archives, Rome.

85. Lionel Holmes and Joseph D'Alessandro, *Portuguese Pioneers of the Sacramento Area,* 11.

86. Ibid., 91; Francis J. Weber, *Encyclopedia of California's Catholic Heritage,* s.v. "Henrique Jose Reed DaSilva"; "A Royal Bishop's Work," *San Francisco Monitor,* July 27, 1907, 1; "Greatest of All Grand Councils," *Catholic Herald,* August 22, 1908, 1. Mela blamed Silveira for the uproar. In a letter to Falconio he complained that he had worked with the Portuguese but that Grace had allowed the Portuguese to come from Fall River and suggested that he had conspired to split the congregation for his own financial gain (May 6, 1909, "Sacramento," Del. Ap. IX, Vatican Archives, Rome).

87. "Feeling High With Portuguese," *Sacramento Bee,* April 20, 1909, 5; "Portuguese Members Strike Against Priest," *Sacramento Union,* April 20, 1909, 3; "Portuguese Make a Reply," *Sacramento Bee,* April 22, 1909, 5.

88. "New Portuguese Church Rising; Catholics Awaiting Dedication," *Sacramento Bee,* August 3, 1912, 10; "St. Elizabeth's Will Be Dedicated; Church Dignitaries Will Officiate," ibid., February 1, 1913, 20.

89. "New St. Mary's Will Face City Park," ibid., May 30, 1914, 10; "Reopening of Italian Church," *Catholic Herald,* August 15, 1914, 8; "Annual Report, 1933," Sacred Heart Parish, Sacramento, ADS.

90. "Mystery Still Shrouds Absent Church Pastor," *Sacramento Bee,* September 20, 1928, 1; "Absconded Priest May Be Returned," ibid., June 1, 1929, 10.

CHAPTER 5 : BUILDING THE CITY BEAUTIFUL, 1890–1930

1. Rowena Wise Day, "Carnival of Lights," 55.

2. The best summary of the transformation of Sacramento politics in response to changing urban conditions is William E. Mahan, "The Political Response to Urban Growth: Sacramento and Mayor Marshall R. Beard, 1863–1914."

3. Davis, *Illustrated History,* 123–26. What is today known as the *Sacramento Bee* was initially published as the *Daily Bee* when it began on February 3, 1857. On January 6, 1890, it began its run under a new title, the *Evening Bee,* and for a time issued a separate *Saturday Bee.* On March 6, 1908, it was again retitled to its current form, the *Sacramento Bee.*

4. "Thank God," *Evening Bee,* March 11, 1893, 1; "Report of the State Capital Planning Commission Upon Its Investigation of the Planning of the Capital of California," 14.

5. The best general study of western boosterism is David M. Wrobel, *Promised Lands: Promotion, Memory, and the Creation of the American West,* esp. 36–38. See also Richard J. Orsi, "Selling the Golden State: A Study of Boosterism in Nineteenth-Century California." An overview of promotional publications can be found in K. D. Kurutz and Gary F. Kurutz, *California Calls You: The Art of Promoting the Golden State, 1870–1940.*

6. Steven M. Avella, "The McClatchy Brothers and the Creation of Superior California."

7. "Substantial Evidences of Sacramento's New Growth"; "Sacramento's Awakening."

8. "New Era Opens for the County of Sacramento," *Evening Bee,* February 13, 1902, 5; Valentine S. McClatchy, "What Is the Matter With Sacramento?" ibid., February 13, 1902, 2; "Sacramento Must Rid Herself of Her Provincialism," ibid., February 14, 1903, 9.

9. The historiographical controversies over the role of the Southern Pacific in California are alluded to in Orsi, *Sunset Limited,* xvi–xvii. He views the Southern Pacific as largely a positive entity that substantially aided California's devel-

opment. The railroad's role in politics is covered in William Deverell, *Railroad Crossing: Californians and the Railroad, 1850–1910*.

10. "The Old Trick," *Sacramento Daily Union*, February 6, 1875, 4; "The Mayoralty," *Daily Bee*, February 6, 1875, 2; "The Mass Meeting," ibid., February 10, 1875, 3. Interestingly, James McClatchy, whose newspaper, the *Bee*, would later become a vocal critic of railroad control of Sacramento, had been one of the supporters of the agreement of 1875 and a speaker at the mass meeting that drafted the articles of "capitulation." See Richard Coke Lower, *A Bloc of One: The Political Career of Hiram W. Johnson*, 8–13, which describes efforts to shake off Southern Pacific control in Sacramento in the early twentieth century.

11. "Sacramento Citizens and the Western Pacific," *Evening Bee*, March 7, 1906, 2; "Western Pacific Opens New Line," *Sacramento Bee*, August 18, 1910, 15; "The Story of the Western Pacific," ibid., August 19, 1910, 1.

12. "Vote for Clinton L. White for Mayor!" *Sacramento Union*, November 4, 1907, 4.

13. "Robinson Submits Report on Beautification of the City," *Sacramento Bee*, November 12, 1908, 12; "Planning a City Beautiful and the Question of Knockers," ibid., November 13, 1908, 4.

14. For copies of the Robinson, Hegemann, and Nolen reports, see "Report of the State Capital Planning Commission," appendixes A, B, and C, 12–29. See also Hegemann, "Report of Dr. Werner Hegemann, Oct. 30, 1913"; Charles Mulford Robinson, "Report on the Improvement of Sacramento"; "Nolen Sends Del Paso Park Plans," *Sacramento Bee*, January 9, 1912, 5; "City Hires Nolen to Plan Parks," ibid., December 19, 1913, 12; and "Professor Zeublin [*sic*] Known Here, Coming," ibid., May 20, 1916, 4.

15. "Reception and Presentation to Rev. Father John Quinn," *Evening Bee*, May 27, 1902, 4.

16. Quinn's Nebraska career is related in Henry W. Casper, *History of the Catholic Church in Nebraska: The Church on the Fading Frontier, 1864–1910*, 193–94. Casper suggests that Quinn asked for his *exeat* "possibly because Bishop O'Connor had misgivings about his administrative and financial competence."

17. The only mention of Quinn's activities in Denver is the newspaper enterprise, found in Thomas J. Noel, *Colorado Catholicism and the Archdiocese of Denver, 1857–1989*, 79. It is unknown when Quinn and Manogue met. However, Quinn later related that he had warmly endorsed Manogue for advancement to episcopal office when Bishop George Conroy stopped in Denver on his return from his visit to the West. "Father Quinn's Sermon" (see chap. 2, n. 56).

18. "Our Own Country: Why Catholics Are Loyal Americans," *San Francisco Monitor*, July 20, 1896, 10.

19. Quinn and McClatchy first clashed when the priest attacked the *Bee's* rival, the *Record-Union,* over the paper's hostile editorializing on the question of the Friar's Lands in the Philippines. See "Of the Philippines: Facts Presented by a Thoughtful Visitor," November 6, 1899, 7; "Our Administration in the Philippines," November 11, 1899, 2; "Duty in the Philippines," November 17, 1899, 2; and "Imperialism and Military Despotism," November 21, 1899, 2. In response, Quinn issued a circular to members of the cathedral parish condemning the report and broadly indicting newspaper coverage of the church. "We Catholics are in this city of Sacramento, victims of an unmannerly press. Every morning and evening we are in danger of finding our religious persons, places, and things most sacred to us made objects of public scorn. We pay twice 66 cents each month for the privilege of learning what fools and how contemptible we are in the eyes of our neighbors." Quinn suggested the possibility of boycotting the offensive papers. A copy of this circular is found in the Quinn Account Book, Cathedral File, ADS. McClatchy fired back, "The language by this priest is as unjust as it is uncalled for, as uncalled for as it is untrue" ("Why This Attack?" *Evening Bee,* November 13, 1899, 4).

20. "Says Justice Is Sacrificed to Commercialism," *Evening Bee,* March 3, 1902, 4; Quinn, "An Earthly Eden," *San Francisco Monitor,* June 23, 1906, 6; "Reception and Presentation to Rev. Father John Quinn," *Evening Bee,* May 27, 1902, 4; "Death Ends the Career of Father John F. Quinn," *Catholic Herald,* December 10, 1921, 1.

21. J. G. Martine was a well-known local businessman. A native of Virginia, Martine was connected to a Sacramento hardware business with one L. L. Lewis. When Lewis closed out the business, Martine became head agent of the Yalupa Land Agency. Later he opened his own general realty business. He also held the position of adjutant general in the National Guard and hence sported the title "General" in his public affairs. See "Loyal Citizen Lost by Death of Gen. Martine," *Sacramento Bee,* May 14, 1913, 11.

22. "Big Land Sale in This City," *Sacramento Union,* February 16, 1906, 12; "More Electric Street Car Lines in and About Sacramento," *Evening Bee,* March 19, 1906, 1, 10. The title to the Dunsmuir property was contested by one of the Conroy family, but ownership was handed to Quinn in an appellate court decision in 1907 ("Father Quinn Wins," *Sacramento Union,* November 8, 1907, 12).

23. Connelly later claimed that he had graduated from Notre Dame, but a search of the records turned up no evidence of any kind of terminal degree.

24. Thomas Spalding, *Premier See: A History of the Archdiocese of Baltimore, 1789–1989,* 292–92.

25. Eugene P. Willging and Herta Hatzfeld, *Catholic Serials of the Nineteenth Century in the United States,* 38–39.

26. "Back in San Francisco," *San Francisco Monitor,* June 16, 1906, 1.

27. John Cantwell to Connelly, July 28, 1909, Chancery Papers. Connelly paid off half the note, and in August 1909 Riordan canceled the remainder of the debt. See also Cantwell to Connelly, August 16, 1909, ibid.; and Connelly to Riordan, August 19, 1909, Riordan Papers.

28. Connelly to Riordan, April 2, 1907, Riordan Papers.

29. "The Importance of the Catholic Press," *Catholic Herald*, March 14, 1908, 1. In early 1930, after Connelly's death, Bishop Robert Armstrong contracted with the popular *Catholic Register* chain, headquartered in Denver, to produce a weekly diocesan paper. In February 1930 the first edition of the *Superior California Register* rolled off the presses. It remained the official medium of the diocese until 1949, when it began to be printed locally and was renamed the *Superior California Catholic Herald*. Later, in April 1960, editor Eymard Gallagher dropped the "Superior California" portion, and it reverted to the name given by its initiator, the *Catholic Herald*.

30. "For a Greater Sacramento," *Catholic Herald*, March 14, 1908, 4.

31. "Northern California," ibid., November 1, 1913, 4.

32. In 1901 the California Constitution was amended to end the taxation of church property that was used "solely and exclusively for religious purposes." The effect of this amendment in Sacramento County was dramatic. In 1900 churches paid taxes on $120,000 worth of property. In 1901 the taxable amount dropped to $96,560, with the Catholic Church paying $6,000 for the cathedral and $3,150 for St. Francis ("Taxation of Churches," *Evening Bee*, July 22, 1901, 5).

33. "Will the Churches Comply With Terms of New Law?" ibid., July 4, 1901, 2.

34. "Has Trustee Devine Bought a Church?" *Saturday Bee*, July 25, 1903, 5; "Catholics of Sacramento to Have Hall of Their Own," *San Francisco Monitor*, December 26, 1903, 249. In the summer of 1908, the association announced plans for a new Catholic Fraternal Hall on the Sixth and L site and contracted architect Frank Schaefer to provide preliminary designs. Schaefer's plans, displayed on the pages of the *Catholic Herald*, projected an elaborate five-story building, complete with banquet, meeting, and lodge rooms; thirty bachelor apartments; and a handsome roof garden ("Sacramento to Have a Magnificent Catholic Building," *Catholic Herald*, July 11, 1908, 1). However, arguments over its location stalled the project ("Discussion of New Catholic Hall Project," ibid., July 18, 1908, 1).

35. Pius Niermann to Theodore Arentz, February 16, 1900; Adrian Wewer to his provincial, March 17, 1900, "St. Francis: Sacramento File," AOFM.

36. Hoelters to Father Commissarius, October 18, 1900, "St. Francis: Sacramento File," AOFM.

37. Oscar Lewis, *Sutter's Fort: Gateway to the Gold Fields*, 203. An additional appropriation of $20,000 was secured in January 1901. See Myrtle Shaw Lord, *Sacramento Saga: Fifty Years of Achievement—Chamber of Commerce Leadership*, 176.

38. Lord, *Sacramento Saga,* 188; "Magnificent Structure in Mission Style to Replace Present St. Francis Church," *Sacramento Bee,* April 11, 1908, 10; Theodore Arentz to Hoelters, January 31, 1908, "St. Francis: Sacramento File," AOFM.

39. Arentz to Hoelters, January 31, 1908; "In the Sacramento Diocese," *San Francisco Monitor,* April 25, 1908, 8; "To Start Work Soon on New Church Edifice," *Sacramento Bee,* May 23, 1908, 4.

40. James A. Harmon, "Brother Adrian Wewer, O.S.F. (1836–1914), Province Architect of the Franciscan Province of the Sacred Heart," copy in "St. Francis: Sacramento File," AOFM. The German-born Wewer was province architect of the Franciscan Province of the Sacred Heart for nearly fifty years. He designed more than one hundred church buildings and an unspecified number of educational institutions and Franciscan friaries throughout the United States. In Sacramento's St. Francis Church, he combined his expertise in neo-medieval church design with the popular mission style prevalent in California architecture at the time.

41. "The New St. Francis Church," *Catholic Herald,* April 18, 1908, 1; "What It Means," ibid., October 24, 1908, 4. See also "Corner Stone of New Church Laid," *Sacramento Bee,* October 19, 1908, 2; and "Corner of Great Temple Is Laid," *Catholic Herald,* October 24, 1908, 1.

42. Tom Cody to "Dear Sir," January 1909, "St. Francis: Sacramento File," AOFM.

43. Ibid.; "Knights of Columbus Mark Anniversary With Banquet," *Sacramento Bee,* February 24, 1909, 3.

44. "Clyde L. Seavey, FPC Aide, Dies in Washington," ibid., August 6, 1943, 1.

45. William Wade, "The Architecture of Small Cities," 46–65.

46. Bonnie Wehle Snyder and Paula J. Boghosian, *Sacramento's Memorial Auditorium: Seven Decades of Memories;* D. Arden Adams, "Building With Unique Tradition Must Step Aside: Famous Old Watson School Going Down," *Sacramento Bee,* November 22, 1924, 16.

47. "Realty Men of State Throng Capital City," *Sacramento Bee,* October 11, 1923, RE1.

48. Banks, "Sacramento Needs More Modern Churches" (see chap. 1, n. 13).

49. C. K. McClatchy to Peter J. DeLay, January 22, 1920, Letter 641, McClatchy Papers; "New Head for Sacramento Diocese," *Catholic Herald,* March 25, 1922, 1.

50. "Bishop Armstrong Appears Before Chamber Board to Give Orphanage Plan," *Sacramento Bee,* March 16, 1931, 10.

51. Brother Z. Joseph Fenlon to Patrick J. Keane, December 18, 1922, "Christian Brothers File," ADS; Conrad Deschler to Tom Westberg, Friday, First Week of Lent, 1976, File 502.82, "History 12th and K," Christian Brothers Archives, St. Helena, California.

52. "Site of Brothers' College Is Placed on Realty Market," *Sacramento Bee,* April 15, 1922, 34; "Cathedral's Sale to Bay City Men in Consideration," ibid., July 5, 1923, 1; "Weinstock, Lubin Home to Be at Twelfth and K," ibid., April 21, 1923, 1; "Bishop's House, Brothers' College Will Be Sold," ibid., March 6, 1923, 1.

53. "Two Large Business Buildings Will Rise in Sacramento Shortly," ibid., January 10, 1924, 1, 18.

54. "Cathedral's Sale to Bay City Men"; "Cathedral," *Catholic Herald,* July 28, 1923, 8. Meanwhile, Keane laid plans to improve the cathedral's interior, at one point announcing an ambitious and costly renovation that included replacing the wooden main altar with marble, new frescoing, and alterations in the sanctuary. See "Cathedral," ibid., January 12, 1924, 8.

CHAPTER 6 : CATHOLIC SOCIAL PROVISION:
THE DEPRESSION AND WORLD WAR II, 1930–1945

1. Bradley Riter, "Modern Sacramento Site Steeped With Old Romance," *Sacramento Bee,* January 4, 1930, A1, A2.

2. Richard Lowitt, *The New Deal and the West.* There is no specific work done on the impact of the Depression in Sacramento, but many of the same trends discussed by William H. Mullins in *The Depression and the Urban West Coast, 1929–1933* were to be found in the California state capital.

3. "Cannery Workers File Claims for Wages in Capital," *Sacramento Bee,* September 6, 1930, 1; "Operators of Cannery Are Sought by Officials," ibid., September 9, 1930, 1; "Canneries' Workers Complain of Low Wages Paid," ibid., June 2, 1933, 1.

4. "Shop Workers to Go Full Time," ibid., December 23, 1930, 18.

5. McGowan, *History of the Sacramento Valley,* 2:256; Steve Wiegand, "Born in the California Gold Rush, Sacramento Became a Metropolis in the 20th Century," *Sacramento Bee,* December 31, 1999, OC1; U.S. Census Bureau figures for 1930. Exact figures were difficult to determine. The percentage noted was calculated by dividing the number of unemployed in Sacramento in 1932, as noted in Wiegand's article (27,000) by the 1930 U.S. Census Bureau's population for the county in 1930 (141,999).

6. "California National Fails to Open Doors Today," *Sacramento Bee,* January 21, 1933, 1. See also "News Travels Fast: Financial Drama Is Enacted," ibid., January 21, 1933, 2; and "California National to Reorganize," ibid., January 22, 1933, 1.

7. "Sacramento Wave."

8. *Hub of Western Industry, Sacramento, California,* 24.

9. "Auto Sales Here in 1932 Total, 2,579," *Sacramento Bee,* January 18, 1933, 14.

10. A good general overview of the history of public policies toward the homeless is to be found in Alice S. Baum and Donald W. Burnes, *A Nation in*

Denial: The Truth About Homelessness, 91–109. See also Walter I. Trattner, *From Poor Law to Welfare State*.

11. M. H. Lewis, *Transients in California*, 143.

12. See Jon L. Jamieson, "General Kelley's 'Army' of 1914," n.p.; "Bummer and Brigands Are Trying to Awe the People of Sacramento," *Sacramento Bee*, March 7, 1914, 1, 10; "Riot Follows Ousting of 'Army': Blood Shed and Cars Are Smashed," ibid., March 9, 1914, 1, 5; and "Army of the Unemployed," ibid., March 26, 1914, 10.

13. C. K. McClatchy, "Merely Some Private Thinks," *Sacramento Bee*, June 6, 1932, 18; "Make Not Sacramento a Magnet for Hoboes," ibid., February 17, 1915, 6.

14. "200 Jobless Fight for 20 Jobs on Waterfront," ibid., February 26, 1931, 1, 16; M. Lewis, *Transients in California*, 147.

15. Davis, *Illustrated History*, 132–33; Willis, *History of Sacramento County*, 140–41.

16. Judge was much loved by a cadre of priests and nuns to whom she was personally generous and supportive in her official capacity. A native of Sacramento, she was a lifelong member of St. Rose Parish and then the cathedral. See "Requiem High Mass Said in Sacramento for Mary Judge," *Superior California Register*, February 4, 1945, 3.

17. McClatchy praised Judge after she turned back some "red" agitators at her office during the depths of the Depression. See C. K. McClatchy, "Merely Some Private Thinks," *Sacramento Bee*, June 6, 1932, 18.

18. Leslie Davies, "Charter Provides for County Welfare Board," ibid., August 1, 1922, 1; "Stranded Families Helped by County," ibid., January 4, 1926, 12.

19. Willis, *History of Sacramento County*, 137–46; "A Home for the Homeless—That Conducted by Peniel Mission," *Record-Union*, November 30, 1900, 3; "Almost a Riot," *Sacramento Daily Record-Union*, May 20, 1885, 3; David Deas, "March Army Troops Had Rowdy Reception in Capital," *Sacramento Bee*, July 25, 1965, B1; "Local Salvation Army Reports That Family Relief Was Extended to 213,881," ibid., March 10, 1934, 7. The Salvation Army moved its location several times but continued a high volume of faith-based service to the poor of Sacramento. It provided emergency lodging for women, a center for mentally disabled men, and a feeding kitchen.

20. Catholic Ladies' Relief Society, No. 1, "Records of Catholic Ladies' Relief Society, No. 1," in *History Book, 1927–1931*, ADS.

21. "Community Chest Virtually Assured Here," *Sacramento Bee*, January 9, 1923, 1; "Community Chest Benefits Numbers, Says Bishop Keane," ibid., February 1, 1924, 17; "Grace Day Home Pleased by Result of Chest's Work," ibid., January 5, 1924, 16; "Death Claims Mrs. Coolot, Leader in Charity Work," *Catholic Herald*, July 30, 1964, 8; "Community Chest Contributions Reach $130,462," *Sacramento Bee*, November 17, 1930, 1, 2.

22. Robert A. Muir, "Sacramento Depression Settlement Survey."

23. "Citizens' Body on Unemployment to Gather Today," *Sacramento Bee*, October 31, 1930, 1, 13; "Unemployed Men Clean Vacant Lots for 1 Meal a Day," ibid., November 24, 1931, 5; "Steady Payrolls Are Pledged by 25 Local Firms," ibid., November 26, 1930, 1, 2.

24. James E. Henley, "Depression, New Deal, War, Government and Economic Growth: The Metropolis Arrives, 1930s–1950s," 99.

25. "City Facing Deficit of $50,000 in 1930 Budget," *Sacramento Bee*, October 13, 1930, 1.

26. "Plan to Change Men's Center Is Dropped by Body," ibid., October 28, 1930, 1; M. Lewis, *Transients in California*, 161.

27. Ann Land Commission, "Minutes," November 4, 1931, SAMCC; "Poor to Receive Staple Groceries As Funds Sink," *Sacramento Bee*, February 5, 1932, 27; Ann Land Commission, "Minutes," February 10, 1932, SAMCC.

28. "Community Chest Is Expected to Be $32,000 Short," *Sacramento Bee*, November 20, 1930, 1, 5; "Chest Directors to Decide Action Tomorrow Noon," ibid., November 14, 1932, 13; "Community Chest Budget for 1933 Cut 35 Percent," ibid., December 13, 1932, 1, 2; Ann Land Commission, "Minutes," February 10, April 19, 1933, SAMCC. The Community Chest survived, in fact, and continued to distribute aid.

29 "Unemployed File New Set of 'Demands' Here," *Sacramento Bee*, February 6, 1931, 14; "Demands of Red Group Refused by Mary Judge," ibid., June 3, 1932, 28; "Unemployed Council Demands Free Meals," ibid., June 6, 1932, 13; "Mob Clashes With Police in Riot at Courthouse," ibid., February 6, 1933, 1; "Mary Judge Says Agitators Here Refuse to Work," ibid., February 8, 1933, 1; James E. Henley, "Wobblies and Communists in Sacramento: The Criminal Syndicalism Trial of 1935."

30. "County Received $23,000 Relief," *Sacramento Bee*, April 4, 1933, 5; "Fight to Oust Mary Judge Is Made by Faction," ibid., June 27, 1933, 1; "Officials Seek Cause for State Relief Attack," ibid., January 24, 1934, 1, 2; "Pastor Demands Probe of Local Relief Program," ibid., April 16, 1934, 1; "Mary Judge Asks Pastor for Showdown on Relief," ibid., April 17, 1934, 3.

31. "Plans for Four County Projects Near Completion," ibid., September 20, 1933, 5; "Cost of County Relief Work Drops One-Third," ibid., January 12, 1935, 8; "Community Chest, City, and Federal Government United to Feed Homeless," *Superior California Register*, January 6, 1935, 3. For a sample of the New Deal–era impact on Sacramento, see "Sacramento County's WPA Accomplishments Are Listed," *Sacramento Bee*, October 17, 1940, 4; "WPA Constructs 274.3 Miles of Road in County," ibid., April 30, 1942, 25; and Luis Grant, "The WPA Gives an Accounting: Several Projects Are Still Under Way Here," ibid., May 9, 1942, 5 (magazine

section). See also William E. Mahan, "Taxpayer Support for Art? The Federal Arts Project in Sacramento, 1937–1941."

32. "New Auditorium to Be Dedicated on Saturday," *Superior California Register,* June 28, 1931, 8.

33. John A. Lally to Robert Armstrong, June 6, 1936, John J. Mitty Papers.

34. John Tumulty to P. J. O'Sullivan, November 2, 1937, "Immaculate Conception File," ADS; Tumulty to Michael Lyons, November 2, 1937, "Sacred Heart File," ADS. Immaculate Conception was given fifteen thousand and Sacred Heart thirty thousand dollars.

35. The story of the financial collapse of the West Coast branch of the Christian Brothers is told in Isetti, *Called to the Pacific,* 339–53. In the midst of the financial crisis, the creditors demanded that all available property be put up for sale—including the Sacramento high school. Bishop Armstrong worked to avert this. See "Christian Brothers File," ADS.

36. "Poor Are Fed by Franciscan Fathers Here," *Sacramento Bee,* January 19, 1934, 13; "Father Keating Thanks All Who Helped Mexican Poor," *Superior California Register,* January 6, 1935, 3.

37. There are many works about Dorothy Day and the movement. One of the best is her autobiography, *The Long Loneliness: The Autobiography of Dorothy Day.* William D. Miller, who knew Day well, wrote both *A Harsh and Dreadful Love: Dorothy Day and the Catholic Worker Movement* and *Dorothy Day: A Biography.* The best volume on the Catholic Worker movement is Mel Piehl's *Breaking Bread: The Catholic Workers and the Origin of Catholic Radicalism in America.*

38. Arthur Ronz to Dorothy Day, February 18, April 20, December 30, 1941, August 26, 1942, W4, box 1, DDCW. Ronz wrote the 1942 letter from a military facility in Monterey.

39. Robert E. Lucey to Robert Armstrong, March 25, 1930, "Social Welfare File," ADS; "Diocese Will Have Catholic Welfare Bureau," *Superior California Register,* August 3, 1930, 8.

40. Catholic Ladies' Relief Society, No. 1, "Report of Grand Deputy Rebecca Coolot to Forty-first Grand Council of the Catholic Ladies' Relief Society, October 15–16, 1930, Marysville," in *History Book, 1927–1931,* ADS; "Bee Writer Gives Vivid Story of What Orphans May Anticipate," *Superior California Register,* April 5, 1931, 9; "New Orphanage Plans Viewed," *Sacramento Bee,* January 16, 1931, 8. With the approval of the priests, Armstrong contacted the Harry R. Bogart fund-raising firm in San Francisco to launch a campaign to raise the money. See "$250,000 Campaign Planned for New Orphanage in Sacramento," *Superior California Register,* February 1, 1931, 10.

41. "Catholics Plan $300,000 Drive for Orphanage," *Sacramento Bee,* February 13, 1931, 1. Welch also arranged for Bishop Armstrong to appear before the

Chamber of Commerce to describe the plans for the new facility ("Story of Drive for Home Funds Told in Detail," *Superior California Register,* July 31, 1932, Dedication no. A).

42. "Bishop R. J. Armstrong Turns First Shovelful of Ground for Sacramento Orphanage," *Superior California Register,* October 25, 1931, 8; "Sacramento Orphanage Model Institution," ibid., August 14, 1932, 7; Elaine E. Feller, "The History and Development of Catholic Social Service in Sacramento," 26–27.

43. "Mrs. Leland Stanford's Generous Gift," *Superior California Register,* April 19, 1900, 5; Sister Gerarda Fawcett, "Memories of Stanford Home," October 1, 1999, Archives of the Sisters of Social Service; "Old Stanford Home Here Is Coming to Life Again: Ballroom Will Be Used," *Sacramento Bee,* December 19, 1936, 6; "Birthplace of Leland, Jr., Now Settlement House, to Be Dinner Scene," *Sacramento Union,* February 27, 1938, c7.

44. See Roger W. Lotchin, *Fortress California, 1910–1961: From Warfare to Welfare.* However, Lotchin makes no allusion to developments in Sacramento.

45. The story of Sacramento's economic transformation during and after World War II is told in Brian Roberts, "Sacramento Since World War II: From Small Town to Megalopolis in Less Than Fifty Years." See also Fonton L. Williams, *Arthur S. Dudley and His Contribution to U.S. Air Defense.*

46. "The Story of McClellan Air Force Base, 1939–1998"; Maurice A. Miller, ed., *McClellan Air Force Base, 1936–1982: A Pictorial History.*

47. Economic Development Council, *Mather Air Force Base,* n.p.; Ron Starbuck, "Sacramento Army Depot History," California State Military Museum, http://www.militarymuseum.org/SacramentoArmyDepot.html; Margaret Krug, "'Father' of Army Depot Recalls Varied Careers," *Catholic Herald,* February 17, 1986, 3. See also "Sacramento Army Depot: 25th Anniversary," 4–5.

48. Transcript of interview with Monsignor Raymond Renwald by Olivia Wheatley, May 15, 1981, St. Thomas More Parish, Paradise, Renwald Papers.

49. "Holy Name Rally Draws Large Crowd to Auditorium Sunday," *Superior California Register,* November 3, 1940, 4; Ronz to Day, February 24, 1942, w4, box 1, DDCW.

50. "Solemn Novena for America to Be Conducted in Capital," *Superior California Register,* May 10, 1942, 3. Novena Catholicism as a means of coping with social distress is treated by John Huels in "The Saturday Night Novena," in which he also discusses the significance of the Sorrowful Mother novena held by the Servite priests at the Basilica of Our Lady of Sorrows on Jackson Street in Chicago.

51. "Girl Workers Seek Board and Room in Sacramento Homes," *Superior California Register,* July 12, 1942, 3. Richard Collins Dwyer was born in San Francisco in August 1915, the son of William and Ethel Dwyer, prominent parishioners of Sacred Heart Parish. His grandfather Thomas Dwyer had been one of Bishop

Manogue's confidants and a benefactor of the cathedral. The Dwyers had become an enormously wealthy family, transferring their fortunes from the brick and river transportation business to a very lucrative cartage firm. His family enjoyed close relationships with the leading clergy of Sacramento, and young Dwyer, during his years as a student at Christian Brothers, had been a server at the Cathedral of the Blessed Sacrament for Bishop Keane. When Bishop Armstrong came to town, the Dwyers became friendly with the new prelate and often hosted him at the posh Del Paso Heights Country Club, where they were members. Later, the Dwyers would often accompany Armstrong on his annual pilgrimages to Bull Meadows in the Marble Mountains of Siskiyou County.

52. "First Year Is Completed by St. Thomas Aquinas Library and Catholic Center in City," ibid., July 23, 1944, 3.

53. Cheryl L. Cole, "A History of the Japanese Community in Sacramento, 1883–1972," 12–13 (see also Wayne Maeda, "The Japanese").

54. Cole's "History of the Japanese Community" covers this pattern of discrimination and cites other sources. She notes especially that the *Sacramento Bee* and especially V. S. McClatchy were particularly vigilant against Japanese settlement in California and in Sacramento (9–16).

55. "Buddhist Temple Established Here," *Evening Bee,* October 7, 1901, 4. This was the second Buddhist temple established in the United States and the first to be incorporated under American laws.

56. Cole, "History of the Japanese Community," 41; Maeda, "The Japanese." Neither of these sources mentions the Catholic mission to the Japanese.

57. "The Real Danger," *Catholic Herald,* May 3, 1919, 4; Joseph Bernard Code, *Dictionary of the American Hierarchy,* s.v. "Albert Breton."

58. M. Liguori Mason(compiler), "Japanese Mission, Sacramento, California." This particular text has the benefit of handwritten corrections and clarifications from Sister Roberta Clauter (1969).

59. William Stoecke, S.V.D., to Thomas Horgan, July 27, 1928, "Japanese Mission File," ADS.

60. "Fine Work Being Done Among the Japanese in Sacramento," *Superior California Register,* March 2, 1930, 10.

61. Mason, "Japanese Mission."

62. Cole, "History of the Japanese Community," 76.

63. Thomas A. Kirby to Mrs. Charles J. O'Connor, June 4, 1942, "Japanese Mission File," ADS; Mason, "Japanese Mission."

64. Gary Y. Okihiro suggests that there was a revival of traditional Japanese religious traditions in the Tulelake camp as a form of passive resistance to the internment ("Religion and Resistance in America's Concentration Camps").

65. Joseph A. Hunt to Kirby, August 16, 1943, "Japanese Mission File," ADS.

CHAPTER 7 : CARVING A SPACE AND CREATING
COMMUNITY: THE CATHOLIC CHURCH AND THE
NORTH AREA, 1940–1970

1. "New St. Philomene's," *Superior California Register,* September 26, 1948, 9.

2. Thomas D. Norris, "Metropolitan Growth in the Sacramento Area During World War II and the Post-war Period," 62; Charles Irish, "Homebuilding Set Pace in Postwar Construction," *Sacramento Bee,* July 6, 1957, C20.

3. Hal Rothman, *Neon Metropolis: How Las Vegas Started the Twenty-first Century,* 293.

4. For a concise summary of a portion of Sacramento's suburban development, see Peter J. Hayes, ed., *The Lower American River: Prehistory to Parkway,* 97–105.

5. "McClellan Is One of Largest Air Force Bases in Nation," *Sacramento Bee,* June 3, 1953, N11; "Here Is What McClellan Base Means to Capital," ibid., June 3, 1953, N11; James J. Brown, "Projects Make Gigantic McClellan Even Bigger," ibid., August 25, 1955, 1.

6. "Rocket Plant Is to Be Erected East of Capital," ibid., December 14, 1950, 1; Douglas Ingells, *The McDonnell-Douglas Story.* For general information about the expansion of the aerospace industry in the American West, see Roger E. Bilstein, "From Colony to Commonwealth: The Rise of the Aerospace Industry in the West."

7. In March 1948, Pacific Telephone and Telegraph began construction of a new communications center in Sacramento at Fourteenth and J. An industrial park, developed north of the city along the American River near Discovery Park, attracted the Crown Zellerbach Paper Company, which began operations there in a ten-square-acre plant in 1949. See "Paper Company Will Build in Industrial Park," *Sacramento Bee,* September 1, 1948, 16; "Procter & Gamble Company Selects Sacramento As Location for New Factory," ibid., May 28, 1951, 1; "Ball Bearing Firm Is Building Plant in North Sacramento," ibid., February 22, 1952, 21; and "Campbell Soup Firm Marks Plant Completion," ibid., December 7, 1954, 2.

8. "City of Folsom Benefits From Huge Expenditures on Dam," ibid., November 19, 1952, F6.

9. This term is borrowed from Kenneth T. Jackson's *Crabgrass Frontier: The Suburbanization of the United States.*

10. James J. Brown, "North Highlands Boom Tops Rapid Growth of Suburbs," *Sacramento Bee,* May 11, 1955, 23. See also Bradley Riter, "Community Mushrooms From Open Fields in Three Years," ibid., June 3, 1953, N2; "North Highlands Gets

Name From Two Subdivisions," ibid., N2; and "Small Home Builder Was Responsible for New Community," ibid., N9.

11. "Plans for Small Home Have Unusual Room Arrangement," ibid., June 2, 1951, 13.

12. Hale Champion, "North Suburbs Pupils Receive Half Education," ibid., May 13, 1949, 1; "County Schools Not Alone in Their Misery," ibid., May 17, 1949, 1; Ralph Bladgen, "Growth Makes Orphans of Cityless Fringes Bordering Sacramento," ibid., September 27, 1955, 1.

13. Public Service Administration, *The Government of Metropolitan Sacramento*, 32. A description of these efforts is in Christian L. Larsen, *Growth and Government in Sacramento*, 3–60.

14. John Cook, "North Highlands: Population Zooms," *Sacramento Union*, June 7, 1959, 1.

15. John Cook, "Rancho Cordova Grew Like Topsy," ibid., May 3, 1959, 1.

16. C. Larsen, *Growth and Government*, 198.

17. Interview with John and Florence Steffen, March 2003. John Steffen, a Procter and Gamble employee, and his wife, Florence, moved to Sacramento from Chicago in the early 1950s. The company found them temporary lodging and also helped the "immigrants" adjust to the unique social and physical conditions of the West through a variety of programs.

18. Samples of this growth include the following: "New Churches of City Go Up in Outlying Areas," *Sacramento Bee*, August 20, 1949, 25; and "Gleaming New Churches—More Than 60 Since 1947—Dot City and County of Sacramento," *Sacramento Union*, February 1, 1953, 16.

19. Hale Champion, "Protestants Combine Efforts to Set Up Churches in County," *Sacramento Bee*, September 19, 1949, 2; Champion, "Steps in Church Cooperative Plan Are Described," ibid., September 20, 1949, 4; Champion, "Comity Plan Reestablishes Community, Church Ties," ibid., September 21, 1949, 20.

20. Rothman, *Neon Metropolis*, 293.

21. Gordon Sabine, *Monsignor Donohoe*, 89–90; interviews with Monsignor John S. McMahon, purchasing agent of the Diocese of Phoenix, 1969–1992, August and December 2005; "New Parish Plant Commands View of Mountains, Lake, City," *Catholic Northwest Progress*, July 6, 1954, clippings, R. G. Seattle, St. Paul, Clippings [1953–1956], Archives of the Archdiocese of Seattle; "Proposed Master Plan for St. Bernadette Parish" (n.d.), R. G. Seattle, St. Bernadette Corres. Gen. [1958–1979], Archives of the Archdiocese of Seattle.

22. Joseph T. McGucken to Earl D. Fraser, February 16, 1962, "St. Joseph Academy File," ADS; Joseph T. McGucken to Carroll O'Sullivan, S.J., April 1, 1958, "St. Ignatius Historical File," ADS (emphasis added).

23. Through additional purchases the Rancho Cordova parish eventually obtained twenty-one acres on which they planned a school, rectory, convent, church, and a girls' high school. See "Ground Broken for New Church," *Sacramento Union,* September 15, 1963, B7. An architect's drawing published in the *Sacramento Bee* showed a typical display of a projected parish master plan. See "In Rancho Cordova," ibid., September 21, 1963, B6.

24. Daniel Twomey to Thomas Kirby, October 8, 1944, "St. Philomene's Historical File," ADS; "Catholic Cleric Says Builders Forget Church," *Sacramento Bee,* August 11, 1955, 1; "Builders Deny Ignoring Church in Subdivisions," ibid., August 13, 1955, 16; "Home Builders Hit for Not Providing Site for Parishes," *Superior California Catholic Herald,* August 11, 1955, 1.

25. "New Catholic Church Will Be Dedicated Sunday," *Sacramento Bee,* September 22, 1948, 18; "Dedication of St. Philomene's September 26th," *Superior California Register,* September 26, 1948, 1; "I.B.V.M. Sisters Accept School in St. Philomene's," ibid., February 6, 1949, 3; "New Sisters Arrive in Diocese," *Superior California Catholic Herald,* August 19, 1949, 1; "St. Philomene's School Plans Eighth Grade," ibid., August 17, 1951, 10 (note that the name of the diocesan newspaper changed from *Superior California Register* to *Superior California Catholic Herald* on August 8, 1949); "$168,206 Low Bid Is Submitted for Catholic Church," *Sacramento Bee,* November 1, 1952, 20; "St. Philomene's Plans Dedication of New Church," ibid., May 28, 1953, 21.

26. "New Parish, St. Ignatius Placed in Care of Jesuits," *Superior California Catholic Herald,* February 25, 1954, 1; "St. Ignatius Raises $277,000 for Convent, Rectory, Church Bldgs.," ibid., June 7, 1956, 10; "Modern Lines," *Sacramento Bee,* February 23, 1957, C24; "Population Growth, Ravages of Time Cause Record High in Diocesan Construction," *Superior California Catholic Herald,* September 25, 1958, 1; "Fast Developing St. Ignatius Parish Completes Church," ibid., September 10, 1959, 1; "New Church of St. Ignatius Loyola on Arden Way Dedicated," *Sacramento Bee,* July 31, 1960, C20; "St. Ignatius Is Dedicated," *Sacramento Union,* August 1, 1960, 9.

27. Interview with Monsignor Cornelius P. Higgins, September 17, 1999, Presentation Parish, Sacramento; "New North Area Parish, Pastor Changes Are Set," *Sacramento Bee,* February 11, 1961, A11.

28. "Church Inauguration at Fair Oaks," *Catholic Herald,* July 9, 1921, 8; "Inaugural Ceremony at Fair Oaks," ibid., July 16, 1921, 8.

29. "The History of St. Mel's Catholic Church, Fair Oaks, California, 1921–1985," n.p.; John Cook, "Fair Oaks Folks Like Status Quo," *Sacramento Union,* April 12, 1959, 1.

30. "Fair Oaks Parish to Build on New Property Site," *Superior California Catholic Herald,* January 30, 1958, 1.

31. "Dedications to Mark Growth of Diocese," ibid., June 11, 1959, 1; "Mercy Sisters' New Home Is 'Across Road' From Door," ibid., August 20, 1959, 1.

32. See untitled photo essay, ibid., August 2, 1956, 1.

33. "New Parish Acquires Ten Acre Site," ibid., February 2, 1956, 1; "North Highlands School Will Be Dedicated on Sunday," ibid., September 27, 1956, 8; "Temporary Church Dedicated Sunday," *Catholic Herald,* October 27, 1960, 1; "St. Lawrence Parish Plans Church Dedication," *Sacramento Bee,* October 20, 1960, A15; "Pallottines Will Open St. Lawrence School," *Superior California Catholic Herald,* August 29, 1957, 1.

34. "Folsom Parish Will Replace 101 Year Old Church," *Sacramento Bee,* March 14, 1958, C2; "Dedication Will Be Set Soon for Folsom Parish Church," ibid., December 4, 1958, C2; "Dedicate Folsom Church Sunday," *Superior California Catholic Herald,* February 19, 1959, 1; "Catholics Plan to Build Folsom School, Convent," *Sacramento Bee,* December 12, 1960, B13.

35. "Parishioners Name Parish in Honor of St. Philomena," *Superior California Register,* January 4, 1948, 7; Reba O'Neil, "In the Beginning . . . St. Philomene's Parish Is Born," *Superior California Register—Easter Edition,* March 28, 1948, 5.

36. O'Neil, "In the Beginning," 5.

37. "St. Ignatius Loyola Parish History, 1954–1979," 5; "Folsom Church Ground-breaking Set March 15," *Superior California Catholic Herald,* March 6, 1958, 1; "$87,923 Bid Wins Contract for New Folsom Church," ibid., March 20, 1958, 1.

38. "Church Sets Dedication of Lourdes Replica," *Sacramento Bee,* May 7, 1958, A5; "Lourdes Grotto to Be Dedicated Sunday," *Superior California Catholic Herald,* May 8, 1958, 1.

39. "The History of St. Mel's Catholic Church, Fair Oaks, California, 1921–1985," 30, 31.

40. *This Is Your Parish, St. John Vianney, Rancho Cordova* (1958), pamphlet in "St. John Vianney Parish Historical File," ADS.

41. "Bishop Will Bless Carmichael's New Church, Sept. 28," *Superior California Register,* September 25, 1952, 1.

42. "St. Ignatius Loyola Parish History, 1954–1979," 11.

43. Eleanor Doyle, "School Partnership in Rancho Cordova," *Catholic Herald,* June 29, 1961, 1.

44. "Bishop Armstrong Makes Appeal to Assure Building of School," *Superior California Catholic Herald,* June 23, 1955, 1; "Whose Responsibility," ibid., June 23, 1955, 3; "New Bishop Armstrong High Makes September 11 Debut With 604 Students," ibid., August 23, 1956, 1; "High School Drive Short $850,000," ibid., February 14, 1957, 1.

45. "Private Girls High to Open in September," ibid., April 28, 1955, 1; "Loretto

High School Will Be Dedicated Sunday by Bishop," ibid., March 1, 1956, 1; "Dedicate Addition to Loretto High," *Catholic Herald,* May 19, 1960, 1.

46. "Jesuit High School Fund Over the Top," *Catholic Herald,* September 27, 1962, 1; "North Area Challenges," ibid., June 21, 1962, 4.

47. For a good overview of the history of the retreat movement in the United States, see Joseph Chinnici, O.F.M., *Living Stones: The History and Structure of the Catholic Spiritual Life in the United States,* 157–71.

48. Interview with the Reverend Neil Parsons, C.P., August 23, 1999, Christ the King Retreat House, Citrus Heights, California.

49. See Bro. Kevin O'Malley, C.P., "A Brief History of the Passionists in Northern California and Western Nevada, 1852–1986"; "Ground Breaking for Catholic Retreat Draws More Than 300," *Sacramento Bee,* April 11, 1949, 12; and "Diocese to Have Retreat House and Monastery," *Superior California Register,* January 11, 1948, 3.

50. "Christ the King Retreat House for Men Is Spiritual Dynamo," *Superior California Catholic Herald,* May 1, 1952, 3; "Retreat House Festival This Sunday Will Raise Funds for New Wing," ibid., May 27, 1954, 10; "Passionist Monastery Blessing This Sunday," ibid., October 24, 1957, 1.

51. "Construction Started on Carmelite Monastery," ibid., May 7, 1953, 10.

52. "How It All Began, Realization of a Dream, the Opening of the Cenacle in Sacramento," ibid., September 19, 1957, 7.

53. "Cenacle Nuns Purchase Site for Women's Retreat House," ibid., May 14, 1953, 1; "First Weekend Retreat Set at Cenacle," ibid., June 24, 1954, 8; "Cenacle Retreat House Blessing Set for July 31st," ibid., July 15, 1954, 1; "1425 Women at Cenacle in Opening Year," ibid., August 11, 1955, 5; *Cenacle History,* 43.

CHAPTER 8 : BUILDING A VISIBLE LATINO PRESENCE IN THE CITY, 1930–1970

1. "Faith of Mexico Is Seen at Impressive Dedication Rites," *Superior California Register,* April 15, 1945, 5. See also "Mexican Church to Be Dedicated in Capital City," ibid., March 25, 1945, 5; and "New Church of Our Lady of Guadalupe Will Be Dedicated," ibid., April 8, 1945, 3.

2. Gina Marie Pitti, "To 'Hear About God in Spanish': Ethnicity, Church, and Community Activism in the San Francisco Archdiocese's Mexican American Colonias, 1942–1965"; Roberto R. Trevino, *The Church in the Barrio: Mexican-American Ethno-Catholicism in Houston.*

3. Galarza, *Barrio Boy,* 200.

4. Rosana M. Madrid, "Narrative History of Mexican/Chicano Community of Sacramento," 26–34.

5. Manuel G. Gonzales, *Mexicanos: A History of Mexicans in the United States,* 113–38.

6. *Mexicans in California: Report of Governor C. C. Young's Mexican Fact-Finding Committee,* 48, 51, 57, 87, 89.

7. Madrid, "Narrative History," 17–25.

8. U.S. Census Bureau; *Journal of Government Information,* vol. 25, issue 5, September 10, 1998, 413–17; Geospatial and Statistical Data Center, University of Virginia Library, Charlottesville.

9. For a general study of *mutualistas,* see Jose Amaro Hernandez, *Mutual Aid for Survival: The Case of the Mexican American.* See also Kaye Lynn Briegel, "Alianza Hispano-Americana, 1894–1965: A Mexican-American Fraternal Insurance Society."

10. "Mexicans Stage Big Celebration at Sacramento," *Sacramento Bee,* September 16, 1929, 10; "Independence of Mexico Observed by Celebration," ibid., September 16, 1930, 1; "Fifteen Jailed in Mexican Festival," ibid., September 17, 1928, 5.

11. Andazola/Salgado/Zuniga File, 85/06 Zuniga Collection, Sacramento Valley Ethnic Survey, SAMCC. Andazola died on July 31, 1980. This file contains obituary clippings in English and Spanish. In his eulogy of her, Father Keith Kenny referred to her as "Enriqueta, la pionera de nuestra colonia Mexicana" ("En Memorium [*sic*] Enriqueta Andazola, September 4, 1980").

12. Nemesio Tony Ortiz, "Sacramento's Mexican Center: A Bitter Lesson to Remember," *El Hispano* (Sacramento), November 11, 1976, 6; "Mexican Center Is Dedicated to Culminate 10-Year Dream," *Sacramento Union,* August 15, 1948, 10; "Ground Is Broken for New Mexican Community House," *Sacramento Bee,* May 5, 1948, 4; "Community Center to Open During Ceremonies This Week," *Sacramento Union,* August 9, 1948, 2; "Mexican Center Will Get Flags at Dedication," *Sacramento Bee,* August 11, 1948, 2; "Mexico Officials Laud Backers of New Center Here," ibid., August 16, 1948, 4.

13. "Andazola Never Lost Her Cultural Pride," *Sacramento Bee,* December 31, 1999, C23.

14. Ortiz, "Sacramento's Mexican Center"; interview with Guadalupe Aguilar conducted by Rosana Madrid, transcribed by Lee Ann Means, January 16 and 25, 1984, 79, Chicano Ethnic Survey, SAMCC.

15. Richard Morefield, "The Mexican Adaptation in American California, 1846–1875"; Antonio Robert Soto, "The Chicano and the Church in Northern California, 1848–1978: A Study of an Ethnic Minority Within the Roman Catholic Church"; Jeffrey M. Burns, "The Mexican American Catholic Community in California, 1850–1980." See also Burns, "The Mexican Catholic Community in California."

16. "In the Matter of the Estate of M. O. V. Ayres, Deceased," in the Probate

Court of Santa Clara County, State of California, August 16, 1879. Ayres also left a small trust fund to one Maggie Ellen Lewis, "a minor of the city and county of Sacramento," directing that if she died before she could take direct control, it was to go to the St. Joseph Orphanage in Sacramento.

17. "Baptismal Register," 1920–1922, St. Mary Church, Sacramento.

18. Madrid, "Narrative History," 65; "Annual Report, 1927," Cathedral of the Blessed Sacrament, ADS.

19. Keane to Thomas O'Donnell, February 20, 1922, Cantwell Papers; "Portuguese and Italian Catholic Churches to Stay," *Sacramento Bee*, April 6, 1923, 12. The nomenclature of these Balkan groups is difficult to track. Before they were forcibly unified into the nation-state of Yugoslavia after World War I, they were referred to in various ways. One was by their distinctive geographic, linguistic, and cultural groups (for instance, Serbs, Croats). Another way was to lump them together as Serbo-Croats. Yet another way was Slavonians—since many apparently did come from the province of Slavonia in the Balkans. Later they would simply be called "Jugo-Slavs" or "Yugo-Slavs." See C. Michael McAdams, "The Croatians of California and Nevada."

20. Timothy Matovina, *Guadalupe and Her Faithful: Latino Catholics in San Antonio From Colonial Origins to the Present*. Father Jose Figols Pero of San Francisco conducted the service in 1910 where "all sermons and prayers . . . [were] rendered in the Spanish tongue" ("Spanish Colony Observes Feast," *Sacramento Bee*, December 14, 1910, 5). When St. Mary's moved to its new location on Seventh and T, the festival continued there ("Feast of Lady of Guadalupe Sunday," ibid., December 12, 1914, 10). Later this site would be the location of Our Lady of Guadalupe Church.

21. John Kouba, S.D.S., "The Hispanic Presence in the Diocese of Sacramento," *Catholic Herald*, November 17, 1986, 4, and November 24, 1986, 4; "Our Lady of Guadalupe Festival Next Sunday in Catholic Church," undated clipping, ca. 1920, from the *Yolo Independent*. This account records the visit of Bishop Grace to the church in Washington (the earlier name for Broderick). The prelate sat on a "specially constructed throne built by the Spanish people." Present also were Agustin Ruiz, vice consul of Mexico, and a small ensemble with organ, violins, and clarinet. "Bishop Keane Will Officiate in Local Catholic Church," undated clipping from the *Yolo Independent*, relates the celebration of 1923. Clippings found in "Our Lady of Guadalupe Historical File," ADS.

22. There are no records about Keating and his work in the Archives of the Diocese of Sacramento.

23. Stephen Keating to D. Rinaldi, September 13, 1926, SA; Keating to "Rev. dear Father," May 14, 1927, SA.

24. "Annual Report, 1927," Cathedral of the Blessed Sacrament, ADS.

25. "Cathedral Summer School," *Catholic Herald,* August 10, 1929, 8; Catholic Ladies' Relief Society, No. 1, "Report of the Works in General, October 1, 1926 to October 1, 1927," in *History Book, 1927–1931,* ADS; Catholic Ladies' Relief Society, No. 1, "Annual Report, October 1931–October 1932," ibid.

26. "Report of Mexican Activities in Sacramento," *Superior California Register,* December 28, 1930, 8; interview with Socorro Falcon Zuniga, daughter of Federico Falcon, July 15, 2005; "Our Lady of Guadalupe," *Catholic Herald,* December 21, 1929, 3; "Mexicans Observe Guadalupe Feast," *Superior California Register,* December 21, 1930, 12.

27. "Report of Mexican Activities in Sacramento," *Superior California Register,* December 28, 1930, 8.

28. Catholic Ladies' Relief Society, No. 1, "Minutes of the Thirty-ninth Session of the Grand Council of the Catholic Ladies' Relief Society of the Sacramento Diocese," in *History Book, 1927–1931,* ADS.

29. These antagonisms were reflected in competition for jobs in Sacramento's canneries, an important source of work for Mexican women. See "Veterans Urge Use of Whites in Canneries Here," *Sacramento Bee,* February 12, 1932, 23; and "Canneries Will Use 'White' Help," ibid., March 16, 1932, 10.

30 See Francisco E. Balderrama and Raymond Rodriguez, *Decade of Betrayal: Mexican Repatriation in the 1930s.* See also Gonzales, *Mexicanos,* 147–49.

31. "Rev. Stephen J. Keating Is Named Diocesan Director of Schools, Bishop Announces," *Superior California Register,* May 31, 1931, 8; "Forming C.Y.O. Group in Sacramento Diocese," *Cathedral Tidings,* September 21, 1934, n.p.

32. Beatrice Griffith, *American Me,* 73–81; "Delinquency War Mapped," April 20, 1943, publication unknown, clipping from Stephen Keating Collection; "Trade Schools Advocated for Mexican Youths," May 16, 1943, ibid.; "Youth Seen As Biggest Business," January 18, 1948, ibid.

33. "S. J. Keating, Probation Officer, Dies at Desk," *Los Angeles Times,* January 17, 1950, A8. Keating's son, also named Stephen, related the account of the adoption of the son.

34. Kouba, "The Hispanic Presence in the Diocese of Sacramento," mentions "El Padre Esteban," and records of his early life are kept in the archives of the Salesian Fathers in San Francisco.

35. Socorro Falcon Zuniga, *Falcon Family Memoir,* copy in "Our Lady of Guadalupe Historical File," ADS.

36. According to various accounts, the Virgin Mary appeared to an Indian peasant, Juan Diego, in December 1531 at the hill of Tepeyac, outside of Mexico City. The Virgin left an imprint of her image on the *tilma* (cloak) of Juan Diego. The image was called Our Lady of Guadalupe and became the national icon of

Mexico. See C. M. Stafford Poole, *Our Lady of Guadalupe: The Origins and Sources of a Mexican National Symbol, 1531–1797.*

37. "$25,000 Campaign Underway for New Church," *Superior California Register,* June 22, 1930, 10.

38. Harry Markham to Sister Frederica, December 18, 1940, "Sisters of Social Service File," ADS.

39. Transcript of interview with Monsignor Raymond Renwald by Olivia Wheatley, May 15, 1981, St. Thomas More Parish, Paradise, California. For a commentary on the Bracero Program, see Tyche Hendricks, "Ex-Braceros Leery of Guest Worker Plan: They Say Senate Bill Needs Assurances on Living Conditions, Pay," *San Francisco Chronicle,* May 30, 2006, A1.

40. "Rev. Carl Willman Arrives for Duty in Diocese Last Week," *Superior California Register,* June 4, 1944, 5; "Pagina Guadalupana: Noticias de la Iglesia de Nuestra Senora de Guadalupe" first appeared in ibid., April 13, 1947, 4, and was signed "Padre Carlo." It contained bits and pieces of local events, announcements of baptisms, first communions, and so on. However, it was discontinued after a few appearances.

41. "Ground Is Broken for New Mexican Community House," *Sacramento Bee,* May 5, 1948, 4.

42. Ibid.

43. Ken Lastufka, "Redevelopment of Sacramento's West End, 1950–1970: A Historical Overview With an Analysis of the Impact of Relocation," 14–23.

44. Rick Kushman, "A Long Struggle for Redevelopment," *Sacramento Union,* August 5, 1984, 1.

45. Lastufka, "Redevelopment of Sacramento's West End," 99.

46. "Her Interior Is Growing Old," *Catholic Herald,* November 7, 1963, 1.

47. Leonard D. Cain, *Housing Discrimination in Metropolitan Sacramento,* 3. Cain notes that by 1960 census tracts in Oak Park had seen substantial growth in its black population: "Oak Park replaced the West End as Sacramento's new 'down town' Negro community" (ibid.).

48. Armando Rendon authored three *Catholic Herald* articles dealing with the influx of Latino/a children into Catholic schools in the central city: "Language Barrier Blocks Student Progress," February 4, 1965, 7; "Local Schools Offer Special Classes for Below Par Students," February 11, 1965, 7; and "Can Language Barrier Be Hurdled?" February 18, 1965, 7.

49. Rendon, "Old Time Residents Move Out," ibid., December 16, 1965, 12; Rendon, "Poverty, Deprivation, Smudge Bus Route," ibid., December 23, 1965, 1.

50. Interview with the Reverend Anthony Maio, August 24, 1999, Vacaville, California (hereafter Maio interview).

51. "Keith B. Kenny File," ADS; "Two Will Be Ordained for Diocese Saturday May 1," *Superior California Catholic Herald,* April 29, 1954, 1; "Bishop Assigns Clergy to New Posts," ibid., April 7, 1955, 1.

52. Eleanor Doyle, "Good Neighbors Become Good Citizens," *Superior California Catholic Herald,* March 8, 1956, 10; "Mexican Center Civic, Welfare Clinic Opens," *Sacramento Bee,* April 25, 1958, A12; "Mexican Center Problem Clinic Starts Operation," ibid., April 29, 1958, C8.

53. "Bishop McGucken Offers Mass for Delta Braceros," *Superior California Catholic Herald,* August 16, 1956, 1.

54. "'Bracero Priests' Set Sacramento Meeting," ibid., February 7, 1957, 1; "Priests Note Dangers to Morals, Justice, in Handling of Braceros," ibid., February 14, 1957, 1.

55. All sacramental activity—baptisms, confirmations, weddings, funerals—that took place at the chapel were officially recorded in the books of the cathedral until Guadalupe became a separate parish in 1969.

56. Maio interview.

57. Ibid. "5th Annual Kermes to Be Held at Mexican Center," *Superior California Catholic Herald,* June 28, 1956, 1; "Mexican Folk to Mark Guadalupe Celebration With High Mass, Parade," ibid., December 2, 1954, 1; "Guadalupe Church to Be Scene of Two High Masses Sunday," ibid., December 9, 1959, 1. The *kermes* became a popular annual event.

58 Maio interview.

59. "4,000 Help Launch New Church Here," *Sacramento Union,* February 17, 1958, 9. The *Bee* insisted on a lower number of attendees ("Nearly 1,000 View Ground Breaking Rites for Church," February 17, 1958, B1).

60. Maio interview. "Church Will Use Building Materials From Mexico," *Sacramento Bee,* January 21, 1956, F19; "Bishop Will Break Ground for Edifice," *Superior California Catholic Herald,* February 6, 1958, 1; "Nearly 1,000 View Ground Breaking Rites."

61. Carlos Gutierrez, "Mexican Artist Finishes Church Mosaic," *Sacramento Bee,* December 6, 1958, A12; Maio interview; Eleanor Doyle, "Mosaic Artistry Reflects Our Lady of Guadalupe," *Superior California Catholic Herald,* December 4, 1958, 1.

62. Gutierrez, "2,000 Witness Mexican Church Consecration," *Sacramento Bee,* December 15, 1958, D1.

63. Richard Rodriguez, *Hunger of Memory: The Education of Richard Rodriguez,* 86.

64. "Holy Angels School Account, 1961," "Cathedral File," ADS.

65. Maio interview; Raymond Renwald to Alden J. Bell, September 11, 1962, "Cathedral File," ADS.

66. "Report to Bishop, January 1967: The Financial Status of the Cathedral and Some Ways and Means to Meet It," "Cathedral File," ADS.

67. "Record-Breaking Crowd Pays Honor to Mary Immaculate," *Superior California Catholic Herald,* May 7, 1959, 1.

68. "Catholic Awakening in Mexico Says Local Priest," *Catholic Herald,* January 4, 1962, 1.

69. "Report—Feb. '62 to March '63," "Cursillos File," Historical Archives, ADS; "Diocese Inaugurates Cursillo Movement," *Catholic Herald,* January 4, 1962, 10.

70. Sr. and Sra. Luis Salinas, Sr. and Sra. Mario Aruajo, Maria Cortex, Jessie Ramirez, and Sr. and Sra. Jose Luis Reyes to Ilustrisimo Sr. Obispo Bell, June 28, 1966, "Cursillo File," Historical Archives, ADS.

71. "Committee for Migrant Workers: Report for 1964," "Migrant Worker File," ADS. As an example, between May and October 1964 they coordinated 210 persons—priests and laypersons—to visit 142 camps scattered through Sacramento, Yolo, Solano, Placer, Sutter, Yuba, and Colusa counties. Here they offered mass, heard confessions, blessed marriages, baptized children, handed out religious articles, offered catechetical instruction, and distributed two to three tons of clothing.

72. Milton E. Ortega to Bishop Alden Bell, "Summary of 1965 Activities," n.d., ibid. Another example of REAP activities was the offering of missions—a Catholic revival of sorts normally held in a parish church. REAP volunteers organized one for migrants in 1965. See "Mission Conducted for Migrant Workers," *Catholic Herald,* October 14, 1965, 10.

73. "Report of Father Edmund O'Neil to Bishop Alden Bell," n.d., "Our Lady of Guadalupe Historical File," ADS; "Grapes of Wrath," *Time,* December 10, 1965, 96.

74. "Farm Workers Converge on Sacramento for Easter Rally," *Catholic Herald,* April 7, 1966, 1; "Welcome Marchers" (editorial), ibid., April 7, 1966, 4; "Delano Farm Workers Kindle Warm Sacramento Welcome," ibid., April 14, 1966, 1, 10. The April 14 *Catholic Herald* carried an extensive photo essay of the rally at the capitol and the service at Guadalupe afterward. See also Art McGinn, "Marchers' Capitol Rally Draws Near," *Sacramento Bee,* April 9, 1966, 1 (includes a photo by Ward Sharrer of lead marchers carrying a huge cross, a banner with the image of Our Lady of Guadalupe, and the American flag); and "6000 Greet Grape March: Huelga Echoes on Mall," ibid., April 11, 1966, 1.

75. "Pastoral Proposal No. 2: Our Lady of Guadalupe Church, March 11, 1965," "Our Lady of Guadalupe Historical File," ADS. The national sanctuary status designated Guadalupe as a shrine for all Spanish-speaking Catholics. Mexican Catholics also had "rights" to be baptized, confirmed, married, and buried in the church.

76. Vatican II (1962–1965) was the general council of the world's Catholic bishops that introduced major reforms for the Catholic Church.

CHAPTER 9 : HOMELESSNESS AND FIGHTING
THE CITY CONSENSUS, 1970–2000

1. Pam Slater, "Making Room for the Winos," *Sacramento Bee,* August 17, 1980, A1; Msgr. Raymond Renwald, "St. Stephen's Story: Hard to Top," *Catholic Herald,* November 11, 1976, 4; Richard L. Dillis to Keith B. Kenny, May 18, 1967, "St. Stephen Historical File," ADS. Even before the single men were turned out, diocesan officials had been negotiating the sale of the St. Stephen property to the city's Redevelopment Agency. See Alden J. Bell to William P. Carmody, June 16, 1966; Carmody to Bell, September 6, 1966; and Bell to Raymond Renwald, August 4, 1967, all in "St. Stephen Historical File," ADS.

2. The literature on homelessness contains a number of works by social scientists. See Baum and Burnes, *Nation in Denial;* Joel Blau, *The Visible Poor: Homelessness in the United States;* Martha R. Burt, *Over the Edge: The Growth of Homelessness in the 1980s;* Peter H. Rossi, *Down and Out in America: The Origins of Homelessness;* and William Julius Wilson, *The Truly Disadvantaged: The Inner City, the Underclass, and Public Policy.* More strictly historical accounts include Todd DePastino, *Citizen Hobo: How a Century of Homelessness Shaped America;* and James Paterson, *America's Struggle Against Poverty in the Twentieth Century.*

3. Martha R. Burt, "Causes of the Growth of Homelessness During the 1980s." Seattle's large homeless population is a good example of this reality in a western city. See Maria Cain, "Listening to the Weak: The Homeless Challenge Us All," *Seattle Times,* March 30, 1987, A15; and Marsha King, "Catholic Agency Does Good—Quietly," ibid., November 30, 1987, B3.

4. Daniel Kemmis, "Cities in the New West," October 27, 2005, http://www.headwatersnews.org/p.kemmis102705.html.

5. "Preparing Sacramento for Post-war"; "Forecasting a City's Future: Sacramento, California," 41.

6. "Forecasting a City's Future," 48.

7. Armando Rendon, "Where Do All the Uprooted People Go?" *Catholic Herald,* November 25, 1965, 1.

8. A series of articles by reporter Armando Rendon for the *Catholic Herald* in December 1965 accentuated the problems created by urban renewal in the Alkali Flats neighborhood directly north of the Cathedral of the Blessed Sacrament.

9. Avella, *Sacramento: Indomitable City,* 152–56.

10. "Capital No Longer Sixth Most Needy City: Study Says Rank Improves Despite More Poor," *Sacramento Bee,* October 26, 1984, B3; LeRoy Chatfield to the author, November 30, 2005 (hereafter Chatfield to author). Social scientists

such as Martha R. Burt have examined the rise of homelessness in the 1980s and studied the issue of housing affordability as "one of the most frequently named culprits in the rise of homelessness" ("Growth of Homelessness," 903). She notes, "Many societal changes converged during the decade to make it increasingly difficult for poor people to maintain themselves in housing." She urges attention to "the two most intransigent factors . . . employment structure and the increasing mismatch between the incomes and cost of living" (931).

11. Chrisanne Beckner, "He's Leaving Home," *Sacramento News and Review,* January 19, 2006, 16.

12. "'Poorhouse' Violates Law, State Supreme Court Says," *Sacramento Bee,* March 5, 1985, A1; "Justices' Poor Judgment," ibid., March 6, 1985, B4; "Goal Is to Help Area Homeless: Sacramento Weighs Small, Scattered Facilities," ibid., March 12, 1985, B1; "Doolittle to Seek Legislation Countering State High Court Rejection of 'Poorhouse,'" ibid., March 13, 1985, B3; "County Apt to End Poorhouse Fight After Ruling, Source Says," ibid., March 29, 1985, B1.

13. "Parishes Share in the Lord's Bounty," *Catholic Herald,* April 11, 1983, 3.

14. Dan Madigan, *25th Anniversary of Sacramento Food Bank Services: Letters From the Hearth,* introduction, n.p.

15. Diane Carnes, "Food Program Is Planned," *Catholic Herald,* January 24, 1974, 1; Father Dan Madigan and Ann Bancroft, "How to Raise Money for Your Parish's Social Services," *Salt of the Earth,* http://salt.claretianpubs.org/issues /prmin; "Volunteers Give Encouragement With Groceries," *Catholic Herald,* January 14, 1982, 3; "Former Market Now Huge Food Bank," *Sacramento Bee,* November 8, 1987, B2; Frances Vitulli, "Downtown Hungry Are Fed," *Catholic Herald,* November 14, 1983, 7, 16.

16. Telephone interview with Fr. Daniel Madigan, March 10, 2006.

17. Ibid.; telephone interview with Tina Thomas, February 22, 2006 (hereafter Thomas interview).

18. As early as 1951 Catherine Buntam and Marian Kemper began a feeding program in the Alkali Flats area on North Twelfth Street. This religiously based organization was serving seven hundred a day in late 1953. See Harriet Smith, "Mom's Faith Keeps Mission Alive," *Sacramento Bee,* December 23, 1953, 11.

19. Much of the foregoing was provided by Chris Delany in a telephone interview, March 14, 2006 (hereafter Delany interview).

20. Rebecca Anne Allahyari, *Visions of Charity: Volunteer Workers and Moral Community,* uses the work of Loaves and Fishes and the Salvation Army in Sacramento as a case study to examine the work of volunteers. She provides some of the best material on the founding and controlling vision of the Delanys. References to the Delanys, including some memories of the Catholic Worker House in Los Angeles and an interview with their daughter Becky, can be found in Rosalie

Riegle Troester, *Voices From the "Catholic Worker,"* 91; the interview with Becky is on 312–32.

21. "Pax Christi Members Arrested in Trident Protest," *Catholic Herald,* May 24, 1989, 6. Delany and three other peace protesters poured human blood on missile parts at the Lockheed Corporation facility in Sunnyvale ("Poured Blood on U.S. Missile Parts," ibid., March 19, 1981, 1). See also Fran Vitulli, "Chris Delany: Life With a Social Activist," ibid., September 10, 1981, 3.

22. Delany interview; Vitulli, "Downtown Hungry Are Fed," 16.

23. Chatfield to author, March 21, 2006.

24. LeRoy Chatfield, *Bakersfield to Boston to Delano, 1963.*

25. Chatfield, *Long Bio: LeRoy Chatfield.*

26. Ibid.; Chatfield, *In the World, Not of the World;* Chatfield, *Boarding School, 1948.*

27. Chatfield to author, March 21, 2006.

28. "Salvation Army's Selected to House the Homeless," *Sacramento Bee,* July 3, 1985, B1. This article described the reaction of Alkali Flat redevelopment leader Marta Bustamente to the designation of the Salvation Army meal center at Twelfth and North B streets to provide emergency housing for single men. "There are people sleeping under stairs, in parks, under bushes now, Alkali Flat is already a dumping ground. Why can't we use East Sacramento or south Sacramento?"

29. [Sacramento] *Loaves & Fishes et al.* v. *City of Sacramento,* 97AS00287 (1997), Exhibit 6 (Sacramento County Courthouse).

30. Frances Vitulli, "Downtown Center Plans Expansion," *Catholic Herald,* January 20, 1986, 1; "Homeless Facilities Lack Permit: Soup Kitchen, Women's Shelter Under Attack," *Sacramento Bee,* October 8, 1987, B1.

31. "Shelter, Food Programs for Poor Seek Permits, City Drops Probe," *Sacramento Bee,* January 23, 1988, B3; "Bishop Blesses Loaves and Fishes Dining Site, Corner Stone," *Catholic Herald,* May 23, 1990, 5.

32. "Loaves and Fishes Plan Backed but Police Chief Opposed, Saying It Will Create a Security Risk," *Sacramento Bee,* March 19, 1988, B2; "Alkali Flats Facility Approved Over Kearns' Protest," ibid., April 15, 1988, B7; "A Place to Find Self-Respect: Clergy Dedicate Sanctuary for Capital Homeless," ibid., May 19, 1989, B1.

33. "Dream Cottages for Homeless May Soon Come True," ibid., July 14, 1994, B1.

34. "Home-for-Homeless Backers Advised by Serna to Back Off," ibid., July 27, 1994, B1; Bill Lindelhof, "A Lenten Call to Aid City's Homeless," ibid., March 2, 1995, B1; Judy Tachibana, "Cottage Industry for Homeless," ibid., December 1, 1995, B1; Robin Eifertsen, "Quinn Cottages to Provide Housing, Hope to Homeless," ibid., May 22, 1997, N1.

35. "Teenagers, the 'Invisible' Homeless, Find Refuge in Center," ibid., July 10, 1994, B1.

36. "Redevelopment OK'D, City Backs Richards Blvd., Vows to Add North Area," ibid., July 19, 1990, B6.

37. Kathryn Casa, "Commerce Challenges Charity: Sacramento Sues Loaves and Fishes Ministry." The resolution of the railroad-yard issue did not come until the waning hours of 2006. See "Railyard Deal Looks Near," *Sacramento Bee,* November 28, 2006, B1; "Rail Village Chugs Ahead," ibid., December 2, 2006, B1; "Sources: City Council Vote Could Cement Railyard Deal," *Sacramento Business Journal,* December 27, 2006; "Railyard Sale Picks Up Speed," *Sacramento Bee,* December 28, 2006, A1; and "Railyard Deal Pulls Into Station," ibid., December 30, 2006, A1.

38. Interview with William Kennedy, director of Northern California Legal Services, March 27, 2006 (hereafter Kennedy interview).

39. "County Cuts General Aid for Poorest," *Sacramento Bee,* May 10, 1995, A1; Chatfield to author; Robert D. Davila, "Loaves and Fishes Takes on City—Mobilizes Supporters in Battle Over Permits," *Sacramento Bee,* August 11, 1995, B1.

40. Davila, "Homeless Project Hits Wall: Neighbors Blow Whistle on Loaves & Fishes Plan," *Sacramento Bee,* July 3, 1995, B1; Deb Kollars, "Bitter Expansion Dispute Clouds Ministry for Homeless," ibid., September 24, 1995, A1. The mill, which had been closed since 1970, had suffered from a series of fires and vandalism. It remained as a wrecked hulk with serious asbestos problems until 2005 when the city supplied $12.5 million in grants and loans to developers Cyrus Youseffi and Skip Rosenbloom for a $28 million apartment complex, providing units for mixed-income applicants, and included funds to demolish the derelict landmark. See "City to Supply $12.5 Million to Fix Up Globe Mills Building," ibid., March 2, 2005, B2; and "Globe Mills Rebirth to Begin," ibid., July 21, 2005, G1.

41. "Trouble Over Loaves & Fishes," ibid., October 4, 1995, B6. The paper also wrote a fairly positive profile of Walter Mueller, an Austrian immigrant who took the initiative in harassing Loaves and Fishes and who often resorted to hot-tempered outbursts and name-calling. At one point an enraged prostitute knocked two of Mueller's teeth out. See Jennifer Bojorquez, "A Bark With Bite: To Protect His Turf, Walter Mueller, the Guardian of Mansion Flats, Isn't Afraid to Let the Fur Fly," ibid., October 26, 1995, F1.

42. Chatfield to author. Someone handed out flyers to street people on the day before Thanksgiving 1995, giving directions to LeRoy Chatfield's south Land Park residence for a free meal. Eight people showed up at the executive director's home. See Steve Wiegand, "Dirty Trick on Downtrodden," ibid., December 1, 1995, B1.

43. Robert D. Davila and Deb Kollars, "Officials Irate at Ad Claiming City Has

27,000 Homeless Kids," ibid., January 26, 1996, A1; Tony Bizjak, "Homeless Ad Takes Center by Surprise: Loaves & Fishes Says It Was Drafted 3 Years Ago," ibid., February 1, 1996, B3; "Homeless Children" (editorial), ibid., February 7, 1996, B7; Bizjak, "Suspended Fine for Loaves & Fishes," ibid., October 1, 1996, B1. For copies of the ad, see *Time*, January 8, 1996, 61; and *Sports Illustrated*, January 15, 1996, n.p., special advertising section located between pages 90 and 100.

44. Tony Bizjak, "Homeless Ad Takes Center by Surprise"; "Loaves & Fishes Falsehood," *Sacramento Bee*, January 27, 1996, B6; Bizjak, "Suspended Fine for Loaves & Fishes."

45. Hannelore Sudermann, "Mayoral Hopeful Unveils Bid to Close Loaves & Fishes," *Sacramento Bee*, February 15, 1996, N7. Hastings, a retired IBM executive, was a neighborhood activist and in his assault on Loaves and Fishes repeated the gross statistic regarding the amount of human waste dumped monthly by the homeless: "twenty six hundred gallons of urine and over ten thousand pounds of bacteria filled excrement." See Tony Bizjak, "Serna Faces 5 Foes in March 26 Election: Hastings Says Special Interests Don't Own Him," ibid., February 25, 1996, A12.

46. Chatfield to author; Thomas interview; Chris Krueger, "Tina Thomas: 2005 SCBA Distinguished Lawyer," November–December 2005, http:///www.sacbar.org/members/saclawyer/.

47. Deb Kollars, "Bid to Keep Park Is Dropped: Loaves and Fishes Throws in Towel, Will Dismantle Expansion," *Sacramento Bee*, April 6, 1996, B1; Kollars, "City Loses Patience on Center for Needy: Loaves & Fishes Faces Crackdown," ibid., August 18, 1996, B1.

48. Deb Kollars, "City, Charity May Try Mediating Dispute," ibid., October 6, 1996, A1; Robert D. Davila, "Talks Ordered on Loaves & Fishes," ibid., October 15, 1996, B1; Davila, "Loaves & Fishes to Abide by Conditions to Begin Mediation," ibid., October 18, 1996, B1; Rebecca Nolan, "Lunches at Center Vex Neighbors: Fremont Park Residents Call for Halt to Meals," ibid., November 14, 1996, N1; Davila, "Food Agency in New Fight: Meals for Needy Assailed," ibid., November 27, 1996, B1.

49. Rebecca Nolan, "Residents Refuse to Stomach 7th Meal," ibid., December 12, 1996, N1; "A Burden to Be Shared" (editorial), ibid., December 31, 1996, B6.

50. Kennedy interview; Tony Bizjak and Deb Kollars, "Frustrated Council Votes to Sue Loaves & Fishes," ibid., January 8, 1997, A1.

51. Tony Bizjak, "Tracing the Roots of the City's Lawsuit: Loaves & Fishes Too Indulgent Toward the Needy, Officials Suggest," ibid., January 9, 1997, A1; "*The People of the State of California* v. *Sacramento Loaves & Fishes*," 96AS05366, Sacramento County Courthouse.

52. Jenifer Warren, "Challenging Charity: Sacramento Sues Burgeoning Pro-

gram for Homeless As 'Public Nuisance,'" *Los Angeles Times*, March 4, 1997, A3; Tim Golden, "Good Works Engender Bad Blood: Sacramento Charity's Success Puts It at Odds With City Council," *New York Times*, March 31, 1997, A10; "Poor Call: Thanks to LeRoy Chatfield's Success in Helping the Needy, Sacramento Is Suing Him"; Casa, "Commerce Challenges Charity"; Emily Bazar, "Help Poor, Don't Sue, Bishop Says—Wants City Action Against Loaves & Fishes Dropped," *Sacramento Bee*, January 22, 1997, B1.

53. Gary Delsohn and Tony Bizjak, "Serna Slams City's Lawsuit Against Loaves & Fishes," *Sacramento Bee*, March 19, 1997, A1.

54. Chatfield to author.

55. Cohen remembered that he had to overcome some discomfort on the part of the other volunteer attorneys with the starkly religious language (telephone interview, March 14, 2006 [hereafter Cohen interview]).

56. Kennedy interview; telephone interview with Gary Smith, March 15, 2006; Chatfield to author.

57. [Sacramento] *Loaves & Fishes et al. v. City of Sacramento*, 97AS00287 (1997) (Sacramento County Courthouse), vol. 2, 4, 7.

58. Wayne Wilson, "City Sues Loaves & Fishes, Seeks to Halt Sunday Feedings, Clinic, Youth Center," *Sacramento Bee*, January 18, 1997, B1; Deb Kollars, "Loaves & Fishes Fires Back With Lawsuit Against City," ibid., March 11, 1997, A1; Cohen interview. The *Sacramento Bee*, which had prodded the whole matter to the boiling point with some of its inflammatory editorials, now withdrew to a more "objective" position and smugly insisted that the lawsuits were the wrong way to go—and pleaded for both sides to call off the lawyers. See "Fewer Lawyers, More Talk," March 12, 1997, B6.

59. Interview with Marc Grossman, March 24, 2006.

60. Chatfield later recognized that the real turning point in the dispute came when city attorney Samuel Jackson met with the council in executive session and asked for a special appropriation of four hundred thousand dollars to defend the city against Loaves and Fishes. "The council members who had voted to sue Loaves were stunned: politically there was no way the council could appropriate such a large sum of money to fight a lawsuit." The dispute went on for a number of months after this dramatic executive session, but Chatfield knew that without the special appropriation, there would have to be a settlement (Chatfield to author, March 22, 2006).

61. Tony Bizjak, "City Seeking Accord on Poor, Talks in Works in Charity Dispute," *Sacramento Bee*, March 28, 1997, A1.

62. Deb Kollars, "Charity: No Meal Deal Yet With City—Loaves & Fishes Wants Suit Dropped," ibid., April 6, 1997, B1.

63. Deb Kollars, "Mediators Brought In," ibid., June 4, 1997, B2; Deb Kollars

and Tony Bizjak, "City, Loaves & Fishes Settle Dispute," ibid., July 2, 1997, A1; "Sacramento and Charity End Homeless Aid Battle," *New York Times*, July 4, 1997, A11.

64. After many years of searching, the center was located in an old North Sacramento post office on Dixieanne Avenue just off Del Paso Boulevard. See Jocelyn Wiener, "WIND Center for Teens Gets a New Home," *Sacramento Bee*, February 21, 2006, B1.

65. Chatfield to author, March 21, 2006.

66. Deb Kollars, "Big August Cutback at Loaves & Fishes: Feud With City Leaves Charity Scrimping," *Sacramento Bee*, June 27, 1997, A1.

CONCLUSION

1. "Embracing the Past: Expansion of City Hall Generates Rave Reviews," *Sacramento Bee*, May 25, 2005, B1; "You Can't Fight City Hall Allure," ibid., July 22, 2005, B1.

2. James Murphy, "Restoration: Preserving the Best From the Cathedral's Victorian Past."

3. The Elks Building was designed by Leonard Starks, "one of Sacramento's most prolific Beaux Arts architects, whose legacy include[s] the U.S. post office building [in downtown Sacramento], C. K. McClatchy High School, and the famed Alhambra Theatre, which was demolished in the early 1970s." See "Glory Restored," *Sacramento Bee*, January 7, 2007, B1; and "He Set Style for the City," ibid., May 10, 2004, A1.

4 In early January 2007, the city council voted to help fund an $18.2 million project to "transform the shuttered Woolworth Building [at Tenth and K streets] into a restaurant and live theater facility." See "City to Help Transform K Street Building," ibid., January 10, 2007, B2; and "Fargo to Run for 3rd Term as Mayor," ibid., January 12, 2007, B1.

5. Gallegos worked as a pastor and often walked the sometimes troubled streets of Sacramento's gang-infested areas to bring about peace. He fearlessly sought out Latino/a youth to end street violence and appointed himself the local chaplain of the Low Riders of Sacramento—a popular Latino young men's club. Gallegos understood that his appointment was a sign in an Irish-run church that Latinos/as had "arrived." See Steven M. Avella, *The Diocese of Sacramento: A Journey of Faith*, 119–20.

BIBLIOGRAPHY

ARCHIVES AND LIBRARIES CONSULTED

Archives of All Hallows College, Dublin
Archives of the Archdiocese of Baltimore
Archives of the Archdiocese of Los Angeles
Archives of the Archdiocese of San Francisco
Archives of the Archdiocese of Seattle
Archives of the Baptist Church, Pacific School of Religion, Berkeley
Archives of the Congregational Church, Pacific School of Religion, Berkeley
Archives of the Diocese of Cheyenne
Archives of the Diocese of Reno
Archives of the Diocese of Sacramento
Archives of the Diocese of Salt Lake City
Archives of the Order of Friars Minor, Santa Barbara Province
Archives of the Sisters of Mercy, Auburn, California
Archives of the Sisters of Mercy, Burlingame, California
Archives of the Sisters of St. Francis of Penance and Charity, Redwood City, California
Archives of the Sisters of St. Francis of Penance and Charity, Stella Niagara, New York
Archives of the Sisters of Social Service, Los Angeles
Archives of the United Methodist Church Conference, Pacific School of Religion, Berkeley
Archives of the University of Notre Dame, South Bend
Archivio Segreto Vaticano, Vatican City
Bancroft Library, University of California–Berkeley
California History Room, California State Library, Sacramento
Cenacle Central Archives, Ronkonkoma, New York
Day, Dorothy. Catholic Worker Collection. Department of Special Collections, Marquette University Archives, Milwaukee
Dominican Archives, St. Albert Priory, Oakland
Raynor Library, Marquette University, Milwaukee
Sacramento Archives and Museum Collection Center, Sacramento
Sacramento Room, Sacramento Public Library, Sacramento

Salesian Archives, San Francisco

Shields Library, University of California–Davis

MANUSCRIPT COLLECTIONS

Benton, Joseph Augustine. Papers. Archives of the Congregational Church, Pacific School of Religion, Berkeley.

Cantwell, John. Papers. Archives of the Archdiocese of Los Angeles.

Chancery. Papers. Archives of the Archdiocese of San Francisco.

Church Federation. Papers. Sacramento Archives and Museum Collection Center.

Manogue, Patrick. Papers. Archives of the Diocese of Sacramento.

McClatchy, Charles Kenny. Papers. Sacramento Archives and Museum Collection Center.

Mitty, John J. Papers. Archives of the Archdiocese of San Francisco.

Owen, Isaac. Papers. California-Nevada Annual Conference, United Methodist Church Conference Archives, Pacific School of Religion, Berkeley.

Renwald, Raymond. Papers. Archives of the Diocese of Sacramento.

Riordan, Patrick. Papers. Archives of the Archdiocese of San Francisco.

Shields, Peter. Papers. Sacramento Archives and Museum Collection Center.

NEWSPAPERS

Catholic Citizen

Catholic Herald

El Hispano (Sacramento)

Freeman's Journal

Los Angeles Times

New York Times

Sacramento Bee

Sacramento Business Journal

Sacramento Daily Transcript

Sacramento News and Review

Sacramento Union (Called the *Daily Union* when it originated on March 19, 1851, this paper merged with the *Sacramento Record,* becoming the *Daily Record-Union* on February 22, 1875. On June 14, 1903, it became the *Sacramento Union*).

San Francisco Chronicle

San Francisco Leader

San Francisco Monitor

Seattle Times

Shepherd Express

Abbott, Carl. *The Metropolitan Frontier*. Tucson: University of Arizona Press, 1993.

Ackermans, Gian. "The History of the Congregation in the Nineteenth Century." Translated by Miranda van Corbag. In *Called by God's Goodness: A History of the Sisters of St. Francis of Penance and Charity in the Twentieth Century*, edited by Gian Ackermans, Ursula Ostermann, and Mary Serbacki. Buffalo: Sisters of St. Francis of Penance and Charity, 1997.

Alexander, Thomas G., and James B. Allen. *Mormons and Gentiles: A History of Salt Lake City*. Boulder: University of Colorado Press, 1984.

Allahyari, Rebecca Anne. *Visions of Charity: Volunteer Workers and Moral Community*. Berkeley and Los Angeles: University of California Press, 2000.

"Annals of This Convent of the Religious Called Sisters of Mercy of Providence, San Francisco, California." 1871. ASMB.

Archer, Mary Urban, O.S.F. *A History of the Holy Name Province of the Sisters of Saint Francis of Penance and Christian Charity, Stella Niagara, New York*. 1987. Typescript in AOFS.

———. "Holy Family Japanese Mission." Sister Urban Archer Research Material (ca. 1969). AOFS.

Armitage, Susan, and Elizabeth Jameson, eds. *The Women's West*. Norman: University of Oklahoma Press, 1987.

Avella, Steven M. *The Diocese of Sacramento: A Journey of Faith*. Belfast: Booklink, 2006.

———. "The McClatchy Brothers and the Creation of Superior California." Paper delivered at the annual meeting of the Western History Association, San Diego, October 2001.

———. "The Personal and Professional in the Work of C. K. McClatchy: The Clash With Peter C. Yorke." *Sacramento History Journal* 2 (Fall–Winter 2002): 9–40.

———. "Phelan's Cemetery: Religion in the Urbanizing West." In *Rooted in Barbarous Soil: People, Culture, and Community in Pioneer California*, edited by Kevin Starr and Richard J. Orsi, 250–315. Berkeley and Los Angeles: University of California Press, 1999.

———. *Sacramento: Indomitable City*. Charleston: Arcadia Press, 2003.

Baird, Joseph Armstrong, Jr. "Architectural Legacy of Sacramento: A Study of Nineteenth-Century Style." *California Historical Quarterly* 39 (1960): 193–207.

Balderrama, Francisco E., and Raymond Rodriguez. *Decade of Betrayal: Mexican Repatriation in the 1930s*. Albuquerque: University of New Mexico Press, 1995.

Baltimore Publishing, comp. *The Memorial Volume: A History of the Third Plenary Council of Baltimore, November 9–December 7, 1884.* Baltimore: Baltimore Publishing, 1885.

Barth, Gunther. *Instant Cities: Urbanization and the Rise of San Francisco and Denver.* New York: Oxford University Press, 1975.

Baum, Alice S., and Donald W. Burnes. *A Nation in Denial: The Truth About Homelessness.* Boulder: Westview Press, 1993.

Bilstein, Roger E. "From Colony to Commonwealth: The Rise of the Aerospace Industry in the West." *Journal of the West* 36 (July 1997): 8–20.

Blau, Joel. *The Visible Poor: Homelessness in the United States.* New York: Oxford University Press, 1992.

Blessing, Patrick Joseph. "West Among Strangers: Irish Migration to California, 1850–1880." Ph.D. diss., University of California–Los Angeles, 1977.

Brauer, Jerald C. "Regionalism and Religion in America." *Church History* 54 (September 1985): 366–78.

Briegel, Kaye Lynn. "Alianza Hispano-Americana, 1894–1965: A Mexican-American Fraternal Insurance Society." Ph.D. diss., University of Southern California, 1974.

Brienes, Marvin. "Sacramento Defies the Rivers, 1850–1878." *California History* 58 (1979): 2–19.

Bruno, Lloyd. *Old River Town: A Personal History of Sacramento.* Sacramento: Suttertown Publishing, 1996.

Buchanan, John G. "Drumfire From the Pulpit: Natural Law in the Colonial Election Sermons of Massachusetts." *American Journal of Legal History* 12 (1968): 232–44.

Burns, Jeffrey M. "Building the Best: A History of Catholic Parish Life in the Pacific States." In *The American Catholic Parish: A History From 1850 to the Present,* edited by Jay P. Dolan, 2:7–136. New York: Paulist Press, 1987.

———. "The Mexican American Catholic Community in California, 1850–1980." In *Religion and Society in the American West: Historical Essays,* edited by Carl Guarneri and David Alvarez, 255–73. Lanham, Md.: University Press of America, 1987.

———. "The Mexican Catholic Community in California." In *Mexican-Americans and the Catholic Church, 1900–1965,* edited by Jay P. Dolan and Gilberto Hinojosa, 129–233. South Bend: University of Notre Dame Press, 1994.

Burns, John F., ed. *Sacramento: Gold Rush Legacy, Metropolitan Destiny.* Carlsbad, Calif.: Heritage Media, 1999.

Burt, Martha R. "Causes of the Growth of Homelessness During the 1980s." Paper given at Fannie Mae Annual Housing Conference, May 14, 1991. Reprinted in *Housing Policy Debate* 2, no. 3 (1991): 903–36.

———. *Over the Edge: The Growth of Homelessness in the 1980s.* New York: Russell Sage Foundation, 1992.

Butler, Anne M. "Mission in the Mountains: The Daughters of Charity in Virginia City." In *Comstock Women: The Making of a Mining Community,* edited by Ronald M. James and C. Elizabeth Raymond, 142–64. Reno: University of Nevada Press, 1997.

———. "There Are Exceptions to Every Rule: Adjusting to the Boundaries— Catholic Sisters and the American West." *American Catholic Studies* 116 (2005): 1–22.

Cain, Leonard D. *Housing Discrimination in Metropolitan Sacramento.* Research Bulletin no. 1. Sacramento: Sacramento Committee for Fair Housing, November 1961.

Carroll, Bret E. "Reflections on Regionalism and U.S. Religious History." *Church History* 71, no. 1 (2002): 120–31.

Casa, Kathryn. "Commerce Challenges Charity: Sacramento Sues Loaves and Fishes Ministry." *National Catholic Reporter* 33, no. 21 (March 28, 1997): 3–4.

Casper, Henry W. *History of the Catholic Church in Nebraska: The Church on the Fading Frontier, 1864–1910.* Milwaukee: Bruce Publishing, 1960.

"The Catholic Parade." *Cathedral Monthly Tidings,* August 1908.

Cenacle History. Ronkonkoma, N.Y.: Cenacle Central Archives, n.d.

Chatfield, LeRoy. *Bakersfield to Boston to Delano, 1963.* Self-published, n.d. In possession of the author.

———. *Boarding School, 1948.* Self-published, n.d. In possession of the author.

———. *In the World, Not of the World.* Self-published, n.d. In possession of the author.

———. *Long Bio: LeRoy Chatfield.* Self-published, n.d. In possession of the author.

Chinese Immigration: The Social, Moral, and Political Effect of Chinese Immigration. Testimony Taken Before a Committee of the Senate of the State of California, April 13, 1876. Sacramento: State Printing Office, 1876. Reprint, San Francisco: R and E Research Associates, 1970.

Chinnici, Joseph, O.F.M. *Living Stones: The History and Structure of the Catholic Spiritual Life in the United States.* New York: Macmillan, 1989.

Clinch, Bryan J. *California and Its Missions.* 2 vols. San Francisco: Whitaker and Ray, 1904.

———. "The Catholics of Russia." *Catholic World* 59 (September 1894): 757–69.

———. "The Formation of the Filipino People." *Yale Review* 10 (May 1901): 53–69.

———. "The Jesuits in American California." Pts. 1 and 2. *Records of the American Catholic Historical Society* 17 (1906): 48–66, 125–43.

———. "The New Ruthenian Archdiocese." *Catholic World* 63 (May 1896): 140–55.

———. "The Truth About the Church in the Philippines." *Catholic World* 69 (June 1899): 289–303.

Cocoltchos, Christopher N. "The Invisible Empire and the Search for Orderly Community: The Ku Klux Klan in Anaheim, California." In *The Invisible Empire in the West,* edited by Shawn Lay, 97–120. 1992. Reprint, Urbana: University of Illinois Press, 2004.

Code, Joseph Bernard. *Dictionary of the American Hierarchy.* New York: Joseph F. Wagner, 1964.

Cole, Cheryl L. "A History of the Japanese Community in Sacramento, 1883–1972." Master's thesis, Sacramento State University, 1973.

———. *A History of the Japanese Community in Sacramento, 1883–1972: Organization, Business, and Generational Response to Majority Domination and Stereotypes.* San Francisco: R and E Research Associates, 1974.

Colville, Samuel. *Sacramento Directory for the Year 1853–1854.* 1854. Reprint, Sacramento: California State Library Foundation, 1997.

Comstock, Timothy F. *An Honorable Heritage: 125 Years of YMCA Service in Sacramento.* Sacramento: YMCA of Greater Sacramento, 1991.

———. *The Sutter Club: One Hundred Years.* Sacramento: Sutter Club, 1989.

Condon, Kevin, C.M. *The Missionary College of All Hallows, 1842–1891.* Dublin: All Hallows, 1986.

Conmy, Peter T. *Seventy Years of Service, 1902–1972: History of the Knights of Columbus in California.* Los Angeles: California State Council Knights of Columbus, 1972.

Connolly, Elaine, and Dian Self. *Capital Women: An Interpretative History of Women in Sacramento, 1850–1920.* Sacramento: Capital Women History Project, 1995.

Conzen, Kathleen Neils. "The Place of Religion in Urban and Community Studies." *Religion and American Culture* 6 (Summer 1996): 108–14.

Copley, John Francis. "Sacramento's Italian Immigrants in 1920." Master's thesis, California State University–Sacramento, 1996.

Cox, Don, et al. *Mercy Hospitals: The First 100 Years.* Carmichael, Calif.: Historic Environment Consultants, 1997.

Daniels, Roger. *The Politics of Prejudice: The Anti-Japanese Movement in California and the Struggle for Japanese Exclusion.* University of California Publications in History, vol. 71. Berkeley and Los Angeles: University of California Press, 1962.

Davis, Winfield J. *An Illustrated History of Sacramento County, California.* Chicago: Lewis Publishing, 1890.

Day, Dorothy. *The Long Loneliness: The Autobiography of Dorothy Day.* New York: Harper, 1952.

Day, Rowena Wise. "Carnival of Lights." In *Sketches of Old Sacramento: A Tribute to Joseph A. McGowan*, edited by Jesse M. Smith, 27–57. Sacramento: Sacramento County Historical Society, 1976.

Deacon, Florence J. "Handmaids or Autonomous Women: The Charitable Activities, Institution Building, and Communal Relationships of Catholic Sisters in Nineteenth-Century Wisconsin." Ph.D. diss., University of Wisconsin–Madison, 1989.

Decker, Kevin Frederic. "Grand and Godly Proportions: Roman Catholic Cathedral Churches of the Northeast, 1840–1900." Ph.D. diss., State University of New York–Albany, 2000.

Delury, John Francis. "Irish Nationalism in Sacramento, 1850–1890." *Golden Notes* 36 (Summer 1990): 1–28.

———. "Irish Nationalism in the Sacramento Region." *Eire-Ireland* 21 (Fall 1986): 27–54.

———. "Irish Nationalism in the Sacramento Region, 1850–1890: Two Paths to Freedom—From Meagher of the Sword to T. P. O'Connor." Master's thesis, California State University–Sacramento, 1985.

Demas, Marilyn K. "Ungraded School No. 2 Colored: The African-American Struggle for Education in Victorian Sacramento." *Golden Notes* 45 (Spring–Summer 1999): 1–89.

DePastino, Todd. *Citizen Hobo: How a Century of Homelessness Shaped America.* Chicago: University of Chicago Press, 2003.

Deverell, William. *Railroad Crossing: Californians and the Railroad, 1850–1910.* Stanford: Stanford University Press, 1973.

Dieringer, Sister Manuela, O.S.F. "St. Stephen's School: Cathedral Parish School." In "Recollections of Sister Manuela Dieringer." October 1976. *Catholic Herald* Files.

Diner, Hasia R. *Erin's Daughters in America: Irish Immigrant Women in the Nineteenth Century.* Baltimore: Johns Hopkins University Press, 1983.

Dingemans, Dennis, and Robin Datel. "Urban Multiethnicity." *Geographical Review* 85 (October 1995): 458–77.

Dion, Maureen, ed. *Pulpit and Pew: A Centennial History of Saint John the Baptist Catholic Parish, Chico, California, 1878–1978.* Chico: St. John the Baptist Parish, 1978. Copy in ADS.

Dolan, Jay P., ed. *The American Catholic Experience: A History From 1850 to the Present.* New York: Paulist Press, 1987.

Doyle, Eleanor. "Catholic Church." *Golden Notes* 11 (January 1965): 5–11.

Doyle, Mary Katherine. *Like a Tree by Running Water: The Story of Mary Baptist Russell, California's First Sister of Mercy.* Nevada City: Blue Dolphin Publishing, 2004.

Dumke, Glenn S. *The Boom of the Eighties.* San Marino, Calif.: Huntington Library, 1944.

Dwyer, John T. *Condemned to the Mines: The Life of Eugene O'Connell, 1815–1891.* New York: Vantage Press, 1976.

———. *The Story of Mount Saint Mary's, Founded 1866, Grass Valley, California.* Grass Valley, Calif.: Historic Preservation Committee, 1980.

Economic Development Council. *Mather Air Force Base.* Sacramento: Sacramento Metropolitan Chamber of Commerce, 1971. Available in the Sacramento Room, Sacramento Public Library.

Edwards, Malcolm. "The War of Complexional Distinctions: Blacks in Gold Rush California and British Columbia." *California Historical Quarterly* 56, no. 1 (Spring 1977): 34–37.

Eifler, Mark A. *Gold Rush Capitalists: Greed and Growth in Sacramento.* Albuquerque: University of New Mexico Press, 2002.

Ellis, William. "Ireland, a Nation." Typescript. In *Occasional Sermons and Addresses by Reverend Father William F. Ellis.* Sacramento: Immaculate Conception Church, Oak Park, n.d.

———. "Sermon Delivered at Cathedral, St. Patrick's Day." Typescript. Available in the Sacramento Room, Sacramento Public Library.

Eminent Victorians. Sacramento: Sacramento Branch, American Association of University Women, 1973. Available in the SAMCC and Sacramento Room, Sacramento Public Library.

Engh, Michael. *Frontier Faiths: Church, Temple, and Synagogue in Los Angeles, 1846–1888.* Albuquerque: University of New Mexico Press, 1992.

Ernst, Eldon G. "American Religious History From a Pacific Coast Perspective." In *Religion and Society in the American West: Historical Essays,* edited by Carl Guarneri and David Alvarez, 3–39. Lanham, Md.: University Press of America, 1987.

———. "The Emergence of California in American Religious Historiography." *Religion and American Culture* 11, no. 1 (2001): 30–52.

Ewens, Mary. *The Role of the Nun in Nineteenth-Century America.* New York: Arno Press, 1978.

Feallock, Kay. "The Kingsley Art Club: One Hundred Years of Support for the Arts." *California History* 70 (Winter 1991–1992): 392–95.

Fecher, Vincent John. *The Movement for German National Parishes in Philadelphia and Baltimore, 1782–1802.* Rome: Gregorian University, 1955.

Feller, Elaine E. "The History and Development of Catholic Social Service in Sacramento." Master's thesis, California State University–Sacramento, 1986.

Findlay, John M. *Magic Lands: Western Cityscapes and American Culture After 1940.* Berkeley and Los Angeles: University of California Press, 1992.

Flanagan, Maureen. "Women in the City, Women of the City: Where Do Women Fit in Urban History?" *Journal of Urban History* 23 (March 1997): 251–59.

Freye, Paul. "Congregational Church." In "Our Pioneer Churches." *Golden Notes* 11 (January 1965): 12–15.

Gaffey, James P. *Citizen of No Mean City: Archbishop Patrick Riordan of San Francisco, 1841–1914*. Wilmington, N.C.: Consortium Books, 1976.

Galarza, Ernesto. *Barrio Boy*. South Bend: University of Notre Dame Press, 1917.

Garcia, Mario T. *Padre: The Spiritual Journey of Father Virgil Cordano*. Santa Barbara: Capra Press, 2005.

Gaustad, Edwin Scott, and Philip L. Barlow. *New Historical Atlas of Religion in America*. New York: Oxford University Press, 2001.

Giffen, Helen S., ed. *The Diaries of Peter Decker: Overland to California in 1849 and Life in the Mines, 1850–1851*. Georgetown: Talisman Press, 1966.

Giggie, John M., and Diane Winston, eds. *Faith in the Marketplace: Religion and the Rise of Urban Commercial Culture*. New Brunswick: Rutgers University Press, 2002.

Goethe, Charles M. *Seeking to Serve*. Sacramento: Keystone Printing, 1949.

Goff, Philip. "Religion and the American West." In *A Companion to the American West*, edited by William Deverell, 286–303. Blackwell Companions to American History. Malden, Mass.: Blackwell Publishers, 2004.

Gonzales, Manuel G. *Mexicanos: A History of Mexicans in the United States*. Bloomington: Indiana University Press, 1999.

"Grapes of Wrath." *Time*, December 10, 1965, 96.

Griffith, Beatrice. *American Me*. Boston: Houghton Mifflin, 1948.

Guilday, Peter K. *A History of the Councils of Baltimore, 1791–1884*. New York: Macmillan, 1932.

Hanchett, William Francis. "Religion and the Gold Rush, 1849–1854: The Christian Churches and the California Mines." Ph.D. diss., University of California–Berkeley, 1952.

Handlin, Oscar. *Boston's Immigrants: A Study in Acculturation*. Cambridge: Harvard University Press / Belknap Press, 1959.

Hartfield, Anne Elizabeth. "Sisters of Mercy, Mothers to the Afflicted: Female-Created Space in San Francisco, 1854 Through the Turn of the Century (California)." Ph.D. diss., Claremont Graduate University, 2003.

Harwick, Susan Wiley. "Ethnic Residential and Commercial Patterns in Sacramento With Special Reference to the Russian-American Experience." Ph.D. diss., University of California–Davis, 1986.

Hayes, Peter J., ed. *The Lower American River: Prehistory to Parkway*. Sacramento: American River Natural History Association, 2005.

Healy, Kathleen, R.S.M., ed. *Sisters of Mercy: Spirituality in America, 1843–1900*. New York: Paulist Press, 1992.

Hegemann, Werner. "Report of Dr. Werner Hegemann, Oct. 30, 1913." Sacramento Room, Sacramento Public Library.

Helmich, Mary A. *Stanford House State Historic Park, Interpretive Plan.* Sacramento: California Department of Parks and Recreation, 1988.

Henley, James E. "Depression, New Deal, War, Government, and Economic Growth: The Metropolis Arrives, 1930s–1950s." In *Sacramento: Gold Rush Legacy, Metropolitan Destiny,* edited by John F. Burns, 98–113. Carlsbad, Calif.: Heritage Media, 1999.

———. "Wobblies and Communists in Sacramento: The Criminal Syndicalism Trial of 1935." *Sacramento History Journal* 5, no. 3 (2005): 38–45.

Hernandez, Jose Amaro. *Mutual Aid for Survival: The Case of the Mexican American.* Malabar, Fla.: Robert E. Krieger Publishing, 1983.

"History and Resume of Founding [of the Young Ladies' Institute]." 1976. Copy in AASF.

"History of Mercy Hospital." N.d. ASMA.

"The History of St. Mel's Catholic Church, Fair Oaks, California, 1921–1985." 1985. ADS.

"History of the School of Nursing, Mercy Hospital, Sacramento, California." N.d. ASMA.

Holden, William M. *Sacramento: Excursions Into Its History and Natural World.* Fair Oaks, Calif.: Two Rivers Publishing, 1988.

Holifield, E. Brooks. "Forum: The Place of Religion in Urban and Community Studies." *Religion and American Culture* 6, no. 2 (Summer 1996): 120–24.

Holmes, Lionel, and Joseph D'Alessandro. *Portuguese Pioneers of the Sacramento Area.* Sacramento: Portuguese Historical and Cultural Society, 1990.

Hoy, Suellen. "Caring for Chicago's Women and Girls: The Sisters of the Good Shepherd, 1859–1911." *Journal of Urban History* 23 (March 1997): 260–94.

———. "The Journey Out: The Recruitment and Emigration of Irish Religious Women to the United States, 1812–1914." *Journal of Women's History* 6 (Winter–Spring 1995): 62–98.

Hub of Western Industry, Sacramento, California. Sacramento: Sacramento Chamber of Commerce, 1944.

Huels, John. *The Saturday Night Novena.* Chicago: Servite Publication, 1975.

Hulse, James W. *The Silver State: Nevada's Heritage Reinterpreted.* 2d ed. Reno: University of Nevada Press, 1991.

Hume, Charles. "The Eagle Theater: First of Gold Rush Theaters." In *Sketches of Old Sacramento: A Tribute to Joseph A. McGowan,* edited by Jesse M. Smith, 169–91. Sacramento: Sacramento County Historical Society, 1976.

Ing, John C., comp. *Sacramento City and County, California.* Sacramento: Sacramento Chamber of Commerce, 1905. Available in the SAMCC.

Ingells, Douglas. *The McDonnell-Douglas Story.* Fallbrook, Calif.: Acro Publishers, 1979. Available in the Sacramento Room, Sacramento Public Library.

Irwin, Mary Ann. "'Going About Doing Good': The Politics of Benevolence, Welfare, and Gender in San Francisco, 1850–1880." *Pacific Historical Review* 68 (August 1999): 365–96.

Isetti, Ronald E. *Called to the Pacific: A History of the Christian Brothers of the San Francisco District, 1868–1944.* Moraga: St. Mary's College of California, 1979.

Jackson, Kenneth T. *Crabgrass Frontier: The Suburbanization of the United States.* New York: Oxford University Press, 1985.

James, Ronald M. *The Roar and the Silence: A History of Virginia City and the Comstock Lode.* Reno: University of Nevada Press, 1998.

Jamieson, Jon L. "General Kelley's 'Army' of 1914." *Golden Notes* 8 (January 1962).

Jones, J. Roy, M.D. *Memories, Men, and Medicine.* Sacramento: Sacramento Society for Medical Improvement, 1950.

Joslyn, D. L. "Sacramento General Shops: Southern Pacific Company—Pacific Lines." Manuscript, David Joslyn Collection, 1948. SAMCC.

Kennelly, Sister M. Berchmans. "Annals" (ca. 1931). ASMA.

Kilde, Jeanne Halgren. "Reading Megachurches: Investigating the Religious and Cultural Work of Church Architecture." In *American Sanctuary: Understanding Sacred Spaces,* edited by Louis P. Nelson, 225–49. Bloomington: Indiana University Press, 2006.

Killen, Patricia O'Connell, and Mark Silk, eds. *Religion and Public Life in the Pacific Northwest: The None Zone.* Walnut Creek, Calif.: Altamira Press, 2004.

King, M. Gertrude. "Early History of Sisters of Mercy in Sacramento, 1905–1911." N.d. ASMA.

Kinzer, Donald L. *An Episode in Anti-Catholicism: The American Protective Association.* Seattle: University of Washington Press, 1964.

Kurutz, K. D., and Gary F. Kurutz. *California Calls You: The Art of Promoting the Golden State, 1870–1940.* Sausalito, Calif.: Windgate Press, 2000.

Lagomarsino, Barbara. "Early Attempts to Save the Site of Sacramento by Raising the Business District." Master's thesis, Sacramento State College, 1969.

Lapomarda, Vincent A., S.J. "Saint Mary's in the Mountains: The Cradle of Catholicism in Western Nevada." *Nevada Historical Society Quarterly* 35 (Spring 1992): 58–62.

Larsen, Christian L. *Growth and Government in Sacramento.* Metropolitan Action Studies no. 4. Bloomington: Indiana University Press, 1965.

Larsen, Lawrence H., and Robert L. Branyan. "The Development of an Urban Civilization on the Frontier of the American West." *Societas* 1 (1971): 33–50.

Lastufka, Ken. "Redevelopment of Sacramento's West End, 1950–1970: A Historical

Overview With an Analysis of the Impact of Relocation." Master's thesis, California State University–Sacramento, 1985.

Laughlin, Corinna. "One Hundred Years Ago: The Cathedral Builders." In *In Your Midst: A Journal of St. James Cathedral Parish.* Seattle: St. James Cathedral, 2004.

L'egare, Armand. "The Great Sacramento Poolroom Battle, 1896–1900." Master's thesis, California State University–Sacramento, 2000.

———. *The Great Sacramento Pool Room Battle, 1896–1900.* Self-published, 2000. Available in the SAMCC.

Leland, Dorothy Kupcha. *A Short History of Sacramento.* San Francisco: Lexikos Press, 1989.

Lewis, M. H. *Transients in California.* San Francisco: State Emergency Relief Administration of California, 1936.

Lewis, Oscar. *Sutter's Fort: Gateway to the Gold Fields.* American Forts Series. Englewood Cliffs, N.J.: Prentice-Hall, 1966.

Limerick, Patricia Nelson. "Believing in the American West." In *The West: An Illustrated History,* edited by Geoffrey C. Ward, 207–13. Boston: Little, Brown, 1996.

Livezey, Lowell W., ed. *Public Religion and Urban Transformation: Faith in the City.* New York: New York University Press, 2000.

Lord, Myrtle Shaw. *Sacramento Saga: Fifty Years of Achievement—Chamber of Commerce Leadership.* Sacramento: Sacramento Chamber of Commerce, 1946.

Lotchin, Roger W. *Fortress California, 1910–1961: From Warfare to Welfare.* New York: Oxford University Press, 1992.

Lower, Richard Coke. *A Bloc of One: The Political Career of Hiram W. Johnson.* Stanford: Stanford University Press, 1993.

Lowitt, Richard. *The New Deal and the West.* Norman: University of Oklahoma Press, 1993.

Luckingham, Bradford. "The Urban Dimensions of Western History." In *Historians and the American West,* edited by Michael Malone, 323–43. Lincoln: University of Nebraska Press, 1983.

[Lunney, M. M. Clare]. "Annals From St. Joseph's Convent." Sacramento. ASMA.

Madigan, Dan. *25th Anniversary of Sacramento Food Bank Services: Letters From the Hearth.* Sacramento: Sacramento Food Bank Services, 2001.

Madrid, Rosana M. "Narrative History of Mexican/Chicano Community of Sacramento." Sacramento: Sacramento Ethnic Community Survey Project, Sacramento History Center, 1984. SAMCC.

Maeda, Wayne. *Changing Dreams and Treasured Memories: A Story of Japanese Americans in the Sacramento Region.* Sacramento: Sacramento Japanese American Citizens League, 2000.

————. "The Japanese." Sacramento Ethnic Survey Study, 1984. SAMCC.

Maffly-Kipp, Laurie. "Eastward Ho! American Religion From the Perspective of the Pacific Rim." In *Retelling U.S. Religious History,* edited by Thomas A. Tweed, 127–48. Berkeley and Los Angeles: University of California Press, 1997.

————. *Religion and Society in Frontier California.* New Haven: Yale University Press, 1994.

Mahan, William E. "The Political Response to Urban Growth: Sacramento and Mayor Marshall R. Beard, 1863–1914." *California History* 69, no. 4 (Winter 1990–1991): 345–71.

————. "Taxpayer Support for Art? The Federal Arts Project in Sacramento, 1937–1941." *Golden Notes* 40 (Fall 1994): 1–46.

Marks, Joseph B., and Lisa J. Sanders. "The Blue Laws Debate: A Sacramento Shopkeeper's Story." *Western States Jewish History* 25 (April 1993): 211–24.

Mason, S. Liguori. "History of the American Foundation, 1874–1924." N.d. Copy in AOFS.

————. Comp. "Japanese Mission, Sacramento, California." Sister Urban Archer Research Material (ca. 1969). AOFS.

Matovina, Timothy. *Guadalupe and Her Faithful: Latino Catholics in San Antonio From Colonial Origins to the Present.* Baltimore: Johns Hopkins University Press, 2005.

Matthews, Donald G. *Religion in the Old South.* Chicago: University of Chicago Press, 1977.

McAdams, C. Michael. "The Croatians of California and Nevada." *Pacific Historian* 21 (1977): 333–49.

McArdle, Mary Aurelia. *California's Pioneer Sister of Mercy: Mother Mary Baptist Russell (1829–1898).* Fresno: Academy Library Guild, 1954.

McCauley, Bernadette. *Who Shall Take Care of Our Sick? Roman Catholic Sisters and the Development of Catholic Hospitals in New York City.* Baltimore: Johns Hopkins University Press, 2005.

McCoy, Florence Nina. "A History of the First Five Years of the Sacramento, California, Turnverein, 1854–1859." Master's thesis, Sacramento State College, 1962.

McCracken, Ellen. "'Cathedrals of the Desert' and 'Sermons in Stone': Fray Angélico Chávez's Contributions to Hispano Church Architecture in New Mexico." *Catholic Southwest* 12 (2001): 75–105.

McGloin, John B., S.J. *California's First Archbishop: The Life of Joseph Sadoc Alemany, O.P., 1814–1888.* New York: Herder and Herder, 1966.

————. "'Philos' (Gregory J. Phelan, M.D., 1822–1902): Commentator on Catholicism in California's Gold Rush Decade." *Records of the American Catholic Historical Society of Philadelphia* 67 (June 1966): 109–16.

———. "Thomas Cian: Pioneer Chinese Priest in California." *California Historical Society Quarterly* 48 (March 1969): 45–58.

McGowan, Joseph A. *History of the Sacramento Valley.* 3 vols. New York: Lewis Historical Publishing, 1961.

McGowan, Joseph A., and Terry R. Willis. *Sacramento: Heart of the Golden State.* Woodland Hills, Calif.: Windsor Publications, 1983.

McKee, Elizabeth A. "The Irish in Sacramento." Sacramento Ethnic Communities Survey, 1984. SAMCC.

Meagher, Timothy J. *The Columbia Guide to Irish American History.* New York: Columbia University Press, 2005.

———. *Inventing Irish America: Generation, Class, and Ethnic Identity in a New England City, 1880–1928.* South Bend: University of Notre Dame Press, 2001.

Meeker, Amanda Paige. "Wright and Kimbrough Tract 24: Review of National Register Eligibility." 2 vols. Master's thesis, California State University–Sacramento, 2000.

Mexicans in California: Report of Governor C. C. Young's Mexican Fact-Finding Committee. San Francisco: State Building, 1930.

Miller, Kerby A. *Emigrants and Exiles: Ireland and the Irish Exodus to North America.* New York: Oxford University Press, 1985.

Miller, Maurice A., ed. *McClellan Air Force Base, 1936–1982: A Pictorial History.* Sacramento: Office of History Sacramento Air Logistics Center, 1982. Available in the Sacramento Room, Sacramento Public Library.

Miller, William D. *Dorothy Day: A Biography.* San Francisco: Harper and Row, 1982.

———. *A Harsh and Dreadful Love: Dorothy Day and the Catholic Worker Movement.* New York: Liveright, 1973.

Moehring, Eugene P. *Urbanism and Empire in the Far West, 1840–1890.* Reno: University of Nevada Press, 2004.

Mooney, Bernice Maher. *The Story of the Cathedral of the Madeleine.* Salt Lake City: Lithografics, 1981.

Morefield, Richard. "The Mexican Adaptation in American California, 1846–1875." Ph.D. diss., University of California–Berkeley, 1955.

Morgan, Sister M. Evangelist. *Mercy Generation to Generation.* San Francisco: Fearon Publishers, 1957.

Muir, Robert A. "Sacramento Depression Settlement Survey." 1935. Available in the SAMCC.

Muller, Dorothea R. "Church Building and Community Making on the Frontier, a Case Study: Josiah Strong, Home Missionary in Cheyenne, 1871–1873." *Western Historical Quarterly* 10, no. 2 (1979): 191–216.

Mullins, William H. *The Depression and the Urban West Coast, 1929–1933.* Bloomington: Indiana University Press, 1991.

Murphy, James. "Restoration: Preserving the Best From the Cathedral's Victorian Past." In *The Cathedral of the Blessed Sacrament,* edited by Mary Cabrini-Durkin, 17–33. Strasbourg, France: Editions du Signe, 2005.

Nagl, Charles E. "A Fight for Survival: Floods, Riots, and Disease in Sacramento." Master's thesis, Sacramento State College, 1965.

Nash, Gerald D. *The American West in the Twentieth Century.* Englewood Cliffs, N.J.: Prentice-Hall, 1973.

———. *The American West Transformed.* Lincoln: University of Nebraska Press, 1985.

Nelson, Louis P., ed. *American Sanctuary: Understanding Sacred Places.* Bloomington: Indiana University Press, 2006.

Noel, Thomas J. *Colorado Catholicism and the Archdiocese of Denver, 1857–1989.* Boulder: University Press of Colorado, 1989.

Norris, Thomas D. "Metropolitan Growth in the Sacramento Area During World War II and the Post-war Period." Master's thesis, California State University–Sacramento, 1982.

North, Diane M. T. "The State and the People: California During the First World War." Ph.D. diss., University of California–Davis, 2001.

O'Connor, Carol. "A Region of Cities." In *Oxford History of the American West,* edited by Clyde A. Milner III, Carol A. O'Connor, and Martha Sandweis, 535–63. New York: Oxford University Press, 1994.

Okihiro, Gary Y. "Religion and Resistance in America's Concentration Camps." *Phylon* 45 (Third Quarter 1984): 220–33.

O'Loughlin, Rev. Thomas. "The Demand and Supply of Priests to the United States From All Hallows College, Ireland, Between 1842 and 1860." *Records of the American Catholic Historical Society of Philadelphia* 94 (1983): 39–60.

Olson, James S. "Pioneer Catholicism in Eastern and Southern Nevada, 1864–1931." *Nevada Historical Society Quarterly* 26 (1983): 159–71.

O'Malley, Bro. Kevin, C.P. "A Brief History of the Passionists in Northern California and Western Nevada, 1852–1986." 1986. In "Religious Priests File," ADS.

Orsi, Richard J. "Selling the Golden State: A Study of Boosterism in Nineteenth-Century California." Ph.D. diss., University of Wisconsin–Madison, 1973.

———. *Sunset Limited: The Southern Pacific Railroad and the Development of the American West, 1850–1930.* Berkeley and Los Angeles: University of California Press, 2005.

Orsi, Robert A., ed. *Gods of the City: Religion and the American Urban Landscape.* Bloomington: Indiana University Press, 1997.

Ottley, Allan R. "Angels Without Wings: The Scarcity of Women in Pioneer Sacramento." *Golden Notes* 38 (Winter–Spring 1992): 25–34.

Oxford, June. *The Capital That Couldn't Stay Put: The Complete Book of California's Capitals.* Fairfield, Calif.: James Stevenson Publisher, 1995.

Pascoe, Peggy. *Relations of Rescue: The Search for Female Moral Authority in the American West, 1874–1939.* New York: Oxford University Press, 1990.

Paterson, James. *America's Struggle Against Poverty in the Twentieth Century.* Cambridge: Harvard University Press, 2000.

Piehl, Mel. *Breaking Bread: The Catholic Workers and the Origin of Catholic Radicalism in America.* Philadelphia: Temple University Press, 1982.

Pierini, Bruce. "Germans in the Sacramento Area." Sacramento County Ethnic History Survey, 1984. SAMCC.

———. "Italian History and Demographics of the Greater Sacramento Area." Sacramento County Ethnic History Survey, 1984. SAMCC.

Pitti, Gina Marie. "To 'Hear About God in Spanish': Ethnicity, Church, and Community Activism in the San Francisco Archdiocese's Mexican American Colonias, 1942–1965." Ph.D. diss., Stanford University, 2003.

Platt, Tony. *What's in a Name? Charles M. Goethe, American Eugenics, and Sacramento State University.* Sacramento: Division of Social Work, California State University, 2004.

Pomfret, John E. "Mark Hopkins' Formative Years in California." *Huntington Library Quarterly* 26 (1962–1963): 57–81.

Poole, C. M. Stafford. *Our Lady of Guadalupe: The Origins and Sources of a Mexican National Symbol, 1531–1797.* Tucson: University of Arizona Press, 1996.

"Poor Call: Thanks to LeRoy Chatfield's Success in Helping the Needy, Sacramento Is Suing Him." *People,* June 9, 1997, 91–94.

"Preparing Sacramento for Post-war." Sacramento Chamber of Commerce, Vertical Files, Counties: Sacramento, Pamphlets, A120. Available in the Sacramento Room, Sacramento Public Library.

Prescott, Gerald. "The California State Fair in the Gilded Age." *Southern California Quarterly* 60 (1978): 17–27.

Public Service Administration. *The Government of Metropolitan Sacramento.* Chicago: Public Administration Service, 1957.

Quinn, D. Michael. "Religion in the American West." In *Under an Open Sky: Rethinking America's Western Past,* edited by William Cronon, George Miles, and Jay Gitlin, 145–66. New York: W. W. Norton, 1992.

Regan, M. Joanna, R.S.M., and Isabelle Keiss, R.S.M. *Tender Courage: A Reflection on the Life and Spirit of Catherine McAuley, First Sister of Mercy.* Chicago: Franciscan Herald Press, 1988.

"Report of the State Capital Planning Commission." Appendices A, B, and C, 12–29. N.d. Sacramento Room, Sacramento Public Library.

Report of the State Capital Planning Commission Upon Its Investigation of the Planning of the Capital of California. Sacramento: California State Printing Office, 1916. Copy in the Graduate School of Design, Francis Loeb Library, Harvard University, Cambridge.

Reps, John W. *Cities of the American West: A History of Frontier Urban Planning.* Princeton: Princeton University Press, 1979.

Ridge, John T. *Erin's Sons in America: The Ancient Order of Hibernians.* New York: AOH 150th Anniversary Committee, 1986.

Riley, Glenda. *Women and Nature: Saving the "Wild" West.* Lincoln: University of Nebraska Press, 1999.

Roberts, Brian. "Sacramento Since World War II: From Small Town to Megalopolis in Less Than Fifty Years." Master's thesis, California State University–Sacramento, 1989.

Robinson, Charles Mulford. "Report on the Improvement of Sacramento." In *Sacramento: City Planning Report,* 1–34. N.d. Available in the Sacramento Room, Sacramento Public Library.

Rodgerson, Eleanor, M.D. *Adobe, Brick, and Steel: A History of Hospitals and Shelters for the Sick in Sacramento and El Dorado Counties.* Sacramento: Sacramento–El Dorado Medical Society, 1993.

Rodriguez, Richard. *Days of Obligation: An Argument With My Mexican Father.* New York: Penguin Books, 1992.

———. *Hunger of Memory: The Education of Richard Rodriguez.* New York: Bantam Books, 1983.

Rogers, Richard C. *The First One Hundred Years of the Sacramento City Schools, 1854–1954.* Sacramento: State Capital Division of California Retired Teachers Association, n.d. Available in the Sacramento Room, Sacramento Public Library.

Roof, Wade, and Mark Silk, eds. *Religion and Public Life in the Pacific Region: Fluid Identities.* Walnut Creek, Calif.: Altamira Press, 2004.

Rossi, Peter H. *Down and Out in America: The Origins of Homelessness.* Chicago: University of Chicago Press, 1989.

Rothman, Hal. *Neon Metropolis: How Las Vegas Started the Twenty-first Century.* New York and London: Routledge, 2003.

Sabine, Gordon. *Monsignor Donohoe.* Tempe: Arizona State University Library, 1988.

Sacramento Army Depot: 25th Anniversary. Lubbock: Boone Publications, 1970.

Sacramento Chamber of Commerce. *Greater Sacramento: Her Achievement,*

Resources, and Possibilities. Sacramento: Kelman, 1912. Available in the California History Room, California State Library, Sacramento.

Sacramento Convention and Visitor's Bureau. *Sacramento: America's Most Diverse City.* Sacramento: Sacramento Convention and Visitor's Bureau, n.d.

Sacramento County, California. Sacramento County Board of Supervisors and Exposition Commissioners, 1914–1915. Available in the SAMCC.

Sacramento County and Its Resources: A Souvenir of "The Bee." 1894. Available in the California History Room, California State Library, Sacramento.

"Sacramento's Awakening." *Great West* 6, no. 19 (October 1907): 6. Available in the California History Room, California State Library, Sacramento.

"Sacramento's Numerous and Beautiful Church Structures." *Great West* 6, no. 5 (October 1907): 15. Available in the California History Room, California State Library, Sacramento.

"Sacramento Wave." *Time,* January 30, 1933.

"St. Ignatius Loyola Parish History, 1954–1979." 1979. ADS.

"St. Stephen's." *Cathedral Monthly Tidings,* September 1908, 5.

"St. Stephen's." *Cathedral Monthly Tidings,* October 1908, 4.

"St. Stephen's Free School." *Cathedral Monthly Tidings,* January 1908, 8, 9.

Sandmeyer, Elmer Clarence. *The Anti-Chinese Movement in California.* 1973. Reprint, Urbana: University of Illinois Press, 1991.

Sarbaugh, Timothy. "Exiles of Confidence: The Irish-American Community of San Francisco, 1880–1920." In *From Paddy to Studs: Irish American Communities in the Turn of the Century Era, 1880–1920,* by Timothy J. Meagher, 161–80. Contribution in Ethnic Studies no. 13. New York: Greenwood Press, 1986.

Schweiger, Beth Barton, and Donald G. Matthews, eds. *Religion in the American South.* Chapel Hill: University of North Carolina Press, 2004.

Self, Robert O. "City Lights: Urban History in the West." In *A Companion to the American West,* edited by William Deverell, 412–41. Blackwell Companions to American History. Malden, Mass.: Blackwell Publishers, 2004.

Severson, Thor. *Sacramento: An Illustrated History, 1839 to 1874.* San Francisco: California Historical Society, 1973.

Shipps, Jan, and Mark Silk, eds. *Religion and Public Life in the Mountain West: Sacred Landscapes in Transition.* Walnut Creek, Calif.: Altamira Press, 2004.

Shortridge, James R. "A New Regionalization of American Religion." *Journal for the Scientific Study of Religion* 16 (June 1977): 143–53.

Sibole, Edna Smith. *135th Anniversary History of the First Methodist Church.* Sacramento: First Methodist Church, 1984. Available in the Sacramento Room, Sacramento Public Library.

Silva, Alan J. "Increase Mather's 1693 Election Sermon: Rhetorical Innovations and the Re-imagination of Puritan Authority." *Early American Literature* 34 (1999): 48–77.

———. "Rituals of Empowerment: Politics and Rhetoric in the Puritan Election Sermon." Ph.D. diss., University of California–Davis, 1993.

"Sisters Chronicle: St. Stephen's Sacramento." N.d. AOFS.

Smith, Martha, and Carol K. Coburn. *Spirited Lives: How Nuns Shaped Catholic Culture and American Life, 1836–1920*. Chapel Hill: University of North Carolina Press, 1999.

Snodgrass, Robert. "History of St. James Cathedral Parish, Seattle, Washington, 1904–1929." Record Group 700, St. James, Publications (108/7), Archives of the Archdiocese of Seattle.

Snyder, Wehle, and Paula J. Boghosian. *Sacramento's Memorial Auditorium: Seven Decades of Memories*. Sacramento: Memorial Auditorium Book Project, 1997.

Soto, Antonio Robert. "The Chicano and the Church in Northern California, 1848–1978: A Study of an Ethnic Minority Within the Roman Catholic Church." Ph.D. diss., University of California–Berkeley, 1978.

"The Southern Pacific Shops, 1863–1950." *Golden Notes* 19 (November 1973): 3–23.

Spadier, Sister Mary Gabriel. "About the Early Mercy Community." Ca. 1965–1966. ASMA.

Spalding, Thomas. *Premier See: A History of the Archdiocese of Baltimore, 1789–1989*. Baltimore: Johns Hopkins University Press, 1990.

Starr, Kevin. *Inventing the Dream: California Through the Progressive Era*. New York: Oxford University Press, 1985.

Stellman, Louis J. *Sam Brannan: Builder of San Francisco*. Fairfield, Calif.: James Stevenson Publisher, 1996.

Stodghill, Ron, and Amanda Bower. "Welcome to America's Most Diverse City." *Time*, posted online August 25, 2002. Or see the print edition, "Where Everyone's a Minority: Welcome to Sacramento, America's Most Integrated City." *Time*, September 2, 2002, 26.

"The Story of McClellan Air Force Base, 1939–1998." In *McClellan A.F.B. Remembered, 1939–1998*, edited by Richard L. Davis, 82–200. Sacramento: McClellan Commemorative Association, 1998. Available in the Sacramento Room, Sacramento Public Library.

"Substantial Evidences of Sacramento's New Growth." *Great West* 6, no. 5 (October 1907): 5, 7. Available in the California History Room, California State Library, Sacramento.

Sullivan, Mary C. *Catherine McAuley and the Tradition of Mercy*. South Bend: University of Notre Dame Press, 1995.

Sweetser, Albion C. *History of the First Congregational Church in Sacramento, California*. N.d. Copy in the Sacramento Room, Sacramento Public Library.

Szasz, Ferenc M. "The Clergy and the Myth of the American West." *Church History* 59, no. 4 (1990): 497–506.

———. *Religion in the Modern American West.* Tucson: University of Arizona Press, 2000.

Szasz, Ferenc, and Margaret Connell Szasz. "Religion and Spirituality." In *Oxford History of the American West,* edited by Clyde A. Milner II, Carol A. O'Connor, and Martha A. Sandweiss, 359–91. New York: Oxford University Press, 1994.

Tarbox, Mary Patricia. "The Origins of Nursing by the Sisters of Mercy in the United States, 1843–1910." Ed.D. diss., Columbia University Teachers College, 1986.

Tentler, Leslie. "On the Margins: The State of American Catholic History." *American Quarterly* 45 (March 1993): 104–27.

Terry, Carole Cosgrove. "Die Deutschen Enwanderer in Sacramento: German Immigrants in Sacramento, 1850–1859." Master's thesis, University of Nevada–Las Vegas, 2000.

———. "Die Deutschen Von Marysville: The Germans in Marysville, 1850–1860." *Psi Sigma Historical Journal* 1 (Spring 2003): 1–3.

———. "Germans in Sacramento, 1850–1859." *Psi Sigma Historical Journal* 3 (Summer 2005): 1–29.

Thompson, Thomas H., and Albert Augustus West. *History of Sacramento County With Illustrations.* Reprint with introduction by Allan R. Ottley. Berkeley: Howell-North, 1960.

Topping, Gary. "Religion in the West." *Journal of American Culture* 3 (1980): 330–50.

Trattner, Walter I. *From Poor Law to Welfare State.* 3d ed. New York: Free Press, 1984.

Trevino, Roberto R. *The Church in the Barrio: Mexican-American Ethno-Catholicism in Houston.* Chapel Hill: University of North Carolina Press, 2006.

Troester, Rosalie Riegle. *Voices From the "Catholic Worker."* Philadelphia: Temple University Press, 1993.

Under the Lamp Post: History of the Young Men's Institute. Oakland: Harrington-McInnis, 1948.

Vandenberg, Marie. "Attitudes and Events Leading Up to the Establishment of the Christian Brothers School in Sacramento, California, 1871–1876." Master's thesis, Sacramento State College, 1968.

Von Brauchitsch, Dennis M. "The Ku Klux Klan in California, 1921–1924." Master's thesis, Sacramento State University, 1967.

Wade, Richard C. *The Urban Frontier: The Rise of Western Cities, 1790–1830.* Cambridge: Harvard University Press, 1959.

Wade, William. "The Architecture of Small Cities." *Architect and the Engineer* (June 1920).

Wall, Barbra Mann. *Unlikely Entrepreneurs: Catholic Sisters and the Hospital Marketplace, 1865–1925.* Columbus: Ohio State University Press, 2005.

Weber, Francis J. *Cathedral of Our Lady of the Angels.* Mission Hills, Calif.: St. Francis Historical Society, 2004.

———. *Catholic California.* Mission Hills, Calif.: St. Francis Historical Society, 1986.

———. *Encyclopedia of California's Catholic Heritage.* Mission Hills, Calif. and Spokane, Wash.: St. Francis Mission Society and Arthur H. Clark, 2000.

Weisenburger, Francis E. "God and Man in a Secular City." *Nevada Historical Society Quarterly* 14 (Summer 1971): 5–23.

West, Richard V. "Edwin Bryant Crocker's Art Gallery in Sacramento." *Nineteenth Century* 5 (1979): 34–39.

Willging, Eugene P., and Herta Hatzfeld. *Catholic Serials of the Nineteenth Century in the United States.* 2d ser., pt. 8, California. Washington, D.C.: Catholic University of America Press, 1964.

Williams, Fonton L. *Arthur S. Dudley and His Contribution to U.S. Air Defense.* Sacramento: McClellan Air Force Base, Sacramento Air Material Area, 1961. Available in the Sacramento Room, Sacramento Public Library.

Williams, Peter W. *Houses of God: Region, Religion, and Architecture in the United States.* Urbana: University of Illinois Press, 1997.

Williams, R. Hal. *The Democratic Party and California Politics, 1880–1896.* Berkeley and Los Angeles: University of California Press, 1994.

Willis, William L. *History of Sacramento County With Biographical Sketches.* Los Angeles: Historic Record, 1913.

Wilson, William Julius. *The Truly Disadvantaged: The Inner City, the Underclass, and Public Policy.* Chicago: University of Chicago Press, 1987.

Wrobel, David M. *Promised Lands: Promotion, Memory, and the Creation of the American West.* Lawrence: University Press of Kansas, 2002.

Zelinsky, Wilbur. "An Approach to the Religious Geography of the United States: Patterns of Church Membership in 1952." *Annals of the Association of American Geographers* 51 (June 1961): 139–93.

INDEX

Italic page numbers refer to illustrations; page numbers with the letter *t* refer to the tables.

ethnic realities, religious bodies as
microcosms of, 6, 10, 120–21, 123–24
Eugene (Ore.), 249
eugenics, 108
Executive Order 9066, 184

Fair Oaks, 204
Falcon, Federico, 225, 226, 228, 229, 235
Falconio, Diomede, 126, 127, 129, 303n86
Fargo, Heather, 269, 272
farmworkers, political activism of, 12,
243–44, 258, 270, 325n74
Father Keith B. Kenny Elementary School,
2
federal aid, Depression-era, 161, 171
federal building, construction of, 57, 59
Federal Emergency Relief Act, 1933, 171
Federal Transient Service, 171
Ferrales, Manuel, 246
floods, recovery following, 21–22, 43–44,
277
Folsom, 192, 207, 253
Folsom Prison, 135, 257
foreign-born persons. *See* immigrants
Foreman, Ferris, 80–81
Franciscan Sisters of Penance and Charity,
10, 75, 78–79, 90–91, 92, 97–99, 101, 123,
124, 183
Francis House, 268, 272
fraternal organizations, 23, 165, 285n25
freeways, building of, 192–93, 231, 232, 255
French Second Empire (1850–1871), 53
Friendship Park, 265, 267

Gabrielli, Virgil, 204–5, 207, 209
Galarza, Ernesto, 105, 119, 217
Gallegos, Alphonse, 1, 279, 332n5
Geisreiter, Bert, 191
Germans and German Americans: as
Catholics, 31, 114, 116–19; German
POWs, 178; immigrants, 103, 115;
political views of, 110, 116
Gilbert, Richard, 273

Globe Mills, 265, 267, 329n40
Goethe, Charles Matthias, 108, 109
Gold Rush: Catholicism in, 29, 53;
Chinese Americans during, 111; church
conditions following, 16; cities created
during, 3, 20; civilizing influences
following, 71; economic development
following, 56; historic commemoration
of, 154; immigrant participation in,
103; Irish migration during, 35; Latinos
prior to, 216; moral climate during,
14; racial discrimination during, 102;
religious communities during, 8, 19
*Gold Rush Capitalists: Greed and Growth in
Sacramento* (Eifler), 4
Gonzales, Manuel G., 217
Gormley, William F., 37–38, 113, 287n62
government reforms: city, 134–35, 140, 152;
county, 195–97
Grace, Thomas: affection for, 101, 278;
cathedral establishment, participation
in, 57, 60, 69, 290n39; child care facility
named after, 97, 98; civic activities of,
40–41, 134; T. Connelly, relations with,
146; death of, 99, 131, 154–55; ethnic
churches and parishes, views on,
115, 117, 122, 125, 126–27, 128, 129, 130,
303n86; fiscal conservatism of, 157; W.
Gormley, relations with, 37; hospital
donation by, 96; Latinos, dealings with,
223, 321n21; national origin of, 33, 113;
on religious tolerance, 41; St. Francis
Church, support of, 150–51; St. Stephen
Church involvement of, 120, 122, 123;
travels abroad, 70
Grace Day Home, 98, 155, 167, 174, 176, 183,
184, 222, 228
Grass Valley, 55, 57, 174, 175
Great Depression: Catholic Church during,
171–76, 186; city development prior to,
134; Croatians on eve of, 132; human
face of, 162–64; impact of, 185–86;
Latino/a population decrease during,

Miranda, Dario Cardinal, 239
mission churches, 148–52
Mistretta, Vito, 180, 186
Mitty, John J., 172
Miwok village, site of, 275, 276
mobility of suburban population, 197, 198
Moore, Thomas, 207
Moreno, Jorge, 245
Mormonism, 15, 19, 283n6
Mormon temple and tabernacle, 57
Mueller, Walter F., 265, 266, 269, 272,
    329n41
mugwump political reformism, 138
Mulbay, Mother Mary Tarcissia, 91, 97
Mulligan, Terrence, 39
multiethnic churches and schools, 120–21,
    123–24
Murphy, Mother, 214
mutualistas (mutual aid societies), 219

Napoléon III, 53
National Council of Catholic Women
    (NCCW), 89, 90
Native Sons of the Golden West, 149, 150
nativist movements, 100, 105–9, 110–11, 132,
    278, 300n36
Naughton, Mother Carmel (Winifred
    Naughton), 85, 86, 96–97
New Deal, 171, 176
New Menace (Ku Klux Klan), 108
newspaper coverage of Catholic church,
    143, 306n19
Niermann, Pius, 148
Nolen, John, 140
nonbelievers, Catholic attitudes toward,
    40, 41
non-Catholic religions, 7–8, 9, 14. *See
    also under name of denomination, e.g.:*
    Protestants
non-Catholics: as cathedral benefactors,
    66; Catholics, relations with, 7,
    10–11, 23, 40–41, 278; Catholic school
    attendance by, 88; mass attendance by,
    29

North Area, 187, 189, 190–91, 192, 193–95,
    194, 196–97, 199–200, 205–6, 208–9, 211
North Area Chamber of Commerce, 196
novena Catholicism, 179, 313n50

Oakland, 258
Oak Park, 251, 255
Old Sacramento (Gold Rush–days theme
    village), 232, 252
O'Neil, Mary Rooney, 85, 89–90
O'Neil, Minnie Rooney, 39, 41, 108
O'Neil, Reba, 206, 207
O'Neill, Charles, 111–12
orphanages, Catholic-run, 174, 175–76,
    312nn40–41
"orthodoxy of everyday life" (term), 70
Our Lady of Guadalupe: Church, 11, 12, 216,
    223, 229–30, 234, 236–46, 247, 321n20,
    325n75; as Mexican national figure, 223,
    228, 239, 240, 322n36; Mission, 227
Our Lady of Lourdes, 207
Our Lady of the Assumption Parish, 208
Our Lady of the Retreat in the Cenacle, 213
Owen, Isaac, 15, 72–73

Pacific Northwest, religion in, 17, 284n11
Papal Volunteers for Latin America, 242
Paris architecture, 53, 61
parishes, establishment of, 187, 189–90,
    190t, 199–201, 202–3, 204–5, 206–7,
    317n23
Passionists, 212, 213
peace protests, 257, 328n21
Perez, Antima, 221
Phelan, Gregory J., 15, 26, 28, 29, 30, 31, 69,
    71, 74–75, 77, 86, 103, 145, 285n28
Phelan, Mother Vincent, 83, 84, 85, 86, 94
Phillipps, Wendell, 34
Phoenix (Ariz.), 200
Pius X, Pope, 182
poor: aid to, 164–71, 173–76, 254–56,
    310n19; policies toward, 248, 274;
    relocation of, 250–51, 255; rise in, 253;
    working, 256

Russell, Mother Mary Baptist, 76, 77, 80, 81, 82, 87, 92
Ryan, Francis DeSales, 36

Sabbath laws, 105, 298n14
Sacramento: description of, 79; history and overview of, 2–5
Sacramento Area Planning Commission, 196
Sacramento Bee (newspaper): American Protective Association (APA) opposed by, 107; anti-Japanese sentiment of, 181, 184, 314n54; Catholic connections, alleged of, 106, 108, 299n20, 299n25; Depression-era news coverage of, 163, 170, 175; on ethnic and national identity, 37, 109; on homelessness, 170, 266, 268, 271, 329n41, 331n58; name changes of, 135, 304n3; overview of, 3; Sacramento promotion by, 154, 160; on suburban expansion, 195, 196. *See also Daily Bee* (newspaper) (*later* Sacramento Bee)
Sacramento Chamber of Commerce, 136, 140, 147, 150, 154, 167, 175, 177, 191, 250
Sacramento City High School, 157
Sacramento Cottage Housing, Inc., 262
Sacramento County Grand Jury, 196
Sacramento County Hospital, 28
Sacramento Food Bank Services, 255
Sacramento Housing and Redevelopment Agency, 262, 264
Sacramento Metropolitan Area Advisory Committee, 196
Sacramento Redevelopment Agency, 231, 247, 326n1
Sacramento Republican Party, 20
Sacramento Social Services Complex, 262
Sacramento Society for Medical Improvement, 93
Sacramento Valley Development Association, 137
Sacramento Women's Council, 73

Sacred Heart Church, 130, 172
Sacred Heart Parish, 255
Saeltzer, Mrs. D. V., Jr., 214
Salt Lake City: architecture in, 52, 57; charities in, 258; homelessness in, 249; religion in, 19, 52, 57; Sacramento compared to, 5–6
Salvation Army: in Depression era, 165, 166, 168, 169, 170, 174, 310n19; homeless, aid to, 168, 169, 254, 260, 328n28; Sacramento arrival of, 165; volunteers, work of, 256, 327n20
San Francisco, 40, 44, 60, 277
San Francisco Monitor, 60–61, 112, 143, 145
Santa Barbara mission, 151
Santo Nombre band, 228
Scanlan, Patrick, 34, 81–82, 83, 117
Schell, Otto, 208
schools: Americanization, role in, 104–5; superintendent, first woman as, 39, 108. *See also* Catholic schools
Seattle (Wash.), 56, 57, 200, 249, 326n3
Serna, Joseph, 252, 253, 257, 259, 262, 263, 263, 264, 266, 267, 270, 271, 272
Serra Hall, 148
Shields, Peter, 17–18
Sierra-Arden Congregational Community Church, 198
Silveira, Guilherme, 129, 303n86
Simmons, Gustavus Lincoln, 94, 95
Sioux Falls (S.Dak.), 56–57
Sisters' Hospital (Mater Misericordiae) (*later* Mercy Hospital), 86, 95–96, 278
Sisters of Charity, 55, 77
Sisters of Mercy, 82; affection for, 101, 278; in Depression era, 174, 176; in health care, 94–97; homeless, aid to, 260, 274; land occupied by, 45, 79–83; Latinos, work with, 225; leadership of, 83–86; C. K. McClatchy praise for, 74; origin of, 33, 75–77; outside Sacramento, 293n21; post–world War II, 213; Sacramento arrival of, 75–77, 99; schools operated

by, 10, 33, 80–92; service training overseen by, 34; teaching by, 78; as urban agents, 86–91
Sisters of Notre Dame of San Jose, 77, 294n22
Sisters of Social Service, 176, 254, 263
Sisters of the Holy Name, 202
Sisters of the Presentation, 76, 77, 203
Slattery, Joseph and Elizabeth, 106
Smith, Gary, 268–69, 270–71
Smith, S. Prentiss, 59
social conditions: in 1960s and 1970s, 253; improving, 135
social control, religion disconnected from, 17, 284n11
social homogeneity, 5
social organizations, Catholic involvement in, 23
social pathologies, foreign-born blamed for, 100, 104, 108
social programs, decline of support for, 251–52
social services: Catholic Church role in providing, 9, 10, 26, 166–67, 277; in Depression era, 160–61, 167–71; overview, 164–65; religious sisters' role in providing, 73, 91, 92. *See also under specific service, e.g.:* child care
social stability, 5
Sociedad de Nuestra Señora de Dolores (*later* Guadalupanas), 222
Southern Pacific Railroad, 47, 138–39, 153, 161, 215, 218, 220, 225, 262, 264, 288n11, 304–5nn9–10, 329n37
Southern Pacific Railroad Company Hospital, 93, 94
south European immigrants, 103
Southside Improvement Club, 143–44
Southside Park, 237, 238
squatters' riots, 21, 284n20
St. Agnes Parish, 200
St. Andrew Parish, 235
Stanford, Jane Lathrop, 50, 176

Stanford, Leland, 50
Stanford Lathrop Home, 174, 176
Stanford Settlement, 255
Stark, Leonard, 220
state capital: Sacramento as, 44, 56, 64, 277; threats to move, 136
state capitol building, 45–46, 57, 63, 66, 68, 140–41
State Emergency Relief Administration (SERA), 162, 171
Steffen, Mother Cecilia, 78
Steffens, Joseph, 46, 57, 59, 69–70
Steinbacher, Henry, 125
Steinberg, Darrell, 267, 269, 272
St. Bernadette Parish (Seattle), 200
St. Elizabeth Church, 130, *131*, 236
Stephens, Russell D., 59, 68–69
Stevenson, R. M., 105
St. Francis Church, 78, 118–19, 148–52, 308n40
St. Francis High School, 185, 210
St. Ignacius Parish, 202–3, 207, 208
St. John Lutheran Church, 261
St. John's parish, 189
St. John the Baptist Church, 207
St. John the Baptist Parish, 205
St. John Vianney Church, 208
St. John Vianney's parish, 201
St. Joseph Academy, 89, 90, 99, 120, 209–10, 222, 225, 228, 233, 236, 278
St. Joseph Church, 172, 178, 254
St. Joseph Convent, 85
St. Joseph School, 33, 87, 88, 172, 222, 233, 240
St. Lawrence Parish, 207
St. Mary Hospital (San Francisco), 92, 95
St. Mary's Church, 129, 130, 222, 223, 237, 321n20
St. Mel mission, 203–4
St. Mel Parish, 189, 207–8
Stoecke, William, 183
St. Patrick Home, 175–76
St. Patrick School, 185